Singapore

Paul Hellander
Peter Turner

Singapore

4th edition

Published by
Lonely Planet Publications
Head Office:	PO Box 617, Hawthorn, Vic 3122, Australia
Branches:	150 Linden Street, Oakland, CA 94607, USA
	10a Spring Place, London NW5 3BH, UK
	71 bis rue du Cardinal Lemoine, 75005 Paris, France

Printed by
SNP Printing Pte Ltd, Singapore

Photographs by
Vicki Beale	Patrick Horton	Arasu Ramasamy
Glenn Beanland	Richard I'Anson	Chris Rowthorn
Paul Hellander	Raffles Hotel	Tony Wheeler

Many of the images in this guide are available for licensing from Lonely Planet Images.
email: lpi@lonelyplanet.com.au

Front cover: Raffles Hotel (Will McIntyre & Deni McIntyre, AllStock)

First Published
June 1991

This Edition
October 1998

National Library of Australia Cataloguing in Publication Data

Hellander, Paul D
Singapore

4th ed.
Includes index
ISBN 0 86442 630 5

1. Singapore – Guidebooks. I. Title.
(Series: Lonely Planet city guide).

915.957045

Paul Hellander

Paul has never really stopped travelling since he was born in England to a Norwegian father and English mother. He arrived in Australia in 1977, via Greece and 30 other countries. He then taught Modern Greek and trained interpreters and translators for 13 years before throwing it all away for a life as a travel writer. Paul joined Lonely Planet in 1994 and wrote our *Greek phrasebook* before being assigned to *Greece* and *Eastern Europe*. Updating *Singapore* was Paul's first assignment in Asia for Lonely Planet. He can be reached at paul@planetmail.net.

Peter Turner

Peter was born in Melbourne and studied Asian studies, politics and English at university before setting off on the Asian trail. His long-held interest in South-East Asia has seen him make numerous trips to the region, and he has also travelled further afield in Asia, the Pacific, North America and Europe. He worked with Lonely Planet as an editor from 1986 to 1993, after which he became a full-time writer. Peter has also worked on Lonely Planet's guides to *Malaysia, Singapore & Brunei, Indonesia, Indonesia's Eastern Islands, New Zealand* and *South-East Asia*.

From the Author

During a frenetic and, more often than not, hot and sticky five weeks of wandering the streets of Singapore, several people came to mind who should be thanked: Elaine Lim of the Singapore Tourism Board and the Sydney office of the STB for a wealth of printed material; Véronique le Petit for her constant stream of tips and advice on eating places and homely hospitality; Matt Donath for information on Singapore Web sites; Evan Jones of Batam for a very helpful lowdown on the Riaus; the efficient and public-spirited people of Singapore for their interest in and assistance with my research; my wife Stella for her continuing support and willingness to hold the fort; and finally Hup Yick for inspiration.

My work, as ever, is dedicated to my sons Marcus and Byron who may one day take inspiration from their father's wanderings.

This Book

The 1st edition of *Singapore* was written by Peter Turner, with additions from Tony Wheeler. Peter also researched and rewrote the 2nd and 3rd editions. This 4th edition was updated by Paul Hellander.

From the Publisher

This 4th edition of *Singapore* was edited at Lonely Planet's office in Melbourne by Andrew Humphreys and Katrina Browning, and proofed by Anne Mulvaney, Rebecca Turner and Darren Elder. The maps were drawn by Glenn van der Knijff, who was also responsible for the design and layout of the book. Leanne Peake helped out with last minute mapping corrections. The cover was designed by Simon Bracken and the illustrations were drawn by Jenny Bowman.

Thanks to Paul Piaia for the climate chart and to Russell Kerr for writing the history section. Many thanks also to David and Pamela Humphreys for their comments and recommendations, and to Paul Hellander for gamely supplying extra material at the eleventh hour.

Warning & Request

Things change – prices go up, schedules change, good places go bad and bad places go bankrupt – nothing stays the same. So, if you find things better or worse, recently opened or long since closed, please let us know and help us to make the next edition even more accurate and useful.

We value all of the feedback we receive from travellers. Julie Young coordinates a small team who read and acknowledge every letter, postcard and email, and ensure that every morsel of information finds its way to the appropriate authors and editors.

Everyone who writes to us will find their name in the next edition of the appropriate guide and will also receive a free subscription to our quarterly newsletter, *Planet Talk*. The very best contributions will be rewarded with a free Lonely Planet guide.

Excerpts from your correspondence may appear in new editions of this guide; in our newsletter, *Planet Talk*; or in updates on our Web site – so please let us know if you don't want your letter published or your name acknowledged.

Thanks

Many thanks to the travellers who used the last edition and wrote to us with helpful hints, useful advice and interesting anecdotes. Your names follow:

Adam Atlas, Jorg Ausfelt, Andy Bolas, Phil Davies, Joey Dunlop, Ingeborg Flagstad, Dr JA Harvey, Markus Herren, Pamela Hines, Jennifer Hor, Mr S Hughes, Paula Hutt, Allen Keme, Shuja Khan, Jackie Laine, Scott Laughlin, Kelvin Law, Simon Lello, Elizabeth Main, Snerharaj Malankad, Anne Manningham, Alan & Shirley Martin, Jon & Phoebe McLeod, GB Morgan, Doug Muir, Vino Naidoo, Elisabeth Obauer, Sue O'Brien, Tracy Pearl, Higgs Piers, Duncan Priestley, Hans Ramlov, Mark Reed, Cassaundra Sledge, Cheryl Tan, Matthew Tonge and Phil & Linda Wotherspoon

Contents

INTRODUCTION 7

FACTS ABOUT SINGAPORE 8

History 8
Geography 14
Climate 14
Ecology & Environment.......14
Flora & Fauna 15

Government & Politics 16
Economy 16
Population 17
People 17
The Peranakans 18

Arts..........................23
Society & Conduct 24
Religion 29
Places of Worship 31
Language 41

FACTS FOR THE VISITOR 44

When to Go 44
Orientation 44
Maps..........................44
Tourist Offices 45
Documents 45
Embassies.....................46
Customs 47
Money 47
Doing Business................50
Post & Communications........51
Internet Resources 54

Books 55
Newspapers & Magazines 57
Radio & TV 57
Photography & Video...........58
Time 58
Electricity 59
Weights & Measures 59
Laundry 59
Health 59
Women Travellers...............59
Gay & Lesbian Travellers 59

Disabled Travellers...........59
Senior Travellers 59
Singapore for Children 60
Libraries 61
Universities..................61
Cultural Centres 61
Dangers & Annoyances 61
Business Hours................61
Public Holidays & Special
Events........................62
Work..........................65

GETTING THERE & AWAY 66

Air 66
Land 69
Sea 71

GETTING AROUND 74

The Airport...................74
Mass Rapid Transit (MRT)....75
Bus 76
Taxi..........................77

Car 77
Trishaw.......................78
Bicycle 79
Walking 79

Boats & Ferries 79
Organised Tours 79

THINGS TO SEE & DO 81

Colonial Singapore.............81
**Walking Tours of
Singapore** 87
Chinatown 97
Little India 98

Arab St 98
Orchard Rd....................99
Jurong........................99
East Coast & Changi 102
Sentosa Island...............105

Other Islands 108
Northern & Central
Singapore 110
Activities 115

PLACES TO STAY 118

Budget 118
Long Term 128

Middle 122

Top End 125

PLACES TO EAT 130

Hawker Food 131
Hawker Centres.............132
Chinese.......................137

Indian 142
**Glossary of Asian Culinary
Terms** 144

Malay & Indonesian...........148
Nonya.........................148
Singaporean 149

Other Asian Cuisine 149   Breakfast, Snacks & Delis ..153   Fruit 155
Western................................152   High Tea 155   Supermarkets 156

ENTERTAINMENT 157

Bars, Bands & Discos 157   Chinese Opera 163   Other Entertainment 163
Cinema 162   Cultural Shows....................163   After Dark 163
Theatre 162   Classical Music 163   Horse Racing 163

SHOPPING 165

Where to Shop 167   What to Buy 169

EXCURSIONS 172

Natural Singapore................172   Kota Tinggi..........................182   Riau Archipelago 184
Malaysia 173   Mersing................................182
Johor Bahru 173   **Indonesia 184**

GLOSSARY..190

INDEX 192

Maps....................................192   Boxed Text 192   Text.....................................192

Introduction

Lying almost on the equator, Singapore is a prosperous city-state that has overcome its lack of natural resources to become one of the powerhouse economies of Asia. In less than 200 years, Singapore has been transformed from a swampy island into a modern industrial nation.

Modern Singapore is a city of concrete, glass, freeways and shopping centres. You can stay at a luxury hotel on fashionable Orchard Rd, eat Italian food, drink Californian wine, buy European designer-label clothes and never know you were in the east at all. But for those who wish to do a little exploring, Singapore offers a taste of the great Asian cultures in a small, easy-to-get-around package.

In the crowded streets of Chinatown, fortune tellers, calligraphers and temple worshippers are still a part of everyday Singapore. In Little India, you can buy the best sari material, freshly ground spices or a picture of your favourite Hindu god. In the small shops of Arab St, the cry of the muezzin can be heard from the nearby Sultan Mosque.

Singapore may no longer be the rough-and-ready port of rickshaws, opium dens, pearl luggers and pirates, but you can still recapture the colonial era with a gin sling under the flashing ceiling fans at Raffles Hotel. Many other fine reminders of Singapore's colonial past remain, despite the island's relentless development.

Perhaps Singapore's greatest treat is the variety and quality of its food. For only a few dollars you can have a bowl of steaming noodles, curry and rice, or delicious satay, all at the same food-stall table. Spend a little more, or a lot more, and Singapore has hundreds of restaurants serving the best Chinese, Indian, Malay and European cuisine.

Some visitors to Singapore see it as just another modern city specialising in instant tours and packaged delights, but a little independent exploration will still uncover enough glimpses of the exotic to keep any visitor interested.

Facts about Singapore

HISTORY

Malay legend has it that long ago a Sumatran prince visiting the island of Temasek
saw a strange animal, which was identified
to him as a lion. The good omen prompted
the prince to found a city on the spot of the
sighting which he named Singapura, or
Lion City in Sanskrit.

This may be a legend, but it is no less
plausible than much of Singapore's official
history. From the arrival in 1819 of Stamford
Raffles – officially declared Singapore's
founder in the 1970s in order to 'neutrally'
settle rival claims by local Malays and
Chinese – to the present, Singapore's past
has been continually moulded to fit political
and economic demands. Nonetheless, beneath the serene surface of gentrified
colonial-era buildings lies an intriguing tale
of the rise and fall of local empires, European colonial 'great games' and the enduring
legacy of 19th century British rule.

Early Empires

Chinese traders en route to India had plied
the waters around what is now Singapore
from at least the 5th century AD. Some
sources claim that Marco Polo visited a
flourishing city in 1292 where Singapore
now stands (though the Venetian's only sure
report is of the city of Malayu – now called
Jambi – on Sumatra).

What is certain, however, is that Singapore was not the first of the great entrepôt
cities in the region. By the 7th century Sriwijaya, a seafaring Buddhist kingdom
centred on Palembang in Sumatra, held
sway over the Straits of Malacca (now
Melaka); by the 10th century it dominated
the Malay peninsula as well. At the height
of Sriwijaya's power, Singapore was at
most a small trading outpost.

Raids by rival kingdoms and the arrival
of Islam spelled the eclipse of Sriwijaya by
the 13th century. Based mainly on the thriving pirate trade, the sultanate of Melaka

quickly acquired the commercial power
once wielded by Sriwijaya. It was a cos-
mopolitan, free port emporium (where,
reportedly, 84 languages could be heard) at
which traders were spared the complex procedures found elsewhere for dealing with
'polluting' foreigners – money spoke first in
Melaka.

Colonial Great Games

Armed with the cross and cannon, the Portuguese took Melaka in 1511, hoping to
drive Islam and its trading hegemony out of
the region. Once the city had fallen to the
mercantile Christians, however, Melaka's
Muslim traders moved on. The equally
ardent Dutch founded Batavia (now
Jakarta) to further undermine Melaka's position, finally wresting the city from their
European competitors in 1641.

In the late 18th century the British began
looking for a harbour in the Straits of
Melaka to secure lines of trade between
China, the Malay world and their interests in
India. Renewed war in Europe led, in 1795,
to French annexation of Holland, prompting
the British (at war with revolutionary
France) to seize Dutch possessions in South-
East Asia, including Melaka.

When, after the end of the Napoleonic
Wars, the British agreed to restore Dutch
possessions in 1818, there were those who
were bitterly disappointed at the failure of
the dream of British imperial expansion in
South-East Asia. One such figure was Stamford Raffles, Lieutenant-Governor of Java.
Raffles soon procured permission to found
a station to secure British trade routes in the
region. The Dutch beat him to his choice of
Riau, an island near modern Singapore, and
Raffles was instructed to negotiate with the
sultan of nearby Johor for land.

Raffles' City Emerges

When Raffles landed at Singapore in early
1819, the empire of Johor was divided.

When the old sultan had died in 1812, his younger son's accession to power had been engineered while an elder son, Hussein, was away. The Dutch had a treaty with the young sultan, but Raffles threw his support behind Hussein, proclaiming him sultan and installing him in residence on Singapore. In Raffles' plans the sultan wielded no actual power but he did serve to legitimise British claims on the island. Raffles also signed a treaty with the more eminent *temenggong* (senior judge) of Johor and set him up with an estate on the Singapore River. Thus, Raffles had acquired the use of Singapore in exchange for modest annual allowances to Sultan Hussein and the temenggong, which ended with a cash buyout of the pair in 1824 and transfer of Singapore's ownership to Britain's East India Company.

The Dutch were unimpressed, but in an 1824 Anglo-Dutch treaty which carved up

Sir Thomas Stamford Raffles (born 1781), founder of Singapore, first stepped foot on the island in 1819 and departed for the last time just four years later. All his notes on the founding, along with accompanying natural history specimens and illustrations, were lost at sea. Back in England, Raffles succumbed to ill health and died at the young age of 45.

spheres of influence in Asia, Singapore remained the property of Britain. In 1826 Singapore, Penang and Melaka became part of the Straits Settlements, controlled by the East India Company in Calcutta but administered from Singapore.

Raffles' first and second visits to Singapore in 1819 were brief, and he left instructions and operational authority with Colonel William Farquhar, formerly the Resident (chief British representative) at Melaka, now Resident of Singapore. Three years later, Raffles returned to run the now thriving colony for a year; his ambitious plans for the city were not being followed by Farquhar.

Raffles' vision amounted to making Singapore the lasting successor to the great entrepôts of the Sriwijayan kingdom, but under the rule of British law and empire. While Raffles was a firm believer in Britain's right to rule, he also preached the virtues of making Singapore a free port, opposed slavery and proclaimed (unenforced) limitations on indentured labour (under which 'coolies' would henceforth be forced to work off the cost of their passage from China for 'no more than two years'). Raffles was also a keen and sympathetic student of the peoples of the region, though in typically colonial fashion he romanticised the distant Malay past while regarding Malays of the present as degraded and lacking the Protestant work ethic (ironically, a position taken by officials in Malaysia and Singapore today).

Raffles initiated a town plan which included levelling one hill to form a new commercial district (now Raffles Place), and erecting government buildings around another, Forbidden Hill (now Fort Canning Hill).

The plan also embraced the colonial practice, still operative in Singapore today, of administering the population according to neat racial categories. The city's trades, races and dialect groups (*bang*) were divided into *kampongs* (villages): Europeans were granted land to the north-east of the government offices, though many soon moved out to sequestered garden estates in the western suburbs; the Chinese, who included Hokkien, Hakka, Canton, Teochew and Straits-born bang, predominated around the mouth of the Singapore River; the (Hindu) Indians were centred around Kampong Kapor and Serangoon Rd; the Arab St area housed Gujarati and other Muslim merchants; Tamil Muslim traders and an assortment of small businesses operated in the Market St area; and the Malay population mainly lived on the swampy northern fringes of the city, where the Sultan Mosque was also located.

How the East Was Won

Recognising the need for cooperation with Chinese communities, Raffles also sought registration of the *kongsi* (clan organisations for mutual assistance known variously as ritual brotherhoods, heaven-man-earth societies, triads and secret societies). Labour and dialect-based kongsi would become increasingly important to Singapore's success in the 19th century as

overseas demand for Chinese-harvested products like pepper, tin and rubber – all routed through Singapore from the Malay peninsula – grew enormously. Singapore's access to kongsi-based economies in the region, however, depended largely on revenues from an East India Company product from India bound for China – opium.

Farquhar had established Singapore's first opium farm for domestic consumption, and by the 1830s excise and sales revenues of opium accounted for nearly half the administration's income, a situation that continued for a century after Raffles' arrival. But the British Empire (which has been called the world's first major drug cartel) produced more than Chinese opium addicts; it also fostered the western-oriented outlook of Straits-born Chinese.

In the 19th century women were rarely permitted to leave China; thus, Chinese men who headed for the Straits Settlement (after 1867, the Crown Colony) of Singapore were likely to marry Malay women. These creole Baba Chinese (the more general term

In 19th century Singapore man-eating tigers were a serious problem. The government was prompted to place a bounty on the animals and tiger hunting became a fashionable pastime. In 1904 a tiger was even shot in the Billiard Room of Raffles Hotel (although this one had escaped from a circus). It was only in 1930 that the last of the island's tigers was dispatched.

Peranakan is now preferred in Singapore) found an identity in loyalty to the Union Jack, British law and citizenship. The British could count on those Babas with capital and a local family to stay put, while other traders were considered less reliable.

The authorities needed all the help they could get, for while revenues and Chinese labourers poured in until the early 1930s (when the effects of the western Depression and fears of political radicalism caused a hiccup), Singapore was continually plagued by bad sanitation, water-supply problems and man-eating tigers, by piracy on the seas, and by the strain of imposing European ideals on an essentially Chinese city. In 1887 the so-called Veranda Riots broke out over a long-simmering dispute about the use of the 'five-foot-ways' (the raised porch area that fronts traditional buildings, replacing pavements). The Chinese claimed the traditional right to use the five-foot-ways for hawking, drying produce, burning sacrificial papers and celebrating festivals; most Europeans wanted the lanes kept clear for pedestrians and for 'sanitary reasons'. The dispute continued into the 1920s, when the health department was finally forced to admit defeat. The domination of European-style footpaths and cleared lanes had to await the modernising reforms of an independent Singapore.

Despite a massive fall in rubber prices in 1920, the ensuing decade saw more boom times. Immigration soared, and millionaires, including Chinese migrants such as Aw Boon Haw, the 'Tiger Balm King', were made overnight. In the 1930s and early 40s, politics dominated the intellectual scene. Indians looked to the subcontinent for signs of the end of colonial rule, while Kuomintang (Nationalist) and Communist party struggles in the disintegrating Republic of China attracted passionate attention. Opposition to Japan's invasions of China in 1931 and 1937 was near universal in Singapore.

Japanese Rule

Singaporean Chinese were to pay a heavy price for opposing Japanese imperialism when General Yamashita pushed his thinly stretched army into Singapore on 15 February 1942. For the British, who had established a vital naval base near the city in the 1920s, surrender was sudden and humiliating. Blame for the loss of Singapore has fallen on everyone from British prime minister Churchill, who failed to divert sufficient forces from the war in Europe to defend Singapore, to squabbling British commanders and the wholesale desertion of Australian troops under the divisive command.

Japanese rule was harsh in the renamed city of Syonan (Light of the South). Yamashita had the Europeans herded onto the Padang, the city green on which they'd once played tennis and strolled; from there they were marched away for internment, many of them at the infamous Changi prison. Chinese Communists and intellectuals, however, were targeted for execution, though there was little method or distinction in the ensuing slaughter. Thousands of Chinese were murdered in a single week. Malays and Indians were also subject to systematic abuse.

As the war progressed inflation skyrocketed. Food, medicines and other essentials became in short supply, to the point where during the last phase of the war, people were dying of malnutrition and disease. The war ended suddenly with Japan's surrender on 14 August 1945, and Singapore was spared the agony of recapture.

Postwar Alienation

The British were welcomed back to Singapore but their right (and ability) to rule was now in question. Plans for limited self-government and a Malayan Union were drawn up, uniting the peninsular states of British Malaya with Crown possessions in Borneo. Singapore was excluded, largely because of Malay fears of Chinese Singapore's dominance.

Singapore was run-down and its services neglected after the war. Poverty, unemployment and shortages provided a groundswell of support for the Malayan Communist Party, whose freedom fighters (of whom the vast majority were Chinese) had emerged as heroes of the war. The Communist General Labour Union also had a huge following, and in 1946 and 1947 Singapore was crippled by strikes.

Meanwhile, the rapid development of Malay nationalism accompanied new political opportunities in Malaya. The United Malays National Organisation (UMNO), which now rules Malaysia, opposed the idea of a Malayan Union, arguing instead for a federation based on the Malay sultanates and opposing citizenship laws which gave equal rights to all races, which would undermine the special status of Malays.

Singapore moved slowly to self-government. The socialist Malayan Democratic Union was the first real political party, but it became increasingly radical and boycotted Singapore's first elections in 1947. After early successes, the Communists realised that they were not going to gain power under the colonial government's political agenda and they began a campaign of armed struggle in Malaya. In 1948 British authorities declared the Emergency: the Communists were outlawed and a bitter guerrilla war was waged on the peninsula for 12 years. There was no fighting in Singapore, but left-wing politics languished under the political repression of Emergency regulations.

Lee Kuan Yew's Singapore

By the early 1950s, the Communist threat had waned and left-wing activity was again on the upswing, with student and union movements at the forefront of the political activity.

One of the rising stars of this era was Lee Kuan Yew, a third generation Straits-born Chinese who had studied law at Cambridge. The socialist People's Action Party (PAP) was founded in 1954 with Lee as secretary-general. A shrewd politician, Lee appealed for support to both the emerging British-educated elite and to radicalist passions – the party included a Communist faction and an ambitious post-Raffles plan of its own: strong state intervention to industrialise Singapore's emporium economy.

Under arrangements for internal self-government, the PAP won a majority of seats in the new Legislative Assembly in 1959, and Lee Kuan Yew became the first Singaporean to hold the title of prime minister.

By the early 1960s Britain had found a way to exit colonial rule in the region. A new state of Malaysia, uniting Malaya with Sabah, Sarawak and Singapore, would balance ethnic numbers and politically unify long-standing economic ties. The arrangement lasted only two years – in 1965 Singapore was booted out of the federation, mainly because Malay fears of Chinese control remained unassuaged. The island was left to fend for itself as the Republic of Singapore. Despite Lee Kuan Yew's public tears and real fears at the messy divorce, both peninsular Malays and Singapore's Chinese were mostly relieved that the marriage of convenience was over.

Making the most of one-party rule in independent Singapore, under Lee's paternal control the PAP set to work moulding its multiracial citizens and fragile state into a viable entity. Industrialisation paid off, and ambitious infrastructure, defence, health, education, pension and housing schemes were rigorously pursued, especially in the 1970s when overseas loans were in ready supply. Housing and urban renovation, in particular, despite their controversial impact on Singapore's physical environment, have been keys to the PAP's success (by the mid-1990s, the city-state had the world's highest rate of home ownership).

Living out social engineering dreams (couched in the anti-western rhetoric of 'Confucianism') recalled from British textbooks, Singapore's leaders also sought order and progress in the strict regulation of social behaviour and identity: banning chewing gum and smoking in public (enforced with hefty fines), installing cameras and automatic locks in lifts to catch public urination in the act, setting up state-sponsored match-making venues and offering financial incentives to well-educated (meaning mostly Chinese) women to have more children.

Singapore-Malaysia Relations

Ever since the untidy divorce in 1965 when Singapore was unceremoniously kicked out of its short-lived union with Malaysia, relations between the two countries have been warm(ish) at best, pretty chilly at worst.

Senior minister and former Singaporean prime minister Lee Kuan Yew didn't improve matters when in early 1997 he suggested that the city of Johor Bahru on the Malaysian side of the Causeway was 'a place of gangsters and car-jackers'. It took a good-will visit the following year by current prime minister Goh Chok Tong to smooth the ruffled feathers.

It's not hard to see why things haven't always been smooth between the two nations. Singapore, the upstart sibling, was dismissed at the time of the separation by Malaysia for refusing to afford the same rights to its own Malay citizens as in Malaysia. Singapore ultimately came out on top with a well-ordered society and a well-run economy, while Malaysia, the big brother, still wrestles with economic woes, unemployment and other social ills that little brother seems to have largely eliminated.

Then there are the niggling unresolved issues like dual territorial claims over a small island in the Singapore Straits, and Malaysian Railways land-holdings on Singapore. There are also petty restrictions on Malay citizens operating freely within Singapore's commercial sector, and vice versa, and there is an unspoken grudge held by the Chinese over positive discrimination in Malaysia in favour of the Bumiputra or native-born Malays.

Notwithstanding, the two nations are more united by common interests than divided by dissimilarities. Talk of reunification does resurface regularly in the press on both sides of the Straits. There has even been a serious proposal by some keen advocates of union to fill in the Straits, using Singapore's technical expertise in landfilling operations to physically join the two nations.

The two will only survive and thrive through tolerance, trade and exchanges of technology and ideas. The prevailing thinking has it that Singapore and Malaysia have to engage in a mutually profitable symbiosis and buck the trend in a region that has had more than its fair share of recent discontent.

Under Lee, high economic growth rates supported political stability, which was further ensured by exiling or jailing dissidents, banning critical publications, controlling public speech (in prime minister Goh Chok Tong's more relaxed, liberalised regime of the 1990s, politicians who raise touchy issues tend to find themselves suddenly convicted of tax evasion) and numbing inquiring minds with possibly the world's blandest media.

Life after Lee

In 1990 Lee Kuan Yew resigned as prime minister (though he still holds the conspicuous position of Special Minister), the same year the Mass Rapid Transit (MRT) subway system – an impressive testament to Singapore's ultra-modernisation and technological capabilities – was completed.

As the century ends, Lee, the 'father of modern Singapore', and Goh's PAP face the situation of all parents. Having reared a population of mobile technophiles for a globalised economy, the children have grown up. Many, especially Indian and Chinese professionals, find better prospects elsewhere; those who remain, like Malay and Chinese youths, are chided for chafing at old expectations.

The Lion City has been given plenty of courage and brains; many Singaporeans seem to feel that what it needs now is a heart.

GEOGRAPHY

Singapore consists of the main, low-lying Singapore Island and 58 much smaller islands within its territorial waters. It is situated just above 1°N in latitude, a mere 137km north of the equator. Singapore Island is 42km in length and 23km in breadth, and together with the other islands the republic has a total landmass of 646 sq km (and growing through land reclamation). The other main islands are Pulau Tekong (24.4 sq km), which is gazetted as a military area but planned to be semi-residential eventually; Pulau Ubin (10.2 sq km), which is a rural haven from central Singapore; and Sentosa (3.3 sq km), Singapore's fun park. Built-up urban sectors comprise around 50% of the land area, while parkland, reservoirs, plantations and open military areas occupy 40%. Remaining forest accounts for only 4%.

Bukit Timah (Hill of Tin), in the central hills, is Singapore's highest point at an altitude of 162m. The central area of the island is an igneous outcrop, containing most of Singapore's remaining forest and open areas. The western part of the island is a sedimentary area of low-lying hills and valleys, while the south-east is mostly flat and sandy.

Singapore is connected to Peninsular Malaysia by a 1km-long causeway. To relieve congestion, a second causeway has opened in the west of the island.

Under current plans, further land reclamation and housing developments will dramatically change Singapore's geography. Land reclamation has already changed the physical geography around the city centre and also in the Tanah Merah and Changi airport area to the east of the island. The small islands south of the Jurong industrial park are steadily being expanded to make room for yet more oil storage facilities.

CLIMATE

Singapore has a typically tropical climate. It's hot and humid year-round and takes some getting used to. Once you are acclimatised, however, it never strikes you as too uncomfortable. The temperature almost

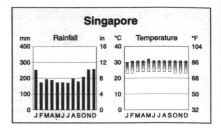

never drops below 20°C (68°F), even at night, and usually climbs to 30°C (86°F) or more during the day. Humidity tends to hover around the 75% mark.

Rain, when it comes, tends to be short and sharp. You may be unlucky and strike rain every day of your visit, but don't believe local legend about it raining every day for months on end. Only about half the days of the year receive rain. Singapore is at its wettest from November to January, and at its driest from May to July. The difference between these two periods is not dramatic and Singapore gets an abundance of rainfall every month.

Being almost right on the equator, Singapore receives on average a steady supply of about 12 hours daylight (less from November to January). Much of the sunshine is filtered through thin cloud but can be intense, nonetheless.

ECOLOGY & ENVIRONMENT

Singapore stands out as an environmentally enlightened country in the region. Though Singaporeans abroad may not always be ideal environmentalists, god forbid that they litter at home. Strict laws control littering and waste emissions, and though industry in the past may have developed with a relatively free hand, Singapore is now much more environmentally aware.

The island, always spotless and well organised, is becoming even cleaner and greener. Though little is left of Singapore's wilderness, growing interest in the ecology has seen new bird sanctuaries and parkland areas gazetted by the government. In such a built-up urban environment, the government has always been aware of the need for sound planning, and ordinary Singaporeans, who perhaps crave wide-open spaces, are increasingly focusing on the environment.

The greatest contribution to a clean environment has been the government's commitment to public transport and control of the motor car. Not content with its impressive MRT rail system and its extensive bus network, the government has an ambitious S$20 billion 'World-class Land Transport System' vision for the 21st century. The MRT network is to more than double in size, while light transit trains and computer-directed buses are intended to increase public transport use from 51% to 75%.

Heavy import duties, registration fees and licensing quotas put a lid on the Singaporean desire to own cars (see The Cost of a Car boxed text in the Facts for the Visitor chapter). As a result, Singapore is remarkably pollution free compared to other cities in Asia, which are beset by choking traffic and car emissions.

But while the island may have made headway in tackling environmental issues at home, it has no control over the actions of its neighbours. The forest fires in Kalimantan and Sumatra in Indonesia in 1997 caused havoc with Singapore's hitherto pristine environment. A heavy smoke haze hung over the island for several weeks providing a gloomy reminder of its precarious position dangling off the tip of the Malaysian peninsula.

FLORA & FAUNA

Singapore was once covered in tropical rainforest, with mangrove and beach forest in the coastal areas. Today only around 300 hectares of primary rainforest and 1800 hectares of secondary forest remain in the centre of the island, in and around the Bukit Timah Nature Reserve. The undeveloped northern coast and the offshore islands are still home to some mangrove forest.

The remaining rainforest is dominated by dipterocarp trees, such as the seraya (*Shorea cutisii*), the most common tree, and the mer-

antis. Other giants include members of the bean family (*Leguminosae*), of which the merbau is one of the best known. The rich biodiversity of the forest is complemented by a large number of ferns.

A lush variety of the island's flora is preserved at the Botanic Gardens, just north of Orchard Rd (see Botanic Gardens in the Things to See & Do chapter for full details).

Although they are now believed to be extinct from the island, tiger, clouded leopard, slow loris, Malayan porcupine and mouse deer all once inhabited Singapore. The animal that you are most likely to see is the long-tailed macaque, known locally as the kera – the grey-brown monkeys that form troupes in forest areas. Squirrels are common and Singapore has several species of flying squirrel, and the tree shrew, which looks like a squirrel but is classified as a primate. The flying lemur is occasionally sighted, as are civet cats (musang) and the distinctive pangolin (also known as the scaly anteater), but these are all nocturnal.

Reptiles, frogs and toads are frequently encountered. The reticulated python, which grows to up to 10m, is one of Singapore's most common snakes, while other island species include the poisonous pit viper and black spitting cobra.

Singapore has over 300 bird species and migrant species are observed in the migratory season from September to May. There's a bird sanctuary with hides at Sungei Buloh in the north-west of the island (see the Sungei Buloh Nature Park section in the Things to See & Do chapter). Common birds in urban areas include the myna, Eurasian tree sparrow, black-naped oriole, yellow-vented bulbul and spotted dove.

Abundant insect life includes numerous species of butterfly and moth, of which the atlas moth is one of the world's largest. Scorpions include the wood scorpion and the large scorpion. Bites are painful but not fatal.

Visitors who want to sample some of Singapore's indigenous flora and fauna should visit Pulau Ubin (see the Northern Islands section in the Things to See & Do chapter), an island off the north-east corner of Singapore. Alternatively, take a hike in the Bukit Timah Nature Reserve (see the Things to See & Do chapter for full details).

GOVERNMENT & POLITICS

Singapore's government is based on the Westminster system. The unicameral parliament has 81 elected members representing 52 electoral divisions. Voting in elections is compulsory. Governments are elected for five years, but a ruling government can dissolve parliament and call an election at any time.

As well as elected members the government has instituted a system that allows it to appoint an opposition. Nonconstituency Members of Parliament (NCMPs) are members who have failed to win enough votes, but are appointed to parliament as runners-up if less than four opposition members are elected. Nominated MPs (NMPs) comprise six prominent citizens that are appointed to give nonpartisan views. NCMPs and NMPs are not allowed to vote on financial and constitutional bills, although they can participate in parliamentary debate.

Singapore also has a president (currently Ong Teng Cheong), who is elected to the position by popular vote. The position is largely ceremonial and real power lies with the prime minister and his government.

The legal system is also based on the British system. The Supreme Court is the ultimate arbitrator and consists of the High Court, the Court of Appeal and the Court of Criminal Appeal. Most cases are heard by the District Courts and Magistrates Courts, except for the most serious criminal or civil hearings.

So in theory Singapore has a democratically elected government and a political system similar to many western democracies. The political practice is somewhat different.

The judiciary's independence is enshrined in the constitution, but many judges are appointed on short tenure and their renewal is subject to party approval. Rulings that have gone against the government have seen new laws quickly enacted by parliament to ensure government victory. The old Communist bogey is used to justify Singapore's Internal Security Act, which is still there to detain outspoken critics. Singapore's Internal Security Department keeps detailed records of its citizens and there is widespread fear of losing jobs, promotional opportunities or contracts through criticism of the government.

The main opposition party is the Singapore Democratic Party (SDP), though the chances of the opposition gaining power are still very remote. As long as the government can keep the economy and the personal wealth of its citizens growing, the opposition is unlikely to gain many converts.

ECONOMY

Singapore has traditionally been seen as one of Asia's four 'dragons' – the Asian economic boom countries of Taiwan, Korea, Hong Kong and Singapore. For over 20 years it has recorded phenomenal growth rates averaging at around 9% (although the recent crisis in South-East Asia has reduced that to under 5%). To add to that, Singapore has a large current account surplus, it is a net creditor, inflation remains low and unemployment is virtually nonexistent.

Singapore's economy is based on trade, shipping, banking and tourism, with a growing programme of light industrialisation. It also has a major oil-refining business producing much of the petroleum for the South-East Asian region. Other important industries include shipbuilding and maintenance, and electronics. Singapore's port vies with Hong Kong to be the busiest in the world.

For many western countries with mounting foreign debt, declining exports and increasing imports, Singapore is seen as a model free-market economy. But while a model economy it may be, its approach is not free market.

Singapore is very definitely a managed economy in the Japanese mould. The government provides direction by targeting

Singapore Highlights

The following is a slightly subjective, but probably accurate list (in alphabetical order) of the top 10 things to see in Singapore.

Boat Quay
Where the nightlife is at its busiest and most visible, and bar and restaurant touts vie for business.
(See page 81)

RICHARD I'ANSON

RICHARD I'ANSON

Little India
Busy, noisy and garrulous, it's almost not Singapore at all. Visit this enclave on Sunday evening and see for yourself. (See page 98)

Bukit Timah Nature Reserve
A jungle haven little more than a stone's throw away from shopping centres and high-rises.
(See page 113)

PAUL HELLANDER

PATRICK HORTON

Pulau Ubin
Singapore's last kampong community. Bring a bike for a leisurely ride and dine on fresh chilli crabs for lunch.
(See page 110)

Changi Airport
Not just a place to arrive at and leave from, Changi is a city unto itself, ultra-modern, efficient and entertaining.
(See page 74)

PAUL HELLANDER

PAUL HELLANDER

Raffles Hotel
Opulent, old-world and affably snobbish, Raffles maintains an air of the Singapore of times gone by.
(See page 83)

Chinatown
The renovated shophouses of Tanjong Pagar and the many restaurants and bars make Chinatown a must on any itinerary.
(See page 97)

RICHARD I'ANSON

PAUL HELLANDER

Sentosa
Love it or hate it, it's fun for a lot of people and the kids will have a whale of a time at Singapore's answer to Disneyland.
(See page 105)

Jurong Bird Park
Worth the trek out west to experience the world's largest enclosed aviary and a great artificial waterfall.
(See page 101)

RICHARD I'ANSON

ARASU RAMASAMY

Singapore Zoo
Arguably the best animal-friendly zoo in the world, where it's the people that feel like the exhibits.
(See page 112)

Revival of the Lion Dance

In the Lion City (Singapura), the lion dance is the most visible and definitive traditional performance art. Far from dying out, the lion dance is undergoing a huge revival and dozens of troupes perform all over the city, year-round. Open-sided trucks seem to be forever cruising the streets to a clash of cymbals, as a troupe goes off to another performance.

Traditionally performing to celebrate the Lunar New Year and other religious events, troupes are now called upon to entertain at birthdays, openings, hotels and corporate events. Once considered the occupation of gangsters, many schools and community groups now have their own lion dance troupes.

BOTH PHOTOGRAPHS BY PAUL HELLANDER

industries for development and offering tax incentives, or by simply telling them what to do. Unions and the labour market are controlled by the government, and there is tough legislation against strikes.

While the government promotes free trade, it always reserves the right to intervene, as it did in 1985 when it closed the stock exchange for three days after a major Singaporean company, Pan Electric Industries, went into receivership.

The Monetary Authority of Singapore (MAS) is a major example of government involvement in the economy. It acts as a central bank and powerful financial market regulator to promote sustained economic growth and provide stability in the financial services sector. Singapore's finance market is one of the largest in Asia and provides 25% of the country's income – to a large degree this is because of the investment stability provided by the MAS.

Singapore does have its share of free marketeers though, and many in the business community want less government involvement in the economy. Singapore wants to assume the role of Asia's finance centre, especially with Hong Kong's handover to mainland China, but investors in 'anything goes' Hong Kong are wary of the more regulated Singaporean markets.

Singapore's restrictive society is also a problem in that it contributes to a brain drain that sees it lose many of its skilled professionals.

Singapore guarantees its citizens decent housing, health care, high standards of education and superannuation, making it a welfare state in comparison with its Asian neighbours. There are no unemployment payments or programmes, but unemployment is negligible and the government insists that anyone who wants work can find it. In fact, Singapore has to import workers from neighbouring countries, particularly to do the hard, dirty work which Singaporeans no longer want any part of.

All workers and their employers make sizeable contributions to the Central Provident Fund (CPF), a form of superannuation that is returned on retirement. Some CPF savings, however, can be used to purchase government housing.

During the 1997/98 currency crisis that almost floored South Korea and Thailand and caused widespread rioting in Indonesia, the Singapore dollar (singdollar) remained reasonably stable and essentially unaffected. However, the longer-term effect of the ensuing reduced trade and tourism with its larger South-East Asian neighbours has yet to be felt.

Singaporeans are no longer feeling quite so complacent about their future wellbeing in a region where shared prosperity is essential for continued growth and stability.

POPULATION

Singapore's polyglot population numbers 3.04 million. It's made up of 77.3% Chinese, 14.1% Malay, 7.3% Indian and 1.3% from a variety of races.

Singapore's population density is high, but the government waged a particularly successful birth control campaign in the 1970s and early 1980s. In fact, it was so successful that the birth rate dropped off alarmingly, especially in the Chinese community. To reverse the trend and further the government's genetic engineering programme, tax incentives were introduced for university-educated women who had children, although at the same time rewards of S$10,000 were offered to those willing to undergo sterilisation.

Later policies offered tax rebates of up to S$20,000 for couples who had a third and fourth child.

PEOPLE

Singapore's character, and the main interest for the visitor, lies in the diversity of its population. Chinatown still has some of the sights, sounds and rituals of a Chinese city, Little India is a microcosm of the subcontinent and on Arab St the *muezzin*'s call from the mosque still regulates the lives of its inhabitants. But modern Singapore is essentially a Chinese city with strong western influences.

continued on page 22

THE PERANAKANS

Origins

The Peranakans are the descendants of early Chinese immigrants who settled in Melaka (Malaysia) and married Malay women. With the formation of the Straits Settlements in 1826, many moved to Penang and Singapore.

The culture and language of the Peranakans (a word which means half-caste in Malay) is a fascinating hybrid of Chinese and Malay traditions. The Peranakans took the name and religion of their Chinese fathers, but the customs, language and dress of their Malay mothers. They also used the terms Straits-born or Straits Chinese to distinguish themselves from later arrivals from China, whom they looked down upon.

The Peranakans were often wealthy traders and could afford to indulge their passion for sumptuous furnishings, jewellery and brocades. Their terrace houses were gaily painted, with patterned tiles embedded in the walls for extra decoration. When it came to the interior, Peranakan tastes favoured heavily carved and inlaid furniture.

Peranakan dress was similarly ornate; Nonyas (the term for a female Peranakan) wore fabulously embroidered *kasot manek* (slippers) and *kebaya* (blouses worn over a sarong), tied with beautiful *kerasong* brooches, usually of fine filigree gold or silver. Babas (the Peranakan male), however, assumed western dress in the 19th century, reflecting their wealth and contacts with the British. The Babas' finery was saved for important occasions such as the wedding ceremony, a highly stylised and intricate ritual exhibiting Malay *adat* (traditional custom).

Upper storey of a beautifully restored terraced row on Peranakan Place, a showcase area for Peranakan architecture.

PAUL HELLANDER

Language

The Peranakan patois is a Malay dialect but one which contains many Hokkien words – so much so, that it is largely unintelligible to a Malay speaker. The Peranakans also included words and expressions of English and French, and occasionally practised a form of backward Malay by reversing the syllables. Fewer than 5000 people now speak the language in Singapore.

Western culture has largely supplanted Peranakan traditions among the young, and the language policies of the government are also accelerating the language's decline. As the Peranakans are considered ethnically Chinese, it is compulsory that children study Mandarin as their mother tongue in schools. Many Peranakans also marry within the broader Chinese community, resulting in the further decline of the Peranakan patois.

Culture

The Peranakans regarded themselves as a cut above the pure Chinese and associated themselves both politically and culturally with the colonial Europeans – a move that was to ultimately lead to their demise during WWII when the invading Japanese army held the Peranakans up in disgrace for aping European attitudes.

Economic depression and rising Asian nationalism effectively sealed the fate of Peranakan culture as a living entity.

Today, societies, such as the Peranakan Association and the Gunong Sayang Association, report growing interest in Peranakan traditions as Singaporeans discover their roots; however, when the older generation passes it is likely that Peranakan culture and language will be consigned to history books.

As it is, Peranakan culture is already today something of a museum piece; the Peranakan Showcase Museum, at Peranakan Place just off Orchard Rd (see the Things to See & Do chapter), offers a look inside a Nonya and Baba house as it was at the turn of the century. The Katong Antique House (Map 8) on East Coast Rd also holds a collection of Peranakan artefacts.

The Peranakan House

More than any other single aspect, the house can be said to symbolise Peranakan culture. It is the setting in which Peranakan art, ritual and tradition are most clearly expressed.

The traditional Peranakan house, with its formal Chinese arrangement and eclectic mix of furnishings, reveals how this unique culture enjoyed a lifestyle that was deeply rooted in Chinese tradition and ritual, and yet was receptive to the cultures of other local communities.

In early 19th century Singapore, the Peranakans first settled in shophouses and terrace houses in the vicinity of Telok Ayer and Amoy Sts, on the eastern fringe of present-day Chinatown. Several families moved into the terrace houses in the Emerald Hill area in the later half of the 19th century. From the turn of the century,

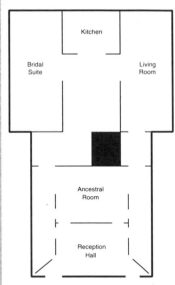

Typical layout of a traditional Peranakan house.

wealthy Peranakans began to move into colonial-type mansions and villas in Katong and Pasir Panjang, while middle-class Babas found new homes in the Siglap, Katong and Joo Chiat areas, where many Babas still reside.

While dispersing throughout Singapore, Peranakan families did attempt to maintain to varying degrees the traditional arrangements of their homes, though, naturally, concessions to modern life were made. Colonial-style living rooms, which were largely absent in the old houses, naturally became an added feature of Peranakan family life.

The traditional Peranakan house was divided into five distinct areas. The **reception hall** was the first room encountered on entering. The Peranakans would worship their deities and formally receive guests in this room. The second room would be the **ancestral room**, the most prestigious room in the house. Pride of place here would usually be taken up by the ancestral altar. The **living room** would be not unlike the living room of today; it would be where the Peranakans relaxed and enjoyed their daily activities. Guests were not normally allowed into this area.

The **kitchen** of a Peranakan household, known as the *perot rumah*, was traditionally located near the back of a terrace house, or in an outhouse of an old detached residence. It was the core space for communal cooking and here gossip and exchange of news was undertaken by the women of the household while the food was being prepared.

Finally, the **bridal suite** was usually set up in the bride's house. Here you were invited to give your blessings as you examined the red and gold-coloured furniture and other dowry gifts provided by the parents of the bride.

The traditional elements of a Peranakan house are rare in modern-day Singapore, although they can still be fairly commonly found in terrace houses in Melaka in Malaysia.

Cuisine

Until recently, Peranakan cuisine was confined to the homes of the few Peranakans that actively practise their culture in contemporary Singapore. However, in recent times there has been a resurgence of interest in Peranakan cuisine, with a number of restaurants now specialising in this unusual blending of Malay and Chinese elements. There's a concentration of Peranakan restaurants in the Katong district (Map 8) – see the Places to Eat chapter. Hawker centres are also increasingly featuring Peranakan food, while cookery books of Peranakan dishes are popular.

Peranakan cuisine typically blends Chinese ingredients with Malay sauces and spices, making original Chinese food seem bland by comparison. It is commonly flavoured with shallots, chillies (fresh or dry), shrimp paste (*belacan*), peanuts, preserved soybeans and blue ginger (*galangal*). Thick coconut milk is used to create the sauce that flavours the prime ingredients.

Examples of Peranakan dishes include *otak-otak*, a wonderful blend of fish and coconut milk, chilli paste, galangal and herbs, all wrapped in a banana leaf; *buah keluak* is a distinctive dish combining chicken pieces with dark nuts imported from Indonesia to produce a rich sauce, while *itek tim* is a classic soup containing duck, tomatoes, green peppers, salted vegetables and preserved sour plums simmered gently together.

Visitors can usually get a taste of distinctive Peranakan *laksa* (noodles in a savoury coconut-milk gravy with fried tofu and bean sprouts) or *mee siam* (rice vermicelli in a spicy-sour gravy) at most food centres.

Nonya desserts are typified by colourful cakes (*kueh*) and sweet, sticky delicacies.

PAUL HELLANDER

The Baba-Nonya Heritage Museum, Melaka, is housed in an attractive terrace of Peranakan houses. Their interiors are preserved as typical 19th century Peranakan residences.

continued from page 17

English is the principal language of education, and growing prosperity sees Singaporeans consuming western values along with western goods. For the government, this divergence from traditional values threatens to undermine the spirit – essentially the work-oriented Chinese spirit – that built Singapore. In an attempt to reverse the new ways of the young, the government runs campaigns to develop awareness of traditional culture and values. These include cultural exhibitions and the compulsory study of the mother tongue in schools.

Government policy has always been to promote Singapore as a multicultural nation in which the three main racial groups (Chinese, Indians and Malays) can live in equality and harmony while still maintaining their own distinct cultural identities. The government strives hard to unite Singaporeans and promote equality, though there are imbalances in the distribution of wealth and power among the racial groups. For the most part, however, the government is successful in promoting racial harmony, a not-always-easy task.

Chinese

The Chinese first settled in the Nanyang, as South-East Asia is known in China, as far back as the 14th century. In the 19th and 20th centuries waves of Chinese migrants in search of a better life poured into Singapore and provided the labour that ran the colony.

The migrants came mostly from the southern provinces: Hokkien Chinese from the vicinity of Amoy in Fujian province; Teochew from Swatow in eastern Guangdong; Hakka from Guangdong and Fujian provinces; and Cantonese from Canton (Guangzhou). Hokkiens and Teochews enjoyed an affinity in dialect and customs, but the Cantonese and Hakkas may as well have come from opposite ends of the earth. The Chinese settlers soon established their own areas in Singapore, and the divisions along dialect lines still exist to some extent in the older areas of the city.

Settlement for the immigrants was made easier by Chinese organisations based on clan, dialect and occupation. Upon arrival, immigrants were taken in by the various communities and given work and housing. The secret societies were particularly prevalent in Singapore in the 19th century; they provided many useful social functions and were more powerful than the colonial government in the life of the Chinese. However, they eventually declined and became nothing more than criminal gangs.

These days, most Chinese are Singaporean born. The campaign to speak Mandarin has given the Chinese a common dialect, but English is also a unifying tongue.

Malays

The Malays are the original inhabitants of Singapore. They are the main racial group throughout the region stretching from the Malay peninsula across Indonesia to the Philippines. Many Malays migrated to Singapore from the peninsula, and large numbers of Javanese and Bugis (from Riau and Sulawesi) also settled in Singapore.

Malays in Singapore are Muslim. Islam provides the major influence in everyday life and is the rallying point of Malay society. The month of Ramadan, when Muslims fast from sunrise to sunset, is the most important month of the Islamic year. Hari Raya Puasa, the end of the fast, is the major Malay celebration.

Islam was brought to the region by Arab and Indian traders in the 15th century, but traditional Malay culture still shows influences of pre-Islamic Hindu and animist beliefs. For example, *wayang kulit*, the Malay shadow puppet play, portrays tales from the Hindu epics of the *Ramayana* and *Mahabharata*.

Malays have traditionally always had a strong sense of community and hospitality, and the *kampong*, or village, is at the centre of Malay life. The majority of Malays live in high-rise districts such as Geylang, but in fast-diminishing rural Singapore and the islands in the north, a few Malay kampongs still exist.

Indians

Indian migration dates mostly from the middle of the 19th century when the British recruited labour for the plantations of Malaya. While many Indians arrived in Singapore, most passed through and eventually settled in Malaya.

In Singapore, approximately 60% of the Indian population are Tamil and a further 20% are Malayalis from the southern Indian state of Kerala. The rest come from all over India and include Bengalis, Punjabis and Kashmiris. The majority of Indians are Hindu, but a large number are Muslim, and there are also Sikhs, Parsis, Christians and Buddhists.

Major Indian celebrations are Thaipusam and Deepavali.

ARTS

Singapore is more normally associated with business and technology than the arts, which have tended to take a back seat to economic development. In the comparatively liberalised environment under Goh Chok Tong, however, the contemporary arts are starting to flourish. Drama, in particular, has taken on a important role in recent times, with productions ranging from English comedy to locally produced plays.

The Substation (see the Entertainment chapter for more details), an avant-garde, alternative arts venue, has been particularly active in the promotion of arts in the city with an all-encompassing programme of events showcasing such diverse activities as Chinese calligraphy and batik painting as well as live jazz and blues concerts.

Chinese Opera

Chinese drama is a mixture of dialogue, music, song and dance. It is an ancient form of theatre but reached its peak during the Ming dynasty, from the 14th to 17th centuries. It went through a decline in the 19th century, though its highest form survived in the Beijing opera, which has enjoyed a comeback in China since the Cultural Revolution. Chinese opera, or *wayang*, in Singapore and Malaysia is derived from the Cantonese variety, which is seen as a more music hall, gaudy style.

What it lacks in literary nuance is made up for by the garish costumes and the crashing music that follows the action. Performances can go for an entire evening but it is usually easy enough for the uninitiated to follow the gist of the action. The acting is heavy and stylised, and the music can be searing to western ears, but a performance is well worthwhile if you should chance upon one. Street performances are held during important festivals such as Chinese New Year, the Festival of the Hungry Ghosts and the Festival of the Nine Emperor Gods.

The band that accompanies the action is usually composed of fiddles, reed pipes and lutes, and drums, bells and cymbals. The scenery is virtually nonexistent, and props rarely consist of more than a table and chairs, but it is the action that is important.

The four main roles are the *sheng, dan, jing* and *chou*. The sheng are the leading male actors and they play scholars, officials, warriors etc. They divide up into *laosheng* who wear beards and represent old men, and *wusheng*, the soldiers and warriors. The dan are the female roles: the *laodan* are the elderly, dignified ladies, the brightly costumed *huadan* are the maids and the *caidan* are the female comedians. Traditionally, female roles were played by men.

The jing are the painted-face roles and they represent warriors, heroes, statesmen, adventurers and demons. Their counterparts are the *fujing*, ridiculous figures who are anything but heroic. The chou is basically the clown.

Lion Dance

This dance is accompanied by musicians who bash cymbals and drums to invoke the spirits. The intricate papier-mâché lion's head is worn by the lead performer while another dancer takes the part of the body. At its best it is a spectacular, acrobatic dance with the 'head' jumping on the shoulders of the 'body', climbing poles and performing acrobatic tumbling. The lion may also be attended by clowns.

The dance is usually performed during Chinese festivals to gain the blessings of the gods. Traditionally a dance troupe would be paid with *ang pow* (red packets of money) held up high to be retrieved with acrobatics. The dragon dance is a variation on the same theme.

Other Performing Arts

Malay and Indian dances sometimes can be seen. *Bangsawan*, or Malay opera, was introduced from Persia and is a popular drama form still performed in Singapore. For details of venues see the Entertainment chapter.

Film

Singapore's film industry is definitely still nascent, but the government is keen to develop the business and attract movie studios to Singapore. The country produced some Malay films back in the 60s and 70s, but that was followed by a long drought of local production broken only in 1991 with *Medium Rare*, based on a true story about an occult murderer. It was followed by the local box office success *Bugis Street* about Singapore's transvestites and notable for getting its nudity and sex scenes past the censors.

At the time of writing, the latest home-grown offering is Glen Goei's *Forever Fever*, a Singaporean remake of the popular 1970s movie *Saturday Night Fever*. Asked why the movie was likely to be a winner leading actor Adrian Tang replied, 'It's got the nipples and naughtiness of *The Full Monty*, the sweet-and-sour sauciness of *As Good as it Gets*, the touchy-feely-goody factor of *Good Will Hunting*, the wham-bam action of *LA Confidential* and the dancing is a helluva lot more exiting than *Saturday Night Fever*'.

Going to the movies is a very popular activity and the annual Singapore International Film Festival is held in April each year featuring films mainly from the Asian region.

Literature

Singapore has recently experienced a literary boom and many young novelists are hard at work writing in English about Singapore. Of the old guard, Goh Sin Tub is a respected writer who has written many books. *Goh's 12 Best Singapore Stories* is widely available. *Juniper Loa* by Lin Yutang is set mostly in the 1920s and is typical of earlier literature looking back at the motherland and the immigrant experience. It is about a young man who leaves China for Singapore and Juniper Loa is the woman he leaves behind.

Of the recent novelists, Philip Jeyaretnem is one of the leading lights and his *Raffles Place Ragtime* is a Singaporean bestseller. *A Candle or the Sun* by Gopal Baratham was published in 1991, after years of rejection by skittish Singaporean publishers. It is about a Christian group that runs foul of the authorities by questioning the government's authoritarianism. *Fistful of Colours* by Suchen Christine Lim, a winner of the Singapore Literature Prize, contrasts the difference and tensions between the modern and traditional, the old and the young in Singapore's ethnic communities. Catherine Lim is another highly regarded writer. Her books, such as *Little Ironies – Stories of Singapore*, are mostly about relationships with Singapore as a backdrop.

The real boom in Singaporean publishing has been in popular fiction. Ghost and horror stories abound in Singapore's bookshops and slightly risqué novels are walking out the door as Singapore discovers, after Goh Chok Tong's relaxation of censorship, that sex sells.

SOCIETY & CONDUCT

Singapore is a society in transition. The change of leadership in 1991 had some effect, though the real dynamic is the younger generation. The society is moving away from its immigrant Chinese outlook as Singaporeans keenly examine and redefine their own, unique identity.

Singapore is often portrayed by outsiders as a soulless money-making machine – an unkind assessment but not without some basis. Cultural pursuits have taken a back seat to technology and economic progress,

The Automated City

If you think that automation and computerisation have crept too far into your daily life, then you had better take a long hard look at Singapore. Here computers, cameras, scanners and bank accounts are all linked in order to keep track of the city-state's three million citizens. Admittedly, it does all make life a little easier for them, too.

All motor vehicles, both two wheeled and four wheeled, are now equipped with in-vehicle units that accept cashcards – stored-value monetary plastic. In order to garner road-toll levies, automatic scanners and cameras mounted on strategically placed gantries record vehicles passing certain key points around the island and request that drivers insert their cashcard into their in-vehicle unit. The appropriate road toll is then automatically deducted. Nonconformists are photographed and mailed a hefty fine.

If your stored-value MRT Farecard is running low on credit, slip it into a machine at the MRT station and top it up. The fee is automatically debited to your bank account. If you don't do it yourself then the barrier gate automatically tops up your card, also automatically deducting the amount from your account.

Tired of the visit to the accountant to file your tax return or, worse still, the long queues at the taxation office? Simple – file your return over the Internet. Looking for a government provided HDB flat? Not a problem, file your request through the Internet. Want to know your school examination results? Check 'em out on the Net. It's a cinch.

The Internet, computerisation and automation are now so all-pervasive in Singaporean society, it's hard to imagine how they ever lived without it. Who said 1984 was passé?

but as the population becomes wealthier, more educated and broad-minded, the restrictive focus on economic development alone is fading.

The government is keen to define the Singaporean identity, especially in its promotion of Asian values. Its neo-Confucian ideals are based on subservience to family and society, hard work and the desire to succeed. This dovetails neatly with the government's authoritarian notions of 'Asian democracy', which argue that western pluralism and democracy are decadent luxuries that Singapore cannot afford. Traditional Chinese culture is stressed, yet Singapore enjoys diverse and growing cultural expression, despite political restrictions.

The widespread use of English and the inheritance of British institutions has meant that Singapore has always been much more western-oriented than other South-East Asian nations. This western orientation, though, has largely been confined to an English-educated elite while the large Chinese-educated working class has traditionally defined Singaporean society. This is changing with a growing middle class and the increasing use of English.

Young Singaporeans have eagerly embraced Levis, Walkmans and western popular culture. But, as in Japan, it is wrong to assume that Singapore is simply aping the west and development will turn it into a European society. Traditional values and customs remain, adapting and blending with the trappings of development. Singaporeans have a confident vision of themselves as a dynamic Asian nation, even if what it means to be Singaporean is yet to be defined.

The great icons of Singaporean culture still tend to be food, but chicken rice or *roti prata* do not a culture make. The nascent but growing interest in the arts has seen a rush of publications examining Singaporean society and traditions, while in other areas, such as theatre and music, Singaporeans examine their identity as never before.

Kiasu or What?

One of the buzz words of the 1990s in Singapore has been *kiasu*. This Hokkien word meaning 'afraid to lose' is best summed up by Mr Kiasu, a Singaporean cartoon hero, whose philosophy includes: Always must win; Everything also must grab; Jump queue; Keep coming back for more; Look for discounts; Never mind what they think; Rushing and pushing wins the race; and Winner takes it all! all! all!

And are Singaporeans kiasu? At the risk of generalising, it's true that they are competitive and a bargain will never pass a Singaporean by, but would the country's economy be so dynamic if they were otherwise? It can sometimes be frustrating trying to get out of a lift or MRT train as fellow passengers push to get off while boarding passengers rush to get in, but it is better than trying to board the subway in New York or Tokyo. Singaporeans haven't inherited the British love of queues and, as in most Asian countries, don't have much time for the deferential excesses of continually saying 'please', 'thank you' and 'sorry', but in a world of plastic smiles and 'have a nice day' the no-nonsense Singaporean approach has something going for it.

Singaporeans have taken the kiasu tag in good humour, as shown by the popularity of Mr Kiasu, and fast-food outlets even offer kiasu burgers. So, when in Singapore, hunt out those bargains, don't pay unless you have to, overindulge at buffets and have a kiasu good time.

Much of it is retrospective – reminiscences of street hawkers or ponderings on the loss of the kampong life – but modern life is also explored, despite official discouragement to question the structure of Singaporean society.

Though the dominant Chinese culture and growing westernisation are the most obvious facets of society, of course Malay and Indian traditions have also shaped Singapore. Traditional customs and beliefs among the various ethnic groups are given less importance or have been streamlined by the pace of modern life, but the strength of traditional religious values and the practice of time-honoured ways remains.

Chinese Customs

The moment of birth is most important for the Chinese and is strictly recorded; it is essential for horoscopes and astrological consultations that are important in later life. Traditionally, only close relatives come to visit after the third day and the household has to undergo purification rites after one month. At this time the child is named, but the name may be changed if it is not deemed to be a prosperous one.

Every family wants at least one boy, as only males can carry out the necessary rituals associated with the worship of the ancestors and the passing of the parents. In the Confucian tradition, children are taught to have great respect for their parents and education is stressed.

Marriages were traditionally arranged and the astrologer consulted to see if the would-be couple were compatible. While the astrologer might still be consulted for an auspicious day, marriages are rarely arranged these days and the Chinese wedding ceremony shows much less tradition. The western tradition of a white wedding is popular, and religion is not really part of the wedding ceremony. In keeping with the Singaporean love of food, wedding receptions are often held at restaurants where guests are treated to a banquet.

Funerals on the other hand are much more traditional, elaborate affairs. The Chinese funeral is one of the most colourful and expensive ceremonies. At a traditional funeral, paper houses, cars, television sets and even paper servants are offered and burnt so that the deceased can enjoy all these material benefits in the next life. The body is dressed in best clothes and sealed in the coffin along with a few valuables. The coffin is placed in front of the ancestral altar in the house, and joss sticks and candles are burnt. Mourning and prayers may go on for three days prior to the funeral, which is an expensive affair involving the hire of professional mourners and musicians who clash cymbals and gongs to drive away the evil spirits. Food and drink is provided to all those who visit the house to pay their respects.

Traditionally, children would mourn the death of a father for three years and white would be worn during this period, but modern life has seen the mourning period greatly reduced. Whatever changes in tradition have occurred, the importance of the grave and its upkeep remains, and most Chinese pay respects to their elders on All Souls' Day.

Chinese New Year is the major festival, and even Chinese who profess no religion will celebrate it with gusto. It is a time for clearing out the old and bringing in the new. The house is given a spring-clean, and all business affairs and debts brought up to date before the new year. It is a time for family, friends and feasting, and ang pow are given to children. Chap Goh Meh is the last day of the Chinese New Year and is the peak of celebrations.

Malay Customs

Adat, or customary law, guides the important ceremonies and events in life, such as birth, circumcision and marriage. When Islam came to South-East Asia it supplanted existing spiritual beliefs and systems of social law, but conversion to Islam did not mean a total abolition of existing customs and beliefs, and many aspects of adat exhibit Hindu and even pre-Hindu influences.

During a birth, evil spirits must be kept at bay and traditional rituals are undertaken to nullify the spirits. For example, in a birth attended by the midwife, the baby is spat on to protect it from the spirits of disease, and the Muslim call to prayer is whispered in the baby's ear. On the seventh day the baby's first hair-cutting (*bercukur*) is performed and the baby is named. If it is later decided that the name does not suit the baby or is hampering its development, the name can be changed.

The circumcision of boys (*bersunat*) is a major event and usually occurs when a boy is aged between eight and 12 years. The boy is dressed in finery and seated on a dais. After feasting, passages from the Koran are read and the boy repeats verses read by the imam. The circumcision occurs the next morning when the boy sits astride a banana trunk and the *mudin*, or circumciser, performs the operation.

The Malay wedding tradition is quite involved and there are a number of rituals which must be observed. The prospective husband dispatches an uncle or aunt to his wife-to-be's house to get the family's permission to marry (*hantar tanda*). Once this is given, the couple are engaged (*bertunang*), and then the actual ceremony (*akad nikah*) takes place.

The bride and groom, dressed in traditional *kain songket* (silk with gold thread), have henna applied to their palms and fingertips (*berinai*). Then in a ceremony with significant Hindu influence (*bersanding*), they 'sit in state' on a dais surrounded by both modern gifts and traditional offerings, such as folded paper flowers in a vase of bath towels, ringed by quail eggs in satin ribbons.

The couple are showered with *bunga rampai* (flower petals and thinly shredded pandan leaves) and sprinkled with *air mawar* (rose-water).

Important ceremonies in family life are accompanied by a feast known as *kenduri*. Guests can number in the hundreds and preparations can take days as many traditional dishes, such as *nasi minyak* (spicy rice) and *pulut kuning* (sticky saffron rice), have to be prepared.

The most important festival is Hari Raya Puasa, the end of the fasting month. This is the equivalent of the Malay New Year and

Caning in Singapore

If proof were needed of Singapore's determination to deal severely with social miscreants, it was unwittingly provided by American teenager Michael Fay.

In 1994 Fay, accused of vandalising cars, received four strikes of the cane in a punishment that not even high-level US government intervention could prevent.

Changi prison is where convicted men, 10 to 15 at a time, are made to squat in a corridor outside the caning room awaiting their turn on a wooden contraption to which they are strapped, bent forward and naked, except for protective padding around their kidneys, and harshly caned across the buttocks by a burly warder using a flexible four-foot long length of rattan – known as the rotan – which has been soaked in water.

The caning which is conducted in a carefully controlled way so as to inflict maximum pain with minimum damage, nonetheless rips into the skin of the buttocks causing immediate blood flow and excruciating pain for the unfortunate victim who often faints from the agony. Caned inmates can usually not sit down for up to three weeks and scarring often lasts for life.

Many thousands of men have received this punishment: 602 prisoners were caned in 1987 (including 115 foreigners), and 616 were caned in 1988 (119 foreigners). In 1992 the number caned grew to 1422, and in 1993 – the latest year for which figures are available – to 3244, or over 60 per week. This seems an almost unbelievable figure for a jurisdiction whose population is just over three million, but the figures are accurate. Just keep your nose clean and you'll avoid a meeting with the man with the rotan – a meeting Michael Fay will never forget.

new clothes are bought, families are reunited and, of course, there is much feasting.

Indian Customs

Most Singaporean Indians come from southern India and so the customs and festivals that are more important in the south, especially in Madras, are the most popular in Singapore.

Traditionally, about 10 days after the birth of a baby the *namakarana*, or name-giving ceremony, is held. An astrologer will be called upon to give an auspicious name, often the name of a god. Boys are very much favoured, as only males can perform certain family rituals. Also, the pernicious dowry system can mean financial ruin for a family with too many daughters.

One of the major ceremonies in the life of a boy of higher caste is the initiation which involves receiving the sacred threads, though this ceremony is generally restricted to the Brahman caste and not widely practised in Singapore. The boy is bathed, blessed by priests and showered with rice by guests. Then three strands of thread, representing Brahma, Vishnu and Shiva, are draped around the boy's left shoulder and knotted underneath the right arm, thus officially initiating the boy into his caste.

Arranged marriages are still common, though the bride and groom have an increasing say in the choice of their intended partner. The day, hour and minute of the wedding are also the preserve of the astrologer. The marriage is usually held at the house of the bride's family, where the couple will be seated on a dais and a sacred flame will be placed in the centre of the room. The final ceremony involves the bridegroom placing the *thali* (necklace) around the bride's neck and the couple circumambulating the fire seven times.

Deepavali, or the Festival of Lights, is the major Indian festival in Singapore and homes are decorated with oil lamps to signify the victory of light over darkness. The spectacular Thaipusam is the most exciting festival.

Dos & Don'ts

Dress The days when arriving travellers could be denied entry to Singapore for having long hair or basically looking scruffy may be long gone, but you will still get scant respect if you turn up looking like you have just emerged from the jungle. Singapore is hot, humid and tropical but young Singaporeans dress smartly. That means the latest fashions from Europe. Denim jeans and Hard Rock Cafe T-shirts are cool too, but so are ties and jackets for dinner and the disco. Only Chinese manual workers, or coffee shop owners, would deign to be seen in public wearing shorts.

Spitting & Such Singapore has strict laws defining appropriate public behaviour. Spitting, urinating in public, chewing gum, jaywalking or even failing to flush the toilet are all misdemeanours that can land you with a fine (see the Fines boxed text in the Facts for the Visitor chapter).

RELIGION

The variety of religions found in Singapore is a direct reflection of the diversity of races living here. The Chinese are predominantly followers of Buddhism and Shenism (or deity worship), though some are Christians. Malays are overwhelmingly Muslim, and most of Singapore's Indians are Hindus, though a sizeable proportion are Muslim and some are Sikhs.

Despite increasing westernisation and secularism, traditional religious beliefs are still held by the large majority. Singaporeans overwhelmingly celebrate the major festivals associated with their religions, though religious worship has declined among the young and the higher educated, particularly the English-educated. In the Chinese community, for example, almost everyone will celebrate Chinese New Year, while the figure for those who profess Chinese religion is around 70%.

An interesting reversal of the trend away from religion is the increase in Christianity, primarily among the English-educated Chinese elite, and the charismatic movements in particular are finding converts.

The government is wary of religion and has abolished religious instruction in schools with the stated aim of avoiding religious intolerance and hatred. The government's stated philosophy is Confucian, which is not a religion as such but a moral and social model. Its ideal society is based on the Confucian values of devotion to parents and family and loyalty to friends, and the emphasis is on education, justice and good government.

Chinese Religion

The Chinese religion is a mix of Taoism, Confucianism and Buddhism. Taoism combines with old animistic beliefs to teach people how to maintain harmony with the universe. Confucianism takes care of the political and moral aspects of life, while Buddhism takes care of the afterlife. But to say that the Chinese have three religions – Taoism, Confucianism and Buddhism – is too simple a view of their traditional religious life.

At the first level Chinese religion is animistic, with a belief in the innate vital energy in rocks, trees, rivers and springs. At the second level people from the distant past, both real and mythological, are worshipped as gods. Overlaid on this are popular Taoist, Mahayana Buddhist and Confucian beliefs.

On a day-to-day level the Chinese are much less concerned with the high-minded philosophies and asceticism of Buddha, Confucius or Lao Zi than they are with the pursuit of worldly success, the appeasement of the dead and the spirits, and the seeking of hidden knowledge about the future. Chinese religion also incorporates what in the west is deemed as superstition; if you want your fortune told, for instance, you go to a temple.

The other important thing to remember is that Chinese religion is polytheistic. Apart from Buddha, Lao Zi and Confucius there are many divinities, such as house gods and gods and goddesses for particular professions. The worship of these gods is the most common form of religious practice in Singapore.

The most popular gods and local deities, or *shen*, in Singapore are Kuan Yin, the goddess of mercy, and Toh Peh Kong, a local deity representing the spirit of the pioneers and found only outside China. Kuan Ti, the god of war, is also very popular and is nowadays regarded as the god of wealth. Offerings of joss sticks and fruit are made at temples but most households also have their own altars.

Integral parts of Chinese religion are death, the afterlife and ancestor worship. At least as far back as China's Shang dynasty, funerals were lavish ceremonies involving the interment of horses, carriages, wives and slaves. The more important the person, the more possessions and people had to be buried with them since they would require them in the next world. The deceased had to be kept happy because people's powers to inflict punishments or to grant favours greatly increased after their death. Even today, a traditional Chinese funeral can be an extravagant event (see Chinese Customs in Society & Conduct earlier in this chapter).

While ancestor worship plays an important role, it is not as extensive as in China, where many generations of ancestors may be worshipped. Singaporean Chinese generally only honour the ancestors of two or three generations, that is, going as far back as their immigrant forefathers.

The most important word in the Chinese popular religious vocabulary is *joss* (luck), and the Chinese are too astute not to utilise it. Gods have to be appeased, bad spirits blown away and sleeping dragons soothed to keep joss on one's side. *Feng shui* (literally 'wind-water') is the Chinese technique of manipulating or judging the environment. Feng shui uses unseen currents that swirl around the surface of the earth and are caused by dragons which sleep beneath the ground.

If you want to build a house, high-rise hotel or find a suitable site for a grave, then you call in a feng shui expert; the wrath of a dragon which wakes to find a house on his tail can easily be imagined! It is said that Lee Kuan Yew regularly consulted feng shui experts when in power, and his luck declined when he insisted on continuing with badly sited land reclamation.

Islam

During the early 7th century in Mecca (in present-day Saudi Arabia), Mohammed received the word of Allah (God) and called on the people to turn away from pagan worship and submit to the one true God. His teachings appealed to the poorer levels of society and angered the wealthy merchant class. By 622 life had become sufficiently unpleasant to force Mohammed and his followers to migrate to Medina, an oasis town some 300km to the north. This migration – the *hejirah* – marks the beginning of the Islamic calendar, year 1 AH or 622 AD. By 630 Mohammed had gained a sufficient following to return and take over Mecca.

The followers of Mohammed spread the word with boundless zeal, using force where necessary, and by 644 the Islamic state covered Syria, Persia, Mesopotamia, Egypt and North Africa; in the following decades its influence would extend from the Atlantic to the Indian Ocean.

Islam is the Arabic word for submission, and the duty of every Muslim is to submit themselves to Allah. This profession of faith (the *shahada*) is the first of the five pillars of Islam, the five tenets in the Koran which guide Muslims in their daily life:

shahada 'There is no God but Allah and Mohammed is his prophet' – this profession of faith is the fundamental tenet of Islam. The shahada is to Islam what The Lord's Prayer is to Christianity.
salah The call to prayer. Five times a day – at dawn, midday, mid-afternoon, sunset and nightfall – Muslims must face Mecca and recite the prescribed prayer.

continued on page 40

Places of Worship

MOSQUES

While much of Singapore's public architecture has Indian roots, and many of the older mosques follow Indian styles (as opposed to Middle Eastern), some newer mosques are modern showpieces of extraordinary design.

Design & Function

Despite their often astounding beauty and seeming intricacy of design, mosques are essentially simple buildings. Their main function is to provide a large space for communal prayer. The largest mosques are the Masjid Jamek, or Friday Mosques, which are intended to provide space for all the Muslims of the area to come together for prayer on Friday, the holy day of the Islamic week.

Smaller, local mosques are used for prayer on other days of the week.

Etiquette for Visitors

Most mosques admit visitors but not usually at prayer times (you'll know it's prayer time by the number of people streaming in). Most Singaporean mosques also admit women visitors (which isn't always the case elsewhere in the Muslim world). Both men and women must dress appropriately, covering their arms and legs – so no shorts or sleeveless T-shirts. A few larger mosques have robes for visitors who are not appropriately dressed. Shoes must be removed before entering.

Built in a Mughal-Indian style, Sultan Mosque is the grandest and most important of the island's 80 or more mosques. Bussorah St, leading to the mosque, is the focal point of festivities during the Muslim fasting month of Ramadan.

RICHARD I'ANSON

PATRICK HORTON

Brightly coloured doors at the Thian Hock Keng Temple.

PATRICK HORTON

Detail of the figures adorning the gopuram at the south Indian-style Hindu Sri Mariamman Temple.

RICHARD I'ANSON

Gopuram detail from the Vishnu-dedicated Sri Srinivasa Perumal Temple.

PAUL HELLANDER

Approaching the main entrance to the Sultan Mosque. Inside a digital display gives the day's prayer times.

RICHARD I'ANSON

The unusual architecture of the Nagore Dhurga Muslim mosque/shrine.

Examples of Mosques

One of Singapore's oldest mosques is the imposing Sultan Mosque (Map 5), close to Arab St, which was originally built in 1825. It's the focus for the island's Muslim community. Not far away, on the corner of Victoria St and Jalan Sultan, is the striking Malabar Muslim Jama-Ath Mosque (Map 5) inlaid with eye-catching lapis lazuli tiles.

In Little India the Abdul Gaffoor Mosque (Map 5) is a simple workaday mosque and the regular call of the *muezzin* is an audible feature of the neighbourhood.

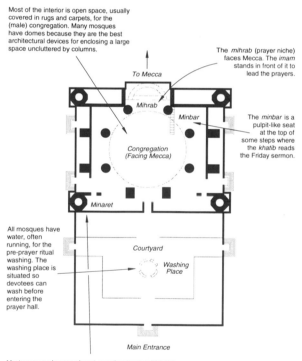

Most of the interior is open space, usually covered in rugs and carpets, for the (male) congregation. Many mosques have domes because they are the best architectural devices for enclosing a large space uncluttered by columns.

The *mihrab* (prayer niche) faces Mecca. The *imam* stands in front of it to lead the prayers.

To Mecca

Mihrab

Minbar

The *minbar* is a pulpit-like seat at the top of some steps where the *khatib* reads the Friday sermon.

Congregation (Facing Mecca)

Minaret

All mosques have water, often running, for the pre-prayer ritual washing. The washing place is situated so devotees can wash before entering the prayer hall.

Courtyard

Washing Place

Main Entrance

Most mosques have a minaret, usually a tower, which the muezzin climbs five times a day to call the faithful to prayer. Increasingly, the muezzin's call is tape-recorded and booms out over loudspeakers. Most older Malaysian mosques are based on Indian designs, so there is usually one minaret rather than several.

CHINESE TEMPLES

Taoism, Buddhism and Confucianism have blended in Chinese religion and, while many temples are theoretically Buddhist or Taoist, it takes a sharp eye to determine which is which. You'll often find statues of the Buddha side by side with statues of Taoist deities. You may also see a statue of Confucius, but a temple devoted entirely to Confucius will be a much quieter and less colourfully decorated place than the usual Chinese temple.

Design & Function

An elaborate Chinese-style roof distinguishes most temples. Some temples are built to a multistorey pagoda design, but many are simpler single-storey buildings.

The Thian Hock Keng Temple is the most important Hokkien Buddhist temple on Singapore. It's laid out on a traditional north-south axis and incorporates numerous shrines to a variety of different deities.

A screen often separates the main entrance from the main hall of the temple, which is a riot of carved, gilded wood, bright cloth and various antiquities such as ceremonial chairs and swords. Incense fills the air, as the lighting of incense sticks accompanies all prayer.

People burn prayers for good fortune, or 'ghost money', to appease evil spirits who might be bothering them or their relatives. Food is offered to ghosts, although after they have tasted it, the food is shared in a communal feast.

PAUL HELLANDER

There are priests, but religious life remains the responsibility of the individual. There are no set times for prayers and no communal services except for funerals. However, the community comes together to observe popular holidays, and noisy parades are held on special occasions.

In Singapore many Chinese participate in Buddhist as well as Taoist festivals, and days such as Buddha's Birthday attract crowds to temples. Noise, colour and a lot of burning incense (sometimes emanating from incense sticks bigger than baseball bats) are features of religious holidays. At other times people pray for success and the basics of life.

Etiquette for Visitors

It is customary to remove your shoes before entering a temple, although this is not always mandatory. Because people are coming and going all the time, often praying for deceased relatives, you should resist the temptation to treat temples as the superb art galleries they often are.

Examples of Chinese Temples

There are many Chinese temples in Singapore, such as the Thian Hock Keng Temple (Map 6) also known as the Temple of Heavenly Happiness. This temple on Telok Ayer St in Chinatown is the oldest (built in 1841) and most colourful temple in the city.

The Kuan Yin Temple (Map 5), on Waterloo St, is one of the liveliest and most popular, with a daily crowd of joss-stick burners and devotees seeking divine intervention in their commercial life.

The Siong Lim Temple (Map 2), near Toa Payoh MRT station, is one of the largest temples in Singapore and includes a Chinese rock garden.

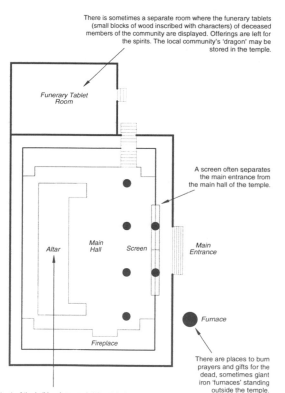

There is sometimes a separate room where the funerary tablets (small blocks of wood inscribed with characters) of deceased members of the community are displayed. Offerings are left for the spirits. The local community's 'dragon' may be stored in the temple.

Funerary Tablet Room

A screen often separates the main entrance from the main hall of the temple.

Altar

Main Hall

Screen

Main Entrance

Furnace

Fireplace

There are places to burn prayers and gifts for the dead, sometimes giant iron 'furnaces' standing outside the temple.

At the back of the hall is a large and elaborately decorated altar, usually containing an image of the deity (or person) to whom the temple is dedicated. In front of the altar is some sort of bench or table where devotees light their incense and pray.

HINDU TEMPLES

As most of the region's Hindus are of south Indian descent, it isn't surprising that Hindu temples in Singapore adopt design elements from south Indian temples.

Design & Function

For Hindus, the square is the perfect shape (a circle isn't perfect because it implies motion), so temples are always based on a square ground plan. Extremely complex rules govern the siting, design and building of each individual temple, based on numerology, astronomy, astrology and religious law. These are so complicated and so important that it's customary for each temple to harbour its own particular set of calculations as though they were religious texts.

Each temple is dedicated to a particular god in the vast Hindu pantheon. The temple is used exclusively for religious rites. However, because Hinduism has so many rites and festivals, there's always something happening and the temple is a de facto community centre.

Etiquette for Visitors

Dress conservatively, remove your shoes before entering and do not attempt to enter the sanctum.

A detail from the highly decorated, colourful and typically south Indian gopuram belonging to the Sri Mariamman temple. The goddess Mariammam is revered for her powers to cure disease and illness.

PATRICK HORTON

Examples of Hindu Temples

The Sri Mariamman Temple (Map 6) in Chinatown is probably Singapore's best known and busiest temple. It is famous for its colourful *gopuram*, or entrance tower, and is built in south Dravidian style. The interior ceiling paintings are particularly vibrant.

Over in Little India is the more functional Sri Veeramakaliamman Temple (Map 5), which has a similarly ornate gopuram, and also the Sri Srinivasa Perumal Temple (Map 5), both on Serangoon Rd. This second temple is also the starting point for the Thaipusam procession to the Chettiar Hindu Temple (Map 6), close to Fort Canning Park.

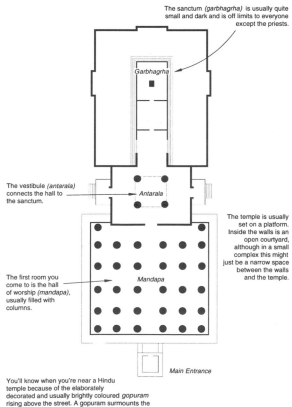

The sanctum *(garbhagrha)* is usually quite small and dark and is off limits to everyone except the priests.

Garbhagrha

The vestibule *(antarala)* connects the hall to the sanctum.

Antarala

The temple is usually set on a platform. Inside the walls is an open courtyard, although in a small complex this might just be a narrow space between the walls and the temple.

The first room you come to is the hall of worship *(mandapa)*, usually filled with columns.

Mandapa

Main Entrance

You'll know when you're near a Hindu temple because of the elaborately decorated and usually brightly coloured *gopuram* rising above the street. A gopuram surmounts the gateway(s) in the walls surrounding the temple.

SIKH TEMPLES

Sikhism doesn't recognise caste or class, so everyone becomes involved in ceremonies. Communal meals are a feature of temple activities.

Design & Function

A Sikh temple is called a *gurdwara*. Outside there is a flagpole, called a *nishan sahib*, flying a triangular flag with the Sikh insignia. There is no special requirement for the design of the building but most use some elements from Punjabi gurdwaras. Sikhs worship only one god and are opposed to idol worship. You'll probably see pictures of the Gurus (the spiritual leaders who founded Sikhism), especially the first, the fifth and the 10th (last) Gurus. The wisdom of the Gurus is contained in the *Guru Granth Sahib*, a book written by Arjun, the fifth Guru, in the early 17th century. It has become an object of veneration in itself and is regarded as the living Guru.

Etiquette for Visitors

The Gurdwara Sahib Yishun is an elegant new Sikh temple in Singapore.

Sikhism is an egalitarian religion and everyone is welcome to enter the temple. However, you must remove your shoes and you are supposed to cover your head.

Examples of Sikh Temples

In general, Sikh temples in this region have until recently been quite modest buildings, such as the Sri Guru Singh Sabha (Map 4) on Wilkie Rd, just south of Little India. Unlike almost all other religions, there was little attempt to reproduce the architectural styles of the religion's birthplace. However, the increasing wealth of the Sikh community has seen some impressive new temples built, such as the Gurdwara Sahib Yishun (Map 2) out in the suburb of Yishun.

Sikhism differs from Hinduism in that there are no caste-related taboos in the preparation and cooking of food. This is an important community ritual, and every gurdwara has a large and cheerful kitchen.

Food prepared in the temple is eaten as a communal meal in the dining hall.

Kitchen & Dining Hall

Guru Granth Sahib

Donations

Prayer Hall

Main Entrance

The *Guru Granth Sahib*, the holy book, is 'woken' in the morning and 'draped' in robes. In the evening it is put to bed. It is the centrepiece of ceremonies.

The temple is always entered by the main door. Sikhs approach the *Guru Granth Sahib* and bow. Money for the upkeep of the temple is usually placed in a box in front of the holy book.

continued from page 30

zakat Originally the act of giving alms to the poor and needy, fixed at 5% of one's income. It has been developed by some modern states into an obligatory land tax which goes to help the poor.

Ramadan The ninth month of the Islamic calendar, when all Muslims must abstain from eating, drinking, smoking and sex from dawn to dusk. It commemorates the month when Mohammed had the Koran revealed to him; the purpose of the physical deprivation is to strengthen the will and forfeit the body to the spirit.

hajj The pilgrimage to Mecca, the holiest place in Islam. It is the duty of every Muslim who is fit and can afford it to make the pilgrimage at least once in their life. On the pilgrimage, the *haji* (pilgrim) wears two plain white sheets and walks around the kabbah, the black stone in the centre of the mosque, seven times.

According to Muslim belief, Allah is the same as the God worshipped by Christians and Jews. Adam, Abraham, Noah, Moses, David, Jacob, Joseph, Job and Jesus are all recognised as prophets by Islam. Jesus is not, however, recognised as the son of God. According to Islam, all these prophets partly received the word of God but only Mohammed received the complete revelation.

Islam came to South-East Asia with the Indian traders from south India and was not of the more orthodox Islamic tradition of Arabia. It was adopted peacefully by the coastal trading ports of Malaysia and Indonesia, and Islam absorbed, rather than conquered, existing beliefs.

Islamic sultanates replaced Hindu kingdoms, though the Hindu idea of kings remained. The traditions of adat (customary law) continued, but Islamic law dominated, while the caste system, never as entrenched as in India, had no place in the more egalitarian Islamic society. Women exerted a great deal of influence in pre-Islamic Malay society, but Islam weakened their position. Nonetheless, Malay women today enjoy more freedom than women do in many other Muslim societies.

Malay ceremonies and beliefs still exhibit pre-Islamic traditions, but most Malays are ardent Muslims and to suggest otherwise would cause great offence. The Koran is the main source of religious law for Malays and, though few are proficient in Arabic, Malay children learn to read it. However, the main medium of religious instruction is Jawi, the Malay language written in the Arabic script.

Hinduism

On first appearances Hinduism is a complex religion, but basically it postulates that we all go through a series of reincarnations that eventually lead to *moksha*, the spiritual salvation which frees one from the cycle of death and rebirth. With each rebirth you can move closer to or further from eventual moksha; the deciding factor is your *karma*, which is literally a law of cause and effect. Bad actions during your life result in bad karma, which ends in lower reincarnation. Conversely, if your deeds and actions have been good you will reincarnate on a higher level and be a step closer to eventual freedom from rebirth. *Dharma*, or the natural law, defines the total social, ethical and spiritual harmony of your life.

Hinduism has three basic practices: *puja*, or worship; the cremation of the dead; and the rules and regulations of the caste system. Although still very strong in India, the caste system was never significant in Malaysia, chiefly because the labourers who were brought here from India were mainly from the lower classes.

Westerners often have trouble understanding Hinduism, principally because of its vast pantheon of gods. In fact, you can look upon all these different gods simply as pictorial representations of the many attributes of a god. The one omnipresent god usually has three physical representations: Brahma, the creator; Vishnu, the preserver; and Shiva, the destroyer or reproducer. All three gods are usually shown with four arms, but Brahma has the added advantage of four heads to represent his all-seeing presence. The four *Vedas*, the books of 'divine knowledge' which are the foundation of Hindu philosophy, are supposed to have emanated from his mouths.

Hinduism is not a proselytising religion since you cannot be converted. You're either born a Hindu or you are not; you can never become one.

Hinduism in South-East Asia dates back 2000 years or more and there are Hindu influences in cultural traditions, such as the wayang kulit (shadow puppet play) and the bersanding wedding ceremony. However, it is only in the last 100 or so years, following the influx of Indian contract labourers and settlers, that it has again become widely practised.

LANGUAGE

The four official languages of Singapore are Malay, Tamil, Mandarin and English. Malay is the national language. It was adopted when Singapore was part of Malaysia, but its use is mostly restricted to the Malay community.

Tamil is the main Indian language; others include Malayalam and Hindi.

Chinese dialects are still widely spoken, especially among the older Chinese, with the most common being Hokkien, Teochew, Cantonese, Hainanese and Hakka. The government's long-standing campaign to promote Mandarin, the main nondialectal Chinese language, has been very successful and increasing numbers now speak it at home.

English is becoming even more widespread. After independence, the government had a bilingual education policy that attempted to develop the vernacular languages and lessen the use of English. However, Chinese graduates found that this lessened their opportunities for higher education and presented them with greater difficulties in finding a job. English was the language of business and united the various ethnic groups, and the government eventually had to give it more priority. It officially became the first language of instruction in schools in 1987. The only communication problems you may have are with older Singaporeans who did not learn English at school.

All children are also taught their mother tongue at school. This policy is largely designed to unite the various Chinese groups and to make sure Chinese Singaporeans don't lose contact with their traditions.

Speak Mandarin, Please!

Singapore is a country with many languages and people, but it is the Chinese who ultimately predominate.

When their forbears came from China they brought with them a number of Chinese languages and dialects, including Hokkien, Teochew, Hakka, Cantonese and Mandarin. So dissimilar are these dialects that they might as well be separate languages. The British temporarily solved the problem by making English the lingua franca of its tropical colony and to a large degree that still remains the case today.

But in more recent times the Singapore government, in an effort to unite its disparate Chinese peoples, has been encouraging minority-language speakers to use the language of administration used by Beijing, namely Mandarin. In this way, it is hoped, disunity and differences can be eliminated and the concept of a Singaporean nation can better be realised.

The campaign was initially targeted at monolingual Chinese-speakers, but over the years it has spread to encompass English-educated Chinese as well who have begun to show an increasing willingness to use Mandarin as their main vehicle for communication in business and pleasure. The government is so intent on its 'Speak Mandarin Campaign' that it even has a Web site where would-be converts can get themselves motivated – it's at www.gov.sg/spkmandarin.

FACTS ABOUT SINGAPORE

Singlish

One of the most intriguing things the visitor to Singapore will notice is the strange patois spoken by the locals. Nominally English, it incorporates linguistic elements from Chinese, Malay and Tamil. Phrases are clipped short, word order is flipped and stress and cadence are unconventional, to say the least. The result is known locally as Singlish.

While there isn't such a thing as Singlish grammar, there are definite characteristics.

First off, there's the reverse stress pattern of double-barrelled words. For example, in standard English the stress would be 'FIRE-fighter' or 'THEATRE company' but in Singlish it's 'fire-FIGHTER' and 'theatre COMPANY'.

Words ending in consonants – particularly 'l' or 'k' – are often syncopated and vowels are often distorted; a Chinese-speaking taxi driver might not immediately understand 'Perak Road' since he pronounces it 'Pera Roh'.

The particle 'lah' is often tagged on to the end of sentences as in, 'No good, lah', which could mean (among other things) 'I don't think that's such a good idea'.

Requests or questions will often be marked with a tag ending since direct questioning is considered rude. So, the question might be 'You want beer or not?', which, of course, comes across to speakers of western English as being extremely rude.

Verb tenses tend to be nonexistent. Future, present or past actions are all indicated by time phrases, so in Singlish it's 'I go tomorrow' or 'I go yesterday'.

Singlish is frowned upon in official use, though you will get a good idea of its pervasive pronunciation characteristics if you listen to the news bulletins on TV or the radio.

The following are some of the most frequently heard Singlishisms:

ah beng – low class, uneducated person with no fashion sense or style; red neck

aiyah! – oh, dear!

alamak! – exclamation of disbelief or frustration, like 'my God!'

ayam – Malay word for chicken; adjective for something inferior or weak

blur – a slow or uninformed person

buaya – womaniser, from the Malay for crocodile

can? – is that OK?

can! – yes! That's fine.

char bor – babe, woman

cheena – old-fashioned Chinese in dress or thinking (derogatory)

go stun – to reverse, as in 'go stun the car'

heng – luck, good fortune (Hokkien)

hiao – vain

inggrish – English

kambing – foolish person, literally 'goat' (Malay)

kaypoh – busybody

kenna ketok – ripped off

kiasee – scared, literally 'afraid to die'; a coward

kiasu – literally 'afraid to lose'; selfish, pushy, always on the lookout for a bargain

kopi tiam – coffee shop

lah – generally an ending for any phrase or sentence; can translate as OK, but has no real meaning; added for emphasis to just about everything

looksee – take a look

makan – a meal; to eat

malu – embarrassed

minah – girlfriend

or not? – general suffix for questions, as in can or not? (can you or can't you?) or go or not? (are you going?)

see first – wait and see what happens

shack – tired

shiok – good, great, delicious

steady lah – well done, excellent; an expression of praise

wah! – general exclamation of surprise or distress

ya ya – boastful, as in 'he always ya ya'

Singapore has developed its own brand of English, humorously referred to as Singlish (see the boxed text opposite). While irate readers write to the *Straits Times* and complain about the decline in the use of the Queen's English, many Singaporeans revel in their unique patois. It contains borrowed words from Hokkien and Malay, such as *shiok* (delicious) and *kasar* (rough), and is often a clipped form of English, dropping unnecessary prepositions and pronouns.

Facts for the Visitor

WHEN TO GO

Any time. Climate is not a major consideration; Singapore gets a fairly steady rainfall
year-round. Your visit may coincide with
various festivals – Singapore has something
happening every month (see Public Holidays
& Special Events later in this chapter). Thaipusam, occurring around February, is one of
the most spectacular festivals or, if shopping
and eating are your major concerns, July is a
good month as the Singapore Food Festival
and the Great Singapore Sale are held.

ORIENTATION

Singapore is a city, an island and a country.
While there are built-up, high-density areas
all around the island, the main city area is
in the south.

The City Raffles founded Singapore on the
Singapore River, and this waterway is still
very much at the heart of the city. Just south
of the river mouth is the Central Business
District (CBD; Map 6), centred around
Raffles Place, and along the river banks are
the popular renovated districts of Boat
Quay and Clarke Quay.

To the south-west, Chinatown (Map 6)
adjoins the CBD, further inland from Robinson Rd. South Bridge Rd runs through the
centre of Chinatown, while New Bridge Rd
further west is the main shopping area.

To the north of the river is the colonial
district (Map 5), which has many reminders
of British rule, as well as a number of top-
end hotels and shopping centres. The famed
Raffles Hotel is on the corner of Bras Basah
and Beach Rds. Between Bras Basah and
Rochor Rds to the north is the main budget
accommodation area, centred on Beach Rd
and Bencoolen St.

Further north are Little India (Map 5),
centred on Serangoon Rd, and Arab St.
Both are interesting, more traditional areas.

From the colonial district, Bras Basah Rd
heads north-west to become Orchard Rd,
Singapore's main tourist area, with dozens
of luxury hotels, shopping complexes,
restaurants and bars. South of Orchard Rd
and west of Chinatown, Havelock Rd is a
quieter and much smaller hotel enclave.

Singapore Island To the west of the island,
Jurong (Map 7) is an industrial area, but it
also contains a number of tourist attractions.
The east coast has some older suburbs and a
major beach park, and at the far east of the
island is Changi international airport. The
eastern and north-eastern parts of the island
are home to some huge housing developments. The central north of the island has
much of Singapore's undeveloped land and
most of the remaining forest. Points of interest include the zoo and a number of parks.
The north-west is less developed, especially
along the coast, which is a live firing area
containing many reservoirs.

Addresses

Unlike many Asian cities, Singapore is well
laid out with signposted streets and logically
numbered buildings. As many of the shops,
businesses and residences are in high-rise
buildings, addresses are often preceded by
the number of the floor and then the shop or
apartment number. Addresses do not quote
the district or suburb. For example, 03-12
Far East Plaza, Scotts Rd is shop No 12 on
the 3rd floor of the Far East Plaza.

MAPS

Various good maps, many in Japanese as
well as English, are available free at tourist
offices, the airport on arrival, most middle
and top-end hotels and some shopping
centres.

Of the commercial maps, *Nelles* and
Periplus are the best. The best reference if
you plan on spending any length of time in
Singapore, or want to rent a car, is the *Sin-
gapore Street Directory*, a bargain at S$10.
It's available at most bookshops.

TOURIST OFFICES
Local Tourist Offices

The Singapore Tourism Board (STB) has two tourist information centres. The first is on the ground floor at its head office (Map 4; ☎ 1-800 738 3778) at 1 Orchard Spring Rd, off Cuscaden Rd at the western end of the Orchard Rd area. The other is at 02-34 Raffles Hotel Arcade (Map 5; ☎ 1-800 334 1335) on North Bridge Rd. Both have a good selection of hand-outs. The big hotels and Changi airport also stock a range of tourist leaflets and free tourist maps. Pick up a copy of the *Singapore Official Guide*, which is updated monthly and has the latest opening hours, prices and bus routes. The STB also produces other excellent publications, such as food, hotel, nightlife and shopping guides.

If you have access to the Internet, the STB's official site (www.newasia-singapore.com) is excellent.

STB Offices Abroad

STB offices overseas include:

Australia
(☎ (02) 9290 2888; fax 9290 2555) level 11, AWA bldg, 47 York St, Sydney, NSW 2000; (☎ (08) 9325 8578; fax 9221 3864) 8th floor, St Georges Court, 16 St Georges Terrace, Perth, WA 6000
Canada
(☎ (416) 363 8898; fax 363 5752) Standard Life Centre, suite 1000, 121 King St West, Toronto, Ontario M5H 3T9
China
(☎ (021) 6248 8145; fax 6248 3150) 202A Hotel Equatorial, 65 Yanan Rd West, Shanghai 200040;
(☎ (0852) 2598 9290; fax 2598 1040) room 2003, Central Plaza, 18 Harbor Rd, Wanchai, Hong Kong
France
(☎ 01 42 97 16 16; fax 42 97 16 17) ONTS Centre d'Affaires Le Louvre, 2 Place du Palais-Royal, 75044 Paris Cedex 01
Germany
(☎ (069) 920 7700; fax 920 8922) Hochstrasse 35-37, 60313 Frankfurt-am-Main
Japan
(☎ (03) 3593 3388; fax 3591 1480) 1st floor, Yamoto Seimei bldg 1-Chome, 1-7 Uchisaiwai-cho Chiyoda-ku, Tokyo 100

South Korea
(☎ (02) 399 5570; fax 399 5574) 9th floor, Young Poong bldg, 33 Sorin Dong, Chongro-ku, Seoul
Taiwan
(☎ (02) 718 5280; fax 719 1049) unit H, 6th floor, Hung Tai Centre, 168 Tun Hwa North Rd, Taipei
UK
(☎ (0171) 437 0033; fax 734 2191) 1st floor, Carrington House, 26-130 Regent St, London W1R 5FE
USA
(☎ 213-852 1901; fax 852 0129) suite 510, 8484 Wilshire Blvd, Beverly Hills, CA 90211; (☎ 212-302 4861; fax 302 4801) 12th floor, 590 Fifth Ave, New York, NY 10036; (☎ 312-938 1888; fax 938 0086) suite 1450, 2 Presidential Plaza, 180 North Stetson Ave, Chicago, Ill 60601

DOCUMENTS
Visas

Citizens of British Commonwealth countries (except India) and citizens of the Republic of Ireland, Liechtenstein, Monaco, Netherlands, San Marino, Switzerland and the USA do not require visas to visit Singapore. Citizens of Austria, Belgium, Denmark, Finland, France, Germany, Iceland, Italy, Japan, Korea, Luxembourg, Norway, Spain and Sweden do not require visas for stays of up to 90 days for social purposes.

Upon arrival, a 14 day or 30 day permit is normally issued depending on your stated length of stay. You can easily extend a 14 day permit for another two weeks but you may be asked to show an air ticket out of Singapore and/or sufficient funds to stay. Further extensions are more difficult but in theory most nationalities can extend their permits for up to 90 days. The Immigration Department head office (Map 3; ☎ 1-800 391 6400) is at 10 Kallang Rd, one block south-west of Lavender MRT station.

Travel Insurance

A travel insurance policy to cover theft, loss and medical problems is a good idea. The policies handled by STA Travel and other student travel organisations are usually good value. Some policies offer lower and higher medical-expense options; the higher ones are chiefly for countries such as the USA which have extremely high medical costs. There is a wide variety of policies available so check the small print.

Some policies specifically exclude 'dangerous activities', which can include scuba diving, motorcycling and even trekking. A locally acquired motorcycle licence is not valid under some policies.

You may prefer a policy which pays doctors or hospitals directly rather than you having to pay on the spot and claim later. If you have to claim later make sure you keep all documentation. Some policies ask you to call back (reverse charges) to a centre in your home country where an immediate assessment of your problem is made.

Check that the policy covers ambulances or an emergency flight home.

Driving Licence
If you will be driving in Singapore, bring your current home driver's licence and an International Driving Permit issued by a motoring association in your country.

Student & Youth Cards
Students should bring their international student card – it's not of much use as student discounts are almost invariably for Singaporeans only, but you might be able to bluff a discount at some attractions. A Hostelling International (HI) card is not worth acquiring as Singapore has no HI hostels but, again, bring it if you have one because flashing it like a student card might bring discounts.

EMBASSIES
Singaporean Embassies
Some Singaporean embassies and high commissions overseas include:

Australia
(☎ (02) 6273 3944; fax 6273 3260) 17 Forster Crescent, Yarralumla, Canberra, ACT 2600
China
(☎ (0106) 532 3926; fax 532 2215) No 1 Xiu Shui Bei Jie, Jianguomenwai, Beijing 100600

France
(☎ 01 45 00 33 61; fax 01 45 00 58 75) 12 Square de l'Avenue Foch, 75116 Paris
Germany
(☎ (0228) 951 0314; fax 310 527) Südstrasse 133, 53175 Bonn
Indonesia
(☎ (021) 520 1489; fax 520 2320) Jalan HR Rasuna Said, Block X/4, Kacling 2, Jakarta
Japan
(☎ (03) 3586 9111; fax 5561 9176) 5-12-3 Roppongi, 5-Chome, Minato-ku, Tokyo 1060032
Malaysia
(☎ (03) 261 6404; fax 264 1013) 209 Jalan Tun Razak, Kuala Lumpur 50400
Netherlands
(☎ (04) 404 2111; fax 404 2460) Weena 607, 3012 CN Rotterdam
New Zealand
(☎ (04) 479 2076; fax 479 2315) 17 Kabul St, Khandallah, Wellington
Thailand
(☎ (02) 286 2111; fax 670 8001) 129 South Sathorn Rd, Bangkok 120
UK
(☎ (0171) 235 8315; fax 245 6583) 9 Wilton Crescent, London SW1X 8RW
USA
(☎ 202-537 3100; 537 0876) 3501 International Place NW, Washington, DC 20008

Embassies in Singapore
Many foreign consulates and embassies are conveniently located around Orchard Rd (Map 4). Addresses for some of them include:

Australia
(☎ 737 9311; fax 735 1242) 25 Napier Rd
Canada
(☎ 325 3200; fax 325 3297) 14-00 IBM Towers, 80 Anson Rd
China
(☎ 734 3200; 735 9639) 11-01/03 Tanglin Shopping Centre, 19 Tanglin Rd
France
(☎ 466 4866; fax 466 8559) 5 Gallop Rd
Germany
(☎ 737 1355; fax 737 2653) 14-01 Far East Shopping Centre, 545 Orchard Rd
Indonesia
(☎ 737 7422; fax 737 5037) 7 Chatsworth Rd
Ireland
(☎ 276 8935; fax 271 8722) 08-06 Tiong Bahru Plaza, 298 Tiong Bahru Rd

Japan
   (☎ 235 8855; fax 733 1039) 16 Nassim Rd
Malaysia
   (☎ 235 0111; fax 835 1267) 02-06, 268 Orchard Rd
Myanmar
   (☎ 735 0209; fax 735 6236) 15 St Martin's Drive
Netherlands
   (☎ 737 1155; fax 737 1940) 04-01, 541 Orchard Rd
New Zealand
   (☎ 235 9966; fax 733 9924) 15-00 Ngee Ann City Tower A, 391A Orchard Rd
South Korea
   (☎ 256 1188; fax 356 1805) 10-03 United Square, 101 Thomson Rd
Thailand
   (☎ 737 2644; fax 835 4991) 370 Orchard Rd
UK
   (☎ 473 9333; fax 475 9706) 100 Tanglin Rd
USA
   (☎ 476 9100; fax 476 9340) 27 Napier Rd
Vietnam
   (☎ 462 5938) 10 Leeden Park

CUSTOMS
Visitors to Singapore are allowed to bring in 1L of wine, beer or spirits duty free. Electronic goods, cosmetics, watches, cameras, jewellery (but not imitation jewellery), footwear, toys, arts and crafts are not dutiable; the usual duty-free concession for personal effects, such as clothes, applies. Singapore does not allow duty-free concessions for cigarettes and tobacco. Importing chewing gum is banned and possession of the stuff is considered an offence.

Duty-free concessions are not available if you are arriving from Malaysia or if you leave Singapore for less than 48 hours (so you can not stock up on duty-free goods on a day trip to Batam in Indonesia).

Drugs, fire crackers, toy currency and coins, obscene or seditious material, gun-shaped cigarette lighters, endangered species of wildlife or their by-products, and pirated recordings and publications are prohibited. The importation or exportation of illegal drugs carries the death penalty for more than 15g of heroin, 30g of morphine, 500g of cannabis or 200g of cannabis resin, or 1.2kg of opium. Penalties for trafficking in lesser amounts range from a minimum of two years in jail and two strokes of the *rotan* (cane) to 30 years and 15 strokes of the rotan. If you bring in prescription drugs you should have a doctor's letter or prescription confirming that they are necessary.

There is no restriction on the importation of currency.

MONEY
Currency
The unit of currency is the Singapore dollar. Singapore uses 1c, 5c, 10c, 20c, 50c and S$1 coins, while notes come in denominations of S$2, S$5, S$10, S$50, S$100, S$500 and S$1000; Singapore also has a S$10,000 note – not that you'll see many.

Why on earth 1c and 5c coins are still in circulation is beyond comprehension, since they are hardly usable and tend to disappear into the deeper recesses of pockets, wallets and purses.

Exchange Rates
The following table shows approximate exchange rates at the time of publication:

Australia	A$1	=	S$0.99
Canada	C$1	=	S$1.12
France	FFr10	=	S$2.73
Germany	DM1	=	S$0.91
Indonesia	1000 rp	=	S$0.11
Japan	¥100	=	S$1.19
Malaysia	RM1	=	S$0.41
New Zealand	NZ$1	=	S$0.84
Thailand	100B	=	S$3.99
UK	UK£1	=	S$2.74
USA	US$1	=	S$1.64

Exchanging Money
Most of the major banks are in the CBD, although there are also a number of major banks along Orchard Rd and local banks are all over the city. Exchange rates tend to vary from bank to bank and some even have a service charge on each exchange transaction – this is usually S$2 to S$3, so ask first. Banks are open from 9.30 am to 3 pm weekdays and until 11.30 am on Saturday.

Moneychangers do not charge fees, so you will often get a better overall exchange rate for cash and travellers cheques with them than at the banks. You'll find money-changers in just about every shopping centre in Singapore. Most shops will accept foreign cash and travellers cheques at a slightly lower rate than you'd get from a moneychanger.

Apart from changing other currencies to Singapore dollars, moneychangers also sell a wide variety of other currencies and will do amazing multiple-currency transactions in the blink of an eye. You can even get good rates for some restricted currencies.

Cash Cash is always useful and usually necessary for the payment of small items like meals in hawker centres, food courts and bars and for buying items from street vendors. However, Singapore is moving more and more towards becoming a cash-less society and in some cases – like hiring cars or paying for hotel bills – cash is considered almost suspect.

Travellers Cheques This time-honoured method of safe money transport is still popular and is always a fail-safe fall-back should the ATMs, credit card dial-up links and cashcard systems of Singapore fail. It is a good idea to always have some travellers cheques as they can often be used instead of direct cash payments in shops and restaurants. Travellers cheques can be bought at post offices in Singapore.

ATMs Most ATMs will accept your credit card from home. It is a good idea to credit your account with cash before you go to avoid any unpleasant surprises when you get back. It also reduces the risk of running out of credit when you most need it. It's a good idea to use only ATMs outside banks for easier retrieval of your card should it be inadvertently swallowed up.

Credit Cards All major credit cards are widely accepted, although you're not going to make yourself too popular after a hard bargaining session for a new camera if you then try to pay for it with plastic. The tourism authorities suggest that if shops insist on adding a credit card surcharge you contact the relevant credit company in Singapore. Most hotels and car-hire companies will insist on a credit card and will probably demand full payment upfront if you cannot produce one.

Cashcards Singaporean citizens or residents with a local bank account can now use cards with a stored cash value. These credit card-sized virtual wallets can contain a stored cash value of up to S$100 and can be topped up at special terminals linked to bank accounts. They can be used at a growing number of establishments but about the only time a traveller will need to use one is at the National Library, where all services must be paid for with a cashcard.

Costs

Singapore is much more expensive than other South-East Asian countries and the strength of the Singapore dollar against most currencies has seen a substantial rise in costs for most visitors.

If you are travelling on a shoestring budget, the prices will come as a shock but you can still stay in Singapore without spending too much money. The great temptation is to run amok in the shops and blow your budget on electrical goods or indulge in all the luxuries you may have craved while travelling in less-developed Asian countries.

Expect to pay S$9 per night or more for a dorm bed and from S$22 to S$45 for a double room in a cheap hotel or guesthouse. Public transport is cheap and you can eat well in Singapore for a reasonable price: a good meal at a food centre can cost less than S$5. So it is possible to stay in Singapore for under S$25 per day, though S$50 is a more realistic minimum. You should be prepared to spend a lot more if you want to eat in restaurants (reckon on S$20 to S$30 for sit-down dining), check out the nightlife or visit a lot of the attractions.

Sights of Singapore: the CBD skyline at dusk (top left); City Hall (top right); Boat Quay and the Singapore River (middle); a Singapore Day performance on the steps of City Hall (bottom left); and the Singapore harbour Merlion lit up at twilight (bottom right).

PATRICK HORTON

PAUL HELLANDER

RICHARD I'ANSON

Getting around Singapore is genuinely easy with options ranging from the rapid, air-conditioned efficiency of the MRT (top), to the cable cars between Mt Faber and Sentosa (middle) or, for a real street level experience, a bicycle trishaw (bottom).

Costs

The cost of items in Singapore's supermarkets is generally on a par with most US, Australian or UK supermarkets. Asian food items are naturally cheap while imported items from Europe or elsewhere tend to be expensive. Cheeses and dairy products are particularly dear, as is alcohol, especially spirits.

The costs of a few basic items are:

Loaf of bread (500g)	S$1.40
Milk (1L)	S$1.60
Imported whisky (70cL)	S$51.70
Cola (1L)	S$1.30
Tiger beer (330mL)	S$2.60
Packet of 20 cigarettes	S$5.60
Rice (5kg)	S$8.45
Packet of noodles (500g)	S$0.75
Unleaded petrol (1L)	S$1.15

If you have more to spend, then most of your cash will be absorbed in hotel bills and restaurants. Mid-range, second-string hotels charge from S$60 to S$100, though hotels at the top of this range are of a pretty good standard. International-standard hotels charge from S$300 and go way up. Depending on discounts available, top-end hotels may offer good value for the facilities on offer.

Tipping & Bargaining

Tipping is not usual in Singapore. The most expensive hotels and restaurants have a 10% service charge, in which case tipping is discouraged. Don't tip at hawker stalls, though the more expensive coffee shops and restaurants that do not add a service charge may expect a tip. Taxi drivers don't expect a tip and may actually round a fare down if it is 10c or 20c above an even dollar – they may expect you, similarly, to round it up. Staff in the international hotels, such as room staff or the doorman who hails your taxi, may expect a tip if they have provided good service.

Bargaining is falling by the wayside in Singapore, but tourists should still expect to haggle for luxury items and souvenirs in some stores. It is unnecessary to bargain for everyday goods or transport, as happens in many Asian countries, though it doesn't hurt to ask about discounts at the more expensive hotels.

Many shops and department stores have fixed prices for clothes and luxury items. A fair number of small shops in the tourist areas, especially electronic shops, don't display prices. In this case bargaining is almost always required, and a request for prices is usually greeted with talk of special offers and the production of a calculator. For antiques, handicrafts and other tourist-oriented items, a price tag doesn't mean you can't bargain, and you usually should.

Some smaller traders put only a small mark-up on goods, while others are very greedy – you need to have some idea of the regular prices. With so many large discount stores and fixed-price shops, it hardly seems worth bargaining in Singapore anymore. See the Shopping chapter for more details.

Taxes & Service Charges

Singapore has a 3% Goods and Services Tax (GST) applied to all goods and services. Visitors purchasing goods worth S$300 or more through a shop participating in the GST Tourist Refund Scheme can apply for a GST refund. These shops display a 'tax refund' sticker, and you must fill in a claim form and show your passport at the shop. The claim form and the goods must then be presented to the relevant counter at Changi or Seletar airports on departure. You then have to mail the customs-stamped form back to the shop, which will post a cheque for the refund.

In addition to the 3% GST, a 10% service charge and 1% 'cess' (government entertainment tax) is added to the bill at the more expensive hotels and restaurants, as well as at most nightspots and bars. This is the 'plus-plus-plus' that follows some quoted prices (as in S$120+++). Some of the cheaper establishments don't add taxes but absorb them into the quoted price, which is 'nett', eg S$70 nett.

DOING BUSINESS

Singapore prides itself on being a dynamic and efficient place to do business. Hardly a week goes by without the press quoting some business survey rating Singapore as the biggest or best in one field or another. If Singapore comes in at 2nd or 3rd then it is exhorted to top the rankings next year.

Leaving Barings Bank and a couple of other scandals aside, Singapore has stable financial markets, a stable government and virtually no corruption, which is something of a rarity in Asia.

Singapore has aggressively attracted foreign investment and big money from overseas has played a large part in the dramatic rise in Singapore's wealth. In recent times, with its high cost of living and rising wages, Singapore has been losing out in the foreign investment stakes to the other boom-time countries of the region, such as neighbouring Malaysia and Indonesia, but reserve-rich Singapore is itself now a large foreign investor.

As a free-trading entrepôt and promoter of foreign investment with minimal restrictions, Singapore is a good place to do business, though it primarily directs its energies and substantial concessions to large investors in export-oriented industries. The domestic economy is very much directed by the government through the auspices of the Economic Development Board (EDB).

Singapore pursues a free-trade policy and, other than the GST for the importation of goods, very few goods are dutiable or restricted for import or export. The Singapore Trade Development Board (STDB; head office (☎ 337 6628; fax 337 6898) 07-00 Bugis Junction Office Tower, 230 Victoria St) has simplified import and export procedures, and trade documents can be processed through TradeNet – an electronic data system.

Singapore bookshops are awash with trade and business publications, and there are various chambers of commerce in Singapore,

such as the Singapore International Chamber of Commerce (Map 6; ☎ 224 1255; fax 224 2785), 10-10-01 John Hancock Tower, 6 Raffles Quay.

The Singapore Telecom White Pages (www.asiapages.com.sg/PhoneBook.htm) and the *Business Times* Web site (www.asia1.com.sg/biztimes) are two good Internet information sources.

The main initial point of contact is the STDB, most of whose overseas offices are located at the Singaporean embassies. STDB offices include:

Australia
(☎ (02) 9233 4211; fax 9233 6492) 12th floor, Overseas Union Bank bldg, 53 Martin Place, Sydney, NSW 2000
China
(☎ (01) 6437 0776; fax 6433 4150) Address as embassy
France
(☎ 01 45 02 13 77; fax 45 02 13 76) Address as embassy
Germany
(☎ (069) 920 7350; fax 920 3522) Goethestrasse 5, 60313 Frankfurt-am-Main
Indonesia
(☎ (021) 522 9274; fax 520 1488) Address as embassy
Japan
(☎ (03) 3584 6032; fax 3584 6135) Address as embassy
Malaysia
(☎ (03) 262 5966; fax 262 5963) 54C, 54th floor, Empire Tower, Jalan Tun Razak, Kuala Lumpur 50400
South Korea
(☎ (02) 736 1207; fax 736 1209) 7th floor, Citicorp Centre bldg, 89-29 Shinmoon-ro, 2-ka Chongro-ku, Seoul 110-062
Taiwan
(☎ (02) 772 1940; fax 781 7648) 9th floor, 85 Jenai Rd, Section 4, Taipei
UK
(☎ (0171) 235 4558; fax 235 4557) Singapore high commission, 5 Chesham St, London SW1P 1RJ
USA
(☎ 212-421 2207; fax 888 2897) suite 21B, 55 East 59th St, New York 10022

Bring plenty of business cards with you to Singapore. Business meetings typically begin with the exchange of cards, which are offered with two hands in a humble gesture signifying that you are presenting yourself to your contact. Expect to be liberally dined and entertained. Establishing personal rapport is important and your business contacts are unlikely to let you languish in your hotel at the end of a working day.

Business Services

A number of business support services exist in Singapore and companies regularly advertise their services in the *Straits Times*. You can rent offices, organise stationery and business cards, arrange phone connections and hire personnel via these outfits.

Translating & Interpreting Services

Translating documents is often a vital and sometimes risky business. The most important thing is to acquire the services of a professional translation service with experience and a proven track record. Your business contract may depend on the accuracy of the final product and you will have no way of knowing whether what you have paid for is good or bad until it is possibly too late.

Interpreting differs from translating in that it is 'live' – you use another person to assist in speech communication as opposed to written communication. This distinction is often blurred in business circles.

Singapore has a wide range of translation and interpretation services listed in the Buying Guide section of the Yellow Pages.

Bear in mind one basic rule when it comes to language and business: if at all possible, 'sell in your *buyer's* language – buy in *your* language'.

Consider utilising translation services from your home country before you approach businesses in Singapore. Having said all that, you are pretty safe using English as the language of communication for transactions in Singapore.

Exhibitions & Conferences

Singapore's main International Convention & Exhibition Centre (Map 6) is 200m east of Raffles Hotel in the colonial district. A new expo centre is being built close to Changi airport but it will not be open for at least another two to three years. Most major hotels have their own mini-convention centres and are well practised in hosting foreign delegations.

POST & COMMUNICATIONS
Post

Postal delivery in Singapore is very efficient and post offices provide a number of services other than selling stamps, including public telephones and the sale of packing material such as padded bags, boxes and bubble wrap. The former main, or general, post office (GPO) on Fullerton Rd near Raffles Place is now closed and letters addressed to post restante c/o GPO are held at the Robinson Rd post office (Map 6), on the corner of McCallum St.

The Comcentre (Map 4), where you can also post letters, at 31 Exeter Rd, very near Somerset MRT station, is open from 8 am to 6 pm weekdays and from 8 am to 2 pm on Saturday. The Changi airport branches in the Terminal 1 and Terminal 2 departure lounges are open from 8 am to 9 pm daily. Otherwise there are some 96 post office branches scattered throughout the island. Normal business hours are from 8.30 am to 5 pm weekdays and from 8.30 am to 1 pm on Saturday.

Postal Codes There is now a six digit postal code system which should be used when addressing mail to and within Singapore. Ask for the *Postal Code Directory* at any post office or call the Postal Code HelpLine (☎ 1-800 240 7678) to find a particular code. Alternatively, visit the Web site (www.singpost.com.sg) for full details.

The system is not surprisingly very efficient. The first two digits are the sector code, which defines a particular area in Singapore, and the last four digits are the delivery point – the house or particular building.

In theory you could address a mail item to someone using the postal code only and it should get there.

Postal Rates Local postage charges for a simple letter or postcard start at 22c for up to 20g, rising to S$1.50 for 500g. An airmail letter to most Asia-Pacific countries costs 60c or 70c for the first 20g, and 25c or 30c for each additional 10g; to Europe and the Americas the cost is S$1 for the first 20g and 35c for each additional 10g. Postcards cost 50c.

Parcels sent by surface mail to countries outside the region cost from S$14 to S$19 for the first kilo, then from S$25 to S$30 for up to 5kg. For parcels up to 10kg the cost is around S$35 to S$40. The main exception to this is for parcels to the USA, which are charged at about double the rate of other destinations.

For full details call the Postage Rate HelpLine on ☎ 165.

Telephone

For such a wired-up city, telephone communications in Singapore fall surprisingly short of being super-efficient. Neither is the service particularly reasonably priced.

Local and overseas calls can be made from public phone booths. A few hotels have free local calls, though most charge around 50c for a 15 minute call and some charge by the minute. The going surcharge on international calls from hotels is 25%.

As well as at public phone booths and hotels, you can make international phone calls at a Telecom centre, such as the ones at 15 Hill St (Map 6), near Fort Canning Park, or 71 Robinson Rd (Map 6), near Raffles Quay, or at selected post offices.

For directory information call ☎ 100; the talking clock is ☎ 1711; and the police emergency number is ☎ 999.

The country code for calling Singapore is 65 and the international access code is 001.

The residential White Pages listings can be found on the Internet at www.asia-pages.com.sg/PhoneBook.htm.

Calls to Malaysia Calls to Malaysia work differently to regular international calls since they are considered STD (trunk or long-distance) calls. To make a call you dial the access code 020, followed by the area code of the town in Malaysia that you wish to call (minus the leading zero) and then your party's number. Thus for a call to 346 7890 in Kuala Lumpur (area code 03) you would dial 020 3 346 7890. Call ☎ 104 for assistance with Malaysian area codes.

Phonecards The easiest way to make a phone call (international or local) is to dial it yourself from a public pay phone, but you'll need a phonecard and a phone which accepts these cards (many pay phones will now operate only with phonecards, not coins). Phonecards come in denominations of S$2, S$5, S$10, S$20 and S$50, and are available at Telecom centres, post offices, 7-Elevens and a number of retail outlets such as newsagents throughout the island.

Credit-Card Phones Credit-card phones are also available (just swipe your Amex, Diners Club, MasterCard or Visa through the slot). At the Telecom centres, there are also Home Country Direct phones – press a country button to contact the operator, then reverse the charges or have the call charged to an international telephone card acceptable in your country. The Home Country Direct service is available from any phone by dialling the appropriate code, listed in the front pages of the phone book.

Mobile Phones Users of mobile phones will find that as long as you have arranged to have 'global roaming' facilities with your home provider, your GSM digital phone will automatically tune into one of Singapore's two digital networks, M1-GSM or ST-GSM. There is complete coverage over the whole island and phones will also work in the underground sections of the MRT rail network. Rates are variable but quite reasonable in comparison with other countries in the region. A cheaper way is to use SMS messaging from mobile phone to mobile phone instead of voice calls. Short messages of up to 150 characters can be sent efficiently and cheaply this way. Contact your service provider for full details.

Fax

Faxes can be sent from all post offices, Telecom centres and hotels but the service tends to be a costly business. Hotels will also normally charge you to receive faxes. The ideal way for business people travelling with their own laptop computers and a mobile phone is to fax directly from your laptop via the phone. Travellers without such means can use a free service via the Internet that covers a large range of countries (see the boxed text on this page).

Email & Internet Access

The simplest way for travellers to get access to email and the Web is to buy time at an Internet cafe. This typically costs anywhere from S$8 to S$11 per hour.

The addresses of some of the most central Internet cafes are:

Challenger Planet Cafe
(Map 6; ☎ 336 7747) Funan Centre 06-00, 109 North Bridge Rd
email: super@challenger.com.sg
Internet: www.challenger.com.sg
Two terminals only (S$8 per hour). It's open daily from 10.30 am to 8 pm.
Cyberheart Cafe
(☎ 734 3877) Orchard Hotel (Map 4), 442 Orchard Rd
email: cyheart@pacific.net.sg
It has 12 terminals charged at S$10 an hour. It's open daily from 11 am to 11 pm.
CyberNet Cafe
(Map 6; ☎ 324 4361) 57 Tanjong Pagar Rd
email: admin@cybertrek.com.sg
Internet: www.cybertrek.com.sg
Plenty of terminals with access time charged at S$8 per hour. A tutorial session for beginners costs S$15 an hour. It's open from 11 am to 10 pm Monday to Saturday, 2 to 7 pm Sunday.
PI@Boat Quay
(☎ 538 1380) The Coffee Bean (Map 6), 52 Boat Quay
email: info@pacific.net.sg
Internet: www.pacific.net.sg
Computer time is charged at S$10 an hour or S$6 for 30 minutes. It's open daily from 11 am to 9 pm, closed Sunday. There are further Pacific Internet cafes at Parco Bugis Junction (Map 5; ☎ 334 3379) and Parkway Parade (Map 8; ☎ 346 3379) on the East Coast.

Free Internet Faxing to Singapore

Singapore is one of a growing number of countries that can be reached via free Internet faxing. This means that you can address an email message to any fax machine in Singapore and it will be delivered without any cost to you or the recipient.

The Internet Fax Company (known commonly as TPC) has a Web site with details (www-usa.tpc.int/tpc_home.html).

The arrangement was set up as an experiment in so-called community faxing. A local node – commonly a university or, in some cases, as in the UK, a major ISP – undertook to receive email and distribute it to a fax machine within a local area for free. It was and still is, to a large degree, a goodwill service and is not tolerant of abuse. In most cases there is a limit to the number of faxes you can send in a week.

How does it work? Let's say you want to fax the Raffles Hotel in Singapore. Raffles' fax number is 339 7650 and Singapore's country access code is 65. You compose an email address as follows:

remote-printer.Raffles_Hotel@653397650.iddd.tpc.int

The first string tells the remote host that this is an email to fax message; the second string indicates the recipient (spaces are indicated by underscores). The address part after the @ sign consists of the country code and fax number followed by a standard Internet address string that doesn't really concern the sender. Send your email and within minutes it will print on the hotel's fax machine. Then again you could always send an email to raffles@pacific.net.sg, but that's another story and you get the point anyway.

Business hotels will often provide Internet access to guests at rates similar to those offered by Internet cafes and the working environment is probably more conducive to business.

Controlling the Internet

One of Singapore's greatest recent dilemmas has been how to liberalise without opening the information floodgates. This is a particularly curly problem when it comes to curbing the essentially anarchical nature of the Internet. On the one hand, the government has decreed that all citizens should be Internet-wired or at least Internet-savvy by 2000. But, on the other hand, it doesn't like all the nasties that go with it – like the criticism of the government there to be read by all in the soc.culture.singapore newsgroup, or the pornographic material that can be found pretty well anywhere you care to look.

Along with China and Vietnam, Singapore is trying to solve this problem through a series of laws and guidelines and through the formation of a regulatory board called the Singapore Broadcasting Authority (SBA). Responsible cyber-citizens who notice antisocial activities on the Net in Singapore are required to notify the SBA. In other words, you have the makings of a voluntary Net police: 1984 comes just 14 years too late.

ISPs ultimately bear the brunt of responsibility for keeping out the cyber-nasties by filtering the good and bad. They are also required by law to report any person or organisation found to be flaunting the rules – a chilling prospect when you consider that you are possibly being spied on the moment you log on to your favourite site. Who knows, the Net police might be knocking on your door just when you least expect it.

The National Library (see Libraries later in this chapter) on Stamford Rd next to the National Museum has a wonderful multimedia centre on the 2nd level where you can access the Internet (Web only) for only S$2 per hour.

Getting Connected If you already have a home Internet Service Provider (ISP) and a laptop computer with a modem and the requisite Internet software, the simplest way to access the Net may be to dial internationally to your home service and access your mail this way. Anything longer and your communication charges will soon add up, not to mention the hotel surcharges. Using a mobile phone linked to your computer with an interface card is a marginally cheaper way.

Most reasonable business hotels will provide a business centre or at least access to a terminal from which you can conduct your affairs. Prices will vary from place to place but they should be in the region of S$10 to S$15 per hour.

If you are planning to stay for a month or longer it may well be worth taking out an Internet account with a local ISP. Hooking up is efficient and painless and you can normally be up and running within 48 hours of registration. You will get a dedicated mailbox and the software to get you started if you haven't already got it. Rates are around S$9.95 per month for 12 hours access time plus S$2.95 per hour thereafter. Flat-rate monthly accounts for S$100 are also available. There is usually a start-up fee of S$40 to S$50.

There are currently three ISPs in Singapore, all offering much the same in the way of services:

CyberWay (☎ 1-800 843 4833)
    email: help@cyberway.com.sg
    Internet: www.cyberway.com.sg
Pacific Internet (☎ 1-800 872 1455)
    email: info@pacific.net.sg
    Internet: www.pacific.net.sg
Singnet (☎ 1-800 838 3899)
    email: sales@singnet.com.sg
    Internet: www.singnet.com.sg

INTERNET RESOURCES

There is a bewildering amount of information on all aspects of Singapore on the Internet. Look via the usual search engines.

Most of the sites given here also provide useful cross links.

Please note that Web site addresses, though correct at the time of going to press, are particularly prone to change.

www.asia1.com.sg
The Web site of Asia One, the company that owns all the papers; the site has links to the *Straits Times*, the *New Paper* and the *Business Times*, among others.
www.changi.airport.com.sg
A detailed guide to Singapore's world-beating airport.
www.geocities.com/TheTropics/7222
A site compiled for visitors by Robin, a Singaporean Chinese; there's a good FAQ section in which travellers' queries are answered.
www.happening.com.sg
An off-beat, online listings magazine with articles, reviews and what's on information; it's updated daily.
www.lonelyplanet.com
This is Lonely Planet's award-winning site, containing destination updates, recent travellers' letters and a useful traveller's bulletin board.
www.sintercom.org
Possibly the best general site for Web links to Singapore's burgeoning Internet community.
www.travel.com.sg
The home site of the Singapore Tourism Board; the text suffers from a surfeit of PRese but there's plenty of good material on shopping, eating, festivals etc.

BOOKS

Most books are published in different editions by different publishers in different countries. As a result, a book might be a hardcover rarity in one country while it's readily available in paperback in another. Fortunately, bookshops and libraries search by title or author, so your local bookshop or library is best placed to advise you on the availability of our recommendations.

Lonely Planet

Lonely Planet publishes a guide to *Malaysia, Singapore & Brunei*, while *South-East Asia on a shoestring* is our overall guidebook to the region. If you're travelling further afield, there are individual guides to all South-East and North-East Asian countries.

Guidebooks

Streets of Old Chinatown by Sumiko Tan is a street-by-street look at Chinatown's buildings, attractions and history with maps, interesting photographs and some restaurant and hotel recommendations. Even though it was published only in 1990, many of the streetscapes have changed dramatically, but the book remains a good read.

1907 Handbook to Singapore by GM Reith is a reprint by Oxford University Press of a British colonial-era book. It concentrates on the public buildings, gardens and clubs, many of which have hardly changed. It comes with the attitudes of the times – Malay is dismissed as a 'primitive language' – but largely avoids reference to Asian cultures.

Bringing things more up to date, the *Handbook for Expatriates* published by Rank Books (1997) is a useful volume for people thinking of coming to live and work in Singapore. It covers such topics as setting up in business, establishing a home and finding a school for the kids. It's concisely written with lots of useful addresses and phone numbers. It's available in Singapore for S$25.75.

History

There are a great number of books available that deal with various events in Singapore's history.

A History of Singapore by CM Turnball is the best choice for a detailed overview of the tropical city-state from its prehistory to the present. It is an excellent scholarly work which is also very readable and a mine of interesting information. The author has also written *A Short History of Malaysia, Singapore & Brunei*.

Singapore: Its Past, Present and Future by Alex Josey deals mostly with recent history. It is very pro-People's Action Party (PAP).

Raffles by Maurice Collis is the straightforward story of the man who founded Singapore.

The fall of Singapore in 1942 and the subsequent Japanese occupation is a well-covered subject. Noel Barber's book *Sinister Twilight – The Fall of Singapore* is an account of the bunglings, underestimations and final heroics that culminated in the rapid collapse of Singapore. *Out in the Midday Sun* by Kate Caffrey tells of the hardships of those who were captured and spent the rest of the war years in prison camps like the notorious Changi camp.

Politics

Lee Kuan Yew – the Man and His Ideas by Han Fook Kwang, Warren Fernandez & Sumiko Tan has been a surprising best seller since its release in November 1997 and stocks in bookstores have even been depleted on a few occasions. It naturally presents the still influential politician in a favourable light, but nonetheless makes for a good read.

Lee Kuan Yew – The Struggle for Singapore by Alex Josey covers all the twists and turns of the former prime minister's rise to power and the successful path along which his PAP has piloted Singapore.

Governing Singapore by Raj Vasil is widely available in Singapore and is as close as you'll get to the official PAP line. It includes interviews with Lee Kuan Yew and Goh Chok Tong.

For an insight into both sides of the PAP story, *No Man is an Island* by James Minchin is one of the best reads available. It's a warts-and-all portrait of Lee Kuan Yew which, unsurprisingly, is hard to find in Singapore.

Chee Soon Juan, the leader of the Singapore Democratic Party, is a thorn in the side of the government. After standing in the 1992 elections against Goh Chok Tong, he was sacked from his academic post for allegedly misusing postage funds and then sued for S$1 million for claiming that his dismissal was politically motivated. His book *Dare To Change: An Alternative Vision For Singapore* roundly criticises the government and offers social-democratic alternatives. It was such a local success that it has been followed by *Singapore: My Home Too*.

Another thorn in the side of the government, and also a former academic at the National University of Singapore, is Christo-

pher Lingle. His article in the *International Herald Tribune*, questioning the independence of the judiciary, resulted in yet another defamation suit in the government's favour. Dr Lingle fled the country and continues the battle in *Singapore's Authoritarian Capitalism*, a damning study of political repression and the 'Asian values' professed by the government.

Nick Leeson's *Rogue Trader* makes fascinating reading from the man who single-handedly brought down Barings Bank through a series of ill-conceived futures speculations (see the Rogue Trader boxed text in the Entertainment chapter). According to Leeson, everyone other than himself is to blame for the fiasco.

People & Society

Tales of Chinatown by Sit Yin Fong is a readable and informative piece on Chinese life. Fong was a journalist in Singapore for many years and writes anecdotal short stories about Chinese customs and beliefs.

Son of Singapore by Tan Kok Seng is the fascinating autobiography of a labourer who grew up in Singapore in the 1950s.

The Babas Revisited by Felix Chia is a classic study of the history, culture and language of the Straits Chinese.

Tiger Balm King by Sam King is an insider's view of Aw Boon Haw, one of the most famous Asian tycoons and founder of Haw Par Brothers, makers of Tiger Balm. This rags-to-riches story is more concerned with examining the Aw household than business exploits.

The Straits Chinese – A Cultural History by Khoo Joo Ee is a detailed chronicle of the Peranakan people from their art to their language.

Fiction

Singapore and Malaysia have long provided a fertile setting for novelists, and Joseph Conrad's *The Shadow Line* and *Lord Jim* both use the region as a backdrop. Somerset Maugham spent time in Singapore writing his classic short stories, many of which were set in Malaya – look for the *Borneo Stories*.

WWII has spawned a number of novels. *Saint Jack* by Paul Theroux is the story of an American pimp in Singapore, while *King Rat* by James Clavell is based on the experiences of POWs in Changi prison. *The Singapore Grip* by JG Farrell was a local best seller and provides an almost surreal view of life in Singapore, which is portrayed as 'fiddling while Rome burned' as the Japanese stormed down the peninsula in WWII.

For a view from the other side, Jiro Osaragi's *Homecoming* is a novel about a Japanese naval officer who goes to Singapore to escape scandal. Much of it is set in Melaka and Singapore in the 1940s. *Southward lies the Fortress* by Lim Thean Soo is about the siege of Singapore as seen through a Singaporean's eyes. Also worth reading is Lim's collection of short stories, *The Parting Gift and Other Stories*.

See under Literature in the Arts section of the Facts about Singapore chapter for more information on home-grown literature.

General

Singapore: A Guide to Buildings, Streets, Places (1988) by Norman Edwards & Peter Keys is dated but still a wonderful architectural guide to Singapore. It has photographs and discussions of Singapore's major buildings, and streetscapes, and also includes plenty of interesting historical and cultural titbits. *A History of Singapore Architecture* by Jane Beamish & Jane Ferguson is another good publication.

Portraits of Places by Brenda SA Yeoh & Luly Kong is an interesting sociological study of changing Singapore, examining selected areas from Orchard Rd to Kampong Wak Selat, the 'last village in Singapore', near Kranji.

David Brazil's *Street Smart Singapore* is a lively look at the Lion City stacked with interesting titbits on its history and culture.

Birdwatchers might want to get hold of *Birds – An Illustrated Field Guide to the Birds of Singapore* written by Lim Kim Seng, a local birdwatcher. Some 350 species from resident to migrant birds are covered in this excellent guide.

NEWSPAPERS & MAGAZINES

Singapore has three Chinese and three English daily newspapers (the latter have a slightly higher circulation). There is also a Malay daily and a Tamil daily.

The English daily newspapers are the establishment *Straits Times*, the *Business Times* and the *New Paper*, an evening tabloid. The *Straits Times* has good regional and foreign news, and some good feature articles. The best independent views on Singaporean politics are found in the readers' letters.

The *New Paper* is a long way behind the *Straits Times* in circulation and is seen as the fun alternative. It is a more staid version of an English tabloid and comes up with some amazingly trite, attention-grabbing headlines. It contains very little news.

The press in Singapore (which is largely owned by the gigantic Singapore Press Holdings) knows its limits and holds off criticism of the government. The foreign media sometimes doesn't know its limits and the government is not above restricting the circulation of foreign publications that do not report to its liking. Nevertheless, *Time*, *Newsweek* and many other foreign magazines are readily available.

RADIO & TV

The state-run Singapore Broadcasting Corporation (SBC) was corporatised in 1994. A slight relaxation of government controls on broadcasting followed, though television censorship is still fairly strict.

The Radio Corporation of Singapore controls most of the radio stations, with 10 stations transmitting in four languages – English, Malay, Mandarin and Tamil – on the AM, FM and short-wave bands. The BBC transmits in Singapore on 88.9 FM.

Singapore has three TV channels: 5, 8 and 12, which broadcast in English, Mandarin, Malay and Tamil. Singaporeans can also pick up Malaysian television – TV1 and TV2 – though reception is notoriously bad.

Channel 8 carries mostly local productions, a booming area. Singapore has been making local news shows, game shows and fairly amateurish dramas for years, but local production is looking healthy and starting to out-rate the many US imports. *Under One Roof* is an enormously popular local sitcom about a middle class family living in a Housing Development Board flat; at the time of writing it's in its fourth year and has already inspired two spin-offs.

Cable television is slowly taking hold though it's not as widespread as might be expected yet. One reason is the high cost of private residence connection fees (though HDB housing connection fees are quite reasonable). Added to that there is a hefty surcharge for every foreign station like CNN or BBC. Don't expect to see these stations unless you are staying in expensive hotels.

PHOTOGRAPHY & VIDEO
Film & Equipment
Film is cheap and readily available. A Kodak 24 exposure roll costs S$4.50, while a roll of Fuji Sensia slide film costs S$8.50. Processing is also reasonably priced: printing and developing a 24 exposure print film will cost around S$11.40, or S$15.60 for 36 exposures. Slide processing costs S$15 for a 36 exposure film.

Technical Tips
The usual rules for tropical photography apply: try to take photographs early in the morning or late in the afternoon. By 10 am the sun will already be high in the sky and colours are easily washed out. A polarising filter can help to keep down the tropical haze. Try to keep your camera and film in a happy environment – don't leave them out in direct sunlight, try to keep the film cool and have it developed as soon as possible after use. Colour film can be developed quickly, cheaply and competently in Singapore, but Kodachrome colour slides are sent to Australia for developing.

Properly used, a video camera can give a fascinating record of your holiday. As well as videoing the obvious things – sunsets, spectacular views – remember to record some of the ordinary everyday details of life in Singapore. Often the most interesting things occur when you're actually intent on filming something else.

Video cameras these days have amazingly sensitive microphones and you might be surprised how much sound will be picked up. This can also be a problem if there is a lot of ambient noise – filming by the side of a busy road might seem OK, but viewing it back home might simply give you a deafening cacophony of traffic. One good rule for beginners to follow is to try to film in long takes and don't move the camera around too much. Otherwise, your video could well make your viewers seasick! If your camera has a stabiliser, you can use it to obtain good footage while travelling on various means of transport, even on bumpy roads. And remember, you're on holiday – don't let the video take over your life and turn your trip into a Cecil B de Mille production.

Make sure you keep the batteries charged and have the necessary charger, plugs and transformer for the country you are visiting. It is possible to obtain video cartridges easily in Singapore, but make sure you buy the correct format. It is usually worth buying at least a few cartridges duty free to start off your trip.

Restrictions
It is advisable to exercise some restraint when taking photographs in places of worship, especially mosques – generally speaking, no one ever objects to photos being taken in Chinese temples. Don't be obvious in taking pictures of people at prayer and avoid using a flash.

TIME
Singapore is eight hours ahead of GMT/UTC (London), two hours behind Australian Eastern Standard Time (Sydney and Melbourne), 13 hours ahead of American Eastern Standard Time (New York) and 16 hours ahead of American Pacific Standard Time (San Francisco and Los Angeles). So, when it is noon in Singapore, it is 8 pm in Los Angeles and 11 pm in New York the previous day, 4 am in London and 2 pm in Sydney.

ELECTRICITY
Electricity supplies are dependable and run at 220V to 240V and 50 cycles. Plugs are of the three-pronged, square-pin type used in the UK. Bring your own adaptors.

WEIGHTS & MEASURES
Singapore uses the metric system, though you may occasionally come across references to odd measurements, such as the *thola*, an Indian weight, or *batu*, the Malay word for mile (literally meaning stone).

There is a metric conversion table inside the back cover of this book.

LAUNDRY
Singapore has plenty of laundries, including the Laundryland chain. There is a Laundryland at 01-06 Orchard Towers (Map 4) at the western end of Orchard Rd – check the telephone directory for other addresses. A large load, including drying and folding, costs around S$10. All major hotels offer a laundry service, which can set you back a small fortune, and most cheap hotels do laundry at more moderate rates.

HEALTH
In Singapore, you can eat virtually anywhere and not worry, and the tap water is safe to drink. Vaccinations are required only if you come from a yellow fever area and Singapore is not a malarial zone. The main health concern is the heat: it is important to avoid dehydration by drinking plenty of fluids.

Dehydration or salt deficiency can cause heat exhaustion. Take time to acclimatise to high temperatures and make sure you get sufficient liquids. Salt deficiency is characterised by fatigue, lethargy, headaches, giddiness and muscle cramps, and in this case salt tablets may help.

Medical facilities in Singapore are of a high standard and are readily available. A visit to a general practitioner costs around S$30. Singapore's public hospitals will accept self-referred patients. Singapore General Hospital (Map 6; ☎ 222 3322) is just south of Outram Rd, near Outram Park MRT.

WOMEN TRAVELLERS
Singapore is probably the safest Asian country to travel in and sexual harassment is very rare. Women are not cloistered in Singaporean society and enjoy much more freedom and equality than in the rest of Asia. Government policy favours sexual equality and abortion is available on request, although not for 'foreign' (non-Singaporean) pregnancies.

GAY & LESBIAN TRAVELLERS
Homosexuality is illegal in Singapore and you can be sentenced to between 10 years and life for engaging in homosexual activities. Singapore isn't completely straight, however, and there is a local gay and lesbian scene. People Like Us (PLU), PO Box 0299, Raffles City post office, Singapore 911710, is the city's grass-roots organisation for men and women. It has monthly meetings and many young professionals attend. For more details email plu-singapore@geocities.com or follow the links from www.utopia-asia.com.

See also under Bars, Bands & Discos in the Entertainment chapter for gay venues or mixed bars and clubs with gay nights.

DISABLED TRAVELLERS
Access Singapore is a guidebook for the disabled produced by the Singapore Council of Social Services. It is available from STB offices (see earlier this chapter for addresses) or contact the National Council of Social Services (☎ 336 1544; fax 336 7732), 11 Penang Rd.

SENIOR TRAVELLERS
Singapore is an ideal destination for senior travellers who want a taste of Asia without the hassles of less-developed countries. The health care system is on a par with any western country, access facilities to hotels and restaurants are excellent and there is a wide range of ready-made tours to cater for all tastes.

Singapore is a remarkably safe city and it's very easy to get around on public transport. The only possible difficulty could be

Singapore on a Shoestring?

Singapore can be a notoriously expensive place to have fun. All theme parks, pretty well all museums and many parks and gardens have some kind of entry fee. The Singaporean business ethos has left scant little to enjoy for free or on the cheap. So what do you do when the bank balance is blown but you really need some R&R without having to pay through the nose for it?

Well, for starters, Sentosa can be enjoyed for as little as S$5, which is all it costs to actually set foot on the island. The monorail and bus transport around Sentosa are free, so are all the walks and pretty decent beaches, and it really is a relaxing place to get away from the city for a while.

Then there is the MRT. For a minimum ticket fee you can, in practice, ride the whole system and see the sprawling HDB housing estates, the rapidly encroaching development of northern Singapore, parks and greenery, and the ever-busy Singaporeans going about their daily life. It is a fascinating cross-section look at Singaporean suburban life.

For the cost of your bus fare and a S$3 return ferry ticket, you can visit still undeveloped Pulau Ubin off Singapore's north-eastern coast. Take a bus to Changi Village and then a bumboat across to this remarkably undeveloped and rural retreat. Visit soon, because there are plans afoot to turn it into an ecological Sentosa.

If you fancy a stroll in what's left of Singapore's primary rainforest, take a walk through Bukit Timah Nature Reserve and enjoy exotic birds, butterflies, monkeys, lemurs and other wildlife. Entry is surprisingly still free, as is entry to the Singapore Botanic Gardens, which are only a short walk from Orchard Rd and are another relaxing haven from the turmoil and humidity of the city.

---

the humid weather which can prove tiring – though travellers on guided tours tend to spend most of their time in air-conditioned buses or buildings. Walking around Singapore can be problematic for the less agile since the footpaths and pavements are often uneven or in many cases nonexistent. In this case, a guided rickshaw tour might be a good solution.

The tourism board puts out a booklet called *Mature Travellers*, though in practice the information it contains is almost equally relevant to younger travellers.

SINGAPORE FOR CHILDREN

Singapore is a safe and healthy country for children, and it is easy and cheap to get around. The food is nutritious and noisy, easy-going hawker centres are an ideal place for wayward young children to commit crimes that would bar them from restaurants. Except perhaps for the heat, Singapore is an ideal family destination.

Singapore's problem is not the lack of attractions for children, but the surplus of them. Every new attraction seems to be yet another theme park and even the old attractions are being tarted up with fairground rides and multimedia displays to keep the kids amused. It won't be long before there's a merry-go-round in the Long Bar at Raffles.

Family attractions top the list of things to do in Singapore. Sentosa is Singapore's big theme park with a host of attractions to keep kids and parents amused. Haw Par Villa has rides and multimedia displays and the children might learn something about Chinese mythology, while Tang Dynasty City is Singapore's biggest cultural theme park. Be warned that by the time you add up entry, rides, food and all the extras, a family will find their wallets considerably lighter, especially if you want to see everything at Sentosa.

The Science & Discovery Centre is packed with knob-twirling, handle-pulling interactive displays that make it a big hit with Singaporean school children, while the Singapore Discovery Centre bills itself as 'fun-filled interactive entertainment for the whole family'.

Singapore Zoo and the neighbouring Night Safari are great for both kids and adults. The Jurong Bird Park and Jurong Reptile Park are also superb for children who love our feathered friends and fierce, scaly creatures.

River cruises are fun and you can include a cruise with a visit to Clarke Quay, which has rides, children's shops and is much more family-oriented than raging Boat Quay further downstream.

For more information on all these places see the Things to See & Do chapter.

LIBRARIES
Singapore has a wide network of public libraries that are well patronised by the island's highly literate society. But unless you are a permanent resident or have some kind of employment or student pass, you can't borrow books from these places. That said, it's still well worth visiting the National Library (Map 4) in the colonial district, just east of Fort Canning Park. Apart from providing a refreshingly cool haven from the heat outside, there is an impressive multimedia centre on the 2nd floor where you can browse the Internet, review CD-ROMs or soak up Singapore Cable-Vision. There is a S$2 charge for these services and you will need to get a cashcard from the service desk on the 2nd floor. There is a bit of paperwork involved and you will need your passport, but it's a relatively painless procedure.

Opening hours are from 11 am to 9 pm on Monday, from 10 am to 9 pm Tuesday to Friday, from 10 am to 5 pm on Saturday and from 1 to 5 pm on Sunday.

UNIVERSITIES
Singapore has two universities and four polytechnics. The National University of Singapore is the older and more prestigious of the two universities, while Nanyang Technological University offers courses in accountancy, business, communication studies and applied science. They are both increasingly hard-wired universities with a policy of providing all students with laptop computers so they can access information by plugging in at scattered information stations, or even attending lectures or seminars via personal video-conferencing.

CULTURAL CENTRES
Cultural centres in Singapore include:

Alliance Française
    (Map 4; ☎ 737 8422) 1 Sarkies Rd
American Association
    (Map 4; ☎ 738 0371) 21 Scotts Rd
Australian & New Zealand Association
    (Map 4; ☎ 734 4902) 19 Tanglin Rd
British Council
    (Map 4; ☎ 473 1111) 30 Napier Rd
German Club
    (Map 7; ☎ 466 9548) 12 First Ave
Goethe Institut
    (Map 6; ☎ 534 5011) 07-00 Nedlloyd House,
    1 Finlayson Green

DANGERS & ANNOYANCES
Singapore is a very safe country with low crime rates. Pickpockets are not unknown, but in general crime is not a problem. This is not surprising, given the harsh penalties meted out to offenders and the fact that hundreds of suspected criminals are held in jail without trial because the government does not have enough evidence to ensure conviction.

The importation of drugs carries the death penalty and, quite simply, drugs in Singapore should be avoided at all costs, not that you are likely to come across them. In case you think the government is bluffing, the tally of executions for drug convictions currently stands at over 40, an astonishing number given the size of Singapore's population.

BUSINESS HOURS
In Singapore, government offices are usually open from Monday to Friday and Saturday morning. Hours vary, starting

Fines

'Singapore is a fine country', said the taxi driver. 'In Singapore we have fines for everything.'

Singapore has a number of frowned-upon activities, and the sometimes Draconian methods of dealing with minor transgressions has caused both mirth and dread among visitors. The famous anti-long-hair campaign is a thing of the past, but it wasn't that long ago that immigration inspections included looking at hair length, and long-haired men were turned away on arrival or given a short-back-and-sides on the spot.

Singapore remains tough on a number of other minor issues, however, and the standard way of stamping out un-Singaporean activities is to slap a S$1000 fine on any offender. Actually, it is very rare that anybody does get fined that amount, but the severity of the fines is enough to ensure compliance.

Smoking in a public place – buses, lifts, cinemas, restaurants, air-conditioned shopping centres and government offices – earns a S$500 fine. You can smoke at food stalls and on the street (as long as you dispose of your butt, of course). The move to ban smoking in private cars was eventually quashed because of the difficulty in enforcing it. A few years ago it was the fashion among Singapore subversives to urinate in elevators but a successful campaign of heavy fines and security cameras has stamped that one out.

Jaywalking is a relatively minor crime – walk across the road within 50m of a designated crossing and it could cost you S$50. The successful anti-littering campaign continues (with a fine of up to S$1000 for dropping even a cigarette butt on the street) and, not surprisingly, Singapore is amazingly clean.

The MRT, Singapore's pride and joy, attracts some particularly heavy fines. Eating, drinking and smoking are forbidden and attract a S$500 fine.

Gum chewing is also a frowned-upon activity in Singapore. Antisocial elements were leaving their gum deposits on the doors of the MRT, causing disruptions to the underground rail services. The sale, importation and even possession of chewing gum is now banned and subject to heavy fines.

---

around 7.30 to 9.30 am and closing between 4 and 6 pm. On Saturday, closing time is between 11.30 am and 1 pm.

Shop hours are also variable. Small shops are generally open from 10 am to 6 pm weekdays, while department stores and large shopping centres are open from 10 am to 9 or 9.30 pm, seven days a week. Most small shops in Chinatown and Arab St close on Sunday, though Sunday is the busiest shopping day in Little India.

For bank opening hours see Exchanging Money in the Money section earlier in this chapter.

PUBLIC HOLIDAYS & SPECIAL EVENTS

The following days are public holidays in Singapore. For those days not based on the western calendar, the months they are likely to fall in are given:

New Year's Day
   1 January
Hari Raya Puasa
   19 January in 1999, 9 January in 2000
Chinese New Year
   Two days (January/February)
Hari Raya Haji
   28 March in 1999, 16 March in 2000
Good Friday
   April
Labour Day
   1 May
Vesak Day
   August
National Day
   9 August

Deepavali
November
Christmas Day
25 December

With so many cultures and religions, there are an amazing number of celebrations in Singapore. Although some of them have fixed dates, the Hindus, Muslims and Chinese follow a lunar calendar which varies annually. In particular, the Muslim festivals vary constantly, moving back 11 days each year. The tourist board puts out a *Festivals & Events* brochure each year and the *Singapore Official Guide* has more specific and detailed listings for each month.

January-February

Ponggal – This is a harvest festival and the time for thanksgiving. It is celebrated by south Indians especially at the Sri Mariamman Temple (Map 6) on South Bridge Rd, where rice, vegetables, sugarcane and spices are offered to the gods.

Chinese New Year – Dragon dances and pedestrian parades mark the start of the new year. Families hold open house, unmarried relatives (especially children) receive *ang pows* (money in red packets), businesses traditionally clear their debts and everybody wishes you a '*Kong hee fatt choy*' (a happy and prosperous new year). Chinatown is lit up, especially Eu Tong Sen St and New Bridge Rd, and the *Singapore River Hong Bao Special* features *pasar malam* (night market) stalls, variety shows and fireworks.

Chingay – This occurs on the 22nd day after the Chinese New Year. Processions of Chinese flag bearers parade down Orchard Rd balancing bamboo flag poles 6m to 12m long. Lion dancers, floats and other cultural performers join in the celebrations.

Thaipusam – This is one of the most dramatic Hindu festivals, in which devotees honour Lord Subramaniam with acts of amazing masochism. In Singapore, Hindus march in a procession from the Sri Srinivasa Perumal Temple (Map 5) on Serangoon Rd to the Chettiar Hindu Temple (Map 6) on Tank Rd carrying *kavadis*, heavy metal frames decorated with peacock feathers, fruit and flowers. The kavadis are hung from their bodies with metal hooks and spikes driven into their flesh. Other devotees pierce their cheeks and tongues with metal skewers or walk on sandals of nails. Along the procession route, the kavadi carriers dance to the drum beat while spectators urge them on with shouts of '*vel, vel*'.

Sugarcane Deliverance

If you are in Singapore during Chinese New Year and chance upon people wandering around with large sugarcanes in their hands, don't be surprised. You are witnessing a cultural manifestation of the Hokkien Chinese people.

The ninth day of the Chinese New Year has special significance for the Hokkiens, who each year celebrate the birthday of Tian Gong (Tee Kong in Hokkien), the God of Heaven. The main celebrations take place at midnight on the day before with offerings of food such as chicken, duck and fruits.

It is also customary to place a pair of sugarcanes at the altar or entrance of the home as a symbol of deliverance. This is a tradition that has its origins in an incident during the era of the Song dynasty (960-1279). The Hokkiens had incurred the emperor's wrath by pledging allegiance to a rebel group. In fear for their lives, they hid in sugarcane fields for eight days, until they were finally pardoned by an emperor made benevolent by the festivity of the season.

Today sellers of sugarcanes make a quick dollar by selling this odd product around the streets of Singapore and yet another Chinese tradition lives on.

In the evening, the procession continues with an image of Subramaniam in a temple car. This festival is now banned in India.

Hari Raya Puasa – The major Muslim events are connected with Ramadan, the month during which Muslims cannot eat or drink from sunrise to sunset. In the evenings food stalls are set up in the Arab St district near the Sultan Mosque. Hari Raya Puasa marks the end of the month-long fast with three days of celebration; in the Malay areas, Geylang Serai is draped in lights for the occasion.

March-April

Qing Ming Festival – On 'All Souls' Day', Chinese traditionally visit the tombs of their ancestors to clean and repair them and make offerings. The San Phor Kark See Temple (Map 2) just south of Ang Mo Kio Ave in the centre of the island receives many visitors.

Hari Raya Haji – This is a Muslim festival in honour of those who have made the pilgrimage to Mecca. Sacrifices of goats and other animals are offered to Allah and the meat is distributed among the poor. Prayers are said at mosques throughout the city.

April-May

Vesak Day – Buddha's birth, enlightenment and death are celebrated by various events, including the release of caged birds to symbolise the setting free of captive souls. Temples such as the Buddhist Lodge (Map 6) on Kim Yam Rd, just off River Valley Rd, and the Temple of 1000 Lights (Map 5) on Serangoon Rd throng with worshippers.

May-June

Birthday of the Third Prince – The child-god is honoured with processions, and devotees go into a trance and spear themselves with spikes and swords during this Chinese festival. Celebrations, if you can call them that, are held at various temples and on Queen St (Map 5), near Bencoolen St.

Dragon Boat Festival – Commemorating the death of a Chinese saint who drowned himself as a protest against government corruption, this festival is celebrated with boat races across Marina Bay.

Singapore Festival of Arts – A biennial event held every even year, this festival has a world-class program of art, dance, drama and music. It alternates with the *Festival of Asian Performing Arts* held every odd year.

July-August

Singapore Food Festival – Celebrating the national passion, this month-long festival throughout July has special offerings at everything from hawker centres to gourmet restaurants.

Great Singapore Sale – Orchard Rd is decked with banners and merchants are encouraged by the government to drop prices in an effort to boost Singapore's image as a shopping destination. It is held for one month around July and usually overlaps in part with the food festival.

Singapore National Day – On 9 August a series of military and civilian processions and an evening firework display celebrate Singapore's independence in 1965.

Festival of the Hungry Ghosts – The souls of the dead are released for this one day of feasting and entertainment on earth. Chinese operas and other events are laid on for them and food is put out (the ghosts eat the food's spirit but thoughtfully leave the substance for mortal celebrants).

September-October

Birthday of the Monkey God – The birthday of T'se Tien Tai Seng Yeh is celebrated twice a year at the Monkey God Temple (Map 6) on Seng Poh Rd opposite the Tiong Bahru Market. Mediums pierce their cheeks and tongues with skewers and go into a trance, during which they write special charms in blood.

Thimithi (Fire Walking Ceremony) – Hindu devotees prove their faith by walking across glowing coals at the Sri Mariamman Temple (Map 6).

Moon Cake Festival – The overthrow of the Mongol warlords in ancient China is celebrated by eating moon cakes and lighting colourful paper lanterns. Moon cakes are made with bean paste, lotus seeds and sometimes a duck egg.

Navarathri – In the Tamil month of Purattasi, the Hindu festival of 'Nine Nights' is dedicated to the wives of Shiva, Vishnu and Brahma. Young girls are dressed as the goddess Kali; this is a good opportunity to see traditional Indian dancing and singing. The Chettiar, Sri Mariamman and Sri Srinivasa Perumal temples (all Map 6) are centres of activity.

October-November

Pilgrimage to Kusu Island – Tua Pek Kong, the god of prosperity, is honoured by Taoists in Singapore who make a pilgrimage to the shrine on Kusu.

Deepavali – Rama's victory over the demon king Ravana is celebrated with the 'Festival of Lights', with tiny oil lamps outside Hindu homes and lights all over Hindu temples. Little India is ablaze with lights for a month to celebrate this most important Hindu festival.

Festival of the Nine Emperor Gods – Nine days of Chinese operas, processions and other events honour the nine emperor gods. The centre of activities is the Kiu Ong Yiah Temple opposite the Singapore Crocodile Farm (Map 2) on Upper Serangoon Rd.

December

Christmas – Orchard Rd celebrates Christmas with shopfront displays and the Christmas light-up, another of the illuminations that Singapore is so fond of.

The Cost of a Car

If you thought owning and running a car in your own country was a costly business, then spare a thought for the Singaporeans: it's bad enough that the cost of housing is sky-high, but owning and running a car in Singapore can really bust the domestic budget.

Anyone wishing to own a car in Singapore must first obtain a Certificate of Entitlement (COE), a document that confers on the holder the right to actually own a vehicle. The COE is acquired through an electronic bidding system which is conducted monthly. The going rate varies but at the time of writing you could expect to fork out around S$25,000 for the right to own a medium-sized car.

Once you have the COE, you can buy the car, which then has to be registered for a fee equivalent to 150% of its open market value. All of which means, taking into account the COE and the cost of registration, that a small family sedan will set you back somewhere in the region of S$78,000.

Add to that the cost of insurance, road taxes, parking fees and the now ubiquitous cash-card system which requires drivers to pay every time they enter the CBD or use certain highways, and being independent with wheels becomes a very expensive proposition.

Nonetheless, Singapore's roads are crowded with expensive, late-model Japanese and European sedans, and the demand does not seem to be abating. Singapore is rapidly running out of land for its people and vehicles. What Draconian measures the governments of the future will introduce to halt this voracious growth can only be imagined.

WORK

Work opportunities for foreigners are limited. While Singapore does have a fairly large expatriate European community, this is more a reflection of the large representation of overseas companies than a shortage of skills in the local labour market. However the vacancies pages of the *Straits Times* are often crammed with job notices – you can read these on its Web site (www.asia1.com.sg/straitstimes) before coming to Singapore.

In the great majority of cases, foreign workers obtain employment before they come to Singapore. One of the main reasons for this is the high cost of accommodation and car ownership, which overseas companies normally cover. There is a slight demand in some professions but Singapore is attempting to fill labour shortages by attracting Hong Kong professionals who may be chaffing under their new political masters and may want out. The overwhelming majority of jobs are for domestic servants (newspapers are full of agencies advertising Filipino house maids) and unskilled labourers.

Some foreigners arrive in Singapore and find work. Business experience and economic training are a bonus, or those with easily marketable job skills can do the rounds of the companies that might be interested. It has become fashionable for some of the restaurants serving western food to employ westerners, and some travellers have picked up temporary work as waiters. Finally, you might want to check out the EDB's Web site (www.singapore.careers.com) where jobs are posted and you might find something suited to your own talents.

Getting There & Away

AIR

Singapore is a major South-East Asian travel hub and a good place to buy air tickets. The overwhelming bulk of international air traffic goes through Changi airport (see The Airport section in the Getting Around chapter).

The airport departure tax (Passenger Service Charge; PSC) from Changi is S$15 and is normally included in the cost of your air ticket.

Travel Agents

Singapore is also a good place to look for cheap plane tickets, and it competes with Bangkok and Penang to be the discount flight centre of the region.

STA Travel (☎ 737 7188; fax 737 2591; sales@sta-travel.com.sg) in the Orchard Parade Hotel (Map 4), 1 Tanglin Rd, is part of the international budget travel chain. It also has offices at the National University of Singapore (Map 7) on Lower Kent Ridge Rd and at the Singapore Polytechnic (Map 7) at 500 Dover Rd.

Other agents worth trying include Harharah Travel (☎ 337 2633) at 171C Bencoolen St, in the same building as the Hawaii Hostel (Map 5), and Airpower Travel (Map 5) (☎ 294 5664; fax 293 1215; airpower@mbox2.com.sg) at 2A Pahang St near Arab St, and on Bencoolen St – the latter has been recommended by many travellers.

All these travel agents sell air, bus and train tickets.

As well as the above, Singapore has hundreds of travel agents all over town for checking prices on flights. Chinatown Point (Map 6) on New Bridge Rd has a good selection of large travel agents on the 1st floor for one-stop shopping for tickets and tours.

Fares Fares vary depending on when and with whom you want to fly. The cheapest fares are likely to be with the least loved airlines (various eastern European ones,

Biman Bangladesh Airlines etc), via inconvenient routes (you're forced to make stopovers on the way) at awkward times (they only fly every other Tuesday at 3 am).

Some typical rock-bottom discount fares being quoted in Singapore include South-East Asian destinations like Bangkok from S$200 one way, Denpasar from S$220 one way or S$370 excursion return and Jakarta from S$120 one way or S$200 return. To the subcontinent, you can fly to Delhi or Kathmandu for S$450 or Madras for S$400, both one-way fares.

Fares to Australia include Sydney or Melbourne for S$500 one way or S$650 excursion return and Perth from S$420 one way or S$500 return. London and other European destinations cost from S$550 one way with the eastern European airlines and from S$620 one way with the better airlines.

One-way fares to the US west coast are around S$650 direct or with a stop in Manila.

Airline Offices Below are some of the major airline offices in Singapore. Check the Business Yellow Pages for any that are not listed here.

Aeroflot
(☎ 336 1757) 01-02/02-00, Tan Chong Tower, 15 Queen St
Air Canada
(☎ 256 1198) 01-10, 101 Thomson Rd
Air India
(☎ 225 9411) 17-01, UIC bldg S, Shenton Way
Air New Zealand
(☎ 535 8266) 24-08 Ocean bldg, 10 Collyer Quay
American Airlines
(☎ 339 0001) 04-01, 108 Middle Rd
British Airways
(☎ 839 7788) 04-02 The Promenade, 300 Orchard Rd
Cathay Pacific Airways
(☎ 533 1333) 16-01 Ocean bldg, 10 Collyer Quay
Garuda Indonesia
(☎ 250 2888) 01-02, 442 Orchard Rd

KLM-Royal Dutch Airlines
(☎ 737 7622) 12-06 Ngee Ann City Tower, 391A Orchard Rd

Lufthansa Airlines
(☎ 737 9222) 05-01 Palais Renaissance, 390 Orchard Rd

Malaysia Airlines
(☎ 336 6777) 02-09 Singapore Shopping Centre, 190 Clemenceau Ave

Pelangi Air
(☎ 481 6302) bldg 24, 960 Seletar Airport West camp

Philippine Airlines
(☎ 336 1611) 01-10 Parklane Shopping Mall, 35 Selegie Rd

Qantas Airways
(☎ 839 7788) 04-02 The Promenade, 300 Orchard Rd

Royal Brunei Airlines
(☎ 235 4672) 04-08, 25 Scotts Rd

Royal Nepal Airlines Corporation
(☎ 339 5535) 03-07, 3 Coleman St

Silk Air
(☎ 542 8111) 03-00 SATS bldg

Singapore Airlines
(☎ 223 8888) 77 Robinson Rd

Thai Airways International
(☎ 1-800 224 9977) 02-00 The Globe, 100 Cecil St

United Airlines
(☎ 220 0711) 01-03 Hong Leong bldg, 16 Raffles Quay

The USA & Canada

Tickets to Singapore in the low season start from as little US$705 return from the US west coast and US$1075 return from the east coast.

Singapore Airlines and others have direct flights but it is usually cheaper to fly via another port, such as with China Airlines via Taipei or Cathay Pacific Airways via Hong Kong.

It is also worth looking into circle Pacific flights. From Los Angeles or San Francisco you can fly Honolulu-Denpasar-Singapore, overland to Bangkok, fly on to Hong Kong or Taipei, and then return to the USA, all for around US$1250. For US$1500, you go via Auckland and the South Pacific. Add another US$200 to include Australia.

The *New York Times*, the *LA Times*, the *Chicago Tribune* and the *San Francisco Examiner* all produce weekly travel sections in

which you'll find any number of travel agents' ads. Council Travel and STA Travel have offices in major cities nationwide.

In Canada, a return ticket from Vancouver starts at US$799 in low season, rising to US$1099 in high season. The magazine *Travel Unlimited* (PO Box 1058, Allston, MA 02134) publishes details of the cheapest airfares and courier possibilities for destinations all over the world from the USA. Travel CUTS has offices in all major cities. The *Toronto Globe & Mail* and the *Vancouver Sun* carry travel agents' ads.

Europe

London has the best deals for flights to Singapore, serviced by a host of airlines. Singapore Airlines, British Airways and Qantas are major carriers, but cheaper tickets are usually with less loved airlines, such as Aeroflot via Moscow or Pakistan Airlines via Karachi for as little as UK£220 one way, UK£399 return. Some of the Arab airlines such as Royal Jordanian and Emirates are other discounters.

For direct flights with Singapore Airlines or Qantas, prices start from around UK£699.

For information on travel agents and special deals, check the Sunday papers and weekly listings magazines such as *Time Out*. London's 'bucket' shops can offer some great deals, but some of these places are fly-by-night operations. Most British agents are registered with the Association of British Travel Agents (ABTA), which guarantees tickets booked with member agents.

Popular and reliable British agents are Campus Travel (☎ (0171) 730 8111), with 41 branches nationwide; STA Travel (☎ (0171) 361 6262); Trailfinders (☎ (0171) 938 3366), with branches in London, Birmingham, Bristol, Glasgow and Manchester; and Crusader Travel (☎ (0181) 744 0474).

Australia

Advance purchase return fares from the Australian east coast to Singapore vary from around A$580 to A$700 return, depending on the season of travel and the length of stay. From Perth, fares are around

A\$600 to A\$940. The 30 day or 45 day excursion fares are the cheapest, while the most expensive is a return ticket valid for over 60 days in the high season, generally from 1 December to 10 January.

Many of the airlines that fly from Australia to Asia, the Middle East and Europe stopover in Singapore. Two of the cheapest are Gulf Air and Lauda Air. Gulf Air flights for around A\$780 are the cheapest on offer and bookings should be made well in advance. Singapore Airlines and Qantas are the main carriers. Both have cheap package tours and good stopover accommodation deals, as does Malaysia Airlines which sometimes has cheap flights to Singapore via Kuala Lumpur.

For cheap tickets, STA Travel has competitive prices for Asian airfares, as does the Flight Centre, another Australia-wide chain which also offers good accommodation discounts.

New Zealand

A number of airlines fly from Auckland to Singapore. Return tickets range from around NZ\$1399 in the low season to NZ\$1460 in the high season. The high season is generally December and January. British Airways, Air New Zealand, Singapore Airlines, Qantas and Garuda Indonesia all fly direct to Singapore, or stopovers are possible in Indonesia and Australia.

Flight Centre and STA Travel are two large discount travel agents with offices throughout the country.

Malaysia

The shuttle service operated by Malaysia Airlines and Singapore Airlines has frequent flights between Kuala Lumpur and Singapore for RM166 (S\$129 from Singapore); seats are available on a first-come, first-served basis. Booked seats cost RM222 (S\$170). Malaysia Airlines also connects Singapore to Kuantan (RM204, S\$158), Langkawi (RM305, S\$237) and Penang (RM255, S\$197) in Peninsular Malaysia, and Kuching (RM287, S\$224) and Kota Kinabalu (RM580, S\$454) in east Malaysia. First class fares are around 40% extra.

Silk Air (☎ 221 2221) has daily flights to/from Kuantan (RM204, S\$158) and Langkawi (RM252, S\$197).

Return fares are double the single fares quoted here. Fares from Singapore to Malaysia are always quoted in Singapore dollars and from Malaysia to Singapore in Malaysian ringgit. With the considerable difference in the exchange rate it is much cheaper to buy tickets in Malaysia so, rather than buying a return fare to Kuala Lumpur from Singapore, buy a one-way ticket and the return leg in Kuala Lumpur.

Going to Malaysia, you can save quite a few dollars if you fly from Johor Bahru rather than Singapore. For example, to Kota Kinabalu the fares are RM418 from Johor Bahru but S\$391 from Singapore. To persuade travellers to take advantage of these lower fares, the SPS (☎ 250 3333) bus service operated by Malaysia Airlines runs directly from the Novotel Orchid (Map 3), 214 Dunearn Rd, to the Johor Bahru airport. It costs S\$12 and takes about two hours. In Singapore, tickets for internal flights originating in Malaysia are only sold by Malaysia Airlines (☎ 336 6777), 02-09 Singapore Shopping Centre (Map 4), 190 Clemenceau Ave, 200m south-west of Dhoby Ghaut MRT.

Indonesia

A number of airlines fly from Singapore to Jakarta for as low as S\$120 one way and around S\$200 return. A flight to Bali costs from S\$220 one way. Garuda Indonesia is the main carrier, though Air France has been offering the lowest prices. Garuda Indonesia also has direct flights between Singapore and Medan, Padang, Palembang, Pekanbaru, Pontianak and Surabaya.

Internal flights are cheaper if tickets are bought in Indonesia. For Pontianak in Kalimantan and some destinations in Sumatra, such as Pekanbaru, it is cheaper to take the ferry to Batam and then an internal flight from there. Garuda Indonesia offers an internal air pass costing US\$300 for three flights, but this is only economical for very long distances.

From Jakarta to Singapore, flights cost from as little as US$65. For international flights, the travel agencies on Jalan Jaksa, Jakarta's budget accommodation area, are good places to look. Indo Shangrila Travel (☎ 625 6080), Jalan Gajah Mada 219G, is a large ticketing agent and often has good deals.

LAND
Malaysia
Bus For Johor Bahru, the air-con express bus operated by Singapore-Johor Express Ltd (☎ 292 8149) departs every 15 minutes between 6.30 am and midnight from the Queen St terminal (Map 3) on the corner of Queen and Arab Sts. It costs S$2.40. Alternatively, the public SBS bus No 170 leaves from the Ban San terminal and costs S$1.10; Bugis MRT station is within walking distance. Bus No 170 can be hailed anywhere along the way, such as on Rochor, Rochor Canal or Bukit Timah Rds.

The bus stops at the Singapore checkpoint, but don't worry if it leaves while you clear immigration – keep your ticket and you can just hop on the next one that comes along. The bus then stops at Malaysian immigration and customs at the other end of the Causeway, 1km away. After clearing the Malaysian checkpoint, you can then catch the bus again (your ticket is still valid) to the Johor Bahru bus terminus on the outskirts of town, or you can walk to town from the Causeway. Moneychangers, whose first offer will usually be less than the going rate, will approach you or there are plenty of banks and official moneychangers in Johor Bahru.

If you are travelling beyond Johor Bahru, it is easier to catch a long-distance bus straight from Singapore, but there is a greater variety of bus services from Johor Bahru and the fares are cheaper.

In Singapore, long-distance buses to Melaka and the east coast of Malaysia leave from and arrive at the bus terminal (Map 3) on the corner of Lavender St and Kallang Bahru, opposite the large Kallang Bahru complex. It is to the north-east of Bencoolen St, near the top end of Jalan Besar. Take the MRT to Lavender then bus No 5 or 61; otherwise it's a 500m walk from the MRT station.

Pan Malaysia Express (☎ 294 7034) has express buses to Kuala Lumpur (S$30) daily at 9 am and 4.30 pm and non-express buses (S$25) at 11 am and 10 pm. It also has buses to Mersing (S$13.10) at 8, 9, 10 am and 10 pm, to Kuantan (S$16.50) at 9 and 10 am and 10 pm, and to Kota Bharu (S$35.10) at 7.30 pm.

Also at the Lavender St bus terminal, Hasry (☎ 294 9306) has standard buses to Kuala Lumpur (S$17) at 8 am, 2 and 9.30 pm and Super VIP coaches (S$25) at 8.30, 9.30, 10 and 10.30 am and at noon, 2.30 and 8.30 pm; and buses to Melaka (S$11) at 8.30 am and 2.30 pm. The journey to Kuala Lumpur takes between five and six hours depending on the bus taken.

Melaka-Singapore Express (☎ 293 5915) has buses to Melaka at 8, 9, 10 and 11 am and 2, 3 and 5 pm. The fare is S$11 for an air-con bus and the trip takes 4½ hours. It is preferable to buy your tickets the day before departure. Many travel agents also sell bus tickets to Malaysia.

For destinations north of Kuala Lumpur, most buses leave from the Golden Mile Complex (Map 3) at the north-east end of Beach Rd; Lavender MRT station is about 500m away. This terminal handles all the buses to Thailand and northern destinations on the way such as Ipoh, Butterworth, Penang and Alor Setar. The trip to Penang costs around S$33 and most buses leave in the afternoon and evening. Bus agents line the outside of the building. Kwang Chow Travel (☎ 293 8977) and Gunung Raya (☎ 294 7711) are two of the bigger agents for Malaysian west coast destinations.

Morning Star Travel (☎ 292 9009) at Lavender MRT station (Map 3) has buses to Kuala Lumpur (S$25) at 8 am and 9 pm, to Penang (S$38) at 8.30 pm, to Alor Setar (S$40) at 9 pm (but in June only) and to Melaka (S$15) at 8.30 am (weekends only). All buses leave from next to the MRT station.

You can also catch buses to Kuala Lumpur from the Queen St terminal (Map 3). Kuala

Lumpur-Singapore Express (☎ 292 8254) has buses to Kuala Lumpur at 9 am, and 1 and 10 pm for S$17.30 or S$22 VIP (seating on the VIP coaches is three across and there is ample room to spread out).

Train Singapore is the southern termination point for the Malaysian railway system (Keretapi Tanah Malayu or KTM). Malaysia has two main rail lines: the primary line going from Singapore to Kuala Lumpur, Butterworth, Alor Setar and then into Thailand; and a second line branching off at Gemas and going right up through the centre of the country to Tumpat, near Kota Bharu on the east coast.

The Singapore railway station (Map 3) (☎ 222 5165 for fare and schedule information) is on Keppel Rd, south-west of Chinatown, about 1km from Tanjong Pagar MRT. The booking office is open from 8.30 am to 2 pm and 3 to 7 pm.

Three trains depart every day to Kuala Lumpur. In order of departure, the *Ekspres Rakyat* leaves at 8.15 am (arrives 2.11 pm), the *Ekspres Sinaran* at 2.25 pm (arrives 8.15 pm) and the *Senandung Malam* at 10.30 pm (arrives 6.20 am). The *Ekspres Rakyat* continues on to Butterworth, arriving at 9.25 pm. There is also a mail train to Kuala Lumpur leaving at 8.15 pm daily. It takes 10 hours.

In addition, there are three ordinary trains to Kluang, Gemas and Gua Musang (on the east coast line to Tumpat) that depart daily at 11.20 am, 6.05 pm and 8.45 am respectively, and an express train to Tumpat (in the very north-east of Malaysia), the *Express Timuran*, at 9.15 pm, which reaches Jerantut at 3.29 am for Taman Negara National Park.

All trains are efficient, well maintained and comfortable, but ordinary and mail trains stop at all stations and are slow. The express trains are well worth the extra money (see the Train Fares From Singapore to Malaysia box). For further details check out the KTM Web site at www.ktmb.com.my or email passenger@ktmb.com.my.

While there is a noticeable jump in comfort from 3rd to 2nd class, 1st class is

---

Train Fares From Singapore to Malaysia

Nonexpress train fares (S$) from Singapore include:

Destination	1st	2nd	3rd
Johor Bahru	4.20	1.90	1.10
Kuala Lumpur	60.00	26.00	14.80
Ipoh	91.50	39.70	22.60
Butterworth	118.50	51.40	29.20
Jerantut	60.00	26.00	14.80
Tumpat	112.50	48.80	27.70

Express train fares (S$) from Singapore include:

Destination	1st	2nd	3rd
Johor Bahru	13.00	10.00	6.00
Kuala Lumpur	68.00	34.00	19.00
Ipoh	100.00	48.00	27.00
Butterworth	127.00	60.00	34.00
Jerantut	68.00	34.00	19.00
Tumpat	121.00	57.00	32.00

---

not much better than 2nd class and considerably more expensive.

You can buy a 30 day rail pass allowing unlimited travel in Malaysia for US$120, or a 10 day pass for US$55. The pass entitles you to travel on any class of train, but does not include sleeping berth charges. Rail passes are only available to foreign tourists and can be purchased at a number of main stations in Malaysia.

From Singapore, there is also a *relbas* (rail bus) service to Kulai, just past Johor Bahru. This train is a different way to get to Johor Bahru, but you should allow up to an hour to buy your ticket and clear customs. The buses are much quicker and more convenient. Trains leave at 8.45 and 11.20 am and 6.05 pm. From Johor Bahru there are seven daily departures for Singapore.

Customs and passport clearances take place at Singapore station for all departures to and from Malaysia.

Taxi Malaysia has a cheap, well-developed, long-distance taxi system that makes travel a real breeze. A long-distance taxi plies between set destinations, and as soon as a full complement of four passengers turns up, off you go. From Singapore, the best bet is to go to Johor Bahru and then take a taxi from there – it's cheaper and there are many more services – but Singapore also has such taxis to destinations in Malaysia.

For Johor Bahru, taxis leave from the Queen St terminal (Map 3). The trip costs S$7 per person, and an extra S$1 if there are long delays at the Causeway. Non-Singaporeans/Malaysians are likely to have to pay more or hire a whole taxi for S$28 since they take longer to clear the border.

Crossing the Causeway The Causeway is the main link between Singapore and the mainland. An impressive piece of engineering in its day, it has difficulty coping with the amount of traffic on weekends, especially on long weekends and public holidays. If you're travelling by private vehicle or taxi, try to avoid these times. Take a bus, as buses sail on past in the express lane while the cars are stuck in the interminable queues.

A new bridge-cum-causeway has been built on the western side of Singapore linking the Singapore suburb of Tuas with Geylang Patah in Malaysia. This new crossing will undoubtedly alleviate some of the bottleneck problems at the main Causeway, but is unlikely to be of immediate usefulness to travellers without their own transport.

Thailand
If you want to go direct from Singapore to Thailand overland, the quickest and cheapest way is by bus.

Bus The main terminal for buses to and from Thailand is at the Golden Mile Complex (Map 3) on Beach Rd. A number of travel agents specialising in buses and tours to Thailand operate from there. Grassland Express (☎ 292 1166) has buses at 7 and 8.30 pm to Hat Yai. Phya Travel (☎ 293 6692) has buses to Hat Yai and Bangkok at 3.30 and 7 pm, with connections to Phuket and Suratthani from Hat Yai. Kwang Chow

Travel (☎ 293 8977) has a bus to Hat Yai and Bangkok at 7.30 pm, or try the many other agents. Most buses leave in the afternoon and travel overnight.

Fares cost from around S$35 to S$45, depending on the quality of service, though all buses are air-con. The S$45 VIP coaches have videos and include a free meal. Most of these buses also stop in Butterworth.

Train The rail route into Thailand is on the Butterworth-Alor Setar-Hat Yai route, which crosses into Thailand at Padang Besar. From Butterworth trains go to/from Singapore. You can take the *International Express* from Butterworth in Malaysia all the way to Bangkok with connections from Singapore. The *International Express* leaves Butterworth at 1.35 pm, arrives in Hat Yai at 4.35 pm and in Bangkok at 8.30 am the following morning. The trip from Singapore to Bangkok costs S$91.70 (2nd class).

A variation on the *International Express* is the *Eastern & Oriental Express*, which departs on alternate Wednesdays, Fridays and Sundays. The train is done out in antique opulence and caters to the well heeled – it's South-East Asia's answer to the *Orient Express*. It takes 42 hours to do the 1943km journey from Singapore to Bangkok. Don your linen suit, sip a gin and tonic and dig deep for the fare: from S$2140 per person in a double compartment, up to S$5510 in the presidential suite. You can also take the train just to Kuala Lumpur or Butterworth for less. For further details call ☎ 323 4390 or fax 224 9265.

SEA
Singapore has a number of ferry connections to Malaysia and the Indonesian islands of the Riau Archipelago. Cruise trips in the region are also very popular with Singaporeans.

The big cruise centre at the World Trade Centre (WTC; Map 2), south-west of the railway station, is the main departure point for ferries and cruises. The WTC is a mini Changi airport with duty free and other shops. A host of agents handle bookings for the ferries, cruises and resorts. To get to the WTC, take the MRT to Tanjong Pagar, then bus No 10, 97, 100 or 131. Bus Nos 65 and 143 go from Serangoon Rd via Orchard Rd to the WTC. From the colonial district, bus Nos 97 and 167 go from Bencoolen St or No 100 goes from Beach Rd.

The Tanah Merah ferry terminal (Map 2) to the east near Changi airport also handles ferries to the Indonesian island of Bintan, and may handle other services in the future. Changi Village, at the far eastern tip of Singapore, also has ferries to Malaysia.

Malaysia

Tanjung Belungkor A ferry operates from Changi ferry terminal (Map 2) to Tanjung Belungkor, east of Johor Bahru. It is primarily a service for Singaporeans going to Desaru in Malaysia. The 11km journey takes 45 minutes and costs S$18/28 one way/return. Ferries leave Singapore at 8.15 and 11.15 am and 2.15 and 5.15 pm; from Tanjung Belungkor departures are at 9.45 am and 12.45, 3.45 and 6.45 pm. From the Tanjung Belungkor jetty buses operate to Desaru and Kota Tinggi.

To get to the Changi ferry terminal, take bus No 2 to Changi Village and then a taxi. The ferry terminal is behind Changi airport just off Changi Coast Rd.

Pengerang From Changi Village (Map 2), ferries also go to Pengerang across the strait in Malaysia. This is an interesting backdoor route into Malaysia. Ferries don't have a fixed schedule, which is most unlike Singapore, and leave throughout the day when a full quota of 12 people is reached. The cost is S$5 per person or S$60 for the whole boat. The best time to catch one is early in the morning before 8 am. Clear Singapore immigration at the small post on the Changi River dock.

Tioman To Tioman, Auto Batam (☎ 271 4866), 02-40 World Trade Centre, is the agent for a high-speed catamaran that does the trip in four hours. Departures are at 8.30 am from the Tanah Merah ferry terminal

(Map 2), and the fare is S$90/148 one way/return. There are no services during the monsoon season from 31 October to 1 March.

Indonesia

Curiously, no direct shipping services run between the main ports in Indonesia and near-neighbour Singapore but it is possible to travel between the two countries via the islands of the Riau Archipelago, the cluster of Indonesian islands immediately south of Singapore.

The two most visited islands are Batam and Bintan, both of which can be reached by ferry from Singapore. Most nationalities are issued a tourist pass for Indonesia, valid for 60 days, upon arrival and do not require a visa. The ferries are modern, fast and air-conditioned, and show movies. From Batam boats go to Sumatra, a popular way to enter Indonesia.

For more information on Batam and Bintan, and onward connections, see the Excursions chapter.

Batam (Pulau Batam) Batam is a resort and industrial park. From Singapore it only takes half an hour to reach Sekupang or 45 minutes to Batu Ampar, both on Batam Island.

Departures are from the WTC (Map 2). The main agents to Batam are Auto Batam (☎ 271 4866) and Dino Shipping (☎ 270 2228), both with offices at the WTC. Between them they have dozens of departures every day to Batam, at least every half-hour from 7.30 am to 8.15 pm. Tickets cost S$17/30 one way/return. Ferries dock at Sekupang, from where you can take a boat to Tanjung Buton on the Sumatran mainland. From there it is a three hour bus ride to Palembang. This is a popular travellers' route to Sumatra.

Ferries also go to Batu Ampar on Batam, which is close to the main town of Nagoya. Departures are roughly every hour from 7.50 am to 8.15 pm. Dino Shipping also has two ferries a day at 9.35 am and 4.45 pm to Nongsa in the north of the island.

Bintan (Pulau Bintan) The same companies that operate ferries to Batam also have ferries to Bintan from the Tanah Merah ferry terminal (Map 2; ☎ 542 7102). From here ferries go to Tanjung Pinang, the main city on the island, at 9.20 and 11.10 am and 1.20 and 3.25 pm. Tickets cost S$39/46 one way/return. The journey takes about 1½ hours. There are also boats to Loban on the west side of Bintan at 8.40 am and 1.25 pm (8.40 am only on Saturday). Loban is connected to Batam by regular local ferries.

For what it's worth you can also sail from Tanah Merah to Johor Bahru in Malaysia once a day and twice on weekends – it's slow (65 minutes) but if it means avoiding the weekend crush at the Causeway, it's probably not such a bad idea.

To get to the Tanah Merah ferry terminal, take the MRT to Bedok and then bus No 35. The taxi fare from the city is around S$12 to S$15.

Karimun (Pulau Karimun) From the WTC (map 2), Auto Batam and Dino Shipping have three ferries daily to Tanjung Balai, the main port on Karimun, another Riau resort island of minor note. The cost is S$28/49 one way/return.

Cruises

There is no shortage of cruises operating from Singapore or including the city in their itineraries. International companies such as P&O, Seven Seas, CTC and Winstar call in at Singapore, but the best deals are with the local operators that offer popular cheap cruises departing from the WTC (Map 2).

Cruises range from a two day/one night package for S$90 twin share to longer cruises to Phuket or Manila. Three day/two night cruises to Penang are very popular

and start from as little as S$492 for two people. The best deals are advertised in the newspaper travel sections, but check for 'administration fees' and 'holiday surcharges'. A S$30 seaport tax is usually payable as well. Contact Channel Holidays (☎ 270 2228; fax 276 9700) for details of the Penang cruise and other good deals.

You could also try Star Cruise (☎ 733 6988; fax 733 8622), 13-01 Ngee Ann City Tower B (Map 4), 391 Orchard Rd, or Morning Star Travel (☎ 292 9009; fax 292 4340), a major agent with offices all over Singapore.

New Century Tours (☎ 732 6765; fax 296 8226) operates the *Leisure World* liner, which has an emphasis on youth and Chinese pop music.

WARNING

The information in this chapter is particularly vulnerable to change: prices for international travel are volatile, routes are introduced and cancelled, schedules change, special deals come and go, and rules and visa requirements are amended. Some airlines and governments seem to take perverse pleasure in making price structures and regulations as complicated as possible. You should check directly with the airline or a travel agent to make sure you understand how a fare (and ticket you may buy) works. In addition, the travel industry is highly competitive and there are many lurks and perks.

The upshot of this is that you should get opinions, quotes and advice from as many airlines and travel agents as possible before you part with your hard-earned cash. The details given in this chapter should be regarded as pointers and are not a substitute for your own careful, up-to-date research.

Getting Around

Singapore is undoubtedly the easiest city in Asia to get around. While other cities like Bangkok, Jakarta and Kuala Lumpur are choked by massive traffic jams and attempt to solve their problems with stop-gap, privately funded public transport systems, Singapore has bitten the bullet and invested huge amounts in an excellent public transport infrastructure.

With a typical mixture of far-sighted social planning and authoritarianism, the government has built a magnificent rail system and controls private cars by a restrictive licensing system and prohibitive import duties that make owning a car primarily a preserve for the rich. The island has excellent roads and an efficient expressway system, and cars entering the central business district (CBD) have to buy special licences.

Singapore also has an extensive bus network and cheap taxis, making getting around a breeze.

The *TransitLink Guide*, S$1.50 from most bookshops, is a good investment if you will be using a lot of public transport. The guide lists all bus and Mass Rapid Transit (MRT) rail routes in a convenient pocket-size format. Maps show the surrounding areas for all MRT stations, including bus stops. Alternatively, the *TransitLink Map* (S$5) maps the whole island with numbered bus routes and MRT stations, but while it's good for outlying districts it doesn't show bus stops in the central city area.

The *Singapore Official Guide*, a free handout from the tourist office, lists Singapore's major attractions and how to reach them by bus and MRT.

THE AIRPORT

Singapore's ultramodern Changi airport (Map 2) is another of those miracles in which Singapore specialises. It's vast, efficient and organised, and was built in record time. It has banking and money changing facilities, a post office (open 24 hours), credit-card phones, free-phones for local calls, Internet facilities, free hotel reservation counters open from 8 am to 11 pm, left-luggage offices (S$3 per bag for the first day and S$4 per day thereafter), nearly 100 shops, restaurants, day rooms (from S$56 for six hours), fitness centres, saunas, showers and business centres. There are free films, audiovisual shows, bars with entertainment, hairdressers, medical facilities, a swimming pool, a mini Science Discovery Museum (in Terminal 2) etc, etc.

Changi is not really one airport but two – Terminal 1 and the newer, even more impressive Terminal 2 – each in themselves international airports to match the world's best. They are connected by the Changi Skytrain, a monorail that shuttles between the two. Terminal 2 is expected to cater for Singapore's increasing air traffic well into the 21st century, but Terminal 1 still handles most of the airlines.

At present the following airlines use Terminal 2: Air France, Delta, Finnair, Malaysia Airlines, Myanmar Airways International, Philippine Airlines, Royal Brunei Airlines, Silk Air, Singapore Airlines and Swissair. All other airlines use Terminal 1. A third terminal is currently under construction, as if the other two weren't already enough.

On your way through the arrivals concourse at Changi, pick up the free booklets, maps and other guides available from stands. They give you a lot of useful information and good quality colour maps of the island and the city centre. There are even guides to the airport and a glossy monthly travel rag, *Changi*.

If you are one of the millions of air travellers fed up with overpriced and terrible food at airports, then Changi is a blessing. It has a variety of restaurants serving a range of cuisines at non-inflated prices. Terminal 2 just pips Terminal 1 for the silver fork award in dining excellence. To find even cheaper food, go to the Singapore hawker food centre on the upstairs level of the car park just outside Terminal 2. The elevator beside McDonald's on the arrival level in Terminal 1 will take you to the basement 'food centre'. It's actually the staff cafeteria but the public can eat there.

Changi airport continues to poll in the various travel-trade magazines as the best airport in the world. You'll understand why when you arrive and are whisked through immigration to find your bags waiting on the other side.

To/From the Airport

Changi is at the eastern end of Singapore, about 20km from the city centre. Airport buses and public buses (catch them in the basement), taxis and the more expensive limousine services run along the expressway into the city centre.

The most convenient bus is the Airbus (☎ 542 1721), running roughly every 20 minutes from 6 am to midnight. Three routes service all the main hotels in the colonial district (the bus also drops off on Bencoolen St), as well as the hotels along Orchard, Tanglin and Scotts Rds. The cost is S$5 (children S$3).

Public bus No 16 operates every eight to 12 minutes from 6 am to 8 pm and takes about half an hour to reach the city. The 16E (Express) also operates from 6 to 9 am and from 5 to 8 pm. The fare on both buses is S$1.50 but bus drivers don't give change so make sure you get some coins when you change money.

As the Express approaches the city, it comes off the flyover into Raffles Blvd and then Stamford Rd. For Beach Rd, get off when you see the round towers of the Raffles City skyscraper on your right, just past the open playing fields of the Padang on your left. A half kilometre further along is the National Museum and the stop for Bencoolen St. The bus then continues up Penang Rd, Somerset Rd and Orchard Blvd (which all run parallel to Orchard Rd).

When heading out to the airport, catch these buses on Orchard or Bras Basah Rds.

Another alternative is to take the No 27 bus (S$1.20, 20 minutes) from Changi to the Tampines Interchange, then hop on the MRT. From Tampines to City Hall costs S$1.40 and takes 25 minutes.

Taxis from the airport are subject to a S$3 supplementary charge on top of the meter fare, which is around S$12 to most places in the city centre. This supplementary charge only applies to taxis from the airport, not from the city.

Seletar Airport (Map 2)

Singapore does have another 'international' airport in Seletar, a small, modern airport more used to corporate flyers and visiting lumin-aries such as Rod Stewart or Henry Kissinger who prefer its anonymity for their occasional visits by Lear jet. Seletar handles at least one international service in the twice daily Pelangi Airlines flights to Tioman Island in Malaysia.

Seletar is in the north of the island, and the easiest way to get there is to take a taxi for around S$11; otherwise bus 103 will take you from outside the National Library to the gates of the Seletar Air Force base from where you change to a local base bus to the airport terminal. Also from the base gates, bus 59 will take you to the nearest MRT station which is Yio Chu Kang. You will be questioned by gate guards before you will be allowed to enter the Seletar base area.

MASS RAPID TRANSIT (MRT)

The ultramodern Mass Rapid Transit (MRT) subway system is the easiest, quickest and most comfortable way of getting around Singapore. It can transport you across town in air-conditioned comfort in minutes.

The MRT was primarily designed to provide a cheap, reliable rail service from the housing estates to the city centre and industrial estates. Most of the 44km of underground track is in the inner-city area, but out toward the housing estates the MRT runs above ground. Not content with this most impressive system, the government has new lines planned with another line to eventually run to Punggol in the north-east and a short but important 6km extension to connect Changi airport into the system.

The trains run from around 6 am to midnight. At peak times, trains run every three to four minutes, and off-peak every six to eight minutes.

Fares & Farecards

You can buy a single-trip ticket or a stored-value card (called a Farecard). Single-trip tickets cost from 60c to S$1.50. Ticket machines take 10c, 20c, 50c and S$1 coins; they also give change. There are also machines that give change for S$2 notes.

Farecards cost from S$10 (plus a S$2 deposit) up to S$50 and they can be purchased from the TransitLink sales offices at MRT stations, the main bus interchanges and at 7-Eleven stores. Farecards can be used on buses as well as the MRT and if you are planning on doing a lot of shuttling around on public transport they work out on average 15% cheaper than cash fares.

You can also purchase special edition souvenir tourist tickets which give you all the benefits of the Farecard for only S$7 (with a stored value of S$6), but they are only valid for the MRT and cannot be topped up. You keep the ticket as a souvenir when you return home.

BUS

While the MRT is easy and convenient to use, for door-to-door public transport it is hard to beat the buses. You rarely have to wait more than a few minutes for a bus and they will take you almost anywhere you want to go.

Bus fares start from 60c (70c for air-con buses) for the first 3.2km and go up in 10c increments for every 2.4km to a maximum of S$1.20 (S$1.50 air-con). There are also a few flat-rate buses. When you board the bus drop the exact money into the fare box. No change is given.

Farecards (see the Fares & Farecards entry) can also be used on buses that have

PATRICK HORTON

It resembles a shoe box on wheels but the Singapore Trolley covers a handy route taking in many of the city's places of interest.

validator ticket machines. Put the card in the validator, select the correct fare and then retrieve your Farecard and bus ticket from the slot below.

There's also something called a Singapore Explorer ticket which at S$5 for one day and S$12 for three days allows unlimited travel on buses.

Tourist Buses

The Singapore Trolley is a grotesque bus made up to look like an old-fashioned tram. Its route takes in the Botanic Gardens, the Orchard Rd area, the colonial district, the CBD, Chinatown and the World Trade Centre with the Trolley stopping at all the major hotels and points of interest. It's a handy route and the bus is certainly distinctive and easy to find. All-day (from 9 am to 4.30 pm) tickets cost S$9 for adults and S$7 for children.

TAXI

Singapore has a good supply of taxis – over 10,000 of them – and it's usually not too difficult to find one, except perhaps during rush hour or at meal times (Singaporeans are not at all enthusiastic about missing a meal).

It is quite easy to recognise Singaporean taxis, although they come in several varieties – the most common being black with a yellow or pale blue roof. Taxis are all metered and the meters are used – unlike in some Asian countries where the meters always seem to be 'broken'. Taxis cost S$2.40 for the first kilometre, then 10c for each additional 240m.

From midnight to 6 am there is a 50% surcharge on top of the meter fare. *From* the airport, there is a surcharge of S$3 for each journey but not *to*. Radio bookings cost an additional S$2.20, or S$3.20 if booked 30 minutes or more in advance. There is also a S$1 surcharge on all trips from the CBD between 4 and 7 pm on weekdays and from noon to 3 pm on Saturday. You may also have to pay a surcharge (see under Restricted Zone & Car Parking in the following Car section) if you take the taxi into the CBD during restricted hours.

Singapore taxi drivers are generally refreshingly courteous and efficient, plus the cars themselves are super-clean since drivers can be fined for driving a dirty cab. Some taxis also accept Visa cards. There are many taxi companies; for radio bookings 24 hours, NTUC (☎ 452 5555) is one of the biggest companies.

CAR

Singaporeans drive on the left-hand side of the road and it is compulsory to wear seat belts. Unlike in most Asian countries, traffic is orderly, but the profusion of one-way streets and streets that change names (sometimes several times) can make driving difficult for the uninitiated. The *Singapore Street Directory* is essential for negotiating the city – see the Maps section in the Facts for the Visitor chapter.

Rental

Singapore has branches of the three major regional rent-a-car operators – Sintat, Hertz and Avis. There are also a large number of small, local operators. If you want a car just for local driving, many of the smaller operators quote rental rates that are slightly cheaper than the major companies. Rental rates are more expensive than in Malaysia, therefore there are expensive surcharges to take a Singaporean rental car onto the mainland. If you intend renting a car to drive in Malaysia for any length of time, it is much better to rent in Johor Bahru.

Rates start from S$100 a day, while collision damage waiver will cost about S$20 per day for a small car such as a Toyota Corolla or Mitsubishi Lancer. Special deals may be available especially for longer-term rental. There are hire booths at Changi airport and in the city. Addresses of some of the main operators are:

Avis
    (☎ 737 1668) Boulevard Hotel, Cuscaden Rd
Budget
    (☎ 532 4442) 26-01A Clifford Centre, 24 Raffles Place
Hertz Rent-a-Car
    (☎ 734 4646) 125 Tanglin Rd

Ken-Air Rent-a-Car
(☎ 737 8282) 01-41 Specialists' Shopping Centre, 227 Orchard Rd
Sintat
(☎ 295 2211) 60 Bendemeer Rd

Restricted Zone & Car Parking

From 7.30 am to 6.30 pm weekdays, and from 10.15 am to 2 pm on Saturday, the area encompassing the CBD, Chinatown and Orchard Rd is a restricted zone. Cars may enter as long as they pay a surcharge. Vehicles are automatically tracked by sensors on overhanging gantries which prompt drivers to insert a cashcard into their in-vehicle unit which then extracts the appropriate toll. The same system is also in operation on certain major highways.

Anyone who doesn't pay the entry toll is automatically photographed by cameras on the gantries and a fine will soon arrive at the car owner's address.

Parking in many places in Singapore is operated by a coupon system. You can buy a booklet of coupons at parking kiosks and post offices. You must display a coupon in your car window with holes punched out to indicate the time, day and date your car was parked.

TRISHAW

Singapore's bicycle trishaws are fast disappearing, although you'll find a few still operating in Chinatown and off Serangoon Rd. Trishaws had their peak just after WWII when motorised transport was almost nonexistent and trishaw riders could make a very healthy income. Today, they are mainly used for local shopping trips or to transport articles too heavy to carry. They rarely venture onto Singapore's heavily trafficked main streets.

The trishaws tend to congregate in large numbers in the pedestrian mall at the junction of Waterloo and Albert Sts (Map 5) at the northern end of the colonial district. You can also usually find them outside major hotels like Raffles. Always agree on the fare

RICHARD I'ANSON

Trishaws relaced Singapore's hand-pulled rickshaws in the 1940s. Sadly, the trishaws are no longer a viable means of negotiating the city's traffic-filled streets and they're now largely relegated to the role of tourist curiosity.

beforehand: a short ride should cost about S$3 and the price goes up from there. Trishaw tours of Chinatown and Little India are operated from a number of the larger hotels.

BICYCLE

Singapore's fast-moving traffic and good public transport system do not make cycling such an attractive proposition, though an increasing number of enthusiasts are regularly seen pounding the tarmac in the outer suburbs. Cycling up to Changi Village and then taking the bike over to Pulau Ubin (see Northern Islands in the Things to See & Do chapter) is also a very popular activity among expat cyclophiles. There is a great mountain bike track encircling the base of the Bukit Timah Nature Reserve for anyone wanting to burn off a few excess kilos. (See the Things to See & Do chapter for further details on Bukit Timah.)

Bicycles can be hired at a number of places on the East Coast Parkway, but they are intended mostly for weekend jaunts along the foreshore. Mountain bikes, racers and tandems are available for around S$3 to S$5 per hour. See the East Coast & Changi section in the Things to See & Do chapter for details. Bikes can also be rented on Sentosa and Pulau Ubin.

WALKING

Getting around the old areas of Singapore on foot has one small problem – apart from the heat and humidity that is. That problem is the 'five-foot-ways'. A five-foot-way, which takes its name from the fact that it is roughly five feet wide, is the walkway at the front of the traditional Chinese shophouse which is usually enclosed, veranda-like.

The difficulty with them is that every shop's walkway is individual. It may well be higher or lower than the shop next door or closer to or further from the street. Walking thus becomes a constant up and down and side to side business, further complicated by the fact that half the shops seem to overflow right across the walkway, forcing you to venture into the street, and bikes or motorcycles are parked across them.

Even newer areas like Orchard Rd suffer from the five-foot-ways syndrome with shopping centre forecourts on different levels. The hazard is exacerbated by the flash but very slippery tiles out the front that every centre seems to see as essential. After a rainstorm on Orchard Rd count the tourists falling.

BOATS & FERRIES

You can charter a bumboat (motorised sampan) to take a tour up the Singapore River or to go to the islands around Singapore. There are regular ferry services from the WTC to Sentosa and the other southern islands, and from Changi Village to Pulau Ubin. You can also take river tours or boat tours around the harbour – see the following Organised Tours section for details.

ORGANISED TOURS

A wide variety of tours can be booked at the desks of the big hotels or through individual operators such as those listed in the *Singapore Official Guide*. Any of Singapore's travel agents can also book tours for you, or you could contact the tourism board (see the Facts for the Visitor chapter for addresses).

Tours include morning or afternoon trips around the city, to Jurong Bird Park, to the east coast or to the island's various parks and gardens. Most tours go for around 3½ hours, though full-day tours are also available. Prices vary depending on how long the tour lasts and the cost of admission to the attractions covered, but most half-day tours cost between S$20 and S$40, while full-day tours can range up to S$70. Tours cover just about all of Singapore, so it's just a matter of finding one that covers your particular interests.

The Singapore Trolley (see under Tourist Buses in the earlier Bus section) allows you to put together your own tour of central Singapore. It plies a set route and you can get on and off where you like. For big spenders, helicopter tours are also available for an unmatchable view of the city. A half-hour from Seletar airport costs S$150 for adults and S$75 for children.

GETTING AROUND

Cruises

River Cruises One of the best ways to get a feel for central Singapore and its history is to take a river cruise. Singapore River Boat (☎ 227 0802) operates a half-hour river tour for S$9 per adult, S$4 per child. It leaves from the Clarke Quay jetty (Map 6), south-west of Fort Canning Park. You can buy tickets at the booth there, and tours leave on the hour from 9 am to 11 pm. The tour goes along the river to the harbour and Clifford Pier and then returns. A taped commentary, complete with weak jokes, gives a good rundown on the history of the buildings along the river.

Harbour Cruises A whole host of operators have harbour cruises departing from Clifford Pier (Map 6), just east of Raffles Place. Companies offer *towkang* (Chinese junk) cruises as well as a number of lunch and dinner cruises. Most of them do the rounds of the harbour, which involves a lot of time passing oil refineries, then a look at Sentosa and the southern islands of St John's, Lazarus and Kusu. The short stop at Kusu is worthwhile and you will get some good views of the city and harbour.

Fairwind (☎ 533 3432) has 2½ hour tours at 10.30 am and 3 pm that cost S$20 for adults and S$10 for children. Its 1½ hour tour at 4 pm costs the same but doesn't stop at Kusu. Watertours (☎ 533 9811) operates tours at the same times for S$24 (morning) and S$29 (afternoon, including tea), and a dinner tour.

J&N Cruise (☎ 223 8217) covers much the same tour route in a catamaran from the WTC. The 1½ hour luncheon cruise at 12.30 pm costs S$35 for adults and S$20 for children, and the two hour cruise at 3 pm costs S$30 for adults and S$17 for children. All prices exclude 3% GST.

All these companies operate dinner and/or evening cruises, as does Resort Cruises (☎ 278 4677). Dinner cruises range from around S$34 to S$80.

It is also possible to charter boats – the Singapore Tourism Board (☎ 339 6622) can put you in touch with charter-boat operators.

RICHARD I'ANSON

ARASU RAMASAMY

ARASU RAMASAMY

PAUL HELLANDER

PAUL HELLANDER

Singaporeans are increasingly coming to appreciate the island's remaining areas of green, which include the Jurong Bird Park and attendant fauna (top left), the East Coast Park with its bicycle paths and recreational facilities (top right), the beautiful Botanic Gardens (middle), and the Chinese and Japanese Gardens (bottom left and right).

Singapore's cultural heritage is preserved in tourist geegaws (top left) and in places like the Haw Par Villa, a popular Chinese mytholology theme park with a series of grotestesque statues and colourful murals (top right and bottom left). Mural detail on Orchard Road (bottom right).

Things to See & Do

Singapore's greatest attraction is its ability to offer a taste of Asian culture in a small, easy-to-get-around package. Minutes from the modern business centre and its towering air-conditioned office blocks are the narrow streets of Chinatown, while across the river is Little India (centred on Serangoon Rd) and the Muslim centre of Arab St.

Further out of the city, the Jurong area has a number of gardens, theme parks and other attractions. The central hills to the north of the city are Singapore's green belt, with some fine parks and the zoo. Sentosa is Singapore's most famous fun-park island, though quieter islands are scattered around Singapore.

COLONIAL SINGAPORE (Maps 5&6)

The mark of Stamford Raffles is indelibly stamped on central Singapore. His early city plans moved the business district south of the river and made the north bank the administrative area. This north bank area is known today as the colonial district and it's where you'll find most of the imposing monuments of British rule – the stone grey edifices of the town hall, parliament and museum, the churches and Victorian architecture. Many of these buildings still serve their original purpose.

The part of the city south of the river is now the central business district (CBD), the commercial heart of Singapore. Its monuments are the skyscrapers of modern finance. Between the colonial district and the CBD is the Singapore River, the site of the first British arrivals and for a long time the main artery of trade.

These areas are easily reached by MRT; get off at either City Hall or Raffles Place stations.

Along the Singapore River

The river, which was once the thriving heart of Singapore, is now a quiet pedestrian precinct – an escape for lunchtime office workers, a spot from which to cast a line for

fish, a favourite backdrop for wedding photography sessions, or a place to dine in one of the bankside terraces or *godowns* (warehouses). The bustling activity of *sampans* (bumboats), cranes, and yelling, sweating labourers has all gone; the new riverfront is a recreational stretch of photo opportunities and colonial restoration.

At the mouth of the river stands Singapore's symbol of tourism, the **Merlion**, a much photographed water spouting, half-lion/half-fish statue. The small park around it is open from 7 am to 10 pm daily.

Heading upstream, **Anderson Bridge** is the first of the old bridges that span the river. The next along is **Cavenagh Bridge**, built in 1869, now for pedestrians only. It provides good access to Empress Place which, named in honour of Queen Victoria, is Singapore's oldest pedestrian area. The Place is surrounded by many reminders of British rule including the **Empress Place building** (1865), an imposing Georgian structure that was once a courthouse and later became government offices. Its most recent function was as a museum, but it is currently undergoing further refurbishment.

Nearby, next to the river at Raffles Landing Site, is **Raffles Statue**, standing imperiously by the water. It marks the place where Stamford Raffles first set foot on the island of Singapore.

Naturally, there are plenty of places to eat along the river. The most popular strip is **Boat Quay**, a picturesque area of restored old shops and renovated terraces stretching between Cavenagh and Elgin bridges. This is one of Singapore's most popular restaurant and nightlife zones and it's abuzz until the early hours of the morning.

Crossing over Elgin Bridge, North Boat Quay leads upriver to **Clarke Quay**. The old Clarke Quay godowns on this bend of the river have been completely rebuilt and the new development is a varied complex of shops and children's amusements. It's another popular dining spot with plenty of eating possibilities ranging from satay stalls to wine bars. There are also floating restaurants on the river.

Unlike Boat Quay, Clarke Quay is fairly family oriented with amusement arcades, toy and children's wear shops, and a playground upstairs. The central square regularly has music and other diversions, like **Clarke Quay Adventure**, a corny riverboat ride attraction, which takes you past alcoves with wax dummies portraying a dubious, raucous history of Singapore. The place is open from 11 am to 10.30 pm; admission is S$5 (children S$3).

On Sunday afternoons a market is held on the pedestrian footbridge across the river.

At Clarke Quay is the jetty for the **riverboat tours**, one of the best ways to explore

RICHARD I'ANSON

The Supreme Court building, the former symbol of British law in colonial-era Singapore.

the river. Singapore River Boat (☎ 339 6833) operates a half-hour tour for S$9 per adult and S$4 per child. Tours leave on the hour from 9 am to 11 pm and tickets can be bought at the jetty.

The Padang

There is no more quizzical a symbol of British colonialism than the open field of the Padang. It is here that flannelled fools played cricket in the tropical heat, cheered on by the Singapore Cricket Club members in the pavilion. At the opposite end of the field is the Singapore Recreation Club, set aside for the Eurasian community. Cricket is still played on the weekends but segregation is, officially, no longer practised.

The Padang was a centre for colonial life and a place to promenade in the evenings. The neighbouring Esplanade Park on the foreshore is still the place for an evening stroll, give or take the odd crane and new foreshore developments. The Padang also witnessed the beginning of the end of colonial rule, for it was here that the invading Japanese herded the European community together, before marching them off to Changi prison.

The Padang is ringed by imposing colonial buildings. The **Victoria Theatre & Concert Hall** (1862) was once the town hall. It is now used for cultural events and is the home of the Singapore Symphony Orchestra. A refurbishment has spruced it up, and a merchandising shop has been added. Check performance times; tickets are often very reasonably priced.

Parliament House (1827) is Singapore's oldest government building. Originally a private mansion, it became a courthouse, then the Assembly House of the colonial government and, finally, the Parliament House for independent Singapore. **High St**, which runs next to Parliament House, was hacked from the jungle to become Singapore's first street, and was an Indian area in its early days.

The **Supreme Court** and **City Hall** are two other stoic colonial buildings on St Andrew's Rd. Built in 1939, the Supreme

RAFFLES HOTEL

The Singapore Sling

A visit to Singapore is considered by many to be incomplete without sampling Singapore's famous cocktail, the 'Singapore Sling'. This colourful and refreshing drink was created at Raffles Hotel in 1915 by a Hainanese-Chinese bartender Ngiam Tong Boon.

Originally, the Singapore Sling was meant to be a woman's drink, hence the attractive pink colour. Today it is very definitely a drink enjoyed by all. Raffles makes a killing by selling rather overpriced and commercially prepared versions of the cocktail in the Bar & Billiard Room (pictured above). However, if you can't make it to the hotel to enjoy this national cocktail, you can make your own.

Ingredients
½ measure gin
¼ cherry brandy
¼ mixed fruit juices (orange, lime or lemon and pineapple)
a few drops of Cointreau & Benedictine
a dash of Angostura Bitters
top with a cherry and a slice of pineapple

Mix all the above, pour into a long glass, find a comfy cane chair on a sunny veranda, grab a Somerset Maugham novel and sip away, making believe that you're in the tropics under a swishing ceiling fan back in the heyday of Singapore's colonial past.

Court is a relatively new addition, and was the last classical building to be erected in Singapore. It is also notable for the building it replaced – the Grand Hotel de L'Europe, which once outshone Raffles as Singapore's premier hotel. City Hall, next door, was where Lord Louis Mountbatten accepted the Japanese surrender in 1945.

Raffles Hotel

Raffles Hotel on Beach Rd is far more than just an expensive place to stay, it's a Singapore institution, an architectural landmark that has been classified by the government as part of the nation's 'cultural heritage'.

Raffles was opened in 1887 by the Sarkies brothers, three Armenians who built a string of hotels which were to become famous throughout the east (these include the Strand in Yangon (Rangoon) and the E&O in Penang, as well as Raffles).

Raffles Hotel started life as a 10 room bungalow, but its heyday began with the opening of the main building in 1899. Raffles soon became a byword for oriental luxury and the hotel featured in novels by Joseph Conrad and Somerset Maugham. Rudyard Kipling recommended it as the place to 'feed at' when in Singapore (but stay elsewhere he added!), and in its Long Bar, in 1915, Ngiam Tong Boon created the Singapore Sling (see the boxed text on the previous page).

More recently, the Raffles underwent extensive renovations and extensions; it had fallen from grace and could no longer compete with Singapore's modern hotels. It reopened in 1991, once again a top hotel, though for some it wasn't the same. While it is true that the Raffles is now a slick exercise in tourism marketing, for many it still oozes the old-fashioned atmosphere of the east as Somerset Maugham would have known it.

The lobby of the restored main building is open to the public (dress standards apply) and high tea is served in the Tiffin Room, though the Writers' Bar next door is little more than an alcove. In the other wings, the Long Bar or the Bar & Billiard Room are the places to sip a Singapore Sling – at S$17 a pop!

The Raffles Hotel Arcade is a collection of expensive shops but, hidden away on the 3rd floor, the **Raffles Hotel Museum** is well worth a look, especially the old postcards. It's open from 10 am to 9 pm and admission is free. Raffles memorabilia is on sale at the museum shop, including the hotel crockery if you can't afford to stay here and nick your own.

Next to the museum, Jubilee Hall theatre puts on *Raffles Revisited*, a multimedia presentation on the history of the Raffles Hotel. Viewing times are at 10 and 11 am, 12.30 and 1 pm, and the cost is S$5 for adults, S$3 for children.

Churches

Some of the most imposing examples of colonial architecture are the churches. **St Andrew's Cathedral** is Singapore's Anglican cathedral, built in Gothic style between 1856 and 1863. It's in the block surrounded by North Bridge Rd, Coleman St, Stamford and St Andrew's Rds. The Catholic **Cathedral of the Good Shepherd** on Queen St is a stolid neo-classical edifice built between 1843 and 1846.

The cathedrals draw a thriving crowd of well-to-do Singaporeans on Sunday, though many of the other churches and religious buildings are being transformed under the auspices of urban redevelopment; the magnificent St Joseph's Institution, a former Catholic boys' school, is now the Singapore Art Museum (see the following section), while the equally impressive former Convent of the Holy Infant Jesus on the corner of Bras Basah Rd and Victoria St, is now a swish restaurant and bar complex.

One of the greats of English literature, Somerset Maugham was a frequent visitor to Raffles and he wrote many of his short stories seated in the shade of the Palm Court. It is Maugham more than any other writer who has shaped popular conceptions of colonial life.

The oldest church in Singapore is the Armenian **Church of St Gregory the Illuminator**, between Armenian and Hill Sts, which is no longer used for services.

Singapore Art Museum (Map 5)
One of Singapore's finest colonial buildings, St Joseph's Institution, near the corner of Bras Basah Rd and Queen St, has been restored and converted into this fine arts museum. Rotating exhibits showcase modern art from Singapore and South-East Asia. Even if the works are not your cup of tea, the building is worth a look and the museum has a good cafe facing Queen St.

The museum is open from 9 am to 5.30 pm daily, closed Monday. Entry costs S$3 (children S$1.50).

Fort Canning (Map 4)
If you continue north-west up Coleman St from the Padang, you pass the Armenian Church of St Gregory and come to Fort Canning Hill, a good viewpoint over Singapore. Once known as Forbidden Hill, it contains the shrine of Sultan Iskander Shah, the last ruler of the ancient kingdom of Singapura. Archaeological digs in the park have uncovered Javanese artefacts from the 14th century Majapahit empire.

When Stamford Raffles arrived, the only reminder of any greatness that the island may once have claimed was an earthen wall that stretched from the sea to the top of Fort Canning Hill. Raffles built his house on the top of the hill, and it became Government House until the military built Fort Canning in 1860. There is little left of the historic buildings that were once on the hill, now it is a pleasant park with an **old Christian cemetery** filled with gravestones which hint at poignant tales of hopeful settlers who died young.

Up on the top of the hill is the **Fort Canning Centre**, a former barracks that now houses the Singapore Dance Theatre.

Also on Fort Canning Hill is the **Battle Box**, which was Singapore's largest underground military operations complex during WWII. Through an impressive audiovisual display visitors are taken back to 15 February 1942, when the decision was made by the British to surrender Singapore to the invading Japanese. It's open daily from 10 am to 6 pm; admission is S$8.

National Museum (Map 4)
The National Museum (also known as the Singapore History Museum) on Stamford Rd traces its ancestry back to Raffles himself, who first conceived of the idea of a museum for Singapore in 1823. It opened in 1849 but then underwent a couple of changes of location to end up in the present building in 1887.

The museum has substantial collections focusing on regional cultures, history and crafts. Exhibits include archaeological finds from the Asian region, articles relating to Chinese trade and settlement in the region, Malaysian and Indonesian arts and crafts, Peranakan artefacts and a wide collection of items relating to Stamford Raffles. The museum also has a superb jade collection donated by the Aw brothers, of Tiger Balm fame.

The trouble with the museum has always been that only a fraction of its collection is on show; the exhibits are rotated and it's pot luck what you see. However, the collections are being dispersed into the many new museums popping up around the city, such as the Singapore Art Museum just to the north-east on Bras Basah Rd and the Asian Civilisations Museum, just around the corner on Armenian St.

The museum is open daily from 9 am to 5.30 pm daily, closed Monday. Admission is S$3. Tours (☎ 1-800 336 1460) for groups of 10 to 12 are available on request. There's a National Museum Shop a short walk away on Armenian St.

Asian Civilisations Museum (Map 6)
Opened in 1997 this museum is housed in a beautifully restored building at 39 Armenian St. It features a permanent display of furniture, ceramics, jade and other arts, which trace the development of Chinese civilisation. A visit here can easily be combined with a

visit to the National Museum, which is a three minute walk away.

It's open from 9 am to 5.30 pm daily, closed Monday. Admission is S$3 for adults, S$1 for children.

Singapore Philatelic Museum (Map 6)

Yet another new museum, this philatelic museum is housed in a colonial building dating from 1908. It holds a well presented collection of rare and not-so-rare stamps from Singapore and around the world. There's also an exhibit tracing the stamp-making process from artwork through to printing. An audiovisual theatre and interactive games provide a high-tech touch.

The museum is on Coleman St; it's open from 9 am to 4.30 pm daily, closed Monday. Entry is S$2, children S$1. Free guided tours start at 11 am and 2 pm.

New Bugis St (Map 5)

For years Bugis St was famous as Singapore's raucous transvestite playground. In a country that banned juke boxes and long hair, Bugis St was proof that Singapore dared to be daring.

Bugis St was never, officially, more than another food stall centre but, in practice, at the witching hour certain young men turned into something more exotic than pumpkins. It was the place to be until the early hours of the morning, to join the crowds and watch the goings on; that is, until Bugis St was totally demolished during the building of the MRT. As has been the case with so many of Singapore's attractions, the answer was to rebuild it, to make it newer and better than ever.

So now Singapore has a New Bugis St, just south-west of Bugis MRT station, complete with new terrace lookalikes and new lock-up wooden stalls with new canvas walkway overhangs. Transvestites are not allowed, and of course New Bugis St is a pale shadow of its former self. Nonetheless it is a pleasant place to hang out in the evenings. Some of the open-air restaurants and bars stay open until 3 am or until the last customers go home. There are fruit and food stalls, and you can pick up a copy watch or

a T-shirt. The large and very popular Bugis Junction shopping centre continues the neo-colonial architecture theme.

Kuan Yin Temple (Map 5)

This temple on Waterloo St is one of the most popular Chinese temples – Kuan Yin being one of the most popular goddesses. Despite dating from only 1982 in its present incarnation, the flower sellers and fortune tellers out the front make it one of the liveliest temples in Singapore.

A few doors away is the **Sri Krishnan Temple**, which also attracts worshippers from the Kuan Yin Temple, who show a great deal of religious pragmatism by also burning joss sticks and offering prayers at this Hindu temple.

Central Business District (Map 6)

Once the vibrant heart of Singapore, **Raffles Place** is now a rather barren patch of grass above the MRT station surrounded by high-rise buildings. There are a few shopping possibilities nearby, including Aerial Plaza (an extension of Change Alley), a collection of small shops and aggressive Indian tailors, from where you can cross Collyer Quay to **Clifford Pier**, the place to hire a boat or catch a harbour tour (see Organised Tours in the Getting Around chapter). Singapore's **harbour** is one of the busiest in the world; there are always boats anchored offshore, with one arriving or departing at least every 15 minutes.

Further south along the waterfront you'll find large office blocks, airline offices, more shops and the **Lau Pa Sat Festival Centre** housed in the Telok Ayer Centre, a fine piece of cast-iron Victoriana that was once a market. It was pulled down during the construction of the MRT but has been restored and now stands on its original site. It has a wide selection of eating places and craft stalls, and cultural performances are occasionally held here. It is particularly lively in the evenings, when adjoining **Boon Tat St** is closed off and hawker carts are set up.

Singapore's disappearing Chinatown is inland from this modern city centre.

continued on page 97

Walking Tours of Singapore

Title page: The prominent tower of Malabar Muslim Jama-Ath Mosque – see the Arab St Walking Tour in this section. (photograph by Paul Hellander)

CITY WALKS

The best way to get a feel for Singapore is to walk around its inner city. Though the ethnic areas are quickly becoming dining and drinking venues rather than repositories of traditional culture, Little India, Arab St and Chinatown are still fascinating areas in which to wander.

Little India Walking Tour

Little India is not very extensive – it is roughly the area bounded by Bukit Timah/Rochor Canal Rd to the south, Lavender St to the north, Racecourse Rd to the west and Jalan Besar to the east. The focus of the area is at the southern end of Serangoon Rd and the small streets that run off it. Here, the shops are wall-to-wall Indian, but only a hundred metres or so away the Chinese influence reappears.

Unfortunately, much of the western side of Serangoon Rd has been flattened and consists of open fields, but there are interesting temples further north. Racecourse Rd has a few shops and some good restaurants down its southern end.

Sunday is the day to visit, when all the temples are buzzing and hundreds of Indian men and Bangladeshi immigrant workers come out to socialise, milling around the streets arm-in-arm or squatting by the side of the road to chat.

The **Zhujiao Centre**, on Serangoon Rd near Buffalo Rd, is Little India's big market. It was known as the KK market (Kandang

The Sri Veeramakaliamman on lower Serangoon Rd is at the heart of Little India, both spiritually and physically.

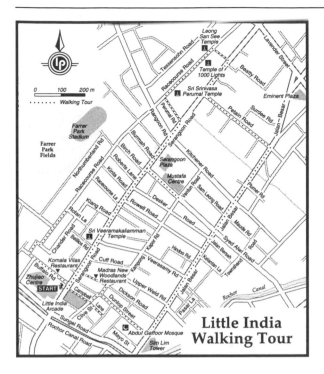

Little India
Walking Tour

Kerbau, meaning 'Cattle Pens', as this was once a cattle-holding area) before it was rehoused in the present modern building. On the ground floor is a 'wet market', the local term for a produce market, and it's one of the liveliest local markets in Singapore, selling all types of fruit and vegetables as well as meat and fish. The hawker centre here has plenty of Indian food stalls. Upstairs, stalls sell a variety of clothes and everyday goods, and you can also buy brassware and Indian textiles.

Across Serangoon Rd is the **Little India Arcade**, representing the new face of Little India. This block of renovated shophouses has its fair share of tourist-oriented souvenir shops, but manages to maintain a traditional atmosphere with Indian textiles, grocery and flower shops. It's a far more successful project than many of the similarly renovated parts of Chinatown.

From here wander around backstreets bearing the names of imperial India, such as Clive, Hastings and Campbell. This is the heart of Little India, with a variety of shops selling spices, Indian music cassettes, saris, religious artefacts and everyday goods for the Indian household. Dunlop St in particular maintains much of its old-fashioned charm. This is also a restaurant area and the best

Restored shophouses on Dalhousie Lane, part of the Little India Conservation District, which encompasses some 900 buildings.

place to sample south Indian vegetarian food; on Buffalo Rd is the famous Komala Vilas restaurant and close by on Upper Dickson Rd is the equally good Madras New Woodlands restaurant (see the Places to Eat chapter).

Apart from the ubiquitous gold shops (gold is a girl's best friend in Asia), there are a few interesting jewellers on Serangoon and Buffalo Rds who make jewellery crafted with traditional designs.

The southern end of Racecourse Rd has the best collection of nonvegetarian restaurants in Singapore, from the tandoori food of north India to Singapore's famous fish-head curry (sounds and looks terrible, tastes delicious).

On the corner of Belilios and Serangoon Rds is the **Sri Veeramakaliamman Temple**, a Shaivite temple dedicated to Kali. It is always popular with worshippers, especially at dusk.

Further north-east along Serangoon Rd is **Serangoon Plaza**. Architecturally, historically and culturally it's a write-off, but the department stores here are good places for bargains. The range may not be extensive, but the fixed prices for electrical goods and other household items are usually as good as you'll find anywhere in Singapore. The **Mustafa Centre** around the corner is a new, larger offshoot crammed with places for bargain hunters.

Also in this area, in the alleyways off Desker Rd, are the infamous brothels. Rows of blockhouse rooms line the alley and a constant parade of men wander up and down. It is fairly seedy but very lively, and the coffee shops with outdoor tables here do a roaring trade. This area is the successor to old Bugis St, without the tourists and carnival atmosphere, and later in the evenings the transvestites strut their stuff.

In complete contrast, the **Sri Srinivasa Perumal Temple** is a large complex dedicated to Vishnu. The temple dates from 1855 but the impressive *gopuram* (tower) is a relatively recent addition, built in 1966. Inside the temple, you will find a statue of Perumal, or Vishnu, and his consorts Lakshmi and Andal, as well as his bird-mount,

Garuda. This temple is the starting point for devotees who make the walk to the Chettiar Hindu Temple during the Thaipusam festival.

Not far from the Sri Srinivasa Perumal is the Sakaya Muni Buddha Gaya Temple, better known as the **Temple of 1000 Lights** (see the Temple of 1000 Lights section in this chapter). It's a glitzy, slightly tacky Thai-influenced temple, but it's popular with visitors. Much more beautiful is the **Leong San See Temple** over the road, a Buddhist and Taoist place of worship with some fine ceramic carvings inside.

From Little India, you can continue your walk south to **Jalan Besar**. The Indian influence begins to wane here. The fine old pastel-coloured terraces with intricate stucco and tiles are Peranakan in style. Of particular note are the terraces on Petain Rd, and those on the corner of Plumer Rd and Jalan Besar.

The Jalan Besar area is home to a number of traditional businesses, while the area around Kelantan and Pasar Lanes is a place to look for antiques. On Sunday a flea market operates, selling everything from old shoes and computer chips to motorcycle parts. If you rummage around you can find old coins, porcelain and brassware.

Just off Jalan Besar on Dunlop St, down towards Rochor Canal Rd, the **Abdul Gaffoor Mosque** is worth a detour for its intriguing fairy-tale blend of Arab and Victorian architecture.

Arab St Walking Tour

The easiest way to begin a tour of the Arab St area is to take the MRT to Bugis station and walk north up Victoria St to Arab St.

Arab St is traditionally a textile district, and while the big merchants inhabit the textile centre on Jalan Sultan, it is still alive with textile shops selling batiks, silks and more mundane cloth for sarongs or shirts. A number of craft shops sell leather bags and souvenirs, and at the end of Arab St near Beach Rd are the caneware shops. Negotiate the five-foot-ways and haggle for the wares.

Sultan Mosque as seen from Bussorah St.

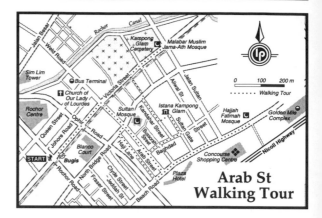

Arab St
Walking Tour

Sultan Mosque (see the Sultan Mosque section in this chapter), the focus for Singapore's Muslim community, is on the corner of Arab St and North Bridge Rd. It is the largest mosque in Singapore and the most lively. You'll also find good Indian Muslim food at restaurants across the street on North Bridge Rd.

One street back, towards the city is **Haji Lane**, a narrow picturesque lane lined with two storey shophouses that contain a number of textile and other local businesses. Kazura, at No 51, is a traditional perfume business with rows of decanters containing perfumes such as 'Ramadan' and 'Aidal Fitri' for the faithful. At the end of Haji Lane turn left onto Beach Rd.

If you have time for a detour north-east along Beach Rd, the **Hajjah Fatimah Mosque** is interesting. A national monument, it was built around 1845 by a Malaccan-born Malay woman (named Hajjah Fatimah) on the site of her home. The architecture shows colonial influences.

Otherwise, turn back up Arab St. Heading north-east along Baghdad St from Arab St, you find more batik and craft shops, and then you cross **Bussorah St**, the new yuppie Arab St. The old terraces have been renovated and flourishing palm trees give the street that Middle Eastern 'oasis look'.

During the month of Ramadan, when Muslims abstain from eating and drinking from sunrise to sunset, this area comes alive with food stalls around dusk when the faithful come to communally break their fast.

At 24 Baghdad St you'll find **stone carvers** crafting the small headstones for Muslim graves, and further along between Sultan Gate and Aliwal St are other stone carvers that also produce carvings for Chinese temples and graves.

If you turn left onto Sultan Gate you come to the historic gates that lead to the **Istana Kampong Glam**. The *istana* (palace) was the residence of Sultan Ali Iskander Shah and was built around

The Malabar Muslim Jama-Ath Mosque, which sits at the corner of the old Malay cemetery.

1840. The Kampong Glam area is the historic seat of the Malay royalty, resident here before the arrival of Stamford Raffles.

The palace isn't open to visitors, but if you walk through the gateway and around to the left a doorway in the palace wall leads you to Kandahar St, behind the Sultan Mosque. Continue up Kandahar St to North Bridge Rd where you'll find a number of venerable Muslim Indian restaurants selling *roti prata* and *biryani*.

Push on north past the restaurants to Victoria St where a right-hand turn brings you to the **Malabar Muslim Jama-Ath Mosque**, a beautiful little building covered in blue tiles that is at its fairy-tale best when lit up in the evenings during Ramadan. Behind it is the old **Kampong Glam cemetery**, where it is said that the Malay royalty is buried among the frangipani trees and coconut palms. Many of the graves have fallen into ruin and are overgrown, but more recent graves are tended, as is evidenced by the cloths placed over the headstones.

Chinatown Walking Tour

You can start a Chinatown walking tour from Raffles Place MRT station in the central business district (CBD). From the station, wander west along Chulia St and south down Phillip St to the **Wak Hai Cheng Bio Temple**. This Teochew Taoist temple is quite run-down but has some interesting scenes depicted under, and on top of, the roof of the main temple.

Continue down Phillip St and over Church St to Telok Ayer St. Up until only a couple of years ago, this was a clamouring district of traditional business, but the blocks around Pekin and Cross Sts are now deserted, awaiting redevelopment. It's amazing how on many of these old Chinese houses, bushes and even large trees seem to sprout straight out of the walls – an indication of the amazing fertility Singapore's steamy climate engenders.

At the junction with Boon Tat St, you'll find the **Nagore Durgha Shrine**, an old mosque built by Muslims from south India in 1829-30. It's not especially significant, but just a little further down the street is the Chinese **Thian Hock Keng Temple**, or Temple of Heavenly Happiness, one of the most interesting temples in Singapore (see the Thian Hock Keng section in this chapter).

Continue walking along Telok Ayer St to the **Al-Abrar Mosque**, which was originally built in 1827 and rebuilt in its present form from 1850-55. A right turn and then another right turn will bring you into Amoy St, a Hokkien area that once catered to sailors and the sea trade. This street has been almost totally modernised and represents the first look at the new Chinatown.

Continue up Amoy St and then turn left (north-west) up Cross St to Club St. A **thieves' market** is held every afternoon in the vacant lot near the corner here. The quiet area around Club St, Ann Siang Rd and Ann Siang Hill was a clove and nutmeg plantation until it became a prime residential area for Hokkien merchants. This area was noted for its highly decorated terraces, a number of which housed the old Chinese guilds, though only a few remain. Ann

The architecturally-confused Nagore Durgha Shrine, in which Chinese towers collide with classical columns and assorted Islamic trappings.

Oiang Hill In particular has some fine terrace houses, both restored and unrestored.

South-west down South Bridge Rd is the **Tanjong Pagar** conservation area, wedged between Neil and Tanjong Pagar Rds. This was the first major restoration project in Chinatown. The beautifully restored terraces accommodate a variety of restaurants and bars. The **old Jinriksha station**, on the corner of Neil and Tanjong Pagar Rds, now a restaurant, is an interesting triangular building that was once the depot for the hand-pulled rickshaws. The **Tanjong Pagar Heritage Exhibition** in the 51 Neil Rd complex is a small, interesting exhibition with old photographs that show what Chinatown used to be like. It is open from 11 am to 9 pm daily; admission is free.

Near Tanjong Pagar, Bukit Pasoh Rd is known as the street of the clans because of the many clan association houses here. Keong Saik Rd is a curving street of old terraces with coffee shops, clan houses and clubs. This street is a hive of ongoing building work, and new hotels and bars are replacing most of the traditional businesses.

Heading back to the centre of Chinatown, north-east up to South Bridge Rd, you enter the **Kreta Ayer district**, the real heart of Chinatown. The street hawkers and many traditional businesses have gone but some of the old atmosphere of Chinatown remains.

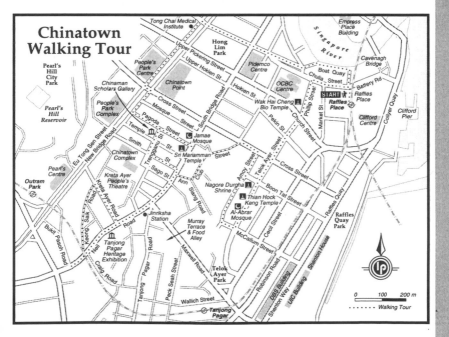

The **Chinatown Complex**, on the corner of Trengganu and Smith Sts, is a lively local shopping and food centre and a popular meeting place outside in the cool of the evening. Along with Smith St, Temple, Pagoda and Mosque Sts are traditionally the heart of old Chinatown, but new developments have destroyed a lot of the atmosphere and Pagoda St is a mess of renovation. Smith St has gold, jade, souvenirs and traditional medicine shops, while Mosque St has a good row of old-fashioned coffee shops. The whole area has plenty of old and new souvenir and trinket shops selling masks, reproduction bronzes, bamboo ware, carvings and silk dressing gowns. Bargain hard.

Upstairs at 14B Trengganu St is the **Chinaman Scholars Gallery**. This living museum is styled as a Cantonese house of the 1930s and includes furniture, clothing, artefacts, photographs and musical instruments from the period. It is open from 9 am to 4 pm daily; admission is S$4 for adults, S$2 for children.

Also in this area is the **Sri Mariamman Temple**, Singapore's oldest Hindu temple (see the Sri Mariamman Temple section in this chapter). The **Jamae (or Chulia) Mosque** on South Bridge Rd is only a short distance from the Sri Mariamman Temple. It was built by Indian Muslims from the Coromandel Coast of Tamil Nadu between 1830 and 1855.

Across New Bridge Rd from Pagoda St is the huge **People's Park Complex** – a modern shopping centre, but with much more local appeal than the general run of Orchard Rd centres.

Further north-east along Eu Tong Sen St is the **Tong Chai Medical Institute**. This architecturally interesting building in the style of a Chinese *godown* (warehouse) is classified as a national monument.

Finish off the walking tour by heading east along North Canal Rd until you hit Boat Quay, where you can quench your thirst with a well-deserved beer.

Traditional Chinese terraces on Ann Siang Hill, now a fashionable address for advertising and architectural companies.

continued from page 86
CHINATOWN (Map 6)

Singapore's cultural heart is Chinatown. Roughly bounded by the Singapore River to the north, New Bridge Rd to the west, Maxwell and Kreta Ayer Rds to the south and Cecil St to the east, it provides a glimpse of the old ways, the ways of the Chinese immigrants that shaped and built modern Singapore.

Much of Chinatown has been torn down and redeveloped over the past 30 years, though the greatest changes have occurred since around 1990. Many of the old colonial shopfronts, which are synonymous with the Chinese on the Malay peninsula, have been restored, or rather ripped down and rebuilt in the same style, under the direction of the Urban Redevelopment Authority.

The redevelopments are faithful to the original, and it is wonderful to see the spirit of the old buildings winning out over the concrete high-rises. The re-creations are now desirable properties commanding high rents. Unfortunately, this has meant that many of the traditional businesses have had to move out and a new, gentrified Chinatown has come into being, composed of fashionable restaurants and expensive shops.

That aside, Chinatown is still a good place to wander around. It contains some of Singapore's most notable temples and there are plenty of eating and shopping possibilities.

See the Chinatown walk in the Walking Tours section of this chapter.

Thian Hock Keng Temple

Also known as the Temple of Heavenly Happiness, this temple on Telok Ayer St is the oldest and one of the most colourful temples in Singapore. The temple was originally built in 1841 and dedicated to Ma-Cho-Po, the Queen of Heaven and protector of sailors.

At that time, this area was on the waterfront and, since many Chinese settlers arrived by sea, it was inevitable that a joss house be built where they could offer thanks for a safe voyage. As you wander through the courtyards of the temple, look for the rooftop dragons, the intricately decorated

The Old Trades of Chinatown

When wandering around Chinatown, you may come across some disappearing trades that have been unique to this area since its inception.

The letter writer will set up a streetside table and pen letters for old Chinese residents who have never learned to read or write. Traditionally, the letter writer would deftly pen the Chinese characters in correspondence destined for relatives back in China; these days he is more likely to be a sign writer, producing lucky scrolls with messages of prosperity and luck to be hung outside houses during the Chinese New Year.

The chop is a Chinese stamp that serves as a signature for documents, and a chop maker will carve them for his customers. Traditionally, the carving was done on bamboo or ivory, though these days plastic is often used. Each chop has a unique imprint, bearing both the design and style of its maker, and cannot be replicated.

Rickshaw drivers have been a part of Chinatown ever since the *jinriksha*, or man-pulled rickshaw, arrived from Shanghai. These were later replaced by the bicycle trishaw, which still plies the streets of Chinatown. Drivers take passengers for short trips between the shopping centres and the nearby housing estates, while the goods trishaw, with a platform at the front, is still a convenient way to transport freight around the back-streets.

beams, the burning joss sticks, the gold-leafed panels and, best of all, the beautifully painted doors.

Sri Mariamman Temple

The Sri Mariamman Temple, 244 South Bridge Rd, right in the heart of Chinatown, is the oldest Hindu temple in Singapore. It was built in 1827, then rebuilt in 1862. The colourful *gopuram* (tower) over the entrance gate clearly identifies this as a temple in the south Indian Dravidian style. A superb collection of colourfully painted Hindu figures gazes out from the gopuram.

Around October each year the temple is the scene for the Thimithi festival, during which devotees walk barefoot over burning coals – supposedly feeling no pain, although spectators report that quite a few hot-foot it over the final few steps!

The temple is open from 7.30 to 11.30 am and from 5.30 to 8.30 pm daily. Admission is S$3, or S$6 if you want to take photos or use a video camera.

LITTLE INDIA (Map 5)

Although Singapore is a predominantly Chinese city, it does have its minority groups and the Indians are probably the most visible, particularly on the colourful streets of Little India along Serangoon Rd. This is another area, like Chinatown, where you can simply wander around and take in the flavours. Indeed, around Serangoon Rd it can be very much a case of following your nose because the heady aroma of Indian spices and cooking seems to be everywhere.

If you want a new sari, a pair of Indian sandals, a recent issue of *India Today* or the *Indian Movie News*, a tape of Indian music or a framed portrait of your favourite Hindu god, then Little India is the place to go.

It's also, not surprisingly, a good place to eat. Since many of Singapore's Indians are Hindu Tamils from the south of India, the streets of Little India hold some superb places to eat vegetarian food.

See the Little India walk in the Walking Tours section in this chapter.

Temple of 1000 Lights

Towards the north-eastern end of Racecourse Rd, at No 366, close to the corner of Serangoon and Beatty Rds, is the Sakaya Muni Buddha Gaya Temple, or the Temple of 1000 Lights. This Buddhist temple is dominated by a brightly painted 15m-high seated figure of the Buddha. The temple was inspired by a Thai monk named Vut-

thisasara. Although it is a Thai-style temple, it's actually very Chinese in its technicolour decoration.

Apart from the huge Buddha image, the temple includes some oddities like a wax model of Gandhi and a figure of Ganesh, the elephant-headed Hindu god. A huge mother-of-pearl footprint, complete with the 108 auspicious marks that distinguish a Buddha foot from any other 2m-long foot, is said to be a replica of the footprint on top of Adam's Peak in Sri Lanka.

Behind and inside the giant statue is a smaller image of the reclining Buddha in the act of entering nirvana. Around the base, models tell the story of the Buddha's life, and, of course, there are the 1000 electric lights that give the temple its name.

Any bus going north-east along Serangoon Rd will take you to the temple.

ARAB ST (Map 5)

Just as Chinatown provides Singapore with a Chinese flavour and Serangoon Rd is where you head to for the tastes and smells of India, Arab St is the Muslim centre. Along this street, and especially North Bridge Rd and side streets with Malay names like Pahang St, Aliwal St, Jalan Pisang and Jalan Sultan, you'll find batiks from Indonesia and sarongs, hookahs, rosaries, flower essences, *hajj* caps, *songkok* hats, basketware and rattan goods.

See the Walking Tours of Singapore section in this chapter for a further description of the Arab St area.

Sultan Mosque

The Sultan Mosque on North Bridge Rd near Arab St is the biggest mosque in Singapore. It was originally built in 1825 with the aid of a grant from Stamford Raffles and the East India Company as a result of Raffles' treaty with the sultan of Johor. A hundred years later, the original mosque was replaced by the present magnificent golden-domed building. The mosque is open to visitors from 5 am to 8.30 pm daily. If you can manage it, the best time to visit is during a religious ceremony.

ORCHARD RD (Map 4)

Orchard Rd is a showcase for modern Singapore and the delights of capitalism. Its rows of modern shopping centres – which range from the Olympian to the hi tech – hold a variety of shops selling everything from the latest in Japanese gadgetry to the antiques of the east. It's on Orchard Rd that you'll also find the majority of the international hotels, the majority of the nightspots and a whole host of restaurants, bars and lounges.

North-west of the busy thoroughfare, you enter the areas of the Singapore elite. Prior to independence, the mansions of the colonial rulers were built here and today the wealthy of Singapore, as well as many expatriates, live in these fine old houses.

Peranakan Place

Among the glass and chrome is Peranakan Place, a complex of old Nonya-Baba shophouses on the corner of Orchard and Emerald Hill Rds.

The **Peranakan Showhouse Museum** is a shophouse filled with artefacts, furniture and clothing which, if traditional Straits Chinese culture interests you, shouldn't be missed. The museum is in a terrace a few doors north of Orchard Rd. Interesting tours of the museum are available on demand (for a minimum of four people) and cost S$10 for adults, S$5 for children. The museum is open from 10.30 am to 12.30 pm and from 2 to 3.30 pm weekdays.

From Peranakan Place, wander north up Emerald Hill Rd, where some fine terrace houses remain. This whole area was once a nutmeg plantation owned by William Cuppage, an early Singapore settler. At the turn of the century, much of it was subdivided and it became a fashionable residential area for Peranakan and Straits-born Chinese merchants. Today, it is a fashionable drinking spot with some good bars.

Peranakan Place is just north of Somerset MRT station.

Istana

The Istana (palace) is the home of Singapore's president and is also used by the prime minister for ceremonial occasions. It was designed in the 1860s as Government House, a neo-Palladian-style monument to British rule. Public works were never a high priority in laissez faire colonial Singapore, but the need to impress the visiting Duke of Edinburgh convinced the island's Legislative Council to approve the building's huge budget. The actual construction was done by Indian convicts transported from Bencoolen on Sumatra. They were paid three to seven times the local coolie rate for their skilled masonry, plumbing and carpentry work.

The Istana is set about 750m back from the road in large grounds. Most of the time the closest you are likely to get to it are the well-guarded gates on Orchard Rd, but the Istana is open to the public on selected public holidays, such as New Year's Day. If you are lucky enough to be in Singapore on one of these occasions, take your passport and join the queues to get in.

House of Tan Yeok Nee

On the corner of Clemenceau Ave and Penang Rd, near Orchard Rd, the House of Tan Yeok Nee was built in 1885 as the townhouse of a prosperous merchant. It's built in a style then common in southern China and is the only building of its kind in Singapore. Although a national monument the house is presently closed to the public and its future is uncertain.

Chettiar Hindu Temple (Map 6)

At the intersection of Tank and River Valley Rds, not far south of Orchard Rd, this temple was completed in 1984 and replaces a much earlier temple built by Indian *chettiars*, or money lenders. It is a Shivaite temple dedicated to the six headed Lord Subramaniam and is at its most active during the festival of Thaipusam, when the procession ends here. Worshippers make offerings of coconuts, which are smashed on the ground to crack them open.

JURONG (Map 7)

Jurong, west of the city centre, is more than just a new housing area. A huge industrial complex has been built on land that was still a swamp at the end of WWII, and today it is the powerhouse of Singapore's economic success story. The Jurong area also has a number of tourist attractions, in Jurong Town itself and on the way to Jurong from the city centre.

Haw Par Villa

This is a Chinese mythological theme park about 10km west from the city centre on Pasir Panjang Rd. It features theatre performances, boat rides and, most notably, a gaudy grotesquerie of figures illustrating scenes from Chinese legends and the pleasures and punishments of this life and the next.

The park was built with the fortune that the Aw brothers made from their miracle cure-all Tiger Balm. Renovations and hi tech additions have changed the face of this still hugely popular monument to bad taste, but the surviving statuary remains its major

attraction. Favourite displays include the '10 courts of hell', where sinners get their gory comeuppance in the afterlife, and the 'moral lessons' aisle, where sloth, indulgence, gambling and even wine, women and song, lead to their inevitable unhappy endings.

The newer attractions include a heart-in-the-mouth roller coaster boat ride and theatres where the inevitable multimedia displays narrate myths and legends. The large, covered amphitheatre has live performances popular with children, and new schedules advertise daily performances such as lion dances and stilt-walking.

Haw Par Villa is popular with Singaporean families – it's fun for the kids, teaches them Chinese mythology and the moral tales scare the bejesus out of any potential miscreants. It costs S$5.00 for adults and S$2.50 for children.

Haw Par Villa is open from 9 am to 6 pm daily. To get there, take the MRT to Buona

RICHARD I'ANSON

A detail from one of the gaudy tableaux at Haw Par Villa.

Vista station, from where you catch bus No 200. Alternatively, from Clementi station take bus No 10.

Jurong Bird Park

This beautifully landscaped 20 hectare park has over 8000 birds from 600 species and includes a two hectare walk-in aviary and artificial waterfall. Exhibits include everything from cassowaries, birds of paradise, eagles and cockatoos to parrots and macaws, and even penguins in an air-conditioned underwater viewing gallery. The nocturnal house includes owls, kiwis and frogmouths. The South-East Asian Birds Aviary is a major attraction and features a simulated rainforest thunderstorm every day at noon. The park also has one of the world's largest collections of hornbills, as well as a walk-through parrot aviary. There is a collection of supposedly talking birds – mynahs and various parrots – but the birds look so bored that it is the visitors that seem to do most of the talking.

You can walk around the park or take the Panorail service – an air-conditioned monorail that does a tour of the park. The Panorail costs S$2.50 for adults, S$1.00 for children.

Admission to the park is S$10.30 for adults and S$4.12 for children. It's open from 9 am to 6 pm weekdays, and from 8 am to 6 pm weekends and public holidays. To get there, take the MRT to Boon Lay station and then catch the No 194 special loop bus or the more frequent No 251. The bird park is on Jalan Ahmad Ibrahim.

You can climb Jurong Hill beside the park for a good view over the area.

Jurong Reptile Park

Formerly known as the Jurong Crocodile Paradise, this theme park has recreated itself to encompass more than just crocs and now boasts a scaly collection of other reptiles and amphibians such as Komodo dragons and giant tortoises.

Although the emphasis is less on crocs than before, there are still plenty of these fierce creatures to be seen and there are

croc-related products on sale. Crocodile wrestling and feeding are two of the supposed highlights. It is open from 9 am to 6 pm daily, and costs S$7 for adults and S$3.50 for children. A trip here is easily combined with a trip to Jurong Bird Park, which is right next door.

Chinese & Japanese Gardens

Off Yuan Ching Rd, the Chinese and Japanese gardens each occupy 13.5 hectares in the vicinity of Jurong Lake.

The Chinese Garden is actually an island. It's colourful and has a number of Chinese-style pavilions and a couple of pagodas. The main attraction is the extensive *penjing* (Chinese bonsai) display.

The less-interesting Japanese Garden (which is almost an island) has large grassed areas and a few buildings. Garden lovers will find Singapore's Botanic Gardens (see later this chapter) of more interest, but the Chinese Garden is very pleasant and a must for bonsai enthusiasts. You can climb to the top of the multistoreyed pagoda – all 176 steps – for a fine view over the two gardens and the surrounding area.

The gardens are open from 9 am to 6 pm daily. Admission to both is S$4.50 for adults and S$2 for children. The Chinese Garden MRT station is a five minute walk from the lake and gardens.

Singapore Science Centre

On Science Centre Rd, off Jurong Town Hall Rd, the Science Centre attempts to make science come alive by providing countless opportunities to try things out for yourself. There are handles to crank, buttons to push, levers to pull, microscopes to look through and films to watch. The centre is primarily designed to encourage an interest in science among Singapore's school children, but it is amazing how many adults compete with the kids to have a go on the hands-on exhibits.

One of the main attractions is the Omni Theatre, next to the main science centre building, with full-blown, three-dimensional whiz-bang Imax format movies covering topics from space flights to roller coaster rides. There is also a planetarium at the centre.

The centre is open from 10 am to 6 pm daily, closed Monday, and admission is S$3 (children S$1.50). Entry to the Imax movies costs S$10 or S$16 for two people.

The easiest way to get to the centre is to take the MRT to Jurong East station and then walk 500m west or take bus Nos 66 or 335 from the station.

Singapore Discovery Centre (Map 2)
This family-oriented centre (☎ 792 6188) is a little off the beaten track at 510 Upper Jurong Rd in far west Jurong, but is worth it if you have children and a few hours to kill. There are exhibits covering Singapore's history including a huge 9m photomap, a five storey high IWERKS movie screen, a motion simulator (S$4), a computerised shooting gallery, virtual parachute jumping and a Children's Adventureland.

Entry to the centre is S$9 for adults, S$5 for children. It's open from 9 am to 7 pm weekdays (closed Monday) and from 9 am to 8 pm weekends and public holidays. Visit on the Internet at www.asianconnect.com/sdc.

To get there take the MRT to Boon Lay and then either the No 192 or 193 bus.

Tang Dynasty City
This multimillion-dollar theme park is a re-creation of old Chang'an (modern-day Xian), the Tang dynasty capital, as it was during China's golden age in the 6th to 8th centuries AD. Behind the massive 10m-high walls, Tang Dynasty City's main street features a courthouse, geisha house and shops, and there are also temples, restaurants and theatres. The mock period-architecture is backed up by 'Silk Road' camel rides, craft demonstrations, performances and displays such as a partial reproduction of the life-size Xian terracotta army.

Like most theme parks it is a bit plasticky, but the size and style of the buildings is impressive. The park also has shops selling tea, antiques and wine, and a wax museum with a talking Mao.

It's open every day from 9.30 am to 6.30 pm; admission is S$15.45 for adults; S$10.30 for children.

Tang Dynasty City is on the corner of Yuan Ching Rd and Jalan Ahmad Ibrahim, near the Chinese and Japanese gardens. Take the MRT to Lakeside station, from where it's a 2km taxi ride, or take bus No 154 or 240.

New Ming Village & Pewter Museum
This pottery workshop at 32 Pandan Rd produces reproduction porcelain from the Ming and Qing dynasties. You can see the craftspeople create their pottery and, of course, you can buy their works. The complete production process is done on the premises and guided tours are available on demand for groups.

New Ming Village is owned by Royal Selangor Pewter. Consequently, the village also has a small pewter museum with some interesting pieces, and the showroom sells an extensive selection of pewter as well as pottery. The pewter is made in Malaysia, but the polishing and hand-beaten designs are demonstrated at the village.

It is open every day from 9 am to 5.30 pm, and admission is free. To get there, take the MRT to Clementi station and then bus No 78 to Pandan Rd.

Singapore Mint Coin Gallery
This gallery, at Singapore's mint on Jalan Boon Lay just east of Boon Lay MRT station, exhibits coins and medals from Singapore and a few coins from around the world. The place is essentially an outlet for the gold medallions that the mint sells, but a few mint sets of Singapore coins are also for sale. Only dedicated coin enthusiasts would want to make the trip out here. It is open from 9 am to 4.30 pm weekdays and admission is free.

EAST COAST & CHANGI (Map 8)
East Coast Park is a popular recreational haunt for Singaporeans. It is the place to swim, windsurf, lie on the sand, rent a bike or, of course, eat. The stretch of beach along

the east coast, south of the East Coast Expressway, was born of reclaimed land and while it wouldn't win any awards as a tropical paradise, it is by far Singapore's most popular beach and has good facilities.

Further inland are the interesting areas of Geylang and Katong, both largely Malay districts, which are rarely frequented by foreign visitors. Geylang is about as close to a 'Little Malaysia' as you'll find, while Katong, centred on busy East Coast Rd, has strong Peranakan influences and offers some interesting dining possibilities.

Changi is known for its international airport and infamous prison, both attractions in their own right. Further out is Changi Village and its nearby beach.

Geylang

If you want to experience Malaysia, the real thing is just across the Causeway. There are Malay areas in Singapore, though its culture is not so obvious nor easily marketed as a tourist attraction.

Geylang Serai is a Malay residential area, but you are not going to see traditional *atap* (thatched-roof) houses or any sarong-clad cottage industry workers. The area is Singaporean high-rise, though there are some older buildings around, especially in the *lorongs* (alleys) that run off Geylang Rd. The lorongs house one of Singapore's most active red-light districts.

Geylang Serai is easily reached by taking the MRT to Paya Lebar station, from where it's a short walk down Tanjong Katong Rd to Geylang Rd, the area's busy main shopping street.

A short walk east along Geylang Rd will bring you to the **Malay Cultural Village** (☎ 748 4700). This complex of traditional Malay-style houses was built as a showpiece of native culture, though it hasn't really taken off as a tourist attraction. On weekends it does attract Singaporean families desperately seeking *kampong* (village) nostalgia, but it is very quiet during the week. Admission is free to wander around the craft shops and bird market or to eat at the satay stalls and restaurants. For S$10 (children

S$7), you can visit the Kampung Days museum and the Legenda Fantasi show. The museum has kampong buildings with waxwork figures, a few artefacts and interesting videos on Malay weddings, games and kampong life. The Legenda Fantasi is a good, whiz-bang show for the kids, with laser effects and a booming sound system telling Ali Baba stories with a Singaporean slant. Performances are held at 8 pm and cost S$5.

Just next door to the cultural village is the **Geylang Serai Market**. It's hidden behind some older-style housing blocks on Geylang Rd, and its entrance is through a small lane that leads to a crowded, traditional Asian market which is yet to be rebuilt as a concrete box. It is a good place to browse and is much more interesting than most of Singapore's new markets. It reaches its peak of activity during Ramadan, when the whole area is alive with market stalls, which set up in the evenings for the faithful after a long day of fasting.

Katong

From the Geylang Serai Market you can head down Joo Chiat Rd to East Coast Rd and explore the Katong district. **Joo Chiat Rd** has a host of local businesses operating during the day, while at night the restaurants and music lounges are popular. Despite some restoration the streetscape has largely escaped the developer and several fine Peranakan-style terraces remain intact, holding around them a little of the atmosphere of old Singapore.

Stop in at Amoy Tea, 331 Joo Chiat Rd, a traditional shop selling a variety of Chinese teas and superbly crafted tea sets. Guan Hoe Soon, at No 214, has Peranakan/Chinese food, and Casa Bom Vento, at No 467, is an interesting Eurasian restaurant.

On Koon Seng Rd, just off Joo Chiat Rd, are some of the finest **Peranakan terrace houses** in Singapore. They exhibit the typical Peranakan love of ornate design; they're decorated with plaster stucco dragons, birds, crabs and brilliantly glazed tiles. *Pintu pagar* (saloon doors) at the front

Kampong Life

A *kampong* is a traditional Malay-style village, with wooden huts on stilts. In the best instances the huts are surrounded by greenery, amid which the villagers live out unhurried lives, with children running wild and languid dogs lazing in the shade.

This all might sound a little idealised, but it's an ideal upon which the Singaporeans are fixated. The word 'kampong' has become synonymous with a slow, relaxed lifestyle which, while still existing in rural Malaysia, has almost completely vanished from rapidly urbanising Singapore.

The symbolic importance of the kampong to Singaporeans cannot be overstated. Confined in 90% of cases to high-rise apartment blocks, Singaporeans have little opportunity to relax in natural surroundings or to revel in any significant personal space. It is hardly surprising then that every weekend middle-class Singaporeans flock en masse to neighbouring Malaysia to enjoy a little piece of tropical Ruritania.

There are, in fact, still a few kampongs in Singapore, mostly in the north-east of the island, on the coast between Sembawang and Punggol. But with iron roofs, electricity and a car parked next to the house, they fall some way short of the untainted idyll of Singaporean yearnings.

Perhaps the closest Singapore comes to the kampong scenario is on Pulau Ubin, which is very rural and very Malay in character. However, developers already have the island in their sights so get there while you still can.

---

of the houses are another typical feature, which allow breezes in while retaining privacy. (For background information on the Peranakans, see the special Peranakan section in the Facts about Singapore chapter.)

Joo Chiat Rd runs into **East Coast Rd**, a well-to-do 'village' shopping stretch that is the centre of Katong. Before land reclamation moved the beach, Katong was a quiet village by the sea. Now East Coast Rd bustles with city traffic and Singapore's modern developments have engulfed the east coast. Despite this Katong still retains its village atmosphere. East Coast Rd is noted for its Peranakan influence, mostly because of the opportunity to sample Peranakan food (also known as Nonya cuisine) and view the fascinating collection of Peranakan antiques in the Katong Antique House at No 208. The Katong Bakery & Confectionery, 75 East Coast Rd, is another local relic from pre-war Singapore. It still serves Nonya cakes and pastries.

It is also worth wandering the back streets of Katong around Joo Chiat and East Coast Rds where you'll find more terraces,

coffee shops and temples. Just off East Coast Rd on Ceylon Rd is the Hindu Sri Senpaga Vinayagar Temple, and about a kilometre away on Wilkinson Rd is the Sri Guru Nanak Sat Sangh Sabha Sikh temple.

East Coast Rd changes its name to **Mountbatten Rd** as it heads into the city and crosses Tanjong Katong Rd, which leads back to Geylang and Paya Lebar MRT station. This area contains a number of grand old villas, such as the Villa Dolce at 164 Tanjong Katong Rd. Mountbatten Rd also has some fine old houses.

From East Coast Rd, bus Nos 12 and 32 head into the city along North Bridge Rd in the colonial district, while bus No 14 goes down Stamford Rd and then Orchard Rd. Coming from the city, bus No 16 can be boarded on Orchard and Bras Basah Rds, and it goes along Joo Chiat Rd, crossing East Coast Rd.

East Coast Park

Stretching along Singapore's east coast on reclaimed land, East Coast Park comes alive on weekends with Singaporeans relaxing by the beach, eating at the seafood outlets or indulging in more strenuous sporting activities. The foreshore parkland has a track running right along the coast for bicycling, jogging or roller blading, and you can hire bicycles, canoes and sailboards. The beach is reasonable, with a continuous sandy stretch and calm waters but, like all of Singapore's beaches, the water is hardly crystal clear.

The **Singapore Crocodilarium**, 730 East Coast Parkway, has a large number of crocodiles crammed into concrete tanks. A shop also sells croc products. It's open daily from 9 am to 5 pm; admission is S$2 for adults and S$1 for children. Nature lovers will want to avoid this place.

Big Splash (☎ 345 1211), 902 East Coast Parkway, is a water fun park with swimming pools and a huge water slide. It's open from 10 am to 6 pm daily.

The **East Coast Recreation Centre** is the big place in the East Coast Park, with bowling, squash, crazy golf, fun rides, a selection of restaurants and food stalls, and bicycle and canoe hire. As well as racers (S$3 per hour) and mountain bikes (S$4 per hour), tandems can be hired.

One kilometre further away from the city is the **East Coast Lagoon**, noted for its seafood. The UDMC Seafood Centre, just west of the lagoon, has a number of restaurants. Also here, east of the lagoon, is the East Coast Sailing Centre (☎ 449 5118), a private club that rents sailboards to the public for S$20 for the first two hours and S$10 for each subsequent hour. Bicycles and canoes can also be hired at the kiosk near the seafood centre.

The only bus is No 401, operating from Bedok MRT station along the service road in the park on Sunday and public holidays. All other buses whiz by on the East Coast Parkway expressway so you'll have to catch a taxi.

Changi Prison Museum (Map 2)

Changi is still used as a prison, but next to the main gate is a museum with a bookshop and a poignant replica of the simple thatched prison chapel built by Allied prisoners during

their horrendous internment at the hands of the Japanese during WWII. Pinned to the chapel are notes from those who lost loved ones in Changi. The small museum features drawings made by the prisoners depicting life in Changi, as well as photographs and other exhibits providing an overview of the war in Asia. The museum is open Monday to Saturday from 9.30 am to 4.30 pm, though you can visit the chapel outside these hours. A service is held each Sunday at the chapel from 5.30 to 6.30 pm.

Changi prison is on Upper Changi Rd near the airport and can be reached by bus No 2 from Victoria St in the colonial district, or pick up the same bus at Tanah Merah MRT station.

Changi Village (Map 2)

Changi, on the east coast of Singapore, is an escape from the hubbub of central Singapore. Don't expect to find traditional kampong houses – the buildings are modern – but Changi does have a village atmosphere. Changi's beach is not exactly a tropical paradise, though it has a good stretch of sand and offers safe swimming. It's popular on weekends but almost deserted during the week. The food in Changi is an attraction, and there are some good seafood restaurants and food stalls near the beach.

From Changi, you can catch ferries to Pulau Ubin (see the Other Islands section later in this chapter). Ferries also go to Pengerang across the strait in Malaysia (see the Getting There & Away chapter).

You can reach Changi Village on bus No 2 from Victoria St in the colonial district; it also passes Changi prison.

SENTOSA ISLAND (Map 9)

Sentosa, just off the south coast of Singapore, is the granddaddy of all Singapore's fun parks. It is Singapore's most visited attraction and it's packed at weekends.

Like its beaches of imported sand, Sentosa is a purely synthetic attraction, but it is a good place for children and there's enough to keep adults occupied. Sentosa has museums, aquariums, beaches, sporting

THINGS TO SEE & DO

facilities, walks, rides and food centres. There's easily enough to do to fill a day and if that isn't enough there's a camping ground, a hostel and two luxury hotels.

Sentosa is open daily from 7.30 am until around 11 pm, or an hour or so later on weekends. Many of the attractions close at 7 pm but cultural shows, plays and music performances are sometimes held in the evenings – check with the tourism board office or ring the Sentosa Information Office (☎ 275 0388). You can also visit Sentosa via the Web at www.sentosa.com.sg.

Basic admission to Sentosa is S$5 for adults (S$3 after 6.30 pm) and S$3 for children under 12. Most of the attractions cost extra and the toll can really add up if you want to see them all.

A free bus service runs around the island, with departures every 10 minutes. There's also a free monorail loop service, which is scenic but slow. You can also get around Sentosa by bicycle; rentals are available from the hire kiosk by the ferry terminal.

Underwater World

This spectacular aquarium is one of Sentosa's most popular attractions. Displays include a turtle pool, moray eel enclosure, reef enclosures with live coral, a theatre showing continuous films and a touch pool where visitors can dip their digits into the pool and fondle the sea life. These exhibits are mere entrées to Underwater World's 'travellator', an acrylic tunnel that takes spectators through the main tanks as all manner of fish swim around in all their natural technicolour glory. There is nothing quite like the sight of a huge manta ray, 60kg grouper, or shark swimming overhead.

The most recent addition to the nautical menagerie is – in the words of Underwater World's own publicity blurb – a 'gigantic, ugly and slimy' exhibit of creatures of the deep featuring a giant octopus, wolf eel and spider crab.

Underwater World is open daily from 9 am to 9 pm, and costs S$12 for adults and S$6 for children.

Images of Singapore

This is a grouping of three small museums in one. The main component is the Pioneers of Singapore waxwork museum, which gives a decent account of Singapore's past and focuses on the traditional cultures of its main communities. The adjoining Surrender Chamber traces the history of the Japanese occupation during WWII – it's surprisingly popular with Japanese tour groups. The newest part is the Festivals of Singapore, which has wax dummy exhibits and explanations of Singapore's many festivals.

Admission to the whole thing is S$5 for adults and S$3 for children; it's open from 9 am to 9 pm.

Fort Siloso

Dating from the 19th century, this was built as a military base and series of gun emplacements linked by underground tunnels. But when it came to the test with the Japanese invasion in WWII, the guns were all pointing in the wrong direction. The island was used by the victorious Japanese as a prisoner-of-war (POW) camp.

From 1989 until 1993, Fort Siloso housed Sentosa's most unusual 'attraction', political prisoner Chia Thye Poh. Arrested in 1966 for allegedly being a Communist, Chia served 23 years in jail before being banished to complete his bizarre sentence among the holiday delights of Sentosa.

A guided walk leads around the gun emplacements, tunnels and buildings, with waxwork re-creations of life in a colonial barracks. A mini sound-and-light show relives the period immediately before the Japanese invasion, and a 'Behind Bars' exhibit focuses on prison life for the POWs. Though not wildly exciting, it is one of Sentosa's more interesting attractions.

Fort Siloso is open from 9 am to 7 pm, and costs S$3 for adults and S$2 for children.

Fantasy Island

This is a huge water theme park with swimming pools, 13 different water rides and 32 slides. Rides range from 'river rafting' to the more terrifying Gang of Four, Blackhole and Kyag slides. There is also an entertainment mall with electronic games. It's great for the kids, bad for the wallet. Entrance costs S$12 (children S$6), lockers are S$1 and floats are S$3 and S$4. Fantasy Island is open from 10 am to 7 pm daily.

Volcano Land

Based on a Mayan city and dominated by a giant, concrete volcano, Volcano Land is Sentosa's tackiest attraction. Singaporean 'Mayan' Indians put on dances and drape snakes around tourist's necks for photos. The show inside the volcano is held every half-hour and takes you through an explorer's tunnel and mock mine-elevator trip to a theatre where even the booming sound effects cannot enliven the dull movie on the evolution of life. The eruption finale is a fizzer and when the exit doors open to reveal the gift shop it is almost a relief. Save your S$10. The volcano 'erupts' every half-hour with a bang and a puff of smoke – you can see it from outside.

Butterfly Park & Insect Kingdom Museum

At the Butterfly Park, you can walk among over 50 species of live butterflies. In the museum there are thousands of mounted butterflies, rhino beetles, *Dynastes hercules* (the world's largest beetles) and scorpions, among other insects.

It is open from 9 am to 6 pm weekdays and until 6.30 pm weekends and public holidays. Entry costs S$5 for adults and S$3 for children.

Asian Village

This collection of craft shops and some food outlets reflects Asia's various cultures. The theme park buildings are vaguely styled after traditional houses. Entry is free, though the rides in the village's entertainment park cost extra. It's open from 10 am to 9 pm.

Other Attractions

The **Maritime Museum** (open from 10 am to 7 pm; adults S$2, children 50c) has exhibits recording the history of Singapore's port and shipping, as well as fishing tools and primitive craft. **Sentosa Orchid Gardens** (open from 9.30 am to 6.30 pm; adults S$2, children S$1) is an orchid garden with a Japanese theme.

Of the free attractions, there's a **Nature Walk** though, in typical Sentosa fashion, it's been livened up in part with dragons and fossils. Long-tailed macaques are common, but hide your food from these aggressive monkeys. You can also wander around the impressive ferry terminal, Fountain Gardens and Flower Terrace.

At night, the **Musical Fountain** spurts water to music and flashing coloured lights, while the **Pasar Malam** (Night Market) stalls sell souvenirs. Nearby is the **Rasa Sentosa Food Centre** – naturally Sentosa

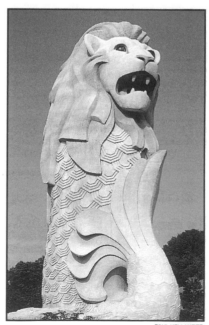

PAUL HELLANDER

The Merlion is the official mascot of Singapore. This Merlion at Sentosa is 11 storeys high.

has a hawker centre – and the ferry terminal also has some dining possibilities.

Other newly completed attractions are an adventure golf theme park and the **Merlion Tower**, a huge Merlion with good views from the top.

Beaches & Recreational Facilities

Sentosa's southern coastline is devoted to beaches: Siloso Beach at the western end, Central Beach and Tanjong Beach at the eastern end. As a tropical paradise, Sentosa has a long way to go to match the islands of Malaysia or Indonesia, but in a case of 'if Mohammed won't come to the mountain' Singapore has imported its beaches from Indonesia and planted coconut palms to give it a tropical ambience. The imported sand does at least make for what are Singapore's best beaches. Pedal cats, aquabikes, fun bugs, canoes and surfboards are all available for hire.

Sentosa has a 5.7km-long bicycle track that loops the island and takes in most of the attractions. Bicycles can be hired at bicycle stations on the track, such as the kiosk at Siloso Beach or at the ferry terminal, and cost from S\$2 to S\$5 per hour.

Sentosa also has a roller-skating rink, which costs S\$2 entry. There are two 18 hole golf courses: Serapong, for members only, and Tanjong, which is open to the public and costs S\$80 for a round on week-days or S\$120 on weekends.

Getting There & Away

Take SBS bus No 65 or 143 from Orchard Rd, or No 61, 84, 143, 145 or 166 from Chinatown to the World Trade Centre (WTC). Tourist buses, such as the Singapore Trolley, also run to the WTC. From the bus terminal across from the WTC take Sentosa Bus Service A. Alternatively, take the MRT to Tiong Bahru station and then Sentosa Bus Service C or M. Services A & C run from around 7 am to 11.30 pm, service M from 4 to 11 pm and on weekends and holidays from 8 am to 11 pm. The cost for any of these buses is S\$6 (children S\$4), including admission to Sentosa.

From Orchard and Bras Basah Rds, Service E runs all the way to Sentosa every 10 or 15 minutes from 10 am to 11.15 pm. The last bus returns from Sentosa at 8.30 pm. The bus costs S\$7 (or S\$5 for children), including admission.

The other alternatives are to take the ferry from the WTC or the cable car.

The ferry used to be the main access to the island before the bridge was built. It is still a most pleasant way to reach Sentosa and costs 80c one way, S\$1.30 return. Ferries operate from 9.30 am to 9 pm.

The cable car leaves from the top of Mt Faber from 8.30 am to 9 pm, or you can board it at the WTC. The one-way fare is S\$5.90 (children S\$3.90), and you can buy tickets for separate stages. The cable-car ride, with its spectacular views, is one of the best parts of a visit to Sentosa. Take the ferry across and then the cable car back to Mt Faber – it is easier walking down Mt Faber than up.

OTHER ISLANDS (Map 2)

Singapore's other islands include Kusu and St John's, Pulau Sakeng and the Sisters' Islands (all south of Singapore), and islands such as Pulau Bukum, which are used as refineries and for other commercial purposes. Further south of Singapore's southern islands are many more islands including the scattered Indonesian islands of the Riau Archipelago (see the Excursions chapter). There are also islands to the north-east between Singapore and Malaysia.

St John's & Kusu Islands

Although Sentosa is Singapore's best known island, there are two others that are also popular with locals as city escapes: St John's (Pulau Sakijang Bendera) and Kusu (Pulau Tembakul). On weekends they can both become rather crowded but during the week you'll find them fairly quiet and good places for a peaceful swim. Both islands have changing rooms, toilet facilities, grassy picnic spots and swimming areas.

St John's Island is much the bigger of the two and has a few safe swimming lagoons, though the water can sometimes be a bit on the dodgy side — hardly surprising given all the passing shipping. There is not much to do here other than walk along its rather uninspiring concrete pathways and relax in its shady picnic areas. You're better off bringing your own picnic, as the culinary offerings are limited to a small cafeteria with limited fare (you can't even get a cold beer!).

Kusu is more interesting but it can be fully explored in no more than an hour. The island has a Chinese temple, the Tua Pek Kong temple, near the ferry jetty, and a Malay shrine, Keramat Kusu, up a steep flight of steps to the top of a hill at the end of the island. Though keramat worship is frowned upon by the Islamic clergy (it's too animistic for their liking), this is Singapore's most popular shrine, especially for childless couples; their prayers for children are marked by the pieces of cloth tied around trees on the way up to the shrine. Kusu is the site of an important annual pilgrimage, honoured by Taoists.

The only real way to see both islands conveniently is on Sunday when you can

hop off the ferry at Kusu, then get on again when it next passes through to St John's. From St John's you can take a ferry back at your leisure. That will give you about an hour and a half on each island, which is more than enough if you just want a taste of the places. On other days you are limited to a half-hour visit to Kusu and over two hours on St John's, as long as you take the 10 am ferry. You are not allowed to stay overnight on either island without permission.

Most of the harbour tours pass St John's Island and stop at Kusu for 20 minutes or so (see Organised Tours in the Getting Around chapter).

The ferries depart from the WTC and the round trip costs S$6.20 (children S$3.10).

Other Southern Islands

Many of the islands on Singapore's southern shore accommodate the refineries that provide much of Singapore's export income. Others, such as **Salu**, **Senang**, **Rawai** and **Sudong**, are live firing ranges. **Pulau Sakeng** has a village and many inhabitants work at nearby **Pulau Bukum**, where the Shell refinery is located.

There are a few off-the-beaten-track islands where you can find a quiet beach. The **Sisters' Islands** are good for swimming and are a popular diving spot with coral reefs nearby. **Pulau Hantu** is also popular.

To reach these islands, you must rent a motorised bumboat from Clifford Pier or Jardine Steps at the WTC. Expect to pay around S$50 per hour. The boats will take from six to 12 people. You can approach individual boat owners or contact the Singapore Motor Launch Owners' Association on the 2nd floor at Clifford Pier, just east of Raffles Place MRT station.

Northern Islands

The easiest northern island to visit is Pulau Ubin, which makes a pleasant day trip and is reached by boat from Changi Village. Pulau Tekong, Singapore's largest island, tends to be forgotten because it is often cut off the eastern edge of Singapore maps (including

Ferry Schedule to Kusu & St John's Islands

Monday to Saturday

| | Depart from | | |
WTC	Kusu	St John's	Kusu
10.00 am	10.45 am	11.15 am	11.45 am
1.30 pm	2.15 pm	2.45 pm	3.15 pm
(last ferry)		(last ferry)	

Sunday & public holidays

| | Depart from | |
WTC	Kusu	St John's
9.45 am	10.20 am	10.35 am
11.15 am	11.50 am	12.05 pm
12.45 pm	1.20 pm	1.35 pm
2.15 pm	2.50 pm	3.05 pm
3.45 pm	4.20 pm	4.35 pm
5.15 pm	5.50 pm	6.05 pm
(last ferry)	(last ferry)	(last ferry)

Kelongs

To the north-east of Singapore in the Straits of Johor, particularly around Punggol and Changi, are the *kelongs*, long arrow-shaped fences erected to trap fish. The kelongs consist of *lawa*, or fishing stakes, which intercept the fish as they come inshore at night on the tidal currents and direct them down a shaft into a netted chamber, the *bunoh mati*, or death chamber. The lawa are made from a palm that gives off a fluorescent glow, which helps direct the fish down into the nets. Powerful lights are used earlier in the evening to attract small fish and plankton into the chamber, which then attract larger fish. Once the large fish are in the bunoh mati, the kelong operators drag them out with nets.

Kelongs are a Malay invention, but the majority of kelong operators are Teochew Chinese, who built larger kelongs with living quarters to make them commercially viable. These fascinating fishing traps are another disappearing sight, since the government doesn't want these untidy things in the water and favours fish farms. Permits for kelongs are not being renewed once they expire, and the remaining kelongs number less than 30.

the one in this book). It is now off-limits since the military took it over in the early 1990s.

Pulau Ubin From Changi Village, you can wander down to the ferry jetty and wait for a bumboat to take you across to Pulau Ubin. You can tell that this is a different side of Singapore by the fact that there's no timetable; you wait for the ferry to fill up and it goes when a quota of 12 people is reached. Pulau Ubin has quiet beaches, a kampong atmosphere and popular seafood restaurants. This rural island is as unlike modern Singapore as you will find. It is also a natural haven for many species of birds which inhabit the mangroves and forest areas.

The best way to explore the island is by bicycle, which can be hired for S$8 to S$15 per day near the jetty. If you ask the bicycle hire operator you may get a hand-drawn map, though the island is small enough to explore without getting lost and there are map boards dotted at strategic locations. Not all the island is open to the public so watch where you go.

You can visit a spectacular disused quarry with granite walls, and a number of temples, including a Thai Buddhist temple and one reached via the beach only at low tide. It is

a peaceful rural scene of fish farms, coconut palms and a few houses. The island's most popular seafood restaurant is the Ubin First Stop Restaurant. Its chilli crabs are exquisite, though a bit on the expensive side at S$22 a pop.

The old bumboat ferries to Pulau Ubin cost S$1.50. They run from 6 am until 10 pm, but you may be in for a wait if there are no other passengers – which is often the case during the week.

NORTHERN & CENTRAL SINGAPORE
Singapore has been dubbed the 'Garden City' and with good reason – it's green and lush, and parks and gardens are scattered everywhere. In part, this fertility is a factor of the climate; you only have to stick a twig in the ground for it to become a tree in weeks! The government has backed up this natural advantage with a concentrated programme that has even turned the dividing strip on highways into flourishing gardens – you notice it as you drive into Singapore from the Causeway.

Despite the never-ending construction, land reclamation and burgeoning HDB estates, Singapore has large areas of parkland and even natural forest. These areas are mostly found to the north of the city in the centre of the island.

Botanic Gardens (Map 3)

Singapore's 127-year-old Botanic Gardens are on the corner of Cluny and Holland Rds, not far from Orchard Rd. They contain an enormous number of plant species, in both a manicured garden setting and in four hectares of primary jungle. The gardens also house the herbarium, where a lot of the work has been done on breeding the orchids for which Singapore is famous. It contains over 12,000 orchids representing some 2000 species and hybrids in all. In an earlier era, Henry Ridley, director of the gardens, successfully propagated rubber tree seeds sent from London's Kew Gardens, after they were smuggled out of Brazil. The Singapore Botanic Gardens pioneered the Malayan rubber boom.

The 54 hectare gardens are open from 5 am to midnight; admission is free. Early in the morning, you'll see hundreds of Singaporeans jogging here.

HDBs

High-rise housing does not have the best of reputations. It's widely viewed as a 1960s social experiment gone wrong and the modern-day associations are of inner-city poverty and migrant ghettos. In Europe and America the high-rises are being torn down. Not so in Singapore.

The state-run Housing Development Board (HDB) is locked into a mammoth construction project, erecting phalanxes of well-built, well-maintained and affordable housing. Modern HDB satellite cities like Toa Payoh, Pasir Ris, Tampines and Bukit Panjang provide homes for nearly 90% of the island's population.

Even so, the rate of construction is having difficulty keeping up with Singapore's booming population. Getting a high-rise apartment has become more difficult in recent years, especially for young families; waits of two years or more are not uncommon. Once acquired, Singaporeans lavish great care and attention upon the flats, ensuring that they remain desirable residences, light years from the urine-smelling, graffitioed blocks of many western cities.

The MRT makes it simple to visit HDB areas. Just jump on a train and pop up somewhere like Toa Payoh, or Tampines (Map 2), where you'll find the big new Century Park shopping mall. True, you won't see any stunning architecture or breathtaking landscapes, and you are equally unlikely to be held spellbound by exoticism, but you will get a good, honest glimpse of what life is like for the overwhelming majority of Singaporeans.

HDB estates are often good places to shop; goods are not subject to the inflated prices of the city centre and buying is straightforward, free of the haggling that goes on in the

popular tourist areas. There are also plenty of decent, unpretentious places to eat – it's in the HDB areas that you may well find Singapore's best *kway teow* or the cheapest chicken rice.

During the early 1980s it was reckoned that HDB blocks were going up at the rate of one apartment every 15 minutes. And still they're building.

PATRICK HORTON

Within the Botanic Gardens is also the **National Orchid Garden** with the world's largest display of orchids featuring over 60,000 plants. It costs S$2 to get in and it's open from 8.30 am to 6 pm.

The gardens can be reached on bus Nos 7 and 174, which run along Stamford Rd and Orchard Blvd. Bus No 106 runs along Bencoolen St and Orchard Blvd to the gardens.

Sunday Morning Bird Singing

One of the nicest things to do on a Sunday morning in Singapore is to go and hear the birds sing. The Chinese love caged birds, as their beautifully ornate bird cages indicate. The birds – thrushes, merboks, sharmas and mata putehs – are treasured for their singing ability. To ensure the quality of their song, the doting owner will feed the bird a carefully

RICHARD I'ANSON
Bird fanciers gathered to talk shop and listen to bird song.

prepared diet and once a week crowds of bird fanciers get together for a bird song session.

The bird cages are hung up on wires strung between trees or under verandas. They're not mixed indiscriminately – sharmas sing with sharmas, merboks with merboks – and each type of bird has its own cage design. Tall and pointy ones for tall pointy birds, short and squat ones for short squat birds.

Having assembled the birds, the proud owners then congregate around tables, sip coffee and listen to their birds go do their thing. It's a delightful scene both musically and visually.

The main bird concert venue (Map 6) is at the junction of Tiong Bahru and Seng Poh Rds on Sunday from around 8 to 11 am; it's only a few hundred metres from the Havelock Rd hotel enclave. The coffee shop here is always well patronised during these mornings.

To get there take the MRT to Tiong Bahru station, then walk 500m east. By bus, take No 123 from Orchard Rd.

Zoological Gardens (Map 2)

At 80 Mandai Lake Rd in the north of the island, Singapore's world-class zoo has over 2000 animals, representing 240 species, on display in almost natural conditions. Wherever possible, moats replace bars and the zoo is spread out over 90 hectares of lush greenery. Exhibits of particular interest are the pygmy hippos, Primate Kingdom, Wild Africa and Children's World. As well as providing a play area, Children's World includes a domesticated animals section where children can touch the animals, see Friesian cow milking demonstrations and sheep dogs in action at the sheep roundup show.

There is a breakfast programme at 9 am and high tea at 4 pm, where you are joined by one of the orang-utans. However, you will be hit for an extra S$13.00 (S$10.30 for children) for the privilege. There are also elephant rides and work performances. At most times of the day, you have a good chance of seeing one of the animal performances or a practice session in the zoo's outdoor theatre. Primates & Reptiles shows

Gin sling-sipping Singapore, as immortalised by the writer Somerset Maugham, is still very much in evidence today in places like the Singapore Cricket Club on the Padang (top), the palm-shaded terraces of Emerald Hill (right) and in fine colonial buildings like that currently housing the National Museum (bottom left). And now Sunday morning bird singing (middle left) is popular in Singapore.

PAUL HELLANDER

RICHARD I'ANSON

RICHARD I'ANSON

RICHARD I'ANSON

RICHARD I'ANSON

ARASU RAMASAMY

The most interesting parts of the city in which to wander are the old ethnic areas like the Malay Muslim surrounds of Arab St (top left; middle left and right) and the shanty streets of Chinatown (top right; bottom left and right).

are held at 10.30 am and 2.30 pm, Elephants & Sealions at 11.30 am and 3.30 pm.

The Komodo dragons are another popular attraction and you can see their feeding frenzy on Sunday afternoon, though in fact they are not all that ferocious.

The zoo is open from 8.30 am to 6 pm daily; admission is S$10.30 (children S$4.60). There is a zoo tram which runs from the main gate and costs S$2.50 for adults and S$1.50 for children.

To get to the zoo, take the MRT to Ang Mo Kio station, and then catch bus No 138.

Night Safari Singapore also has an impressive Night Safari, on a 40 hectare site next to the zoo in secondary forest. Open from 7.30 pm to midnight daily, walking trails criss-cross the park and allow a unique opportunity to view nocturnal animals. The park is divided into a number of habitats, focusing mostly on Asian wildlife, and special lighting picks out the animals. With 1000 animals representing 100 species, the Night Safari is not as diverse as the zoo, but wandering the trails at night is a recommended experience.

There is also a tram, including commentary, which loops through the park and stops near the East Lodge restaurant at the far side of the park. Noisy, camera-flashing passengers can spoil the ride, despite being exhorted to keep quiet and avoid flash photography. The western side of the park is only accessible by tram. To explore all the park, it is best to do a complete loop and then walk the trails. The complete East Loop walking trail is 2.8km in length and takes about an hour to complete.

The Night Safari costs S$15.45 for adults or S$10.30 for children under 12 years. The tram ride costs an extra S$4 (children S$3). The entrance is directly opposite the zoo entrance.

Getting to the Night Safari is the same as for the zoo. In addition, the Bus Plus Zoo service (S$5, children S$3) picks up on Orchard, Bras Basah and Scotts Rds from 6.30 to 8.30 pm. The return buses run until 11 pm.

Mandai Orchid Gardens (Map 2)
Singapore has a major business in cultivating orchids and the Mandai Orchid Gardens, beside the zoo on Mandai Lake Rd, is the best place to see them – four solid hectares of orchids. The gardens are open from 8.30 am to 5.30 pm daily; admission is S$2 for adults, 50c for children.

Bukit Timah Nature Reserve (Map 2)
Singapore is not normally associated with nature walks and jungle treks, but they can be enjoyed at this 81 hectare nature reserve. It is the only large area of primary forest left in Singapore, and is a haven for Singapore's wildlife. The reserve also boasts the highest point in Singapore, 162m Bukit Timah.

The reserve is run by the National Parks Board and at the entrance to the reserve is a visitors centre with an exhibition hall containing interesting displays on Singapore's natural history.

The most popular walk in the park is the summit walk along a paved road to the top of Bukit Timah. Even during the week it attracts a number of walkers, though few venture off the pavement to explore the side trails. The road cuts a swathe through dense forest and near the top there are views across Peirce Reservoir, though they are partly blocked by the dense vegetation.

The best trails to explore the forest and see the wildlife run off the summit road. Try the North View, South View or Fern Valley paths, where it is hard to believe that you are in Singapore. These paths involve some scrambling over rocks and tree roots in parts, but are easily negotiated. A good suggestion would be to take the North View path and loop back via the Seraya Loop and Jungle Fall paths. It is a moderate walk, though strenuous in parts and can easily be done in about an hour. An alternate return route to the visitors centre is via the Tuip Tuip and Rock paths.

The park has over 800 species of native plants, including giant trees, ferns and native flowers. Wildlife is difficult to see, though long-tailed macaques and squirrels are in abundance. Flying lemurs, reticulated pythons and birds, such as the racquet-tailed drongo and white-bellied sea eagle, inhabit the reserve. Try to pick up either one of the two editions of *A Guide to the Bukit Timah Nature Reserve* explaining the reserve's flora and fauna (available at Mobil and BP petrol stations and some book-shops).

The exhibition hall is open from 8.30 am to 6 pm, and entry is free. It is a good idea to bring a water bottle if you intend going on some extended walks. A towel and even a change of clothes are also worth bringing as the walks are testing in parts and the con-ditions are hot and very humid (there are changing rooms and showers near the park entrance).

To get to Bukit Timah take bus No 171 or 182 – both run along Orchard and Stamford Rds in the colonial district and pass Newton MRT station. Get off just past the 12km mark at the large, yellow Courts Mammoth Super Store on Upper Bukit Timah Rd. The en-trance to the park is on the other side, about 1km along Hindhede Drive.

Sungei Buloh Nature Park (Map 2)

This 87 hectare wetland nature reserve is home to 140 species of birds, most of which are migratory. From the visitors centre with its well-presented displays, trails lead around ponds and mangrove swamps to hides for observing the birds. The bird life, rather than the walks, is the main reason to visit and the area is mostly former orchard and fish ponds.

Sungei Buloh is open from 7.30 am to 7 pm weekdays and from 7 am to 7 pm on weekends and holidays. Admission is S$1 for adults (children 50c). Audiovisual shows on the park's flora and fauna are held at 9 and 11 am, 1 and 3 pm. Guided walks are held at 9.30 am and 4 pm, weather per-mitting. Allow yourself three hours to do the park justice.

The park is in the north-west of the island, overlooking the Straits of Johor. Take the MRT to Choa Chu Kang station, then bus No SS7 to the Woodlands Interchange, then bus No 925.

Other Parks

Despite Singapore's dense population, the island possesses many small parks and gardens.

MacRitchie Reservoir (Map 2) has a 12 hectare park area with a jogging track, ex-ercise area, playground and tea kiosk. It is a pleasant retreat from the city, and popular with joggers. A band often plays on Sunday (check the newspapers). To the north of MacRitchie Reservoir is **Upper Seletar Reservoir** (Map 2), where paddle boating is possible, and further east is **Lower Seletar Reservoir** (Map 2), where you can go fishing.

For MacRitchie Reservoir take bus No 167 from Stamford Rd, No 132 from Orchard Rd or No 156 from Bishan MRT station. For Upper Seletar take bus No 138 from Ang Mo Kio MRT station. For Lower Seletar, take the MRT to Yishun, then any of bus No 851, 852, 853, 854 or 855.

Off Kampong Bahru Rd, the 116m-high Mt Faber forms the centrepoint of the pleas-ant **Mt Faber Park** (Map 2). The hillside slopes offer fine views over the harbour and the city. To get there, take the cable car up from the WTC. Mt Faber can conveniently be visited in conjunction with a trip to Sentosa.

Pasir Ris Park (Map 2) on the north-eastern coast is for the most part a manicured park with a narrow stretch of beach. The park also has a wooden walk-way that goes through a mangrove swamp area which is good for bird watching. The park is often empty during the week, but comes alive on weekends and holidays. To get there take the MRT to Pasir Ris and then bus No 350 to the resort, only a short walk from the beach.

Bukit Batok (Map 2), also known as Little Guilin, is a former quarry, now a hilly outcrop and lake around which a park has been created. It's often compared to the spectacular limestone formations and lakes of Guilin in southern China, hence the name – truth be told, it's a pale imitation. The park is near Bukit Gombok MRT station, 14km north-west of the city.

Holland Village (Map 7)

If you're wondering what the life of an expatriate is like, head for Holland Village. It's on Holland Rd, a westerly continuation of Orchard Rd, and services the garden-belt suburbs of the well-to-do.

Holland Village is, in fact, just a suburban shopping centre where foreigners can shop, sip coffee and feel at home, but it has a definite village community atmosphere. It is best known for its host of fashionable restaurants and watering holes, concentrated on Lorong Mambong, just back from the main road. The Holland Shopping Centre is a modern complex and a good place to shop for antiques, furnishings and crafts, such as porcelain ware, batik and wood carvings.

The nearest MRT station is Buona Vista, about a 15 minute walk along Buona Vista Rd from Holland Village. Or take bus No 7, 105 or 106 from Penang Rd/Orchard Blvd.

Temples

The central city areas of Singapore provide plenty of opportunities to experience colourful religious architecture, but a couple of temples of note are found in the outer areas.

Siong Lim Temple (Map 2) This is one of the largest temples in Singapore and includes a Chinese rock garden. It was built in 1908 but includes more recent additions. It features Thai Buddha statues and 2000kg incense burners. Next to the main temple is a monastery, and next to that is another temple featuring a gigantic Buddha statue. It's at 184E Jalan Toa Payoh, north of the city centre, about 1km east of Toa Payoh MRT station.

Kong Meng San Phor Kark See Temple (Map 2) This is the largest temple in Singapore and covers 12 hectares. A modern temple, it is impressive in its size and design, though its main function is as a crematorium: funerals, complete with paper effigies, are frequent. There's an attached old people's home, reminiscent of the old 'death houses' that used to exist in Chinatown; old folk were once packed off to death houses

towards the end of their lives to avoid the possible bad luck of a death in the home.

The temple is on Bright Hill Drive, about 1.5km west of Bishan MRT station.

Kranji War Memorial (Map 2)

Near the Causeway off Woodlands Rd, the Kranji War Memorial includes the graves of thousands of Allied troops who died in the region during WWII. The walls are inscribed with the names of those who died and a register is available for inspection. It can be reached by bus No 182 from Somerset Rd.

Sun Yatsen Villa (Map 2)

This old villa (built in the 1880s) was the one-time residence of the Chinese revolutionary Republican leader Sun Yatsen (who following the overthrow of the Qing dynasty became president of post-Imperial China in 1912). The house is a fine example of a colonial Victorian villa. Inside are personal items and photographs of Sun Yatsen, while upstairs is a Chinese library.

The villa is on Ah Hood Rd, about 500m south of Toa Payoh MRT station. Bus No 145 from Balestier Rd passes this way.

ACTIVITIES

Singapore's private clubs and country clubs have excellent sporting facilities but there are also fine public facilities, such as those at Farrer Park near Little India, and a host of commercial ventures.

Archery

Contact the Archery Club of Singapore (☎ 258 1140) at 5 Bintang Walk.

Badminton

Badminton is popular in South-East Asia and the region has produced more than a few world champions in the sport. Courts at the Singapore Badminton Hall (☎ 344 1773), 102 Guillemard Rd, are open from 8 am to 11 pm; bookings are essential.

Bowling

Tenpin bowling is very popular in Singapore. The cost per game is around S$3 to

S$3.80; shoe hire is around 50c. Check the Buying Guide Yellow Pages for a full list. Some alleys include:

Singapore Tenpin Bowling Congress
(☎ 355 0136) 01-01 Balestier Plaza, 400 Balestier Rd
Superbowl
(☎ 221 1010) 15 Marina Grove, Marina South

Cricket
The Singapore Cricket Club (☎ 338 9271), Connaught Drive, holds matches every weekend on the Padang from March to October. The club is for members only but spectators are welcome.

Cycling
Recreational cycling ranges from a leisurely peddle along the foreshore of the east coast to mountain biking at Ulu Pandan.

The easiest riding possibilities are along the east coast and at Sentosa and Pulau Ubin. Bikes can also be hired at these places.

Bukit Timah has two mountain bike trails, 7km in all, running around the edge of the nature reserve between Chestnut Ave and Rifle Range Rd. The trails cut though jungle and abandoned quarry sites and, though hilly in parts, are well surfaced.

The Ulu Pandan Boy's Brigade Mountain Bike Track is a challenging, unpaved 4km trail for jungle and mud adventure. It is opposite the Singapore Polytechnic on Dover Rd.

Two Wheel Action (☎ 463 2143) organises Sunday rides in collaboration with the Singapore chapter of the Hash House Harriers. You bring your own bike and meet at a pre-ordained point for a casual ride to some location on the island. Cost is S$10 per session, or S$100 annual membership. Weekend rides to the Riau Archipelago in Indonesia are also arranged for around S$140 all-inclusive.

Golf
Singapore has plenty of golf courses, though some are members only or they don't allow visitors to play on weekends. A game of golf costs around S$90 on weekdays, and from S$100 to S$220 on weekends. Club hire is expensive. The following courses have 18 holes, except for Changi, Seletar and Warren, which are nine hole courses:

Changi Golf Club
(☎ 545 5133) Netheravon Rd
Jurong County Club
(☎ 560 5655) 9 Science Centre Rd
Keppel Club
(☎ 273 5522) Bukit Chermin
Marina Bay Golf & Country Club
(☎ 221 2811) 6 Marina Green
Raffles Country Club
(☎ 861 7655) 450 Jalan Ahmad Ibrahim
Seletar Country Club
(☎ 481 4745) Seletar Airbase
Sembawang Country Club
(☎ 257 0642) Sembawang Rd
Sentosa Golf Course
(☎ 275 0022) Sentosa Island
Singapore Island Country Club
(☎ 459 2222) Upper Thomson Rd
Warren Golf Course
(☎ 777 6533) Folkestone Rd

Singapore has driving ranges at the Parkland Golf Driving Range (☎ 440 6726), 920 East Coast Parkway, and Green Fairways (☎ 468 8409), Bukit Turf Club, Fairways Drive. The cost here starts from S$3 for 48 balls.

Squash
Most of the island's country clubs have squash courts. Fees are between S$7 and S$9 per hour. Some of the public courts include:

East Coast Recreation Centre
(☎ 449 0541) East Coast Parkway
Kallang Squash & Tennis Centre
(☎ 440 6839) Stadium Rd
West Coast Recreation Centre
(Squash ☎ 778 8966) 12 West Coast Walk

Swimming
Singapore has a number of beaches for swimming – try East Coast Park, Changi Village, Sentosa or the other islands. Singapore also has plenty of public swimming

pools; admission is S$1 or S$1.20 on weekends. The addresses of some of the public swimming pools are:

Bishan Swimming Complex
(☎ 353 6617) 14 Bishan St
Farrer Park Swimming Complex
(☎ 299 1002) Dorset Rd
River Valley Swimming Complex
(☎ 337 6275) River Valley Rd

Tennis
Tennis courts cost from S$3 to S$6 per hour to hire. Rates, like squash, are from S$7 to S$9 per hour. Courts available include:

Farrer Park Tennis Courts
(☎ 299 4166) Rutland Rd

Singapore Tennis Centre
(☎ 442 5966) 1020 East Coast Parkway

Water Sports
The East Coast Sailing Centre (☎ 449 5118), 1212 East Coast Parkway, is the place to go for windsurfing and sailing. Sailboards cost S$20 for two hours hire; lessons are available. The centre also rents laser-class boats for S$20 per hour. Sailboards and aquabikes are also available for hire on Sentosa.

For water-skiing, William Water Sports (☎ 282 6879) at Punggol Point in the north of the island rents boats, a driver and gear for S$65 per hour. Cowabunga Ski Centre (☎ 344 8813), 10 Stadium Lane, Kallang, is the home of the Singapore Water Ski Federation and offers lessons and equipment.

Places to Stay

Singapore has a wide variety of accommodation in all price categories. You can get a dormitory bed in a guesthouse for S$8, a room in a cheap Chinese hotel for around S$35, pay from S$120 up to S$300 for a room in an 'international-standard' hotel, or shell out S$6000 for the best suite at Raffles. Hotel standards are usually high but so are prices; Singapore is the most expensive city in South-East Asia in which to stay, with rates that put it up there with other expensive cities around the world.

Hotels can be categorised into three groups: 'top end', for which the main centre is along Orchard Rd; 'mid-range', a term which encompasses the better cheap Chinese hotels and a lot of smaller, relatively new air-con hotels scattered throughout the city; and 'budget', which are those places that cost under S$50. These cheaper places are found mainly in the colonial district, particularly along Beach Rd and Bencoolen St.

Hotel rates have fluctuated dramatically over the past few years. Prices depend very much on what the market will bear, and when visitor numbers and hotel occupancy rates are high, you'll pay dearly at the top end of the scale. At other times, the big hotels offer large discounts. The same is true to an extent for mid-range and the cheaper top-end hotels, but price variations are less dramatic. On the other hand, room rates for budget accommodation are very stable.

In the major hotels, a 3% GST, 1% government tax and 10% service charge are added to your bill. This is the dreaded 'plus-plus-plus' which follows the quoted price (eg S$140+++), while 'nett' means that the price includes tax and service charge. The hotels stipulate that you should not tip when a service charge applies. The 4% taxes (GST and government taxes) also apply to the cheaper hotels but are usually included in the quoted price.

PLACES TO STAY – BUDGET

Budget accommodation is accounted for by guesthouses and an ever-shrinking number of cheap Chinese hotels.

Guesthouses are typically just residential flats or office space partitioned up into dormitories and cubicle-like rooms. Overcrowding tends to stretch the limited facilities, and the rooms really are small – just spartan boxes with a fan. In addition, everybody else staying there will be a traveller, just like yourself. On the other hand, they're good sources of information, good places to meet people and you won't find any cheaper accommodation.

New guesthouses are constantly opening up, and the services they provide are improving. Dormitory beds cost from S$8 and rooms from S$20, though most rooms go from around S$25 to S$30, ranging up to S$50 for hotel-standard rooms with air-con, attached bath and TV. Free tea and coffee are standard offerings, and a basic breakfast is usually thrown in. Singapore does not have an official youth hostel.

Guesthouses do move around, usually in search of cheaper rents or under eviction notices initiated by other tenants in the building. The guesthouses listed in this chapter are the more conveniently located and well-established ones. Others tend to come and go, so keep your eyes open, or just wander around Bencoolen St or Beach Rd with a backpack and you're sure to get plenty of offers. Touts at the bus and railway stations may also offer accommodation. Some places don't advertise and are merely residential flats that rent out rooms on an ad-hoc basis. They can offer some of the best accommodation and are good options for long-term visitors.

The other budget option is the cheap Chinese hotels. Most of these places have seen better days but they do have more character than the guesthouses. Rooms range from around S$30 to S$65. This will get you a fairly spartan room with a bare floor, a few pieces of furniture, a sink and a fan. Toilets are usually shared but you often get hot water in the showers. Couples should always ask for a single room – this usually means just one double bed, whereas a double has two. Singapore also has three YMCAs, though these are more mid-range options, and two inconveniently located camping grounds.

The main budget area is in the colonial district bounded by Bras Basah, Rochor, Beach and Selegie Rds. Bencoolen St has traditionally been the backpackers' centre in Singapore, and while it still has a number of guesthouses, most of the old buildings and Chinese hotels have fallen to the wrecker's ball. Many backpackers' places have relocated to the Beach Rd area. Other cheap possibilities can be found in Chinatown, and further north in Little India and nearby Jalan Besar. There are also a number of cheap hotels out in the *lorongs* (alleys) of Geylang, east of the city, but most travellers find them far too inconvenient.

Bencoolen St Area (Map 5)
Bencoolen St has very little character left but it's within walking distance of the city centre, Orchard Rd and Little India.

To get there from Changi airport take public bus No 16 or 16E, which will both drop you on Stamford Rd. Get off near the National Museum, cross Stamford Rd and walk north through the small park to Bras Basah Rd and Bencoolen St. From the railway station, bus No 97 stops on Stamford Rd. From the Lavender St bus station, almost all buses that run along Jalan Besar also go down Bencoolen St. The nearest MRT station is Dhoby Ghaut, about 10 minutes walk away.

Guesthouses Singapore's original backpackers' centre is at 46-52 Bencoolen St. There's no sign at all; go around the back and take the lift. Almost the entire building is devoted to guesthouses, some of which have been running for almost 20 years. The place is completely traveller-worn – filthy stairwells, graffiti-adorned lift etc – though some of the places offer reasonable rooms.

At the top, at least in elevation, *Lee Boarding House* (☎ 338 3149; fax 333 1997) has its reception at No 52 on the 7th floor but it has rooms on other floors. It's a large place with beds in basic dorms for S$9 or beds in less crowded air-con dorms for S$10. Rooms range from standard singles/doubles with fan for S$22/28 and air-con rooms from S$30/45, right up to some good hotel-style rooms with air-con and bathroom for S$45 to S$60. *Peony Mansions* (☎ 338 5638; fax 339 1471), one of the original guesthouses, is on the 4th floor. Dormitory beds cost S$8 (or S$9 with air-con), a single room with fan costs S$18 and a double with fan S$22. Double rooms with air-con cost from S$30 to S$45. The dorms aren't great but the rooms are reasonable and many have been upgraded. There are other guesthouses in the block, like *Latin House* (☎ 339 6308) on the 3rd floor at No 46, which is an anonymous place with run-down rooms.

On the other side of Bencoolen St, between the Strand and Bencoolen hotels, is *Bencoolen House* (☎ 338 1206) at No 27. The reception area is on the 7th floor. Dorm beds cost S$7, a few singles cost S$20 but most rooms cost from S$25 up to S$45 for air-con. It's a bit run down but OK.

In the thick of things, the *Peony Mansion Travellers' Lodge* (☎ 334 8697; fax 334 7014), 131A Bencoolen St, is a popular place with an excellent 24 hour Indian restaurant downstairs. It has a variety of reasonable rooms from S$25 for a fan room with two bunk beds to S$50 for rooms with air-con and shower.

Green Curtains (☎ 334 8697), also at No 131A, is an offshoot of Peony Mansions with well-maintained rooms. The S$25 fan rooms are fairly small and dark but better rooms range up to S$45.

Another centre for guesthouses is at 171 Bencoolen St. *Goh's Homestay* (☎ 339 6561; fax 339 8606), up a long flight of stairs to the 3rd floor at 169-D, has an eating/meeting area where you can get breakfast, snacks and

PLACES TO STAY

drinks. The rooms are clean but small, without windows and fairly pricey at S$36/46 for singles/doubles; dorm beds cost S$14. There is Internet access at S$6 per hour. The *Hawaii Hostel* (☎ 338 4187) on the 2nd floor at 171-B is an impersonal place with 10-bed dorms for S$10, pokey singles for S$25 and better air-con doubles for S$35. Basic breakfast is included.

Hotels Redevelopment in the area has seen the demise of most of the old hotels. The *San Wah* (☎ 336 2428; fax 334 4146), 36 Bencoolen St, is a little better than the cheapest Chinese hotels and many of the rooms have air-con. It has a pleasant courtyard area set back from the street. Fan/air-con doubles cost S$50/55.

At 260-262 Middle Rd, near the corner of Selegie Rd, is the good, spotlessly clean *Sun Sun Hotel* (☎ 338 4911). It's a cut above the other traditional Chinese hotels and some rooms have their own balconies. There's a handy confectionery shop downstairs. Singles/doubles cost S$40/45, air-con doubles cost S$50. There is a discount for stays over three days.

Beach Rd (Map 5)

Beach Rd, a few blocks from Bencoolen St toward the (ever-receding) waterfront, is another centre for cheap hotels. If you aspire to the Raffles but can't afford it, at least you can stay nearby. From Changi airport, bus No 16 or 16E can drop you near the towering Raffles City shopping centre, opposite the Padang, from where it's a short walk to Beach Rd. From the railway station and the World Trade Centre (WTC) take bus No 100. Bus Nos 82 and 107 run down Beach Rd from the Lavender St bus station and pass the Golden Mile Complex bus station on Beach Rd, only a 10 minute walk from the cheap hotels. The Beach Rd area is about halfway between City Hall and Bugis MRT stations.

Guesthouses *Lee Travellers' Club* (☎ 339 5490), on the 6th floor of the Fu Yuen building at 75 Beach Rd, with more rooms on the other floors, is a large, popular place which is less cramped than some of the competition. It costs S$8 for a place in an eight bed, air-con dorm; singles start at S$15, though most rooms are air-con doubles for S$35 and S$40. It's one of the better guesthouses and has a small kitchen for guests' use.

Willy's (☎ 332 1585), 494 North Bridge Rd, is a reasonable if cramped place, with dorm beds for S$8 (S$12 with air-con) or better air-con doubles for S$30 and S$38. *Waffles Homestay* (☎ 334 1608), 490 North Bridge Rd, is on the top floor of an Indian restaurant and two doors down from Willy's. It's a friendly place with dorm beds for S$8 and S$12, and a few basic double rooms for S$26.

In between Willy's and Waffles is the *Sunderbone Homestay* (☎ 333 9335) where most rooms are taken by long-term guests. Prices are the same and facilities are similar to the two above places since they're all run by the same management. Enter all three via the front restaurants or via the back lane after hours.

Liang Seah St, which runs into Beach Rd, has a couple of guesthouses that are holding on in the face of the surrounding redevelopment. The popular *New Backpackers' Lodge* (☎ 338 7460) at No 18A is in an old terrace with Chinese hotel-style rooms, but chopped in half and without any furniture. It has lost a bit of its shine and can be crowded. A dorm bed with air-con costs S$8 and most rooms go for S$25. Breakfast is included. The *Cozy Corner Lodge* (☎ 333 4656), at No 2A nearer to Beach Rd, is a good place that tries harder and offers a slightly better standard of rooms. Dorm beds cost S$9, double rooms cost S$25 with fan. Don't be surprised though, if by the time you read this they too have moved – possibly to Peony Mansions.

Hotels The hotels here are all of a similar basic standard: traditional Chinese hotels with wire-topped walls, shuttered windows, a few pieces of furniture and a basin with running water. They're a bit down-at-heel but good for the price.

The *Shang Onn* (☎ 338 4153), 37 Beach Rd at the corner of Purvis St, is a little more expensive than the other places. Singles/doubles cost S$30/34. The rooms are very clean and have character but not much else.

At the corner of Liang Seah St and North Bridge Rd is the *Ah Chew Hotel* (☎ 336 3563), a very traditional old Chinese hotel. The S$30 non-air-con rooms are basic, but at least the eyeball-sized holes in some of the rooms have been taped over. The old guys who run the place are very friendly, and the shared bathrooms are spotless.

Chinatown (Map 6)
Chinatown is an interesting area to stay and it has a few cheap hotels, most of which are within walking distance of the railway station, and Outram Park and Tanjong Pagar MRT stations.

Guesthouses The friendly *Chinatown Guest House* (☎ 220 0671), 5th floor, 325D New Bridge Rd, opposite Pearl's Centre, has dorm beds for S$12 and reasonable rooms ranging from S$30 to S$50 with air-con. It's about the cheapest option in Chinatown and handy for Outram Park MRT station.

Hotels On Peck Seah St, just off Maxwell Rd, there are a couple of carpeted, air-con hotels. At the *New Asia Hotel* (☎ 221 1861; fax 223 9002) at the corner of Maxwell Rd and Peck Seah St, most rooms are small but reasonable value at S$40/58 for singles/doubles, S$5 extra with TV. A couple of doors down at 10 Peck Seah St, the *Air View Hotel* (☎ 225 7788; fax 225 6688) is a bit better than the New Asia, and charges S$60 for doubles or S$75 with two double beds. All rooms have a shower and TV.

Little India & Jalan Besar (Map 5)
Little India and Jalan Besar have a few cheap hotels and a growing number of mid-range establishments. It is perhaps not as convenient as the other areas, but it is a lively and animated area and its proximity to the Lavender St bus station is convenient if you arrive by long-distance bus from Malaysia.

Guesthouses There is at least one remaining guesthouse in Little India on Roberts Lane: the popular *Ali's Nest* (☎ 291 2938), at No 23, is run by the friendly Ali, who lived in the Netherlands and speaks Dutch. Beds in a dorm containing four to eight beds, are S$9. A few small singles go for S$20, or better doubles cost S$30. Breakfast is included in the price and safety lockers are available for guests.

Hotels The *Little India Guest House* (☎ 294 2866) at 3 Veerasamy Rd is just off Serangoon Rd in the heart of Little India. It is more a small hotel than a guesthouse. Small, well-appointed singles/doubles with shared bathroom but no air-con cost S$38/50.

Jalan Besar has a few cheap hotels, but this is not a convenient location unless perhaps you arrive at the Lavender St bus station and just can't be bothered looking further.

Nearest to the bus station, just down Jalan Besar at No 383, the *Kam Leng* (☎ 298 2289) is a rather run-down old hotel with rooms at S$30 with fan and S$36 with air-con. At No 290A, the architecturally interesting *International Hotel* (☎ 293 9238) has singles without a bath for S$35 or large doubles for S$40 or S$50 with bath. Most rooms have balconies.

Other Areas
Camping The best place for camping is on Sentosa (Map 9) where pre-erected four-person tents cost S$12 per night plus 3% tax. Camp beds cost an extra 50c each. The site caters primarily for groups but individuals can stay by booking in advance through the Sentosa Information Centre (☎ 270 7888). The nearby youth hostel is only open to organised groups; an air-con bunk room for up to 12 people costs S$120.

There's also the good *East Coast Campsite* on East Coast Parkway (Map 2), at the 5km marker, but officially you must book three months in advance and obtain a permit from the People's Association (☎ 340 5113) on Stadium Link, opposite the National Stadium.

PLACES TO STAY

The Ys Singapore has three YMCAs, which take men, women and couples. They provide good mid-range accommodation and, though not the bargain they used to be, are still very popular. Advance bookings in writing with one night's deposit are usually essential. Book at least six weeks in advance for the YMCA International and around three weeks in advance for the others. Non-YMCA members must pay a small charge for temporary membership.

The *YMCA International House* (Map 4; ☎ 336 6000; fax 337 3140; hostel@ymcasin. org.sin) is at 1 Orchard Rd, opposite Bras Basah Park in the colonial district. It's a handy location and the place has good facilities, including a fitness centre, roof-top swimming pool, squash and badminton courts and a billiard room. There's also a restaurant, which offers a cheap daily set meal, and a McDonald's. All rooms have air-con, TV, telephone and attached bathroom, but are of a fairly average mid-range standard and becoming expensive at S$101 for a single, S$118 for a double, S$141 for a family room and S$152 for a superior room. All prices are nett and include breakfast. A bed in a dorm costs S$28. Despite the high rates, the rooms are often booked well in advance.

The *YWCA Fort Canning* (Map 4; ☎ 338 4222; fax 337 4222; ywcasin@singnet. com.sg) at 6 Fort Canning Rd, close to Dhoby Ghaut MRT, offers good accommodation though it's still pricey for a 'Y'. Dorm beds cost from S$35 to S$45, while a standard single room is a whopping S$110.

The *YMCA Metropolitan* (Map 4; ☎ 737 7755; fax 235 5528; hostel@mymca.org.sg), 60 Stevens Rd, also has decent rooms, a pool and cafe. It is a good 15 minute walk north of Orchard and Tanglin Rds, and less conveniently located than the other two 'Y's. Singles/doubles with bathroom, TV and air-con range from S$64 to S$98 for a 'pool view' room.

Guesthouses Orchard Rd (Map 4) has a number of guesthouses and private apartments that occasionally take in travellers. It

is worth keeping an eye out for these places as they can be well located and can offer a better class of guesthouse.

Hotels The *Mayfair City Hotel* (Map 6; ☎ 337 4542; fax 337 1736), 40-44 Armenian St, behind the National Museum, is on one of Singapore's oldest streets and within walking distance of many attractions. Good rooms with air-con, shower and TV cost S$60/70 for singles/doubles.

The *Mitre Hotel* (☎ 737 3811), 145 Killiney Rd, is the cheapest hotel anywhere near Orchard Rd (500m to the north). It would have to be the most dilapidated fleapit in Singapore, but that said it does have a good deal of character. It is in an old villa, with large grounds, set back off the street. The dingy bar on the ground floor is popular with the oil-rig workers who stay here. Rooms range from S$22 for a rough single with fan to S$36 for a passable double with air-con and bath.

PLACES TO STAY – MIDDLE

Singapore is experiencing a mini boom in mid-range accommodation. New hotels are springing up in Chinatown, Little India and the colonial district to cater for independent visitors who want a little luxury but not the price tag of the five-star hotels. Most of the new hotels have well-appointed rooms with bathroom, hot water, air-con, phone and TV but forego the trimmings of the big hotels and offer rooms only.

The cheaper hotels listed here are mostly second-string, older places which have comfortable rooms but could do with a face-lift. Others come close to matching the top-end hotels, but lack the restaurants, bars and the Filipino band playing in the lobby.

Colonial District (Maps 5&6)

The *New 7th Storey Hotel* (☎ 337 0251; fax 334 3550) at 229 Rochor Rd, at the northern end of the colonial district, is an older, upmarket cheapie. Reasonable budget rooms with air-con, TV, telephone and carpeting cost S$65, or S$80 with bathroom. It's close to Bugis MRT station but the immediate area around the hotel is bereft of much else other than lawn.

The *South-East Asia Hotel* (☎ 338 2394; fax 338 3480), 190 Waterloo St, is quiet and offers good value for money. All rooms have air-con, bathroom, TV and phone. Doubles cost S$70, or S$86.50 with two double beds. This is the hotel for the lazy sightseer – within 200m you'll find a Buddhist temple, Hindu temple, market, food stalls and a shopping centre. The street is also alive with flower-sellers and fortune-tellers during the day.

Waterloo Hostel (☎ 336 6555; fax 336 2160), 55 Waterloo St, is not your average hostel. Part of the Catholic Centre, it's quiet and well run, and offers very good air-con singles/doubles with TV, phone and fridge for S$63/68, or S$73/83 with bath. The tariff includes breakfast.

Modern-style hotels with air-con and bathrooms include the *Strand Hotel* (☎ 338 1866; fax 336 3149), 25 Bencoolen St, diagonally opposite the backpackers' centre. Its excellent, upgraded rooms provide a good alternative to the top-end hotels and cost S$95 for a double. The hotel has a coffee shop and bar.

The *Metropole Hotel* (☎ 336 3611; fax 339 3610), on Seah St behind the Raffles, is an older three star hotel that has lost its shine, but it has a good coffee shop and restaurant called The Barn. Rooms have had a minor face-lift and start at S$100/115 plus 14% for singles/doubles.

The *Beach Hotel* (☎ 336 7712; fax 336 7713), 95 Beach Rd, has double rooms for S$95, S$105 and S$120. The rooms are well appointed and many of the attached bathrooms have baths, but the hotel has no coffee shop or other facilities.

Little India (Map 5)

Although Little India is a less convenient area for visiting Singapore's attractions, the hotels here are currently the best buys in this range.

The pick of the bunch is the tasteful *Perak Lodge* (☎ 296 9072; fax 392 0919; perlodge@singnet.com.sg), 12 Perak Rd, a

small, private guesthouse in a renovated Peranakan-style building. Its wooden-floored, air-con singles/doubles start at S$80/90, breakfast included.

About 300m around the corner from the Perak Lodge is the handy *Mayo Inn* (☎ 295 6631; fax 295 8218) at 9A Jalan Besar. Rooms are reasonably sized and very clean, but those overlooking the main street are noisy. Singles/doubles go for S$80/90. The *Boon Wah Hotel* (☎ 299 1466; fax 294 2176), at 43A Jalan Besar on the corner of Upper Dickson Rd, has reasonable singles/doubles with air-con, TV and bathroom for a moderate S$52/63.

Close to Serangoon Rd, the *Tai Hoe Hotel* (☎ 293 9122; fax 298 4600) at 163 Kitchener Rd is a modern, bustling hotel offering excellent rooms with bathroom, TV, phone and bar fridge. Opening rates of S$68/78 for singles/doubles make it one of the best mid-range buys in Singapore, but prices may rise.

The small *Kerbau Hotel* (☎ 297 6668; fax 297 6669) at 54/62 Kerbau Rd offers spotless singles/doubles with bathroom, phone and TV for S$70/80. Rooms are on the smallish side and those on the ground floor are windowless – the more expensive upstairs rooms are better.

The multistorey *Broadway Hotel* (☎ 292 4661; fax 291 6414), 195 Serangoon Rd, is one of the oldest of the hotels in Little India, but well maintained. The rooms have air-con, TV and bathrooms, and cost S$80/90 (S$90/100 for deluxe). The hotel has a good Indian restaurant.

Slap-bang in the heart of Little India is the newish and very attractive *Grandmet Hotel* (☎ 297 8797; fax 297 8171) at 65A-75A Desker Rd. Air-con singles/doubles start at S$57/80. There is a convenient restaurant of the same name underneath the hotel.

Two blocks down at 44 and 44A Rowell Rd is the *Comfort Hotel* (☎ 295 4225; fax 295 3140); its single rooms are on the small side and facilities are pretty minimal, but it's clean and close to restaurants and shops. Singles/doubles cost S$85/100.

The *Mustafa Hotel* (☎ 295 5855; fax 295 5866), 145 Syed Alwi Rd, is the hotel for shoppers. It is above the Mustafa Centre, a large department store bustling with bargain hunters. Newish, quite luxurious rooms are good value. Singles/doubles go for S$90/105.

Other newish hotels include the large *Fortuna Hotel* (☎ 295 3577; fax 294 7738), 2 Owen Rd, with some of the best rooms costing from S$112, and the *Starlet Hotel* (☎ 392 3933; fax 392 7833), one block south at 301 Serangoon Rd, with modern singles/doubles with TV, phone and fridge for a reasonable S$78/98. The smaller *Penta Hotel* (☎ 299 6311; fax 299 9539) on Birch Rd has fairly cramped singles/doubles from S$78/89. All three hotels regularly offer discounts, making them a good option.

Also at the top of this range, the *Dickson Court Hotel* (☎ 297 7811; fax 297 7833), at 3 Dickson Rd over near Jalan Besar, is a boutique hotel with 51 well-appointed rooms from S$105 to S$155 plus 14%. Designed around new shophouses, it has style but some of the rooms are small and dark. There's also a restaurant and bar.

Orchard Rd (Map 4)
You can find a few reasonably priced hotels around Orchard Rd. On Kramat Rd, one block north of Orchard Rd, the *Supreme Hotel* (☎ 737 8333) is a decent mid-range place and a good deal for the location, with doubles for S$85.

Lloyd's Inn (☎ 737 7309; fax 737 7847), 2 Lloyd Rd, is a small but modern hotel less than 10 minutes walk south from Orchard Rd along Oxley Rd. It's in a quiet street among old villas and the rooms are spread out, motel style, around the reception building. Well-appointed doubles cost S$85, or a double with fridge is good value at S$95. Bookings are advisable.

In the quiet residential area to the north of Orchard and Tanglin Rds are some good hotels, but they are a little out of the way. The *Sloane Court Hotel* (☎ 235 3311; fax 733 9041), 17 Balmoral Rd, is a pleasant Tudor-style hotel in a garden setting with an

English pub. The singles/doubles are comfortable but nothing special and cost S$80/90 plus 14%.

A few hundred metres from the Sloane Court is the *VIP Hotel* (☎ 235 4277; fax 235 2824) at 5 Balmoral Crescent. The rooms (which cost S$99) are a little run down, but the hotel has a swimming pool.

Next to the Shangri-La Hotel, the *RELC International House* (☎ 737 9044; fax 733 9976; relcih@singnet.com.sg), 30 Orange Grove Rd, has large well-appointed doubles with balcony and fridge from S$110, after discount, making them good value. RELC stands for Regional English Language Centre, and the bottom floors of this place are devoted to conference rooms and teaching facilities while the top floors are given over to accommodation.

Chinatown (Map 6)
Chinatown's renovated terraces are also home to a number of mid-range hotels offering rooms with character, but because of the terrace design the cheaper rooms are often windowless. Prices are high in these small hotels, and given that some are charging close to top-end hotel rates while at the same time offering limited facilities, expect discounts.

Dragon Inn Chinatown (☎ 222 7227; fax 222 6116), 18 Mosque St, is in a row of renovated shophouses. The rooms have air-con, bath and TV, but the small singles for S$65 are dark and many are located around the noisy air-con shaft. The doubles are much better at S$98 or S$118 for the larger rooms.

The cute *Damenlou Hotel* (☎ 221 1900; fax 225 8500), 12 Ann Siang Rd, has character and a good cafe. Rooms cost from S$100 to S$120 but some are better than others so it pays to look at a few.

At the southern edge of Chinatown near Outram Park MRT station, the *Chinatown Hotel* (☎ 225 5166; fax 225 3912), 12-16 Teck Lim Rd, is a good small hotel with a guesthouse feel. After discount, singles/doubles can be had for S$88/98, including breakfast in the lobby dining area. The larger *Royal Peacock Hotel* (☎ 223 3522; fax 221 1770), 55 Keong Saik Rd, is more luxurious and has a stylish bar/cafe. All rooms have mini-bars and VCRs can be requested; singles/doubles cost S$130/140, but some of the rooms are dark so check before you move in.

Other Areas

Other mid-range places can be found in less convenient locations. Towards the east coast, Geylang and Katong (Map 8) have a few moderately priced hotels. These are interesting areas in which to stay but they're a long way from most of Singapore's attractions. In the Geylang district, the *Lion City Hotel* (☎ 744 8111; fax 748 7622), 15 Tanjong Katong Rd, is a very good hotel and only a short walk from Paya Lebar MRT station. Standard/deluxe doubles cost S$125/145 after discount.

Hotel 81 (☎/fax 348 8181) at 305 Joo Chiat Rd in Katong is a newish hotel in renovated shophouses. Spotless rooms cost S$59 weekdays and S$79 at weekends but some rooms are windowless. The more up-market *Chancellor Hotel* (☎ 742 2222; fax 348 8677) at 181 Joo Chiat Rd is also in a renovated old building. Rooms start at around S$84 plus taxes.

PLACES TO STAY – TOP END

The rates for Singapore's international standard hotels constantly change as they ride the roller coaster of supply and demand. Discounts are not usually available if you walk in off the street, but it is always worth asking. Travel agents overseas should be able to secure good deals on accommodation. If you book in advance yourself, fax or phone the sales offices of the hotels and ask for the corporate or discount rates to avoid paying walk-in rates.

If you arrive by air, the Singapore Hotel Association (SHA; ☎ 339 9918; fax 339 3795) operates an outlet at Changi airport and keeps an up-to-the-minute list of available rooms. You don't pay extra for the service and you will be quoted the current discount rates.

Hotels Online

A growing number of hotels can now be contacted by email for booking enquiries, and where email addresses are available we have listed them.

In addition, an ever increasing number of hotels have their own Web pages where you can view the hotel and retrieve further information on room rates, possible discounts and any in-house facilities offered.

The Singapore Hotels Association (SHA; email shamail@singnet.com.sg) has an extremely useful Web site (www.asianconnect.com/sha), where you can browse a comprehensive selection of hotels on its listings. Many have colour photographs and online booking facilities.

As a rough demarcation line, 'top end' refers to hotels where a standard double room costs over S$120 a night. Singapore's best hotels generally cost over S$200 a night, and many are designed to cater for expense-account travellers. Naturally, all these hotels will be air-conditioned and have bathroom, TV and mini-bar, and in almost all cases there will be a swimming pool and a variety of restaurants, coffee shops and bars. They are all of international standard and often there is little to distinguish one from the other – the choice boils down to price and which part of town you want to stay in.

The hotels at the lower end of this range are of a good standard but are either getting a little old or lack the extensive facilities of the larger hotels. Singapore has a number of 'super luxury' hotels that in price and standards are more than a cut above the mere international-standard hotels. Singapore also has a couple of hotels with definite oriental flavour and style, notably the Goodwood Park in the Orchard Rd area and, of course, Raffles in the colonial district. A few new boutique hotels have sprung up in renovated terraces and while they don't have pools or a host of restaurants and bars, they have character, which is something many of the concrete-and-glass high-rise hotels lack.

Unless otherwise stated, all prices are '+++', that is you have to add the 10% service charge, 3% GST and 1% government tax on top of the rates we quote. The prices we give are the published rates for a standard single room; all these hotels have more expensive 'deluxe' and 'superior' rooms, which are normally larger or have a better view, and many also have suites.

These prices should be used as a guide only, as Singapore hotel rates are subject to large variations.

Orchard Rd (Map 4)

Orchard Rd is where everyone wants to stay, and consequently hotels tend to be a little more expensive here than elsewhere. This is very much the tourist centre of Singapore, with a profusion of hotels, airline offices and shopping centres. The area is well serviced by the MRT, with Somerset and Orchard stations both on Orchard Rd.

The *Cockpit Hotel* (☎ 737 9111; fax 737 3105) has a good location just off Orchard Rd at the city end. It's looking a little weary and the facilities are limited but it is comparatively moderately priced at S$190 for a single room.

Some cheaper, smaller hotels can be found to the north and west of the western end of Orchard Rd, near Scotts and Tanglin Rds – an easy walk to the action.

The *Ladyhill Hotel* (☎ 737 2111; fax 737 4696) on Lady Hill Rd is a moderately priced low-rise place with an attractive garden setting. The best rooms with private balconies overlooking the pool are in the chalet block. Singles cost from S$170 to S$210.

The *Garden Hotel* (☎ 235 3344; fax 235 9730; garden@pacific.net.sg) at 14 Balmoral Rd has a pleasant covered courtyard atrium area and a courtyard pool. Single room rates run from S$160 to S$180.

The *Hotel Asia* (☎ 737 8388; fax 733 3563; hotasia@singnet.com.sg) does have a very good location, on Scotts Rd close to the action on Orchard Rd, but considering its age and lack of facilities, it is probably a bit overpriced with singles costing from S$180 to S$210.

The *Cairnhill Hotel* (☎ 734 6622; fax 235 5598) at 19 Cairnhill Circle is a short walk from Orchard Rd. In terms of quality it's a notch below most of its peers but it is reasonably priced at S$210 for a single.

The *Hotel Phoenix* (☎ 737 8666; fax 732 2024; rsvp@phoenix.com.sg), 277 Orchard Rd across from Le Meridien Singapore (which itself is a very good hotel but only worth considering if you can get a large discount), is at the lower end of the price range for the Orchard Rd area and lacks a lot of facilities; the big plus is that it sits over Somerset MRT station. Singles go for S$250.

The *Imperial Hotel* (☎ 737 1666; fax 737 4761), 1 Jalan Rumbia, enjoys a hill-top location near River Valley Rd within walking distance of the city end of Orchard Rd. Single room rates are a healthy S$330.

Most of the top hotels are at the western end of Orchard Rd around Scotts and Tanglin Rds.

The *Omni Marco Polo* (☎ 474 7141; fax 471 0521), just off Tanglin Rd, is moderately priced for its superior facilities, while the impressive *Regent* (☎ 733 8888; fax 732 8838), 1 Cuscaden Rd, is edging into the super luxury category with singles starting at S$350.

The *Traders Hotel* (☎ 738 2222; fax 831 4314; thsbc@singnet.com.sg), located between the Imperial and Marco Polo, is typical of the new breed of Singaporean hotels – well-appointed rooms but with pared back facilities to give a reasonable single room rate from S$235.

The *ANA* (☎ 732 1222; fax 732 2222; anahotel@singnet.com.sg), just west of Tanglin Rd at 16 Nassim Hill, is a more expensive joint done out in old-world decor. Their single room rates start at S$300.

On the corner of Scotts and Orchard Rds, the *Singapore Marriott Hotel* (☎ 735 5800; fax 735 9800), formerly The Dynasty, has had a complete recent makeover. It's exceedingly opulent but expect to fork out S$380 and upwards for a bed here.

The *Mandarin Singapore* (☎ 737 4411; fax 737 2361), decked out in restrained oriental style, is another top hotel. It's halfway along Orchard Rd at No 100; single room rates are S$300 and upwards.

Sheraton Towers (☎ 737 6888; fax 737 1072; anssh2@po.pacific.net.sg), 39 Scotts Rd, pedals yet more opulence and it's a big favourite with business types who can pass on the tab. Single room rates cost from S$370 and upwards.

The *Melia at Scotts* (☎ 732 5885; fax 732 1332; meliasct@pacific.net.sg), next to Sheraton Towers and near Newton MRT station, is popular with tour groups. Published single room rates start at S$260 but travel agents can usually get good discounts here.

The *Goodwood Park Hotel* (☎ 737 7411; fax 732 8558), 22 Scotts Rd, was designed by the architect responsible for Raffles. If anything, it is more ornate and more delightful even than its more famous sibling. It began life as the Teutonia Club for the German community in Singapore, and was also the base of the Australian army commission investigating Japanese war crimes. As you'd expect, beds here don't come cheap – a single room will set you back a minimum of S$385.

Colonial District (Maps 5&6)
The colonial district's real estate may not be as prestigious as Orchard Rd but most of the hotels here are more convenient for most of Singapore's attractions.

The *Bayview Inn* (☎ 337 2882; fax 338 2880), 30 Bencoolen St, is a good, three star hotel among the backpackers' guesthouses. While it doesn't have a big lobby or a profusion of restaurants, it does have a roof-top swimming pool and good rooms. Published single room rates start at S$150 but regular discounts make it a good buy.

The *Hotel InterContinental* (☎ 338 7600; fax 338 7366) is a new hotel in the Bugis Junction complex. Shophouse rooms out the front recreate the style of the complex, and high-rise rooms are also decorated in period style. It has plenty of class and all the trimmings of a top hotel. Singles start at S$325.

The *Peninsula Hotel* (☎ 337 2200; fax 339 3847) and its sister hotel the *Excelsior* (☎ 338 7733; fax 339 3847), both on Coleman St, over toward the business centre of Singapore, are moderately priced with published room rates starting at around S$215.

The *Carlton Hotel* (☎ 338 8333; fax 339 6866; carltsin@singnet.com.sg), 76 Bras Basah Rd, has excellent facilities and offers discounts on its rather pricey advertised rates, which are currently upwards of S$300 for a single.

The *Allson Hotel* (☎ 336 0811; fax 339 7019), 101 Victoria St, is another very good tourist hotel and regular discounts make it reasonable value. The opening price for a single here is S$230. Both the Allson and the Carlton are close to City Hall MRT station.

The twin, 73 storey *Westin Stamford Hotel* (☎ 339 6633; fax 336 5117; westin1@singnet.com.sg) and *Westin Plaza Hotel* (phone/fax as for Westin Stamford Hotel), built over the Raffles City shopping centre and City Hall MRT station, are the tallest hotels in the world. With countless restaurants and lounges, and two roof-top swimming pools, these two are also among the best hotels in Singapore. A single here will set you back anywhere between S$325 and S$400.

Nearby, on the edge of the colonial district, the massive Marina Square complex holds a cluster of super luxury hotels including the *Marina Mandarin* (☎ 338 3388; fax 339 4977), the *Oriental* (☎ 338 0066; fax 339 9537) and the *Pan Pacific* (☎ 336 8111; fax 339 1861; panpac@pacific.net.sg), all with lobbies that owe their inspiration to Hollywood special effects movies. The *Ritz-Carlton Millenia* (☎ 337 8888; fax 338 0001) next door is even more plush and more expensive: starting rates for singles are S$320 at the Marina Mandarin but reach as high as S$550 at the Ritz.

The venerable *Raffles* (☎ 337 1886; fax 339 7650; raffles@pacific.net.sg), at the junction of Bras Basah and Beach Rds, is as much a tourist attraction as it is a hotel. In recent times it has undergone massive renovations to restore its grandeur and it's now

PAUL HELLANDER

ringed by new extensions. To the purist it ain't the old Raffles but the restorations are faithful to the original spirit. The bars and restaurants are still redolent of the days when the Orient was almost always prefaced with the adjective 'mysterious'. And what other hotel can claim that a tiger was once shot in the billiard room? The limited number of beautiful antique-decorated rooms are only for those with money to burn: period suites cost some S$6000 per night. Alternatively, you can slum it in a regular suite for S$650.

Chinatown (Map 6)

If you want to experience the atmosphere of Chinatown, the futuristic *Furama Hotel* (☎ 533 3888; fax 534 1489; fhs60@singnet. com.sg), 60 Eu Tong Sen St, is right in the centre of things. Singles cost from S$200 to S$220.

The *Duxton* (☎ 227 7678; fax 227 1232; duxton@singnet.com.sg) in the Tanjong Pagar area is a boutique hotel in a renovated terrace. Rooms are furnished in an opulent, antique style and the suites have an attractive mezzanine bedroom. Singles start at S$280.

Other Areas

In Little India and the Arab St area there are a few good, reasonably priced hotels.

The *New Park Hotel* (Map 5; ☎ 291 5533; 297 2827; newpark@singnet.com.sg) on Kitchener Rd in Little India is popular with tour groups and close to good shopping. Published single room rates are S$230.

The *Albert Court Hotel* (Map 5; ☎ 339 3939; fax 339 3252), on Albert St at the southern edge of Little India, is a boutique hotel in a new shophouse redevelopment. It's a bit on the small side and lacks many of the extras that are found in the bigger hotels, but the dining court centre next to the hotel is a bonus. Starting rates for singles are S$180.

The *Golden Landmark Hotel* (Map 5; ☎ 297 2828; fax 298 2038) at the corner of Victoria and Arab Sts close to Bugis MRT station, has Middle Eastern inspired architecture. Its rates are very competitive, with singles starting at S$180.

The *Hotel Equatorial* (Map 3; ☎ 732 0431; fax 737 9426), 429 Bukit Timah Rd, and the *Novotel Orchid* (☎ 250 3322; 250 9292), just across the road at 214 Dunearn Rd, are about 2km north of Orchard Rd. Both hotels have shuttle bus services to Orchard Rd but because they are a long way from anywhere they often offer big discounts. Singles officially kick in at S$188 and S$220 respectively. These hotels are certainly worth considering if you have a car and want to travel around the island as they are handy for Singapore's expressways.

LONG TERM

For medium to long-term stays, Singapore has a number of serviced apartments, or it is possible to rent rooms in private apartments. Rents are very high and an apartment in the sought-after areas close to the city will cost upwards of S$1000 per week. There are cheaper apartments and even small houses much further out for lower rents but, even so, they still don't come cheap.

For many foreign workers on term contracts, serviced apartments are a no-fuss form of accommodation and as cheap, if not cheaper, than renting an apartment. The cheapest option of all is to rent a room in an apartment with a local family. The guesthouses usually know of some options.

Expect to pay around S$200 per week for a room in an apartment, though this varies depending on the standards and amenities available.

Another option is a serviced apartment in a hotel. For your money you get the amenities of a hotel, laundry facilities and car parking, and the apartments will be suites with separate bedroom, a small kitchen and a living/dining room. The cheaper places have essential furniture and cooking utensils, but are fairly bare. Many have one month minimum stays, though some can be rented by the week, making them good alternatives to hotel rooms.

Some hotels offering this option are the *Perak Lodge* in Little India with a comfortable superior room with TV, fridge, room safe and Internet access if required. For a minimum stay of one month expect to pay around S$2000. The *Novotel Orchid* has one bedroom apartments from S$3000 per month, the *Imperial*, slightly more expensive, and the *Plaza*, with apartments starting at S$3800. Two bedroom apartments will usually cost an extra 50%.

The better hotels have more luxurious suites for around S$4500 to S$6000 per month. The *Orchard*, *Carlton*, *Oriental* and *Pan Pacific* hotels all have suites.

Other serviced apartment blocks usually have swimming pools, gyms and most of the amenities of hotels, with similar rates. Some to try include: *Liang Court Regency* (☎ 337 0111), 177 River Valley Rd; *Palm Court* (☎ 235 0088), 15 Cairnhill Rd; and *Karakouen Orange Court* (☎ 738 1511), 6C Orange Grove Rd.

PLACES TO STAY

Places to Eat

Singapore is far and away the food capital of Asia. When it comes to superb Chinese food, Hong Kong may be a step ahead, but it's Singapore's sheer variety and low prices which make it so good. Equally important, Singapore's food is accessible – you don't have to search out obscure places, you don't face communication problems and you don't need a lot of money.

Alternatively, if you want to make gastronomic discoveries, there are lots of out-of-the-way little places where you'll find marvellous food that few visitors know about. The Singaporean enthusiasm for food (and economical food at that) is amply illustrated by newspaper and magazine articles on the best hawker stalls in the city. Everyone has their favourite chicken rice or roti prata stall, tucked away in one of the hundreds of hawker centres that dot the city.

Recommendations

The sheer variety of food is overwhelming. To get to grips with it, you first have to know what types of food are available, and then where to find them. This chapter offers lots of pointers and we include a couple of sets of dining recommendations of our own. Beyond that, the Singapore Tourism Board's *Singapore Official Guide* and *Eating Out in Singapore* booklets are good introductions to Singaporean food, and they also include restaurant recommendations. The annual *Singapore's Best Restaurants* is a selection of fine restaurants, chosen by a survey of *Singapore Tatler* magazine subscribers, a decidedly well-to-do bunch. Moderately priced restaurants are increasingly included. Other publications come and go, but every newspaper and magazine has a food section listing the latest gastronomic discoveries and promotional offers.

Dining Options

Dining possibilities range from streetside hawker stalls to five-star hotel restaurants,

with a whole gamut of possibilities in between. In a hawker centre you can eat excellent food for under S$5. This is the real Singaporean dining experience not to be missed. (See the special Hawker Centre section later in this chapter.)

Next up the scale are the coffee shops, or *kopi tiam* ('kopi' is Malay for coffee and 'tiam' is Hokkien for shop). These spartan, open-fronted restaurants with marble-topped tables often have similar food to the hawker centres, and within each coffee shop you may find two or three different stalls serving their own specialities. Other coffee shops are more restaurant-like and the menus are more extensive; the food may be as good as a top restaurant and cost a fraction of the price. The old coffee shops, typically housed in a terrace or under an old hotel, are a dying breed.

Restaurants run the full range from glorified coffee shops to luxury restaurants. The price increases with the quality of the decor and the efficiency of the service. Unlike most Asian cities where western chain food is a luxury item, Singapore's Asian and western chain restaurants are reasonably priced.

All the luxury hotels have a selection of restaurants, and they house most of Singapore's fine dining establishments, though they are facing increasing competition from new restaurants springing up all over town. It may be sacrilegious to say so, but Singapore has too many restaurants. It is quite likely that many places will not survive the current boom.

Mid-range and expensive restaurants normally add a 10% service charge and 4% tax. Many restaurants offer good value set lunches and more expensive set dinners, which allow you to try a number of dishes as you stuff yourself to the eyeballs at very reasonable prices. Many restaurants have lunch and dinner buffets, but the big hotels are the traditional buffet specialists.

In the listings that follow we categorise restaurants firstly by cuisine, then area and finally by price. Generally speaking cheaper restaurants come first and more expensive ones follow.

HAWKER FOOD
For general information on the etiquette of hawker centres and a description of the kinds of food they offer, see the special Hawker Centres section.

Central Business District (Map 6)
Near the waterfront towards Chinatown is *Lau Pa Sat Festival Market*, on Raffles Quay near Raffles Place MRT station. It's housed in the renovated Telok Ayer market building, a wonderful example of intricate Victorian cast-iron architecture in the railway station mould. It has some souvenir stalls and occasionally stages cultural exhibits, but the main emphasis is on the favourite Singaporean pastime – food. Hawkers inside serve Nonya, Korean and western food, as well as the more usual fare; and the famous Zam Zam restaurant has opened a very popular Indian Muslim stall. There are also some restaurants with bars here. Lau Pa Sat is more sanitised and expensive than the usual hawker centres, but as part of the re-creation of old Singapore, quasi-mobile hawkers set up in the evenings on Boon Tat St, where the dining is cheaper and cooler than inside.

Orchard Rd (Map 4)
The *Newton Food Centre*, at the north-eastern end of Scotts Rd, near Newton MRT station, is popular with tourists and therefore tends to be a little more expensive, but it is lively and open 24 hours. Eat there while you can – it is destined for redevelopment in the near future.

The *Kopitiam* food centre in the basement of Le Meridien Singapore is new on the scene and offers local, Japanese and Western foods. It's also open 24 hours.

The *Marché* Swiss food centre in the basement of the Heeren building is a combined Swiss eatery and delicatessen with Swiss dishes such as rösti, cheeses, sausages and pasta. Diagonally opposite, in the basement of the Cineleisure Orchard complex, is the Hollywood-inspired *Food Junction* with a steel and neon ambience and Asian food stalls named after movie stars.

The *Scotts Picnic Food Court* in the Scotts Shopping Centre on Scotts Rd, by the Hyatt Regency, is a glossy food court, and the stalls offer a variety of international Asian cuisine, including Thai and Japanese.

Orchard Emerald Food Court in the basement of the Orchard Emerald Shopping Centre has a varied selection of Asian food, as do the food stalls downstairs in *Orchard Towers*, at the corner of Orchard and Claymore Rds, and the *Food Life Food Court* on the 4th floor of the Wisma Atria Shopping Centre. The latter is small but has a good selection of local dishes and 'moderne decor' from the 50s. The *Asian Food Mall* in the basement of Lucky Plaza has a good range of local hawker favourites and it's as cheap as you'll find anywhere.

Colonial District (Map 5&6)
The *Albert Centre*, Albert Rd between Queen and Waterloo Sts, is an extremely good, busy and central centre which has all types of food at low prices. At the corner of Bencoolen and Albert Sts, in the basement of the Sim Lim Square complex, is the *Tenco Food Centre*, a very clean establishment.

Victoria St has a good selection of hawker centres. *Victoria St Food Court*, near the Allson Hotel, is a notch up from most food centres. It has an air-con section at the back and a bar with draught beer. The food is cheap and good, and you can get western-style breakfasts here. A few doors away, the *Koh Fong Restaurant* is not a restaurant but a grouping of food stalls around open-air tables. Across the road in the Bras Basah Complex, the *Xiang Man Lou Food Court* is a small, air-con food court with Malay and Indian tandoori stalls which also offer some Chinese favourites. It is open 24 hours.

continued on page 136

HAWKER CENTRES

Undoubtedly, the most original, cheap and entertaining way to eat is at a hawker stall. This is not only where most locals eat when they are not 'eating out', but it is where you will find Singaporean food at its most inventive and tasty.

A hawker stall was traditionally a streetside kitchen cart with a few chairs and tables scattered around for the customers. In recent years, the Singapore authorities have moved all the impermanent and 'untidy' stalls into permanent hawker centres where fixed stalls, tables and chairs are the order of the day.

For a beginner though, eating at a hawker centre can still be a frustrating experience. Firstly, there is an enormous choice of foods from a number of regional cuisines. Selecting something you like can be a hit and miss affair until you have got the hang of it. Understanding the process by which you get a meal and a drink can also be confusing, as can fathoming the unwritten hawker etiquette. Here, in a few easy steps, is how to go about getting the best out of your own hawker experience. For a rundown of recommended hawker centres, see the main text in the Places to Eat chapter.

Selecting a Centre

Typically you will end up at a hawker centre near your hotel, though some, like the *Newton Food Centre*, are worth travelling for. There are centres, like the *Lau Pa Sat Festival Market*, that cater as much for tourists as they do for locals and they tend to be brighter and more accommodating for newcomers. Others, like the *Maxwell Road Hawker Centre* in Chinatown or the *Haig Road Market &*

Typical hawker centre seating (in this case, it happens to be the Newton Food Centre) – communal, alfresco and plastic, for quick and easy cleaning.

ARASU RAMASAMY

Cooked Food Centre in Katong, ply their trade mainly to locals and can be a little rougher around the edges; that said, the food is as good, if not better, than their more sanitised counterparts.

Food centres are gentrified hawker centres, usually found in the air-con basements of large shopping centres. While the food is as good as that served up in the hawker centres, the food centres themselves tend to be rather bland, plastic places in which to eat, lacking the liveliness of the outdoor venues. But after a hot, sticky shopping session they can be blissful oases of cool.

Selecting a Stall

The best way to select a stall is to browse and see what takes your fancy. Most stalls will specialise in some kind of food dish, such as *congee* (porridge), offal, noodles or fish. There will usually be a sprinkling of Chinese, Indian, Malay and Muslim stalls, though Chinese cooking tends to dominate. A healthy crowd of patrons is usually a good sign that a particular stall is worth trying.

Communication can occasionally be a problem; the best strategy is usually to smile and point at whatever you want, letting the stall-holder know whether you want a small, medium or large serving. Most stallholders are helpful and willing to assist in making choices.

Typical Dishes

Typical hawker food includes *chye tow kway* (carrot cake), a vegetable and egg dish, tasting something like potato omelette (and totally unlike the western idea of carrot cake); that should cost just S$2 to S$3 for a serving.

Indian *biryanis* are common and cost around S$3, or you can have a *murtabak* (see the Glossary of Asian Culinary Terms later in this chapter for descriptions of dishes) for around S$2. Chicken rice and *char siew* (roast pork) will always be available, as will all the usual Cantonese dishes like fried rice (S$1.50 to S$3), fried vegetables (S$3) and sweet and sour pork (S$3 to S$5).

There will often be Malay or Indonesian stalls with satay from 40c to 45c a stick, and *mee rebus* and *mee soto*, both for around S$2. *Won ton mee*, a substantial soup dish with shredded chicken or braised beef, costs from S$2 to S$3. You may also find *chee chong fun*, a type of stuffed noodle dish, which costs from S$2 to S$4 or more, depending on whether you order with prawns, mushrooms, chicken or pork. *Popiah* (spring rolls) and *laksa* (spicy coconut-based soup) are other staples, but there's also a whole variety of other dishes and soups.

To finish up you might try a fruit salad for S$2 or a *pisang goreng* (fried banana) for 50c.

Where to Sit

You can basically sit anywhere, though at busy times your choice will be dictated by what's available. It's probably a good idea to

PAUL HELLANDER

The food at the hawker stalls is all cooked on the spot in front of you, so there's never any question of how fresh it is.

PAUL HELLANDER

grab a table first and then leave one of your party (assuming there are two or more of you) to hang on to it while the others foray for food. The food stall will often want to know what table you are sitting at so make a note of its number, if it has one. At a larger table don't be surprised if you end up being joined by strangers, as table-sharing is accepted hawker centre etiquette. Of course, you will get odd looks if you move onto someone's table when there are patently lots of other empty spaces.

What to Drink

Drinks are served at drink stalls. You can find beer (S$8 for a large bottle) but far more refreshing are the juices made to order from fresh fruit. These cost anywhere between 80c and S$2, depending on the type of fruit. Other alternatives include sugarcane juice or *ais kacang* (see the Drinks boxed text later this chapter).

More often than not someone will approach you and ask if you want a drink – if not, just go and get one yourself.

Cutlery

Cutlery – spoons, forks and chopsticks – is normally located at a central station, from which you help yourself. Chinese food is normally eaten with chopsticks with a spoon for the soups; Malay/Indonesian food with a spoon, and a fork to help out. With food purchased from the Indian stalls, fingers may be the best option. Just watch what others are doing and follow suit.

Note that some cutlery stands are Muslim-only, which means that you take and return your utensils to the specific Muslim section. This is so that forbidden food, such as pork, does not come into contact with Muslim utensils. Do observe this rule if you come across it.

Paying the Bill

You pay for your food or drink when it is brought to your table or when you take delivery of it directly from the stall. Tipping is not expected.

PAUL HELLANDER

Hawker stalls are often devoted to just one particular food type – in the case shown here it's chicken rice. However, equally often there is no explanatory signboard and it can be difficult to work out just what the food on offer actually is.

continued from page 131

The new *Parco Bugis Junction* centre on North Bridge Rd has an excellent food court in the basement, right near the entrance to Bugis MRT station. It is more expensive than most, but has a good range and is great for Japanese food.

Food Paradiz (Map 4), in the basement of the Paradiz Centre on Selegie Rd, is another good air-con food court.

The *Tropical Makan Palace* in the basement of the Beach Centre, 15 Beach Rd, is close to Raffles and the budget accommodation area. It has food stalls in the air-con section or you can eat outside.

Just north of the river on Hill St, the large *Hill St Food Centre* is popular, and across the road the *Funan Centre* has a very good air-con food court on the 7th floor.

Little India (Map 5)
On Serangoon Rd at the start of Little India, the large *Zhujiao Centre* is a market with a number of food stalls. As you would expect, Indian food dominates. Opposite the market, the newer, air-con *Hastings Food Court* in the Little India Arcade has vegetarian and non-vegetarian food, as well as Keralan specialities and north Indian tandoori food.

Over on Jalan Besar are the *Berseh Food Centre*, halfway between at the corner of Jalan Berseh, and the lively *Lavender Food Centre*, at the end of Jalan Besar near Lavender St, which is good for seafood and stays open until the early hours of the morning.

Chinatown (Map 6)
The Chinatown area has a number of excellent food centres. The *People's Park Food Centre* is good as is the *Maxwell Road Hawker Centre*, an old-fashioned centre at the corner of South Bridge and Maxwell Rds. The pigs' trotters in black bean sauce is a speciality.

Some of the best Chinese food stalls are on the 2nd floor of the *Chinatown Complex* at the corner of Sago and Trengganu Sts, where there is also a market. Try *Fu Ji Crayfish*, the stall where crayfish hor fun costs only S$3, or a superb crayfish (actually

---

Hawker Centres on the Web

For Singaporeans, eating is a national pastime. So it's no surprise that a society as technologically literate as this one should have dozens of Web sites devoted to the burning issues of where and what to eat. Check the Unofficial Food Page at www.sintercom.org/makan/index.html for a site devoted to hawker centres. Categories include the 'Hall of Fame' and 'Hall of Shame', and a 'Lost & Found' full of heart-rending pleas for information on the whereabouts of hawker stalls that people are trying to locate.

---

scampi) or prawn claypot with vegetables and rice costs around S$5.

The *Fountain Food Court*, 51 Craig Rd, is a different type of food centre in keeping with the new Chinatown. You can dine in air-conditioned comfort, and the nouveau decor includes sand-blasted and bag-painted walls. The food is good, but some dishes are at restaurant prices. It serves satay and other Malay food, popiah and kueh (cakes), and good (and cheap) congee.

Other hawker centres can be found alongside the *Tanjong Market*, not far from the railway station, and at the *Amoy Food Centre*, where Amoy St meets Telok Ayer St.

The famous *Satay Club* has finally fallen into the hands of redevelopers, but many of the vendors have relocated from opposite the Padang to Read St at Clarke Quay where over a dozen vendors fan their charcoal grills. The satay here is still the best in Singapore; just make sure you specify how many sticks (40c a time) you want or they'll assume your appetite is much larger than it is. It's at its liveliest in the evening. Clarke Quay also has an air-con food court.

Other Areas
The *Taman Serasi Food Centre* (Map 2) has one of the best settings – it is next to the Botanic Gardens north-west of the city

centre on Cluny Rd, just off Napier Rd. The stalls are predominantly Malay. Try the roti john, a type of fried sandwich with chilli, washed down with the fabulous soursop fruit juice.

The *Rasa Singapura Food Court* is a collection of hawkers selected in a special competition to find the best stalls for each dish. It used to be on Tanglin Rd but most of the hawkers have moved to the Bukit Turf Club (Map 7) on Turf Club Rd and they have taken the name with them. During the week, it's open for lunch and dinner until 11 pm. On weekends, it's open all day until midnight but you have to pay entry to the races until 6 pm.

Over in Katong the *Sin Hoi Sai Eating House* (Map 8) on East Coast Rd does a roaring trade with the locals who spill out onto the street each night. There are several cuisines to tempt you here, but BBQ fish seems to be quite prominent.

Diagonally opposite the Malay Cultural Village in Katong is the *Haig Road Market & Cooked Food Centre* (Map 8), a bit of a mouthful, but there are plenty of delicacies to whet your appetite in this fairly new hawker centre.

CHINESE

Singapore has plenty of restaurants serving everything from a south Indian rice plate to an all-American hamburger, but naturally it's the Chinese restaurants that predominate. Many cater for family and work groups, and offer banquets for eight or more people. They offer a wonderful opportunity for groups to try a whole range of dishes at reasonable prices. Even at the à la carte restaurants, dishes are meant to be shared, and restaurants offer small, medium and large servings to cater for different size groups. The prices of dishes quoted in this section are for small servings or for average prices for lunch or dinner for one or two persons.

Cantonese

Cantonese food is the most widely known of China's diverse cooking styles. It is famous for its dim sums, sweet and sour dishes, wonton soups and spring rolls. Its cooking is characterised by quick stir-frying in light oil using subtle seasonings and only the freshest of ingredients. Culinary connoisseurs used to spicier Asian cuisines might consider it bland, or even occasionally too sweet, but it probably suits untrained western palates more easily than other regional Chinese cuisines. Cantonese food is, not surprisingly, well represented in Singapore with a large variety of outlets.

On Orchard Rd, the small pedestrian street of Cuppage Rd (Map 4) between Centrepoint and Cuppage Plaza is a good little restaurant strip for cheap eats. The eastern side is lined with various Chinese coffee shops with tables on the pavement.

For cheap dim sum a good bet is the *Tiong Shan Eating House* (Map 6), an old-fashioned coffee shop at the corner of New Bridge and Keong Saik Rds in Chinatown. A plate of dim sum costs around S$2 and other dishes average S$3. It is as good as you'll find anywhere.

More expensive dim sum can be had in more luxurious air-con surroundings at the *Regency Palace* (Map 5; ☎ 338 3281) in the Plaza by the Park, 51 Bras Basah Rd, in the colonial district. The prices are reasonable and most plates cost about S$2 to S$4. Many of the big restaurants offer dim sum, but remember that dim sum is a lunchtime or Sunday breakfast dish – in the evening these restaurants change to other menus.

The famous *Fatty's Eating House* (☎ 338 1087) at 01-33 Albert Complex (Map 5) on Albert St, near the corner of Bencoolen St, has been popular with westerners ever since Fatty became a favourite with British troops stationed in Singapore during the Emergency. The food is consistently good and moderately priced. Most dishes cost around S$5 to S$8, but can go up to S$20 or more for crab. The restaurant is always crowded, but the ever-busy staff turn the tables around quickly so you shouldn't have to wait long.

The *Hillman* (Map 6; ☎ 221 5073), 159 Cantonment Rd, near Outram Park MRT station, is an open-fronted restaurant with a

PLACES TO EAT

Recommended Eating

With Singapore's super-abundance of dining options, coming up with any kind of 'top restaurants' list is an almost impossible task. Having said that, for what it's worth, following is a list of 10 places that this author has enjoyed eating at (all of these places are described more fully in the main text).

They appear in ascending order of expense.

Lau Pa Sat Festival Market (Map 6), Raffles Quay, Chinatown. Possibly the most atmospheric hawker centre in town and almost certainly the best organised. You can find *any* kind of food here.

Newton Food Centre (Map 4), Newton Rd. A very lively and animated eating centre that captures the fun of outdoor eating as it used to exist in the old Satay Club.

Beautiful Myanmar Restaurant (Map 6; ☎ 222 1665), 11 Mosque St, Chinatown. Excellent cheap food catering mainly to the local Burmese community.

House of Sundanese Food (Map 8; ☎ 345 5020), 218 East Coast Rd, Geylang. It requires something of an effort to get out here, but it's worth it for excellent west Javanese food at very reasonable prices.

Fatty's Eating House (Map 5; ☎ 338 1087), 01-33 Albert Complex, Albert St. Still popular after all these years – as witnessed by the lines of foreigners waiting for a table. A good feed is guaranteed.

Hillman (Map 6; ☎ 221 5073), 159 Cantonment Rd, Chinatown. A bit out of the way but worth the trek for the claypot specialities.

Delhi Restaurant (Map 5; ☎ 296 4585), 60 Racecourse Rd, Little India. A slightly upmarket Indian eatery. A hard choice given the quality of the nearby restaurants, but a good choice nonetheless.

Chilli Buddys (Map 4; ☎ 732 9108), 180 Orchard Rd. One of the few places you can dine alfresco on Orchard Rd, and this author's favourite for a lunchtime nasi goreng.

Sketches (Map 5; ☎ 339 8386), Parco Bugis Junction, 200 Victoria St. A great place for DIY pasta dishes. Handy for shopping and grabbing a relaxing lunch.

The Moomba (Map 6; ☎ 438 0141), 52 Circular Rd, Boat Quay. A great Australasian restaurant close to the pubs on Boat and Clarke quays. Expensive, yes, but perfect for a more unusual and special night out.

Paul Hellander

good reputation. You can have a decent meal for under S$15 per person. Pot-cooked dishes are their speciality – try the pot beef.

The *Esquire Kitchen* (Map 5; ☎ 336 1802), 02-01 Bras Basah Complex in the colonial district, is a moderately priced aircon place with typical red Chinese decor and good food. It serves excellent value set lunches and dinners.

Grand City (Map 4; ☎ 338 3622), 07-04 Cathay building, is a more expensive restaurant and has a varied menu with good seafood and chicken dishes. It's near Dhoby Ghaut MRT station, right at the eastern end of Orchard Rd.

Tsui Hang Village (Map 6; ☎ 338 6668), 02-142 Marina Square, 6 Raffles Blvd, is a popular Hong Kong-style restaurant. You can fill yourself on a good set lunch for around S$40 for two, or the set dinners cost from S$60; à la carte meals are available. It also has a branch at the Hotel Asia (Map 4), 37 Scotts Rd, near Orchard Rd.

Hainanese

Chicken rice is a common and popular dish all over town. Originating from Hainan, a large island off the southern coast of China, it is a dish of elegant simplicity, and in Singapore you can find it at most hawker centres and food courts.

Yet Con (Map 5; ☎ 337 6819), 25 Purvis St, is claimed by many to be the best of all Singapore's chicken rice eateries. A similarly popular, but more expensive location is in the *Mandarin Singapore* (Map 4) on Orchard Rd.

Loy Kee Chicken Rice (Map 5) in the basement of Parco Bugis Junction is eagerly sought out by lunchtime diners who are prepared to queue up for their treat. Not too far away at the Beach Centre at 15 Beach Rd you can try chicken rice at *Good Family* (Map 5), another popular and good value Hainanese eating place.

Xiang Yuan (Map 5), in the basement of an apartment block right opposite Bugis MRT station on the south side of Victoria St, is another quietly appreciated location for locals in the know where you can get some pretty decent Hainanese dishes.

Hokkien

Despite the large number of Hokkien in Singapore, Hokkien food is not all that popular since dishes tend to be simple and rather heavy. The one shining exception here is Hokkien mee, which is considered by many to be Singapore's national dish.

Beng Thin Hoon Kee (Map 6; ☎ 553 7708) on the 5th floor of the OCBC Centre on Chulia St is popular and has moderately priced dishes, including Hokkien seafood. It is a short walk from Raffles Place MRT station.

Hunanese

Hunanese cuisine is essentially represented by three establishments in Singapore, all of them in the mid-range to expensive price bracket. Hunanese flavours are those of subtle seasonings and spicy tastes sharpened by the liberal use of dark soy sauce.

The *Charming Garden* (☎ 251 8149) at the Novotel Orchid Hotel (Map 3), 214 Dunearn Rd, is the main contender for the role of specialist in this field. Its pigeon soup in a bamboo tube is one of its more unusual specialities.

The *Cherry Garden* (Map 6; ☎ 331 0538) in the Oriental Singapore on Marina Square includes Hunanese cooking along with Szechuan cuisine, while the *Spice Garden* (☎ 732 4122) at Le Meridien Singapore (Map 4) on Orchard Rd mixes Hunanese with Cantonese cuisine. A meal for two will work out at about S$85 though the Spice Garden's buffet lunch is a better deal at around S$28 per person.

Shanghainese

Shanghainese cuisine is similar to the cuisine of Beijing but tends to be sweeter and oilier with pork, cabbage and soybean featuring prominently on the menu.

If you are looking to try it out, the cuisine is represented at the lower end of the price scale at popular *Zhu Chang Fen* in the basement of the Parco Bugis Junction centre (Map 5) and at the upper end of the scale by the *Chang Jiang* (☎ 734 7188) in the Goodwood Park Hotel (Map 4) on Scotts Rd. At the latter, decor is opulent and dress code applies. Braised Wuxi spare ribs are on the specialities list and make sure you ask for the deep-fried buns (man dou) to mop up the sauces. A meal for two will set you back a steepish S$130.

Szechuan

Spicy Szechuan, or Sichuan, food is popular with Singaporeans and restaurants are fairly common, though usually expensive.

The cheapest would have to be the *Magic of Chongqing Hot Pot* (Map 4; ☎ 734 8135) on the 4th floor of the Tanglin Shopping Centre, offering a simple rustic eating ambience. Hot pot or steamboat features prominently here and the 'eight treasure tonic tea' is perfect for cleansing the palate. A set dinner costs S$23.80 while a set lunch goes for a very reasonable S$17.90.

Next in line price-wise is the *Dragon City Sichuan* (☎ 254 7070) in the Novotel Orchid Hotel (Map 3) on Dunearn Rd. It has fairly old-fashioned Chinese decor but the food is topnotch. Try the chef's favourite fried prawns with dried chilli. Dinner will cost two people about S$60.

Further along in price is the *Min Jiang* (☎ 730 1704) in the Goodwood Park Hotel (Map 4) on Scotts Rd. Szechuan hot and sour soup should be sampled here as well as the steamed dumplings. A romantic meal for two costs an impressive S$160.

Teochew
The Teochew from south-eastern China near Guangzhou (Canton) are famous for their food stalls, for their fiery temperament and for inventing the steamboat – a kind of Chinese fondue cooking. Their delicious braised duck with soy sauce and fresh chillis is a well-known regional speciality.

Among the many coffee shops on China-town's Mosque St (Map 6) you'll find a good selection of simple Teochew food served in very traditional restaurants. Menus are hard to come by but a request for suggestions and prices will be readily answered, and the prices are low. The *Chui Wah Lin* (☎ 221 3305) at 49 Mosque St is basic but OK and has very good porridge – try the duck porridge for S$3.

Liang Kee (Map 6; ☎ 225 5415) at 16 Murray Terrace is another good Teochew eatery. A tasty crayfish sambal goes for S$16. The *Ellenborough St market* (Map 6), across from Clarke Quay in Chinatown, is also noted for its Teochew food stalls.

For moderately priced Teochew food in luxurious surroundings, try the *Teochew City Seafood Restaurant* (Map 4; ☎ 733 3338), 05-16 Centrepoint at 176 Orchard Rd. Braised goose and pomegranate chicken are a couple of the restaurant's specialities. Dinner for two works out at about S$50.

For Teochew opera while you eat, head up to the *House of Teochew Taipan* (☎ 334 8743) at 02-47/48 Parco Bugis Junction centre (Map 5) on Victoria St. Its vegetarian rolls and Pom Pom chicken are favoured by clients. Reservations are always necessary and prices are on the higher side – up around the S$70 mark for two.

Yunnanese
There is really only one place in Singapore specialising in Yunnanese cooking and it's the *Yunnan Kitchen* (Map 6; ☎ 338 3001) on Clarke Quay. It's a very popular restaurant and it pays to reserve a table. Mushrooms are a Yunnan speciality and the Yunnan Kitchen does a few dishes featuring the tasty fungus. Try wholepiece matsutake mushroom. Prices are mid-range to high with a decent feed for two coming out at around S$70.

Vegetarian
On Bencoolen St in the colonial district, the Fortune Centre (Map 5) is a good place for cheap vegie food. On the ground floor are the *ABC Eating House* and *Yi Song* food stalls, which have cheap vegetarian food in air-con surroundings. On the 4th floor, the *Eastern Vegetarian Food* coffee shop, offers rice or noodles with three selections from S$2.

The *Fut Sai Kai* (Map 5; ☎ 298 0336) at 143, 147 and 153 Kitchener Rd in Little India is a spartan old coffee shop with an air-con restaurant next door. Most main dishes cost around S$8 to S$10.

Similarly priced is the *Kwan Yim* (☎ 338 2394), another traditional, long-running vegetarian restaurant. It's at 190 Waterloo St in the South-East Asia Hotel (Map 5) in the colonial district.

Chinatown has some moderately priced vegetarian restaurants, including the *Happy Realm* (Map 6; ☎ 222 6141) on the 3rd floor of Pearl's Centre on Eu Tong Sen St, which is one of the best around. Main dishes cost around S$5 to S$6 and it has good claypot dishes. *Loke Woh Yeun* (Map 6; ☎ 221 2912), 20 Tanjong Pagar Rd, is another reasonably priced restaurant in Chinatown where you can have a meal for under S$15. While it mostly caters for vegetarians it also has chicken and prawn dishes.

Over in the colonial district at 143 Victoria St is the popular *Yuan Xiang Vegetarian Food* (Map 5) restaurant, in the Koh Fong Restaurant complex. It's cheap, with dishes in the S$4 to S$5 range and within walking distance of the backpackers' area of Beach Rd.

Lingzhi Vegetarian (☎ 734 3788) is popular with health-conscious eaters. It offers a wide range of atypical dishes like sautéed Japanese mushroom, asparagus and macadamia nut in a potato basket, or braised monkey-head mushroom with celery and dried chilli. Two people can eat handsomely and originally for about S$40. It's at 400 Orchard Rd in the Orchard Towers (Map 4).

Seafood

Singapore has another variation on Chinese food – seafood. In Singapore it's simply superb, whether it's prawns or abalone, fish-head curry or chilli crabs. Most of the specialists are some distance out from the city centre but the trip is worthwhile. Seafood isn't cheap, and prawns or a whole fish or crab start at just under S$20 per dish. Many places don't have set prices, but base them on 'market price' and the size of the fish. Make sure you check the price first.

The Bugis St area in the colonial district also has a couple of hustling, reasonably priced seafood places and it is a pleasant place to dine under the stars and people watch. Other cheaper dishes at fixed prices are available from the menus.

The *UDMC Seafood Centre* (Map 8) at the beach on East Coast Parkway has a number of seafood restaurants and is very popular in the evenings. The food and the setting are good, but the staff tend to hustle a bit at some of these places, so definitely check the prices first.

Punggol Seafood (☎ 448 8511), located in the new marina just east of the UDMC, is one of the better known restaurants here, having had a loyal following for years at its rural location at Punggol on the north-eastern coast (before housing developments forced it to move). The food is still excellent, though slightly expensive at around S$35 a head.

Long Beach Seafood Restaurant (☎ 445 8833), 1018 East Coast Parkway, is one of Singapore's best known seafood restaurants. It's famous for its black pepper crabs and 'live drunken prawns' (soaked in brandy). It's a casual, huge restaurant next to the Singapore Tennis Centre and it also has a branch at UDMC Seafood Centre (Map 8).

The smart and casual *Snappers* (Map 6; ☎ 434 5281) in the Ritz-Carlton Millenia at 7 Raffles Ave is one of the city's breeziest and more expensive fish eateries. The emphasis is on east-west fusion dishes though there are other, more straightforward fish dishes on the menu. Two will dine here for around S$150-plus.

Something Different

Tanjong Pagar, to the south of Chinatown, has a number of Chinese tea houses, where the emphasis is on the art and presentation of tea drinking. Take your shoes off at the door, and as you sit on cushions on the floor the waitress will bring you a tea set, complete with burner and kettle of boiling water, and demonstrate the art of tea preparation.

Tea Chapter (Map 6; ☎ 226 1175), 9A Neil Rd, boasts Queen Elizabeth and Prince Philip among the clientele. Dim sum snacks are served for around S$2 per plate, and the extensive range of Chinese teas costs from S$6 to S$15. It is open daily from 11 am till 11 pm. A few doors away at No 23, *Yixing Yuan* (Map 6) offers a small dim sum lunch for around S$7, or you can have dim sum for around S$2 to S$3 per plate, washed down with the tea of your choice. Both tea houses have shops that sell expensive tea and tea paraphernalia.

If you have a passion for durian, Asia's notoriously pungent and often forbidden fruit, you can try it in various guises at *Durian Chendol* (Map 6), Clarke Quay, a place touted as Singapore's first (and probably only) durian restaurant.

Snackworld (Map 4; ☎ 732 6921), 01-12/13 Cuppage Plaza, and the annexe outside on Cuppage Terrace off Orchard Rd, has crocodile on the menu, starting at S$25 a plate, if you can stomach the thought of eating the wildlife (actually it is farmed and, of course, it is supposed to taste like chicken). It has a wide range of dishes at some of the best prices in town.

The *Imperial Herbal Restaurant* (☎ 337 0491) in the Metropole Hotel (Map 5), 41 Seah St near Raffles, is an unusual restaurant with an extensive range of dishes cooked with medicinal herbs. You can order dishes recommended by the resident herbalist, and sample weird and wonderful things like scorpions and deer penis. Expect to pay about S$40 per person.

INDIAN

There are three types of Indian food in Singapore: south Indian, Indian Muslim and north Indian.

South Indian food is mostly vegetarian and Little India is the main centre for it. Here, you can get a thali – an all-you-can-eat rice plate with a mixture of vegetable curries – for less than S$5.

Indian Muslim food is something of a hybrid. It is the simpler south Indian version of what is basically north Indian food. Typical dishes are biryani served with chicken or mutton curry, roti and murtabak. This kind of food can be found all over Singapore but the main centre is on North Bridge Rd (Map 5) opposite the Sultan Mosque. Indian Muslim food is also well represented in the hawker centres; you can have a superb chicken biryani for just S$2.50 to S$3.50.

For the rich north Indian curries and tandoori dishes, you have to go to more expensive restaurants. They can be found all around Singapore, but Little India has a concentrated selection of very good restaurants on Racecourse Rd (Map 5), where you'll pay considerably less than at Indian restaurants in the more fashionable areas.

To sample eat-with-your-fingers south Indian vegetarian food, try the famous and very popular *Komala Vilas* (Map 5; ☎ 293 6980), 12-14 Buffalo Rd. It was established soon after the war and has an open down-

stairs area where you can have masala dhosa (S$1.50) and other snacks. The upstairs section is air-conditioned and you can have an all-you-can-eat rice meal for S$5. Remember to wash your hands before you start, use your right hand and ask for eating utensils only if you really have to! On your way out, try an Indian sweet from the showcase downstairs.

Two other rice-plate specialists are *Sri Krishna Vilas* (Map 5) at 229 Selegie Rd and *Ananda Bhavan* (Map 5) at 219-221 Selegie Rd (the southern extension of Serangoon Rd).

A main contender in the local competition for the best south Indian food is the *Madras New Woodlands Restaurant* (Map 5; ☎ 297 1594) at 14 Upper Dickson Rd off Serangoon Rd. A branch of the well-known Woodlands chain in India, New Woodlands serves freshly prepared vegetarian food in very clean air-con rooms. The yoghurt is particularly good. Prices are about the same as at Komala Vilas.

Racecourse Rd, a block north-west of Serangoon Rd, is the best area in Singapore for non-vegetarian curry. The *Banana Leaf Apolo Restaurant* (Map 5; ☎ 293 8682), 56 Racecourse Rd does superb Indian food, including Singapore's classic fish-head curry. It is newly renovated with gleaming granite and air-con luxury, but prices are still cheap with set meals at S$5.50 for vegetarian, S$6.50 for non-vegetarian and S$17 for fish-head curry.

The very popular *Muthu's Curry Restaurant* (Map 5; ☎ 293 2389) at 78 Racecourse Rd also specialises in fish-head curry and other seafood dishes. Rice plates vary from S$4 to S$6 depending on what you choose from the counter, and fish-head curry starts at S$16 for a serve to be shared among a table of diners.

In the same block along Racecourse Rd are some good north Indian restaurants, with typically dark decor. They serve the cheapest, and some of the best, Indian tandoori food in Singapore. *Delhi Restaurant* (Map 5; ☎ 296 4585) at 60 Racecourse Rd has Mughlai and Kashmiri food, with curries from S$5 to S$12. Expect to pay around S$20 per person for a substantial meal with bread and side dishes. The food is excellent and this restaurant is always popular. If it is full, its sister restaurant a few doors down at No 48, *D' Deli Pubb & Restaurant* (☎ 294 5276), has the same fare with a bar at the front.

Just around the corner is *Andhra Curry* (Map 5; ☎ 293 3935), 41 Kerbau Rd, with tasteful decor in a renovated Peranakan terrace. Inexpensive vegetarian and non-vegetarian set meals are offered for lunch and dinner, but the most popular part of the restaurant is the food stall area in a beer garden setting out the front.

Another cheap north Indian restaurant in Little India is the small *Delhi Restaurant* (run by the same people responsible for the Delhi Restaurant at 60 Racecourse Rd), in the Broadway Hotel (Map 5) at 195 Serangoon Rd. It has curries and kormas for around S$4.50 and breads such as naan. Over at 35 Jalan Besar on the east side of Little India is the little known but very good *Bobby-O Claypot Curry* (Map 5; ☎ 298 5782) which does some wonderful north and south Indian dishes and some Iranian specialities, all without monosodium glutamate (MSG) and at very economical prices.

For cheap Muslim food (chicken biryani for S$3.50, as well as murtabak and fish-head curry), there are a couple of cheap, venerable establishments on North Bridge Rd (Map 5) in the Arab St area, opposite the Sultan Mosque. Each has the year of foundation proudly displayed on its signs out the front. The *Victory* (established 1910) is at 701 North Bridge Rd, the *Zam Zam* (established 1908) is at No 699 and further along at No 791-797 is the *Islamic*. The *Jubilee Classic Restaurant*, 749 North Bridge Rd, slightly more upmarket in renovated and air-conditioned surrounds, serves the same Muslim dishes and a few more at very reasonable prices.

There's a small, basic Indian Muslim place called *OM Moosa Restaurant* (Map 5) under the backpackers' guesthouses at 129 Bencoolen St in the colonial district. It has very good food and specialises in fish dishes, including fish-head curry, but has chicken and vegetable items too. Meals are around S$4 and it's open 24 hours.

In Chinatown, a similarly lively and cheap 24 hour restaurant is the *Tasree Restaurant* (Map 6) at 323 New Bridge Rd, opposite Pearl's Centre.

In the Orchard Rd area, *Maharani* (☎ 235 8840) is on the 5th floor of the Far East Plaza (Map 4), 14 Scotts Rd. It serves north Indian cuisine and both the food and service are good. You can eat well for S$20 per person and lunch buffets are offered on weekends.

The Orchard Rd area also has a vegetarian Woodlands restaurant, the *Bombay Woodlands Restaurant* (Map 4; ☎ 235 2712), B1-01 Tanglin Shopping Centre, 19 Tanglin Rd. The decor is very Orchard Rd and the prices are about three times what you pay in Little India but the buffet lunches are still reasonable value.

Boat Quay has a selection of more expensive north Indian restaurants for dining inside or overlooking the river. *Maharajah* (Map 6; ☎ 535 0122) at No 41 is one of the cheaper options with curries for around S$8 to S$14. A good meal costs S$25 or less per person. The fashionable *Royal Bengal* at No 72 is lavishly decorated in colonial style, as are the staff. The food is not just Bengali, and a meal will cost around S$35. The marginally cheaper *Hazara* is a small 'north Indian frontier restaurant' at No 57, with Indian antiques and efficient service. The food is very good, though the serves are small.

Possibly the best Indian restaurant in town is the *Cashmir* (Map 4; ☎ 735 5506) on the 4th floor of Ngee Ann City at 391 Orchard Rd. Its subtly elegant dining area is enough to win points before you even order your food, while the dishes are touted as 'fine food fit for moghuls'. Biryani rice with mutton is the speciality but prawn masala vies competitively for the title of top dish. A meal for two should not exceed a reasonable S$70.

continued on page 148

PLACES TO EAT

Glossary of Asian Culinary Terms

achar – Indian vegetable pickle
ais kacang – similar to *chendol* but made with evaporated milk instead of coconut milk; also spelt *ice kacang* (Malay/Indonesian)
aloo gobi – potato and cauliflower dish (Indian)
ayam goreng – Malay fried chicken

bak chang – local rice dumpling filled with savoury or sweet meat and wrapped in leaves
bak choy – variety of Chinese cabbage that grows like celery, with long white stalks and dark green leaves
bak kutteh – local pork rib soup which has hints of garlic and Chinese five spices
beef rendang – beef stewed with spices and coconut milk (Malay/Indonesian)
belacan – fermented prawn paste used as a condiment
belacan kankong – green vegetables stir-fried in prawn paste
biryani – a north Indian dish of rice and meat, seafood or vegetables
brinjal – aubergine or eggplant (Indian)

carrot cake – omelette-like dish made from radishes, egg, garlic and chilli; also known as *chye tow kway*
chapati – griddle-fried wholewheat bread (Indian)
char siew – sweet roasted pork fillet
chendol – local dessert, which is a cone of ice shavings topped with coloured syrups, brown sugar syrup and coconut milk filled with red beans, attap seeds and jelly
cheng ting – dessert consisting of a bowl of sugar syrup with bits of herbal jelly, barley and dates (Chinese)
chicken rice – dish where the rice is cooked in a clay casserole with pieces of chicken, Chinese mushroom, Chinese sausage and soy sauce; also known as claypot rice
chilli padi – variety of small chilli which is extremely hot
choi sum – popular Chinese green vegetable, served steamed with oyster sauce
chye tow kway – see carrot cake
claypot rice – see chicken rice
congee – Chinese porridge

daun kunyit – turmeric leaf (Malay)
dhal – a dish of pureed lentils (Indian)
dhosas – light, crispy jumbo-sized pancakes brimming with potatoes, onions and spices (Indian)
dian xin – called *dim sum* in Cantonese; refers to Chinese sweet and savoury buns, dumplings and mini-dishes served at breakfast and lunch
dim sum – see *dian xin*
dow see – fermented, salted black beans (Chinese)

es avocado – chilled avocado shake (Malay/Indonesian)
es delima – dessert of water chestnut in sago and coconut milk (Malay/Indonesian)

GLENN BEANLAND

Shark's fin soup, a Cantonese speciality.

GLENN BEANLAND

Gongbao jiding *is the most famous Szechuan dish.*

GLENN BEANLAND

Eggplant, raita *and* chapatti, *a simple Indian meal.*

Prawn sambal, *a Malaysian dish.*

Nasi lemak, *a typical Malaysian breakfast.*

Cucumber pickle, a Nonya condiment.

fish-head curry – red snapper in curry sauce; a famous Singapore Indian dish

fish sauce – liquid made from fermented anchovies and salt; used widely in South-East Asian cooking

gado gado – cold dish of bean sprouts, potatoes, long beans, *tempeh*, bean curd, rice cakes and prawn crackers, topped with a spicy peanut sauce (Malay/Indonesian)

galangal – ginger-like root used to flavour various dishes

garam masala – sweet, mild mixture of freshly ground spices, usually black peppercorns, coriander seeds, cumin seeds, cloves and black cardamom (Indian)

gari – pickled ginger (Japanese)

garoupa – white fish popular in South-East Asia

gathat – large pan, similar to a Chinese wok (Indian)

ghee – clarified butter used for cooking (Indian)

gingko nut – meaty nut used in soups and desserts, or roasted and chopped for sauces, salads and meat dishes

gula jawa – brown palm sugar sold in thin blocks (Malay)

gulab jumun – fried milk balls in sugar syrup (Indian)

Hainanese chicken rice – local speciality; chicken dish served with spring onions and ginger dressing, soup and rice boiled in chicken or coconut oil

halal – food that has been prepared according to Muslim dietary laws

hoisin sauce – thick seasoning sauce made from soybeans, red beans, sugar, flour, vinegar, salt, garlic, sesame, chillies and spices; sweet-spicy and tangy in flavour (Chinese)

Hokkien mee – yellow noodles which are fried with sliced meat, boiled squid, prawns and garnished with strips of fried egg (Chinese)

hokkigai – surf clam (Japanese)

hotategai – scallop (Japanese)

idli – steamed rice cake (Indian)

ikan bilis – small deep-fried sardines (Malay/Indonesian)

kaen cud – soup (Thai)

kaen paad – curry (Thai)

kaen phet kai – hot chicken curry (Thai)

kai tom kha – lemon grass chicken soup with coconut milk (Thai)

kang kong – water convolvulus, thick-stemmed type of spinach (Chinese)

kari ayam – curried chicken (Malay/Indonesian)

kecap – soy sauce (Indonesian/Malay)

keema – spicy minced meat (Indian)

kemiri – candle-nut; waxy nut similar to macadamia (Malay/Indonesian)

kepala ikan – fish-head, usually in a curry or grilled (Malay/Indonesian)

khao – rice (Thai)

Kobe beef – fat-marbled, top quality Japanese beef produced from hand-reared, milk-fed cattle

kofta – minced meat or vegetable ball (Indian)

korma – mild Indian curry with yoghurt sauce

kueh mueh – Malay cakes
kway teow – local broad rice noodles (Chinese)

laksa – local spicy coconut soup of thin white noodles garnished with bean sprouts, quail eggs, prawns, shredded chicken and dried bean curd; also called *Nonya laksa* to differentiate it from *Penang laksa*, which has no coconut milk and a prawn paste-based gravy
laos – see *galangal*
larb – minced chicken or pork flavoured with spices, herbs and lime (Thai)
lassi – yoghurt-based drink (Indian)
lemon grass – called *takari* in Thai and *sereh* in Indonesian, it has long, spear-shaped, grass-like leaves; the taste of the stalk is a strong lemon-citrus
lombok – type of hot chilli (Malay)
lontong – rice cakes in a spicy coconut-milk gravy topped with grated coconut and sometimes bean curd and egg (Malay/Indonesian)
lor mee – local dish of noodles served with slices of meat, eggs and a dash of vinegar in a dark brown sauce

maki – rice hand-rolled in seaweed (Japanese)
mee pok – flat noodles made with egg and wheat (Chinese)
mee rebus – yellow noodles served in a thick sweetish sauce made from sweet potatoes, garnished with sliced hard-boiled eggs and green chillies (Malay)
mee siam – white thin noodles in a sourish and sweet gravy, made with tamarind (Malay)
mee soto – noodle soup with shredded chicken (Malay)
mi krob – crisp, thin noodles with shrimp, egg and sweet and sour sauce (Thai)
miso – a paste made from cooked fermented soybeans (Japanese)
morel – mushroom of *genus Morcella*
mulligatawny – spicy beef soup (Indian)
murgh – chicken (Indian)
murtabak – *roti prata* which has been filled with pieces of mutton, chicken or vegetables (Indian)

naan – tear-shaped leavened bread baked inside a clay oven (Indian)
nasi biryani – saffron rice which has been flavoured with spices and garnished with cashew nuts, almonds and raisins (Malay/ Indonesian)
nasi goreng – fried rice (Indonesian)
nasi lemak – rice which has been boiled in coconut milk (Malay)
nasi padang – term referring to Malay rice and the accompanying meat and vegetable dishes (Malay)

pak krasan – leafy cabbage-like legume unique to Thailand
pakora – vegetable fritter (Indian)
phrik – chillies (Thai)
pilau – rice fried in ghee and mixed with nuts, then cooked in stock
pla thot sam rot – fried garoupa with sweet and sour sauce (Thai)
poo paad gari – curried crab (Thai)
popiah – vegetarian rice cakes
poppadom – Indian cracker

raita – side dish of cucumber, yoghurt and mint used to cool the palate (Indian)
rendang – spicy Indonesian coconut curry with beef or chicken
rijstaffel – literally 'rice table'; a buffet of Indonesian dishes (Dutch)
rogan gosh – stewed mutton in a rich sauce (Indian)
roti prata – flat round pancake-like bread (Indian)

saag – spicy chopped spinach dish (Indian)
sake – Japanese rice wine
salam – plant the leaves of which are used much like bay leaves in cooking (Malay)
sambal – sauce of chilli, onions and prawn paste which has been fried (Malay)
sambar – fiery mixture of vegetables, lentils and split peas (Indian)
santen – coconut milk (Malay)
sashimi – raw fish served in slices, accompanied by *wasabi*, pickled ginger and soy sauce (Japanese)
satay – pieces of chicken, beef or mutton which are skewered onto wood sticks and grilled (Malay/Indonesian)
shabu-shabu – Japanese version of hot pot or steamboat
som sa – citrus fruit unique to Thailand
soto ayam – spicy chicken soup with vegetable and potatoes
steamboat – style of cooking in which meats, seafood and vegetables are dipped into a pot of boiling clear stocks and cooked at the table (Teochew Chinese)

tandoori – Indian style of cooking in which marinated meat is baked in a clay oven
taro – vegetable with leaves like spinach, stalks like asparagus and a starchy root similar in size and taste to the potato
tau hui – by-product of soybean, served as a local dessert with sugar syrup
teh tarek – local tea made with evaporated milk, which is literally 'pulled' or 'stretched' from one glass to another
tempeh – preserved soybeans which have been deep-fried (Malay)
teppanyaki – chicken, beef and seafood grilled on a hotplate (Japanese)
thali – buffet of rice, curried vegetables, soup, curries and bread (Indian)
tikka – small pieces of meat and fish served off the bone and marinated in yoghurt before baking (Indian)
tofu – soybean cake (Japanese)
tom yum kung – hot and sour, spicy seafood soup (Thai)

vindaloo – fiery Indian vinegar-based curry

won ton mee – a soup dish with shredded chicken or braised beef

yakitori – meat, chicken or vegetable satays glazed with sweet soy and mirin sauce (Japanese)
yam – Thai word for 'salad'; *yam nua* is the popular Thai beef salad
yu char kway – deep-fried Chinese bread sticks
yu tiao – deep-fried pastry eaten for breakfast or as a dessert

zensai – Japanese appetisers

continued from page 143
MALAY & INDONESIAN
Though Malay food is easy to find throughout Singapore, dedicated Malay restaurants are far from abundant. The occasional stall or two at some of the food centres serves Malay food, and satay is easily found. Indonesian food shares many similarities with Malay cuisine, though some dishes such as gado gado are uniquely Indonesian.

The Orchard Rd area has a number of good restaurants. *Bintang Timur* (Map 4; ☎ 235 4539), 02-13 Far East Shopping Centre, 14 Scotts Rd, has excellent Malay food at excellent prices. You can try a good range of dishes and eat your fill for S$20 or less. *Tambuah Mas* (Map 4; ☎ 733 2220), 04-10/13 Tanglin Shopping Centre, 19 Tanglin Rd, is cheap and has a good selection of seafood dishes and Indonesian favourites, such as rendang, gado gado and chendol. Another good Indonesian restaurant is *Sanur* (Map 4; ☎ 734 2192), 04-17/18 Centrepoint, 176 Orchard Rd. Most mains are S$7 to S$10 and range up to S$20 for whole fish.

Pancha Sari (Map 6; ☎ 338 1032), 03-239 Marina Square, is a reasonably priced Indonesian restaurant in the colonial district. Most mains cost from S$6 to S$10 and you can eat well for under S$20.

If you like the fiery food of north Sumatra, there are a few nasi padang specialists, the best known being *Rendezvouz*, 02-19 in the Raffles City Shopping Centre (Map 6) on Bras Basah Rd in the colonial district. The good and cheap *Rumah Makan Minang* (Map 5) is at the corner of Muscat and Kandahar Sts, behind the Sultan Mosque on Arab St, in a renovated shophouse.

Slap-bang in the middle of Peranakan Place is *Chilli Buddys* (Map 4; ☎ 732 9108) at 180 Orchard Rd and home to the 'hottest in and outdoor restaurant'. Chilli Buddys specialises in, well, chillis and the menu features a good selection of chilli-style dishes and also lists a whole bunch of fascinating stories about chillis. A mean, chilli-laced nasi goreng will set you back about S$13.50.

House of Sundanese Food (Map 8; ☎ 345 5020), 218 East Coast Rd, specialises in west Javanese cuisine. Try a number of dishes, nasi padang-style, many of which cost around S$4. The chicken dishes are particularly good, or try the charcoal-grilled whole fish for around S$20. There is also a branch at 55 Boat Quay, but it is not as good as the one on East Coast Rd.

The Geylang district in the east coast area has plenty of Malay eateries. For Malay food stalls during the day, go to the *Geylang Serai Market* (Map 8) on Changi Rd. This is the predominantly Malay area in Singapore, and it's worth a visit just to see the market, which is more traditional than the new complexes. To get there, take the MRT to Paya Lebar station and walk east along Sims Ave to Geylang Serai.

About 1km from Geylang Serai Market, *Casa Bom Vento* (Map 8; ☎ 348 7786), 467 Joo Chiat Rd, is an interesting restaurant serving Eurasian food, which is a mixed cuisine basically Malay in origin with a Portuguese bent. Try the beef smor (pepper steak) or the debal (devil curry), a traditional post-Christmas dish of leftover meats and vegetables cooked up in a fiery curry. Mains cost around S$6 to S$10.

More expensive is *Azizas Restaurant* (Map 5; ☎ 235 1140), 180 Albert St, just south of Little India. It serves authentic Malay meals and is regarded as one of Singapore's top Malay restaurants.

NONYA
For a description of Nonya cuisine see the Peranakan special section on page 18.

The *Nonya & Baba Restaurant* (Map 6; ☎ 734 1382) is one of the best restaurants in which to try Nonya food at reasonable prices. Most mains cost from around S$6 for small claypots up to S$15 for large serves. A variety of snacks and sweets are also available. It is at 262-4 River Valley Rd, near the corner of Tank Rd, west of Fort Canning Park. Dhoby Ghaut MRT station is a 15 minute walk away.

In Holland Village (Map 7), west of the city, the *Baba Cafe* (☎ 468 9859), at 25B

Lorong Liput, has good value food in an attractive setting.

In Chinatown, *Blue Ginger* (Map 6; ☎ 222 3928), 97 Tanjong Pagar Rd, is a trendy two storey shophouse serving authentic Nonya food at realistic prices. There is an impressive range of menu items including ikan masak assam gulai, a tamarind-flavoured fish curry which should be tried. Dinner for two is around S$60 and the crowd is mainly young business people and expats.

One of the other good places to go for Nonya food is east of the city in the Geylang and Katong districts. *Guan Hoe Soon* (Map 8; ☎ 344 2761), 214 Joo Chiat Rd, is a long-running, moderately priced restaurant noted for its Nonya dishes. Though air-conditioned it's really just a glorified coffee shop.

The *Peranakan Inn* (Map 8; ☎ 440 6194), 210 East Coast Rd, is one of the cheapest places in Singapore to eat Nonya food in an air-con setting. Most dishes cost S$4 to S$6, and more expensive seafood dishes are around S$15.

The *Hok Tong Hin Restaurant* (Map 8), at the corner of East Coast and Ceylon Rds, is a hawker-style coffee shop where you can get a superb laksa for only S$2.50. The *Carlton Restaurant* (Map 8), at the corner of East Coast Rd and Lorong Stangee, is similar.

During the day, try the Nonya kueh (Nonya cakes) and curry puffs at the *Katong Bakery & Confectionery* (Map 8; ☎ 344 8948), 75 East Coast Rd. This is a wonderful, old-fashioned bakery and cake shop, a real throwback to the Singapore of yesteryear. If you prefer more sanitised surroundings, East Coast Rd also has plenty of new cake shops for takeaways.

SINGAPOREAN

Surprisingly there is only one place that calls itself a 'Singaporean' restaurant and that is *Ah Hoi's Kitchen* (☎ 831 4373) in the Traders Hotel (Map 4) at 1A Cuscaden Rd, just off the west end of Orchard Rd. The establishment has a coffee shop setting and dishes run from stingray in chilli sauce to belacan kangkong. It's a casual laid-back place but a bit on the pricey side nonetheless.

OTHER ASIAN CUISINE
Burmese

If you fancy something different, the *Beautiful Myanmar Restaurant* (Map 6; ☎ 222 1665) at 11 Mosque St in Chinatown is a small, friendly and modern establishment that caters for mainly Burmese clients Its house speciality is Yangon dun bouk (golden rice with a choice of meats). Also worth ordering is the spicy and supposedly very healthy mjin khwa thoke salad full of green chillis, vegetables and crunchies. You can eat well for under S$20, beer included.

Japanese

While you can spend a small fortune at a Japanese restaurant, you can also find food at moderate prices.

The *Cold Storage supermarket* in the Takashimaya department store at Ngee Ann City (Map 4), Orchard Rd, has a great takeaway bar for sushi and sashimi at very low prices. Also in Takashimaya, *Nogawa* (☎ 735 9918) on the 4th floor is a reasonably priced Japanese restaurant with sushi from S$4 and mains for around S$15 to S$18.

A few food courts also have teppanyaki grills with a dining bar. *Sumo* in the basement at Parco Bugis Junction centre (Map 5) in the colonial district, does grills for around S$6 to S$10, as well as S$15 set meals. *Teppanyaki Place*, in the food court at the Tanglin Mall (Map 4) on the corner of Tanglin and Napier Rds, has set meals from S$6.90 and grills at S$16 for two.

Small Japanese restaurants displaying plastic-glazed meals in the window can be found all around Singapore. *Restaurant Hoshigaoka* is a chain of Japanese restaurants, with branches at 03-45 Centrepoint (Map 4) and 01-18 Wisma Atria (Map 4) on Orchard Rd, and 03-237 Marina Square (Map 6). Small set meals, such as tempura and sushi, cost around S$20.

Izumi (Map 6; ☎ 534 3390), 48 Boat Quay, is a more expensive option but worth it. Cheaper set dinners for S$30 are also available.

For top-of-the-range Japanese food, try the *Keyaki* (☎ 434 8335) in the Pan Pacific

More Recommended Eating

Two English expatriates, who have spent much of the last six years eating their way round Singapore's various hawker centres, coffee shops and restaurants, offer the following as places always worth going back to (in no particular order):

Esmirada (Map 4; ☎ 735 3476), Peranakan Place. A Greek-influenced place that does excellent salads (S$14.50 for a Greek salad big enough to share) and barbecued meat/vegetable skewers. Reservations are recommended at weekends.

Q Hue (Map 7; ☎ 471 6501), Pasir Panjang Rd, 200m south-east of Haw Par Villa. Great for wine and Spanish tapas served in a pleasant outdoor courtyard.

Paulaner Bräuhaus Restaurant & Microbrewery, Wheelock Place (Map 4; ☎ 737 8884) on Orchard Rd and also Millenia Walk (Map 6; ☎ 337 7130) on Temasek Blvd. German cuisine; try the pork knuckle or sausage platter – delicious and excellent value at S$20 each. The beer is made on the premises.

Cha Cha Cha (Map 7; ☎ 462 1650), 32 Lor Mambong, Holland Village. A Mexican restaurant popular with expats and young Singaporeans. Go for the beef burritos (S$12) followed by strawberry margaritas.

Jumbo Seafood (☎ 442 3435), 1206 East Coast Parkway, at the UDMC Seafood Centre (Map 8). It has an excellent and deserved reputation for reasonably priced seafood – which means it's usually crowded even when next door is empty.

Wee Nam Kee (Map 6; ☎ 256 4051), 275 Thomson Rd, opposite Novena MRT. A typical, traditional coffee shop that does excellent Hainanese chicken rice, dumplings, lemon chicken and hotplate beancurd. Two people can eat well for S$25.

Komala Vilas (Map 5; ☎ 293 6980) on Upper Dickson St or *Madras New Woodlands* (Map 5; ☎ 297 1594) on Buffalo Rd, both off Serangoon Rd. Two great cheap 'n' cheerful, vegetarian south Indian places where you can eat for under S$6 a head.

Istanbul Corner (Map 4), 5 Koek Rd, off Orchard Rd. Cheap Turkish fare (S$6 to S$12 per dish) with a clientele of Turks and local tourists. Try the fattoush, humous with pitta bread or lamb shwarma.

Kopitiam Food Court, Le Meridien Singapore (Map 4), Orchard Rd. A 24 hour coffee house-style food court with over 53 stalls. Try the sizzling hotplate stall or Macpherson's BBQ Seafood for fresh crab.

Michelangelo's Restaurant (Map 7; ☎ 475 9069), 60 Jalan Merah Saga, Holland Village. Serves a sort of hybrid Australian-Italian cuisine, with excellent seafood pasta, spinach salad, lamb and a good (though pricey) selection of wines. It's definitely worth a splurge for the consistent high quality of the food. Reservations are recommended.

David & Pamela Humphreys

Singapore Hotel (Map 6) on Raffles Blvd, east of the Padang. Dinner here will cost anywhere between S$80 and S$150 depending on what you have. Kobe beef is one of the house specialities.

Korean

Seoul Garden is a Korean chain with branches at 05-01 Shaw Centre (Map 4), 1 Scotts Rd, in the Orchard Rd area, and 03-119 Marina Square (Map 6) in the colonial district, among others. The Korean BBQ set lunches for around S$12 and the slightly more expensive set dinners are excellent value.

Tanjong Pagar Rd in Chinatown also has a number of Korean restaurants, and Clarke Quay has riverside Korean BBQ stalls. The Clarke Quay *towkangs*, refurbished Chinese junks moored on Singapore River, also have Korean and other BBQs. A good feed with beer will cost around S$20.

Korean Restaurant (Map 4; ☎ 235 0018) in the Specialists' Shopping Centre between Orchard Rd and Somerset MRT is considered one of Singapore's best restaurants. Complimentary Korean pickles are served to all diners before the meal and the most popular meal is the US short rib BBQ beef, though there are plenty of other Korean dishes to choose from including the excellent ginseng chicken soup. Lunch will set you back about S$40 a head.

Taiwanese

For Taiwanese food try the reasonably priced *Goldleaf* (Map 6) at 24-24A Tanjong Pagar Rd in Chinatown. A speciality is chicken covered in whole fried chillies. You can eat very well for less than S$20.

Lung Yee Family Restaurant (Map 8) in Katong at 199 East Coast Rd, gets good write-ups in the local press for its home-style Taiwanese fare. Porridge is only S$3 and other dishes you could try are fairy duck, imperial chicken and drunken prawns all at reasonable prices.

Thai

The Golden Mile Complex (Map 5) at 5001 Beach Rd, just north-east of Arab St, is a modern shopping centre catering to Singapore's Thai community. Here you'll find a number of small coffee shops serving Thai food and Singha beer. Prices are cheap – you can get a good meal for S$4 or S$5. If you are willing to pay a little more there's the *Pornping Thai Seafood Restaurant* (☎ 298 5016), which is a notch up in quality, and has a bar and an extensive Thai menu.

Parkway Thai (☎ 737 8080) in Centrepoint (Map 4), 176 Orchard Rd, has an extensive menu – small mains range from S$8 up to S$15 for seafood.

Cuppage Thai Food Restaurant (Map 4; ☎ 734 1116), 49 Cuppage Rd, is not the greatest Thai restaurant but it has set dinners for two at S$28 and S$38, and a pleasant alfresco setting just off Orchard Rd.

Baan Thai (Map 4; ☎ 735 5562), 04-23 Ngee Ann City on Orchard Rd, is one of the better Thai restaurants in Singapore, with good-sized mains for around S$14 to S$20. Try their green curry.

Over in Geylang you will find the best Thai food in this part of the island at *Lemongrass* (Map 8; ☎ 443 1995). The fried fish with home-made sweet Thai sauce is one of its specialities. Prices are in the S$15 to S$20 range for main courses. The restaurant is at 899 East Coast Rd and takes a bit of getting to without a taxi.

The mid-range to expensive *Pimai Thai* (☎ 431 1064) restaurant in the Hotel Intercontinental (Map 5) at 80 Middle Rd is perhaps Singapore's best Thai restaurant. It has a warm, wooden, earthy interior with attentive service. Roasted red curry duck is one of the house specialities, but the menu is large enough to make the choice difficult. Two can eat here for around S$60.

Vietnamese

There are a couple of pretty decent Vietnamese restaurants within striking distance of the Orchard Rd area. First is the *Me Kong Restaurant* (Map 4; ☎ 834 1211) on the 4th floor of Ngee Ann City at 391 Orchard Rd. The ambience is a bit sterile and the restaurant has large windows allowing passers-by to look in, but the food is good. The menu also has plenty of Chinese dishes. Prices are mid-range.

The *Saigon* (Map 4; ☎ 235 0626), 15 Cairnhill Rd, has a more relaxed and casual environment with bamboo and rattan furniture. It's a great place for groups and people looking for a fun night out. There are over 70 Vietnamese dishes on offer with spring rolls and deep-fried soft shell crab being among the most popular. Set meals are available for about S$29 per person.

WESTERN
Fast_Food
Yes, you can get western food in Singapore. There are over 50 *McDonald's*, found all over town. It's good to see that the corporate smile and 'have a nice day' haven't really caught on in Singapore – you can be served with the same brusque efficiency as you would find in any Singaporean coffee shop.

There are also *A&W Restaurants*, *KFC*, *Burger King*, *Dunkin'Donuts*, *Dennys*, *Pizza Hut*, *Baskin Robbins* and *Swensen's Ice Cream* outlets – obviously there's no shortage of western fast food.

French
A number of restaurants do a pretty good job of convincing you that you're in France, even though you're almost on the equator.

La Cascade (Map 6), 7 Ann Siang Hill Rd in Chinatown, is a cheaper French place with set lunches for S$11.80 and set dinners for S$48.

Le Restaurant de France (☎ 733 8855) at Le Meridien Singapore (Map 4), 100 Orchard Rd, is one of the better French restaurants in Singapore. Or, you may like to take a credit card or two to *Maxim's de Paris* in the Regent Hotel (Map 4), 1 Cuscaden Rd. The best value is the dinner buffet for S$95.

Italian
Gone are the days when Italian food was only available at a few super-expensive restaurants or chain stores serving soggy pizza and insipid pasta.

Boat Quay (Map 6) near Chinatown has its fair share of Italian restaurants. One of the best for the money is *Pasta Fresca* (☎ 469 4920) at 30 Boat Quay which has a huge range of authentic pastas from S$10 and small pizzas from S$12 to S$15. It's open 24 hours. This restaurant is part of a chain, which also has an outlet on the 4th floor of Shaw House (Map 4), 350 Orchard Rd.

Neighbouring Boat Quay Italians include *Luna Luna* (☎ 538 2030), which specialises in seafood, and *Al Dente Trattoria* (☎ 536 5366), which serves primarily pasta and pizza.

Sketches (☎ 339 8386) in the Parco Bugis Junction centre (Map 5) at 200 Victoria St is an unusual kind of 'design-your-own' Italian pasta restaurant in which you create your own dish from a tick-off menu. Meals are tasty and cost about S$13.50 for a big pasta creation. It's very close to Bugis MRT station.

Ristorante Bologna (☎ 338 3388), in the Marina Mandarin in the Marina Square complex (Map 6), is one of the best and most expensive Italian restaurants in town.

Other Western Cuisine
Hard Rock Cafe (Map 4; ☎ 235 5232), 50 Cuscaden Rd, near the corner of Orchard and Tanglin Rds, is popular for American-style steaks, BBQ grills and ribs. Main meals cost around S$20, and snacks such as burgers cost around S$8. The restaurant finishes serving around 10.30 pm when the bands start, but there is a small snack bar that stays open.

Planet Hollywood (Map 4; ☎ 732 7827) features a shop, a darkish and freezing-cold air-con bar and a more enticing restaurant with American-style lunch deals for around S$20. It's at 541 Orchard Rd on the ground floor of the Liat Towers.

Bob's Tavern (☎ 467 2419), 17A Lorong Liput, Holland Village (Map 7), to the west of the city, is an English-style pub popular with expats who for some reason miss English food. It serves good steaks, fish and chips etc. Main meals cost around S$20. You can drink at the bar, or dine outside on the veranda.

Steak houses are mostly run by chains such as *Ponderosa* (☎ 336 0139) with branches at 02-232 Marina Square (Map 6); and 02-20 Raffles City Shopping Centre (Map 6). The *Sizzler* chain is also moving into Singapore, but the biggest chain is *Jack's Place* with restaurants all over town, including 03-18/19 Wisma Atria (Map 4), 435 Orchard Rd and 01-01 Bras Basah Complex (Map 5).

Many other cuisines are represented in Singapore. For German food, there is the *Bräuhaus Restaurant & Pub* (Map 4; ☎ 250 3116), United Square, 101 Thomson Rd, to the north of the city centre, and the *Treffpunct Cafe*, B2-09 Tanglin Shopping Centre (Map 4) in the Orchard Rd area, which is a small deli serving German sausages.

The Moomba (Map 6; ☎ 438 0141) at 52 Circular Rd, just behind Boat Quay, is an Australian New Age restaurant that gets the thumbs up from locals and visitors alike. Fusion cuisine is the trend here combining emu or kangaroo with Szechuan sauce or done char siew-style. There is a great selection of Australian wines. Prices are on the high side though.

Istanbul Corner (Map 4), 01-11 Cuppage Plaza, 5 Koek Rd, right near the corner of Orchard Rd, is one of the few Middle Eastern restaurants in Singapore and it's pretty cheap.

Olea (Map 7) at 833 Bukit Timah Rd near Holland Park serves Greek food. The menu is comprehensive but prices are a bit on the high side.

El Felipes Cantina (☎ 468 1520), 34 Lorong Mambong in Holland Village (Map 7), is an old favourite that has large serves and moderate prices. Tex Mex dishes cost around S$12 to S$15, and innovative mains with a Spanish touch are slightly more expensive. Next door, the similar *Cha Cha Cha* (☎ 462 1650), 32 Lorong Mambong, is the most popular Mexican restaurant in town, as much for the margaritas as the good food.

Alkaff Mansion (Map 3; ☎ 278 6979), west of the city at 10 Telok Blangah Green, has ambience plus-plus-plus. It's a restored old mansion offering Dutch rijsttafel (rice table) with an endless parade of dishes served with a touch of colonial theatre for a whopping S$65. It's popular with tour groups. Much cheaper but still allowing you to take in the serene surroundings and the graciousness of the mansion is high tea for S$18 and the western and Asian buffets which cost S$28 for lunch and S$35 for dinner.

A few of the places mentioned in the Entertainment chapter also do good food, notably *Brewerkz*, the *Saxophone Bar & Grill* and *JP Bastiani's*.

BREAKFAST, SNACKS & DELIS

The big international hotels have their large international breakfast buffets (from around S$20 to S$25), of course, but there are still a few old coffee shops which do cheap Chinese and Indian breakfasts – take your pick of dhosas and curry or yu-tiao and hot soy milk.

Roti chanai with a mild curry dip is a delicious and economical breakfast available at the *OM Moosa Restaurant* (Map 5), 129 Bencoolen St in the colonial district. Most of the old coffee shops can rustle up toast and kaya (egg and coconut jam) without too much difficulty.

There are many places which do a fixed-price breakfast – Continental or American. Try the *Silver Spoon Coffee House* at B1-05 Park Mall (Map 4), 9 Penang Rd, immediately south of Dhoby Ghaut MRT station.

The *Golden Dragon Inn* (Map 5) on Bencoolen St is a Chinese coffee shop on the 2nd floor of the Fortune Centre that does a reasonable job of western grills. If you crave cholesterol for breakfast, ham and eggs costs only S$3, and later in the day steak or prawns with chips and eggs served on a sizzler costs S$6.

One of the nicest breakfasts is undoubtedly *Breakfast with the Birds* (☎ 265 0022) at Jurong Bird Park (Map 7), to the west of the city. The buffet breakfast costs about S$12 (admission is extra) – the waffles are great.

For western-style pastries, head for the *Café d'Orient de Délifrance* (Map 4) at Peranakan Place on Orchard Rd – the croissants and coffee here are hard to beat. This is the original store with the best setting, but you can find branches everywhere in Singapore.

Old Chang Kee is a chain that specialises in that old favourite, curry puffs. There is one at the Lau Pa Sat Festival Market (Map 6) and another at the corner of MacKenzie and Niven Rds, near Selegie Rd. Opposite the

Drinks

Life can be thirsty in Singapore, so you'll be relieved to hear that drinks are excellent, economical and readily available.

There are a wide variety of soft drinks from Coca-Cola, Pepsi, 7Up and Fanta to a variety of F&N flavours, including sarsaparilla (for root beer fans). Soft drinks generally cost around S$1.

You can also find those fruit-juice-in-a-box drinks all over town, with both normal fruit flavours and oddities like chrysanthemum tea.

Beer drinkers will probably find Anchor Beer or Tiger Beer to their taste, although the minimum price for a large bottle of beer is at least S$8. Travelling Irish may be surprised to find that Guinness has a considerable following in Singapore – in part because the Chinese believe it has a strong medicinal value and in part because it has a higher alcohol content than beer. ABC Stout is a cheaper local equivalent.

Sipping coffee or tea in a Chinese cafe is a time-honoured pursuit at any time of the day or night. If you want your tea, which the Chinese and Malays make very well, without the added thickening of condensed milk, ask for *teh-o*. Shout it – as it's another of those words which cannot be said quietly. If you also don't want sugar, you have to ask for *teh-o kosong*, but you're unlikely to get it as the Singaporeans simply cannot believe anyone would drink tea that way.

Fruit juices are popular and very good. With the aid of a blender and crushed ice, delicious concoctions like watermelon juice can be whipped up in seconds. Old fashioned sugarcane crushers, which look like grandma's old washing mangle, can still be seen in operation. Most food centres have a fruit stall, which serves juice in a glass or in a plastic bag to take away.

Half-way between a drink and a dessert are *chendol* and *ais kacang*. An ais (ice) kacang is rather like an old-fashioned sno cone but the shaved ice is topped with syrup and condensed milk, and it's all piled on top of a foundation of beans and jellies. It tastes terrific!

Chendol is somewhat similar, with shaved ice, coconut milk and funny, gooey green noodles.

Other oddities? Well, the milky, white drink in clear plastic bins at drink sellers is soybean milk, which is also available in soft-drink bottles. Medicinal teas are popular with the health-minded Chinese.

At juice stalls, pick your fruit, or fruit combination, and it's whipped up into a drink before you.

TONY WHEELER

Old Chang Kee, the *Selera Restaurant*, at 15 MacKenzie Rd, has even better curry puffs – possibly the best in town. Try its range, washed down with coffee in an old-style kopi tiam.

Singapore has plenty of delis that cater for lunching office workers and snacking shoppers. In the Orchard Rd area, *Aroma's Deli*, 01-05 Tanglin Shopping Centre (Map 4) on Tanglin Rd, has good coffee and a changing deli menu. *Seah Street Deli* at Raffles Hotel (Map 6) is slightly misnamed. This is Singapore's answer to a New York deli – pastrami, bagels and rye at higher than average prices but still excellent.

HIGH TEA

Most of the coffee shops in the big hotels do 'high tea', featuring local cakes and snacks and all the tea or coffee you can drink. They are usually buffet affairs held in the afternoon, around 4 pm, of course, and can be good value as well as delightful eating experiences. Add 14% in taxes to the following prices.

Cafe Oriental (Map 6) in the Amara Hotel near Chinatown has a Nonya buffet, one of the most popular cuisines for high tea, for S$10 from 3 to 6 pm during the week.

The *Coffee Lounge* at the exclusive Goodwood Park Hotel (Map 4), in the Orchard Rd area, has a good Nonya kueh buffet from 3 to 5.30 pm for S$13.80. The *Cafe Espresso*, also at the Goodwood Park Hotel, has an English high tea for S$18.50.

The *Bar & Billiard Room* at the Raffles (Map 6) has high tea from 3.30 to 5 pm featuring Asian and Continental food. Though expensive at S$25, it is affordable for Raffles.

Coleman's Cafe in the Peninsula Hotel (Map 6), just north of the Padang, is particularly good value at S$7.50 for a range of savoury hawker favourites, but it's available only on Saturday from 3.15 to 6 pm.

The *Kaspia Bar* at the Hilton International (Map 4) on Orchard Rd does a good English high tea from 3 to 6 pm weekdays. Buttered crumpets, scones with jam and cream, sandwiches and cheeses are featured. It costs S$16.50.

The *Melting Pot Cafe* at the Concorde Hotel (Map 6), west of Chinatown, has the longest high tea in town – from noon to 5 pm weekends – for an afternoon of decadence costing S$13.80.

FRUIT

If you're already addicted to tropical fruit, Singapore is a great place to indulge your passion. If you've not yet been initiated, there could hardly be a better place in the world to develop a taste for exotic flavours. In Singapore, the places to go for an easy introduction are the fruit stalls which you'll find in food centres or sometimes on the streets.

Slices of a variety of fruits (including those dull old apples and oranges) are laid out on ice in a colourful and mouthwatering display from which you can make a selection for just 30c and up. You can also have a fruit salad made up on the spot from as many fruits as you care to choose. Some tastes to sample include:

Durian The region's most infamous fruit, the durian is a large oval fruit about 25cm to 30cm long, although it often grows larger. The durian is renowned for its phenomenal smell, a stink so powerful that first-timers are often forced to hold their noses while they taste.

When the hardy, spiny shell is cracked open, pale white-green segments are revealed with a taste as distinctive as the smell. Durians are so highly esteemed that great care is taken over their selection and you'll see gourmets feeling them carefully, sniffing them reverently and finally demanding a preliminary taste before purchasing.

Mangosteen One of the finest tropical fruits, the mangosteen is about the size of a small orange or apple. The dark purple outer skin breaks open to reveal pure white segments shaped like orange segments but with a sweet-sour flavour which has been compared to a combination of strawberries and grapes.

Nangka/Jackfruit This enormous watermelon-sized fruit hangs from trees and when opened breaks up into a large number of bright orange-yellow segments with a slightly rubbery texture. Externally, the nangka is covered by a green pimply skin, but it's too big and too messy to clean to make buying a whole one worthwhile.

Papaya Originating in Central America the papaya, or pawpaw, is about 30cm or so in length and the bright orange flesh is somewhat similar in texture and appearance to pumpkin but related in taste to a melon. The numerous black seeds in the centre are said to have a contraceptive effect if eaten by women.

Pomelo This large grapefruit-cross is the most common citrus fruit in South-East Asia. It has a thick, yellowish skin and a pink flesh that is sweeter than grapefruit.

Rambutan In Malay, the name means 'spiny'. Rambutans are the size of a large walnut or small tangerine and they're covered in soft red spines. You peel the skin away to reveal a very close cousin to the lychee with cool and mouthwatering flesh around a central stone.

Starfruit Known in Malaysia as blimbing, the starfruit takes its name from the fruit's cross-sectional star shape. A translucent green-yellow in colour, starfruit has a crisp, cool and watery taste.

Zirzat Sometimes known as soursop or white mango, the zirzat has a warty green outer covering and is ripe and ready to eat when it begins to look slightly off – the fresh green skin begins to look blackish and the feel becomes slightly squishy. Inside, the creamy white flesh has a deliciously thirst-quenching flavour with a hint of lemon.

SUPERMARKETS

Singapore has plenty of supermarkets selling everything from French wine and Australian beer to yoghurt, muesli, cheese and ice cream. *Cold Storage* is one of largest supermarket chains, with well-stocked supermarkets in the basements of Takashimaya at Ngee Ann City and Centrepoint, both on Orchard Rd (Map 4). Another is at Parco Bugis Junction (Map 5) on Victoria St in the colonial district. There is also an excellent French supermarket, called *Carrefour*, at Suntec City (Map 6) which is so big that the staff go round on rollerblades.

For late-night groceries, *Smart*, on the northern side of the Marina Square complex (Map 6), is open 24 hours. You'll find *7-Eleven* stores (which are also open 24 hours) all over town including at 75 Victoria St, in the colonial district, and on Orchard Rd in Centrepoint (Map 4).

Entertainment

Singapore's nightlife is burgeoning, as the young middle class spends its increasing wealth on entertainment. It's not of the Bangkok 'sex and sin' variety, nor does a wild club scene exist, but the huge number of bars and discos are becoming increasingly sophisticated. Pool, wine and cigars are now cool.

Boat Quay is packed nightly until the early hours of the morning, but Orchard Rd and Chinatown also have their fair share of good bars. Smoking is permitted in bars, though if food is also served all smoking is restricted until after meal times.

The live music scene in the bars is less healthy. It's very limited with few venues and only a small roster of bands and performers. For better bands, you have to go to the clubs and discos, where a cover charge normally applies. At such places dress is smart casual, drinks are expensive and the bands mostly play covers. Almost every four star hotel has a Filipino band playing in the lobby, every five star hotel has a jazz band, and even many three star hotels can muster up a piano.

Highbrow entertainment such as classical music, ballet and theatre can also be enjoyed in Singapore, as well as Chinese opera and tourist-oriented cultural shows.

The free tourist magazines and the local newspapers have limited entertainment sections. The *Straits Times* is good for cultural and special events, while *Eight Days*, the weekly television and entertainment magazine, has the best listings. For nightlife look out for the free, twice-monthly *I-S Magazine*.

BARS, BANDS & DISCOS
The time to drink is during happy hour, which is usually from around 5 to 8 or even 9 pm. At these times drinks are as cheap as half price. Most of the bars also serve food and serious drinking is done outside meal times, but you can grab a stool at the bar anytime.

Many bars feature bands. With live music imports still dominate – mostly Filipino bands but occasionally western musicians – playing jazz, pop covers, old favourites or, just occasionally, something more risqué like the blues.

Singapore has hardcore bands like Stompin' Ground, but they won't be playing on Orchard Rd. It is difficult to see original Singaporean performers singing about life in the Housing Development Board (HDB) estates, or dissatisfaction with the oppressive nature of Singaporean society, but they do exist and Singaporean music is developing its own identity.

Popular artists such as Dick Lee and Kopi Kat Klan laid the foundation for performing songs with Asian themes delivered in a Singaporean voice.

The best place to see local pop performers is probably *Substation* (see Theatre later in this chapter); call to see what's on.

Singapore has no shortage of discos. They tend to be big on decor and are yuppie hang-outs with strict dress codes. A few dance party clubs exist but they are fairly tame. A cover charge of around S$15 to S$20 applies on weekdays and S$25 to S$35 on weekends. Women often pay less.

Some venues don't have a cover charge, but drinks are expensive and you can expect to pay around S$10 for a glass of beer. Those that do have a cover charge usually include the first drink free. For most venues, 10% service charge and 4% government tax are added to the drinks and the cover charge.

Orchard Rd (Map 4)
The Orchard Rd area is still the main centre for nightlife, with a host of bars and pubs mainly in the hotels and hidden away in the shopping centres.

One of the biggest discos, *Fire*, 04-19 Orchard Plaza, 150 Orchard Rd, is teenage techno heaven. The cover charge is S$12 for girls (S$21 on weekends), S$15 for boys

(S\$24 on weekends). Under the same management and the favourite in Singapore at the moment is *Sparks*, level 7, Ngee Ann City. The dance floor jumps to the biggest music system in town, and everything stops for the dazzling laser show. For something quieter in the same complex, try the *Jazz Evergreen*. The *World Music Bar* also gets some interesting bands. Cover charges range from S\$15 during the week to S\$25 on weekends.

Orchard Towers, 400 Orchard Rd, has a concentration of venues. It has been tagged the 'Four Floors of Whores', which, though there are a few bar girls, makes it sound more risqué than it actually is. *Top Ten* on the 4th floor is a large barn of a place with Manhattan skyline decor and an affluent clientele. It is primarily a disco but a band alternates brackets. Entry costs S\$22 on Friday, S\$28 on Saturday and S\$17 for the rest of the week. *Ginivy*, on the 2nd floor of Orchard Towers, has two types of music – country and western. It's a casual place with middle-aged cowboys and a smattering of bar girls. In a similar vein, but smaller and quieter, is *FB's* on the 3rd floor, featuring football and Foster's.

If you fancy yet another Irish pub with expensive pints of Guinness or Kilkenny then *Muddy Murphy's* in the basement of the Orchard Hotel Shopping Centre is a handy hangout for Celtic expats. The top bar is narrow and smokey and only opens in the evening.

Anywhere, 04-08 Tanglin Shopping Centre, 19 Tanglin Rd, is a long-running rock 'n' roll venue. The band, Tania, has been playing here since 1981 and features a cross-dressing lead singer. The band has a regular following of mostly expats and can belt out a song when they try. This place has a casual, convivial atmosphere and no cover charge.

Hard Rock Cafe, 50 Cuscaden Rd, has the usual rock memorabilia and good atmosphere. It has better bands than most venues – including one of the best Singapore bands, Jive Talk – and occasionally imports some big names from overseas. The music and cover charge starts, and the ash trays come out, after 10.30 pm when the dining stops. Entry is S\$15 (free on Sunday) – otherwise get there early. It stays open until around 2 or 3 am.

Opposite the Hard Rock Cafe in the basement of the Ming Arcade, *Cave Man* is a cool little bar with graffiti everywhere and modern music on the jukebox. Not a lot happens, but it's a casual bar for conversation. The *Makati*, on the 7th floor, is a large, smokey Filipino disco with no cover charge.

Brannigan's, in the Hyatt Regency, is a popular, casual pick-up spot, with a mixed clientele and its fair share of bar girls. Good bands play until 1 or 2 am, and happy hour is from 5 to 8 pm. It is packed on weekends.

Emerald Hill Rd has a collection of bars in the renovated terraces just up from Orchard Rd. *No 5* at, you guessed it, 5 Emerald Hill Rd, is very popular with a largely tourist clientele and its chilli vodka has a mean reputation. The bar is crowded or you can drink at the tables outside, while acoustic music plays upstairs. Next door at No 7, *Que Pasa* is a popular tapas bar with a Spanish theme and smokers will enjoy the snazzy upstairs smoking room.

Next along at No 9, *Ice Cold Beer* has the coldest beer in town and lots of different brands. You can even watch movies for free upstairs. Also upstairs and at Peranakan Place on the corner of Emerald Hill and Orchard Rds, *Papa Joe's* is another popular place with a covers band on the weekend and a first drink cover charge.

Nearby, the *Saxophone Bar & Grill*, 23 Cuppage Terrace, near the corner of Orchard Rd, is a small place with some good blues, jazz and funk music and an outside, alfresco dining area (the food is good French/Continental but a little pricey). It's so small that musician O'Donel Levy and his R&B band have to play on a platform behind the bar, but you can sit outside and listen to the music after the dining finishes. There is no cover charge.

Fabrice's World Music Bar at the Singapore Marriott, 320 Orchard Rd, is home to some interesting bands with music ranging from reggae and African to Latin American.

Vincent's Lounge, at 6/F Lucky Plaza (200m east of Orchard MRT), is a small gay pub that is popular any night of the week.

Singapore River (Map 6)

The renovated banks of the Singapore River in the centre of town are the happening place in Singapore, especially Boat Quay. Further along the river, Clarke Quay is less frenetic and a little more spread out with several colourful streets, all with their fair share of watering holes and restaurants.

Boat Quay Is there life after Boat Quay? This place has become so incredibly popular that the rest of Singapore seems dead in comparison. The crowds start coming around 6 pm for a quiet drink or a meal, and keep growing through the night. Weekends are busy until 2 or 3 am, while weekdays are marginally quieter and most bars close

PAUL HELLANDER

A quiet moment at Boat Quay before sundown brings the nightlife crowds.

by 1 am. Boat Quay attracts everyone from the rich and famous to young Singaporean kids vomiting into the gutter after a night of over-indulgence.

Boat Quay has so many bars that you can just wander along until one takes your fancy. At the eastern end, *Harry's*, at No 28, gets going early in the evening as city workers flock for happy hour until 8 pm. Corporate high-fliers and wannabees, mostly expat, bullshit each other over beer and are joined later in the evening by a mixed, upmarket crowd who come for the jazz bands. Singapore's cocktail barmen haven't yet invented the Nick Leeson Slammer, but if they did it would be at Harry's or *Escobar*, a few doors down at No 37. These places finish up around midnight.

Just around the corner, *Molly Malone's*, 42 Circular Rd, is an Irish pub and a good place for a change of pace. It has a real pub atmosphere with Guinness on tap and traditional Irish bands upstairs. It closes at midnight and on Sunday.

Back on Boat Quay, *Culture Club*, at No 38, sometimes has decent bands, as does the newer *España*, at No 45. *Exclusiv 56*, at No 56, is a quieter bar with an older clientele and jazz on the jukebox.

Rootz, at No 60, is popular with young Malays and has reggae and hip-hop music. Further along are the *Riverbank*, at No 69, and *Shoreline*, very popular with young Singaporeans. They stay open until 2 am during the week and 3 am on weekends when everything else is closed.

Right at the end of Boat Quay near the bridge, *The Coffee Bean*, at No 82, is a hip coffee shop with an attached Internet section (known as PI@Boat Quay) with banks of terminals for surfing the net. It closes at midnight.

Clarke Quay Though the quieter cousin of Boat Quay, Clarke Quay has a good selection of places for a beer. The bars are not so overwhelmed by crowds and they tend to be more convivial.

The *Crazy Elephant*, beside the river at Trader's Market, is the most happening bar,

Rogue Trader – Nick Leeson

When the beer is flowing at Harry's, on Boat Quay, the talk among the expat regulars still frequently returns to the subject of one of the bar's most infamous patrons. On 23 February 1995 Nicholas William Leeson, general manager at Barings Futures Singapore, a shade short of his 28th birthday, disappeared from his office having single-handedly wrought a disaster of catastrophic financial dimensions.

He had totally wiped out the 233-year-old Barings Investment Bank in a cumulative series of ill-conceived investment gambles on the derivatives market – a game that few in financial circles knew much about nor cared to master. He bet heavily on the future direction of the Nikkei index, which he hoped would rise at the beginning of 1995. With the Japanese economy on a gradual slide, and coupled with the Kobe earthquake, Leeson's financial gambles on the Nikkei went from bad to ruinous.

All this time Leeson had managed to persuade his superiors that he was making money for Barings when, in fact, he was losing money by the barrow-load. Since he acted as both front-office trader and back-office settlements manager he was able to disguise his manoeuvrings, while at the same time pulling in an enormous salary of his own. By December 1994, the cumulative debt in the ultimately inauspiciously numbered account, No 88888, had topped $512 million. By the end of his gambling spree he had cost Barings $1.3 billion.

Nick Leeson was a working class Londoner with a thirst for the good life and a brash ability to persuade others that he was doing fine in what is viewed generally as a high-risk financial activity. When the chips were down he finally skipped Singapore. He was arrested in March 1995 while on a stopover in Germany and extradited back to Singapore where he was tried and sentenced to six and a half years. He now languishes in Changi prison.

Nick Leeson, the man who was once expelled from Harry's for baring his backside, now has a lot of time on his hands to remember and rue his high-flying life in Singapore's adrenaline-driven financial markets.

A movie documenting the events was in production at the time of writing. It promises to be a fascinating insight into one of Singapore's juiciest scandals.

Harry's, now exchanged for a jail cell by former patron Nick Leeson.

PAUL HELLANDER

with some decent rock bands (and a Sunday night blues jam) and plenty of room on the pavement outside for chatting. The *Wild West Tavern*, upstairs, is decked out like a saloon and is popular for country music of sorts, though the band seems more intent on playing old pop covers. *Dancers: The Club* entertains the Dream Team nightly and is open from 8 pm on weekends. *JP Bastiani's* (☎ 339 0392), 01-13 Clarke Quay, is a wine merchants with a very chic wine bar where high fliers like to be seen.

The *towkangs* (Chinese junks) moored on the river at Boat Quay house moderately

RAFFLES HOTEL

PATRICK HORTON

PATRICK HORTON

RICHARD I'ANSON

PAUL HELLANDER

PAUL HELLANDER

Three of Singapore's most visited sights: the elegance of Raffles Hotel (top left and right); the bustle of Boat Quay and the river (middle left and right); and the much loved phoniness of Sentosa's beaches and myriad attractions (bottom left and right).

RICHARD I'ANSON

PAUL HELLANDER

RICHARD I'ANSON

RICHARD I'ANSON

RICHARD I'ANSON

RICHARD I'ANSON

Entertainment Singapore style.
Top: Chinese New Year lights on North Bridge Rd (left); Chingay Festival (right).
Middle: The Chinese Dunhuang Dance Troupe (left): Chingay Festival parade (right).
Bottom: The Thiapusam Festival, one of the highlights of the Indian calendar (left and right).

priced restaurants with bars that sometimes have acoustic music. Music also plays at the central square near the Satay Club.

The newish *Brewerkz* (☎ 438 7438), in the Riverside Point Centre at 30 Merchant Rd, just south of the river across from Clarke Quay, is a micro-brewery-cum-restaurant offering no less than five locally produced boutique beers. The India Pale Ale is the most popular. The place also does a pretty honest lunchtime special for S$15, which includes starter and main course *and* two large glasses of beer of your choice.

Chinatown (Map 6)

The Tanjong Pagar area in Chinatown has a number of pubs in the renovated terraces, though in recent years they have lost a lot of their clientale to Boat Quay.

Duxton Hill has a string of bars that are pleasant, if relatively quiet places to have a drink. *Elvis' Place*, 1A Duxton Hill, is lined with Elvis memorabilia, though it has foregone the 50s music and is much like any other bar. The *Cable Car*, at No 2, is done out like a San Francisco cable car, while further along at No 10 the *Flag & Whistle* is a quiet English-style pub.

The pick of the pubs in this area is the *JJ Mahoney Pub* at 58 Duxton Rd. It has a big range of beers, including Murphys on tap. There's a band on the ground floor, a games room bar on the 2nd floor and karaoke on the 3rd.

The liveliest night spot in Tanjong Pagar is *Moon Dance*, 62 Tanjong Pagar Rd, with a busy dance floor and a club atmosphere. It is also a popular gay venue: Thursday night is women's night, Friday is men's. It's open until 2 am Monday to Thursday, and until 3 am on Friday and Saturday.

Two gay karaoke pubs also on Tanjong Pagar are *The Babylon*, 52 Tanjong Pagar, with a young crowd, and the *Inner Circle Pub*, which attracts mostly Chinese in groups of friends.

Closer to Outram Park MRT station, the *Butterfly Bar & Cafe*, 55 Keong Saik Rd, is a funky little place with post-modern decor and happy hour until 8 pm.

Colonial District (Maps 5&6)

Of course you can have a drink at *Raffles Hotel*, at the Long Bar or in the Bar & Billiard Room, where that infamous tiger was supposedly shot. One of the favourite pastimes in the elegant Long Bar is throwing peanut shells on the floor – swinging stuff. The Bar & Billiard room is laid back, and you can recline in the wicker chairs, tickle the ivories or chug-a-lug outside on the patio. In the evenings both bars have light jazz from 7.30 pm and serve food. Avoid the overrated and expensive Singapore Sling – it comes out of a barrel – and it's the butt of local jokes.

The place to be seen these days is *Chijmes*, a bar and restaurant complex on Bras Basah Rd just round the corner from the stuffy Raffles Hotel. This is a converted church and convent complex built between 1855 and 1910 that now boasts some pretty classy European-style bars and restaurants. The *Fountain Court*, with gurgling water, stone walls and greenery all dominated by a rather imposing Gothic chapel is a very atmospheric spot for a pre-dinner cocktail, while *Father Flanagans* – yet another Irish pub – serves a mean but pricey pint of Guinness stout for S$13.

Next to Father Flanagans, *Jump* is a hot bar where things really happen after 10 pm. Smart dress code applies.

The *Compass Rose*, on the 70th floor of the Westin Stamford Hotel, 2 Stamford Rd, has stunning views and prices to match. After 8.30 pm a minimum charge of S$15 applies. This is not the place to don jeans.

Somerset's, in the Western Plaza next door, is a jazz venue – probably *the* jazz venue in terms of playing proficiency.

The bar in the lobby at the *Marina Mandarin Singapore* has jazz in the evenings in salubrious and impressive surroundings.

A less pretentious and much cheaper place to drink is *New Bugis St*, one block south of Bugis MRT. You can have a beer at the food stalls under the stars until 3 am, or whenever everyone goes home. If you want to pay more, there are a couple of places that have karaoke and bad Filipino bands.

ENTERTAINMENT

For something different, the *Boom Boom Room* (☎ 339 8187), 3 New Bugis St, is a supper club affair with a cabaret and Singapore's only regular stand-up comic. There's a cover charge of S$17 on weekdays, S$23 at weekends.

Other Areas

Zouk (Map 6), 17-21 Jiak Kim St, near the Havelock Rd hotels, is a legendary dance club housed in an old *godown* (warehouse) by the Singapore River. A cover charge of around S$30 applies on weekends, S$25 for ladies. Next door, *Velvet Underground* has great music and is groovily designed, with a more mature crowd than Zouk. Friday and Saturday nights are gay friendly.

Just off River Valley Rd, about an 800m walk west of Clarke Quay, is Mohamed Sultan Rd, home to a sprinkling of popular late-night bars. Of these the *Next Page Pub* (Map 6) is the rowdiest and most popular with a gregarious expat crowd that is renowned for getting up onto the bar to boogie after a few frozen margaritas. You can rave, play pool or just chill out until 3 am. *Zeus* and the *Venue*, in the same street, offer retro and house music to a mainly younger clientele on weekends. Don't bother checking in to these places until way after 9 pm.

Not far from Arab St on Beach Rd, the Concourse shopping centre is home to a couple of restrospective theme pubs on its basement level – the 50s *Elvis at The Concourse* and the 60s *Pyschedelic Cafe Pub*, both decked out with memorabilia.

Wala Wala Bar & Grill, on Lorong Mambong out in Holland Village (Map 7), to the west of the city, has one of those sin machines that were banned for many years in Singapore – a jukebox. It's an American-style restaurant and bar popular with expats. Happy hour is from 4 to 9 pm.

For a quieter drink in Holland Village, *Bob's Tavern*, 17A Lorong Liput, has a good, relaxed, English pub atmosphere.

CINEMA

There are plenty of cinemas in Singapore, most of which screen only mainstream Hollywood fare. Chinese kung fu films and all-singing, all-dancing Indian movies are also popular. There are multi-theatre cineplexes at *Shaw Towers* and at the *Shaw Centre* on Scotts Rd, near the corner of Orchard Rd. *United Artists Theatre* is a four screen cineplex at Bugis Junction on Victoria St in the colonial district.

Alternative cinema has just a couple of outlets in the *Picture House* in the Cathay building (Map 4), 6 Handy Rd, at the city end of Orchard Rd, and *Jade Classics* in Shaw Towers (Map 5), 100 Beach Rd, 200m north-east of Raffles.

Singapore has an annual film festival and the various expatriate clubs also show movies. The *Alliance Française* (☎ 737 8422), 1 Sarkies Rd, often has movies open to the public, some with English subtitles.

As part of Goh Chok Tong's liberalisation, Singapore has introduced an R rating, so that previously banned movies showing nudity are allowed a screening if the content is of artistic merit. These movies are for over 21-year-olds only.

THEATRE

The nascent theatre scene is starting to come of age as Singaporeans become more interested in cementing their identity. More local plays are being produced, and alternative theatre venues such as the *Substation* (Map 6; ☎ 337 7800; email admin@substation.org.sg), 45 Armenian St, are helping to foster an interest in theatre. Plays, workshops, poetry readings and visual art exhibits are held here.

The main venues for theatre are the *Drama Centre* (Map 4; ☎ 336 0005) on Canning Rise, just north-west of Fort Canning Park; the *Victoria Theatre* (Map 6; ☎ 336 2151), Empress Place, opposite Boat Quay; and the *Kallang Theatre* (Map 3; ☎ 345 8488), opposite the National Stadium on Stadium Rd.

Performances range from local and overseas plays staged by a variety of local theatre companies to blockbusters such as *Phantom of the Opera* and *Les Misérables*. Some of the hotels, such as the *Hilton* and

Raffles, also stage theatre performances from time to time, although invariably these include dinner as part of the package and it makes for a pricey evening.

The Singapore Festival of Arts, which features many drama performances, is held every second year around June. Music, art and dance are also represented at the festival, which includes a Fringe Festival featuring plenty of street performances.

CHINESE OPERA
In Chinatown or in the older streets of Serangoon Rd and Jalan Besar, you may chance upon a *wayang* – a brilliantly costumed Chinese street opera. There's nothing subtle about these noisy and colourful extravaganzas, where overacting is very important. The best time of year to see one is around September during the Festival of Hungry Ghosts. They are often listed in the 'What's On' section of the *Straits Times*.

CULTURAL SHOWS
At the *Mandarin Singapore* (Map 4), on Orchard Rd, there is an Association of South-East Asian Nations (ASEAN) night every evening at 8 pm. It features dancing and music from all over the region. The show costs S$24 for adults and S$15 for children; including dinner it is S$48 for adults and S$26 for children.

CLASSICAL MUSIC
High-brow entertainment can be found at the *Victoria Concert Hall* (Map 6; ☎ 338 4401), the home of the Singapore Symphony Orchestra, opposite the Padang. Very reasonably priced tickets start at S$8, or more depending on the visiting musicians. The SSO programme is informative and comprehensive and can be picked up for free at offices of the Singapore Tourism Board or at the Victoria Concert Hall.

OTHER ENTERTAINMENT
The big hotels have cocktail lounges and there are some Chinese nightclubs scattered around the city centre. The *Neptune Theatre Restaurant* (Map 6), Collyer Quay, has a Chinese cabaret, Cantonese food and hostesses. It is glitzy but just this side of seedy and the shows are as risqué as Singapore will allow. The *Red Lantern Beer Garden*, downstairs, is definitely seedy, and has a band at lunchtime and in the evening, cheap meals and reasonably priced beer.

Lido Palace, in the Concorde Hotel (Map 6), part of the Havelock Rd cluster of hotels, also has a Chinese cabaret and dance hostesses. In the same vein is *Golden Million Nite-Club*, in the Peninsula Hotel (Map 6) on Coleman St, just north of the river.

AFTER DARK
If you're worried that Singapore is simply too squeaky clean for belief, you may be relieved to hear that there's a real locals-only, low-class, red-light district stretching along the laneway behind Desker Rd between Jalan Besar and Serangoon Rd in Little India (Map 5). Rows of blockhouse rooms have women standing in doorways while a constant stream of men wander past. Outside, hawkers sell condoms and potency pills, and makeshift tables are set up with card games to gamble on.

Desker Rd is also the successor to Bugis St and late in the evening transvestites strut their stuff. It doesn't have the atmosphere of old Bugis St, but it is lively and the coffee shops, such as the *Choon Huat*, 2 Desker Rd, and the *Hong Fa*, nearby, are interesting places to sit out on the pavement for noodles or a beer.

The predominantly Malay district of Geylang (Map 8), just east of the city, is full of houses and bars operated by organised Chinese gangs who 'employ' women of all nationalities, including Indonesians, Indians and the occasional Caucasian. They are found in the lorongs off Sims Ave. Of course, Singapore caters to business needs, and there is no shortage of 'health centres' and escort services.

HORSE RACING
The horse-racing calendar is part of the Malaysian circuit and races are held in Singapore once a month at the *Bukit Turf Club*

(Map 2), on Bukit Timah Rd. At other times, races are broadcast on the huge video screen. The racecourse is to be redeveloped for housing and is slated to move to Woodlands in the future.

The races are usually held on weekends and admission is S$5.15, or S$10.30 under the fans in the stand. If you are going to blow your dough at the races then you might as well spend S$20.60 for a seat in the air-conditioned members' stand – it gets very hot in the ordinary section on a crowded race day. Show your passport and buy a ticket for the members' at the tourist information booth outside. The only drawback is that you cannot get down to view the horses from the sealed-off members' stand.

The Bukit Turf Club produces a racing calendar that is available at the tourism board offices; or ring ☎ 469 3611 for information. All betting is government-controlled, and the minimum win or place bet is S$5. A lot of money passes through the windows on race days, which regularly attract about 30,000 punters. Despite government crackdowns, race fixing is growing with the popularity of the sport.

Be sure to dress properly – no shorts, sandals or T-shirts are allowed. The turf club also has a good hawker centre.

Shopping

One of Singapore's major attractions is shopping. The sheer range is impressive and prices for many goods are still competitive with other discount centres, but these days, with tariffs dropping everywhere around the world, Singapore is not the bargain centre it once was. 'Duty free' and 'free port' are somewhat throwaway terms. Remember that not everything is loaded down with import duty in your own country and Singapore also has some local industries to protect.

There are still plenty of bargains to be had on all sorts of goods, but there are also a number of guidelines to follow if you want to be certain to get your money's worth. First of all, don't buy anything unless you really want it and don't buy anything where the hassle of getting it back home will cost you more than the savings you make.

Prices & Bargaining

It may seem like stating the obvious, but before you leap on anything as a great bargain, find out what the price really is. If you're going to Singapore with the intention of buying a camera or CD player, for example, check what they would cost you back home first. Depending on your country of residence, Singapore may have few bargains to offer – Americans will find cheaper prices at home for many goods.

When you reach Singapore, shop around to find out what the 'real' price is. Fixed-price shops are increasingly becoming the norm but bargaining is still often required, especially in the tourist areas. Many of the small shops, such as electronic and souvenir shops, don't display prices and you are expected to bargain. Even when prices are displayed it doesn't always mean that prices are fixed. The Singapore Tourism Board (STB) introduced a scheme under which shops display tags marked as fixed price or recommended price. Labels marked 'I'm tagged with a recommended price' means bargaining is allowed. Only a few shops

follow this convention. If you are unsure, always ask if 'discounts' are available.

It's wise to shop around and compare prices. You can check prices with the main agent or showroom in Singapore or at a big fixed-price department store where the price is unlikely to be rock bottom, but is most likely to be in the ball park.

If you arrive by air, check the prices of electronic goods, watches etc at the airport duty-free shops. Expect prices in the shops in town to be 10 to 20% less than at the airport. Newspapers are always full of ads for consumer goods and they are not only good for checking prices but also to see where the sales are on.

It is better to frequent larger discount shops offering fixed prices if you are not practised at bargaining and don't know prices. Except for antiques, handicrafts and souvenirs, where bargaining is almost always required, good deals can be found without having to haggle.

If you do have to bargain, the secret is to stay good-humoured and to try to make them move rather than you. Your first gambit can be 'Is that your best price?', for their opening offer almost certainly won't be. Then make an offer below what you are prepared to pay and move to the price you want through counter offers. You have to give the impression that if the price isn't right you can happily do without the goods or that you will try the shop next door.

Be careful though: by entering into a bargaining routine you are tacitly implying that you are seriously interested in buying the item. Don't start a bargaining session if you have no real interest in buying. A retailer can quickly become very annoyed with you for wasting his or her time, if you are perceived to be bargaining just for the hell of it.

Guarantees

Guarantees are an important consideration if you're buying electronic gear, watches, cameras etc. Make sure your guarantee is international – usually this is no problem but check it out before you start haggling. A national guarantee is next to useless – are you going to bring your calculator back to Singapore to be fixed? Finally, make sure that the guarantee is filled out correctly with the shop's name and the serial number of the item written down.

As important as the guarantee is the item's compatibility back home. You don't want to buy a brand or model for which there are no spares or agents back home.

Buyer Beware

Singapore has stringent consumer laws and the government wants to promote the island as a good place to shop, however, you should be wary when buying.

This is particularly true in smaller shops if you push for too good a deal. A shopkeeper may match your low price but short-change you by not giving you an international guarantee or the usual accessories. For example, you may be offered a very low price for a camera, only to find that the guarantee is only good for Singapore, the batteries and case are extra and the price quoted is for a brand-name body with a no-name lens.

Make sure you get exactly what you want before you leave the shop. Check your receipts and guarantees and make sure they are dated and include serial numbers and the shop's stamp.

Check for the right voltage and cycle when you buy electrical goods. Singapore, Australia, New Zealand, Hong Kong and the UK use 220V to 240V at 50 cycles, while the USA, Canada and Japan use 110V to 120V at 60 cycles. Check the plug – most shops will fit the correct plug for your country.

Singapore enforces international copyright laws so being palmed off with pirated goods is not really a problem. You should be wary but the only real instances of this are the copy-watch sellers who will offer you a 'genuine imitation Rolex' for a ridiculously low price and make no pretence of its authenticity.

If you have any problems take your purchases back to the shop, though many, particularly the small ones, are not noted for their after-sales service. If you fail to get satisfaction from your point of purchase then contact the Small Claims Tribunal (☎ 535 6922; fax 455 5994) or the STB. The Small Claims Tribunal is at the Apollo Centre, 05-00, 2 Havelock Rd, and tourist complaints are usually heard within two or three days. The STB's *Singapore Official Guide* lists 'errant traders' that have been found guilty of tourist rip-offs. Traders in Lucky Plaza on Orchard Rd and in the Sim Lim Tower in the colonial district seem to figure regularly.

Service

In Singapore you buy on one basis only – price. The goods (high-technology goods that is) are just the same as you'd get back home, so quality doesn't enter into it. You're not going to come back for after-sales service, so service doesn't come into the picture either. You're not there to admire the display or get good advice from the assistants. In Singapore it's price, price, price.

Consequently, Singapore's shops can be quite unexciting places – 99 times out of 100 it's simply a case of pack the goods in. Nor are the staff always that helpful or friendly – they may be a long way behind Hong Kong shop assistants when it comes to out-and-out rudeness, but a few shopping trips in Singapore will soon indicate why the government runs courtesy campaigns so often.

GST

Almost all goods and services are levied with a 3% Goods and Services Tax (GST). A tax refund on goods worth S$300 or more can be applied for through shops participating in the GST Tourist Refund Scheme. These shops will display a 'tax refund' sticker, though often it is more hassle than it is worth. For more details see the Money section in the Facts for the Visitor chapter.

Great Singapore Sale

In an effort to reverse Singapore's declining image as a bargain hunters' destination, the

STB and Orchard Rd traders promote the Great Singapore Sale, held every year in July. Many stores offer discounts at this time but, again, it pays to shop around.

WHERE TO SHOP

Singapore is almost wall-to-wall with shops and, while there are certain places worth heading to for certain items, shopping centres usually have a mixture of shops selling electronics, clothes, sporting goods etc. Shopping centres are found all over town, but, of course, Orchard Rd is famous for its profusion of shopping possibilities.

Orchard Rd (Map 4)

The major shopping complexes on and around Orchard Rd have a mind-boggling array of department stores and shops selling whatever you want. The prices aren't necessarily the best, but the range of goods is superb and this is certainly a good place for high quality, brand-name items. The following is an overview and is by no means exhaustive.

Starting at the city end, Park Mall on Penang Rd, which runs parallel to Orchard Rd, has household fittings and decor shops, and a few oddities like a teddy bear shop, a recent fad in Singapore.

Orchard Point, Orchard Plaza and Cuppage Plaza, clustered together near Somerset MRT station, have a variety of shops and food outlets. Next along is Centrepoint, one of the liveliest shopping centres, with good bookshops on the 4th floor, carpets on the 5th floor, and Marks & Spencer and Robinsons department stores. The Cuppage Centre behind Centrepoint has food outlets and an adjoining wet market.

Past Peranakan Place, Orchard Emerald has watches and electronics, and the basement has a large supermarket, food stalls and restaurants. Next door, OG is a straightforward department store.

Across Orchard Rd next to Somerset MRT station, the Specialist's Shopping Centre is older and quieter. It has the John Little department store and also a good range of sporting goods shops.

On the corner of Orchard Rd and Orchard Link is Ngee Ann City, which houses the large Takashimaya department store. The basement is great for food, especially Japanese food, while the individual shops are dominated by Cartier, Harrods and other exclusive outlets.

Opposite Ngee Ann City, The Paragon and The Promenade are two other upmarket shopping centres with many designer boutiques. A little further west and much more downmarket is Lucky Plaza, a bustling, hustling place with dozens of shops crammed together. It's good for cheap clothes, bags and shoes, but bargain hard and shake off the touts and pesky tailors. Opposite Lucky Plaza is Wisma Atria, which has an Isetan department store and lots of boutiques.

On the corner of Scotts and Orchard Rds is Tang's, one of Singapore's oldest established department stores. Scotts Rd is becoming the preferred shopping area for Japanese visitors and this is noticeable in the Shaw Centre with its large Isetan department store and Kinokuniya bookshop. Also on Scotts Rd, the Scotts Shopping Centre has plenty of boutiques and an excellent food court in the basement. The Far East Plaza is a big shopping centre with electronics and a bit of everything.

At the top of Orchard Rd, the Far East Shopping Centre has some sporting shops that cater for golfers and cyclists. The Forum Galleria is dominated by Toys 'R' Us, with other children's gear specialists in the same centre.

Tanglin Rd is quieter and has far fewer of the hard-sell commercial enterprises of the kind found on Orchard Rd. The Tanglin Shopping Centre has Singapore's best selection of expensive Asian arts and antiques. It's well worth a browse and some refined bargaining if you want to buy.

Colonial District (Maps 5&6)

Raffles City is architecturally one of the most impressive shopping centres in Singapore and has some interesting small shops, as well as the Sogo department store. East of Raffles City, Marina Square has a huge array of shops in a massive complex which also includes three hotels and plenty of restaurants.

Raffles Hotel has a shopping area, which, as you would expect, is firmly upmarket with designer clothes and the like. Stamford House, on the corner of Stamford Rd and Victoria St, is a beautifully restored building with a host of shops for furniture, paintings, home fittings and nick-nacks.

Bugis Junction is a fairly new shopping centre on Victoria St that has breathed some life into the area. Built on the old Bugis St above Bugis MRT station, it comprises shophouse recreations covered by an atrium, the large Seiyu department store and the Hotel Inter-Continental.

On Bencoolen St, Sim Lim Square is known as the place to buy computers and electronic goods. Sim Lim Tower across Rochor Canal Rd is a big electronic centre with everything from capacitors to audio and video gear. These two centres are popular with tourists looking for bargains so the first asking price is often higher than elsewhere.

Other possibilities in the colonial district are the Albert Complex and Fou Lu Shou Complex just off Rochor Rd, and on Selegie Rd you'll find a variety of shops in the Paradiz Centre and Parklane Shopping Mall.

Chinatown (Map 6)
Chinatown is a popular shopping area with more local flavour. The People's Park Complex and People's Park Centre are good places to shop. They form a large complex with plenty of electronics, clothing and department stores. The electronics are only as cheap as you make them. The Chinatown Complex has an interesting market for everyday goods and cheap shops.

Chinatown Point specialises in craft shops. The quiet Riverwalk Galleria, just west of Boat Quay, has arts and crafts shops, while on Smith St you'll find craft and souvenir shops.

Other Areas
In Little India (Map 5) the Serangoon Plaza department stores have electrical and every-

day goods at honest prices. They have proved so popular for cheap electronics, clothes and household goods that the large Mustafa Centre department store has opened around the corner on Syed Alwi Rd.

Arab St (Map 5) is good for textiles, basketware and South-East Asian crafts.

East of the city is Parkway Parade (Map 8) on Marine Parade Rd, a large, general shopping centre that is popular with beachgoers. It has some larger discount shops for electronics.

Housing estate areas have plenty of shopping strips for cheaper clothes and household items, and bargaining is the exception rather than the rule. Try Ang Mo Kio, Bedok, Clementi, Toa Payoh, Geylang – all easily reached by MRT. Tampines has the big Century Park shopping mall.

Department Stores
Singapore has a wide variety of department stores offering both their own brand goods and other items, generally at fixed prices, which is ideal if you've had enough of bargaining. They include shops like CK Tang, Isetan, Metro or Yaohan, all with branches along Orchard Rd. Some of the department stores in Singapore include:

CK Tang
 320 Orchard Rd
Daimaru
 Liang Court, 177 River Valley Rd
Galeries Lafayette Liat Towers
 541 Orchard Rd
Isetan
 Shaw Centre, 1 Scotts Rd
 Wisma Atria, 435 Orchard Rd
John Little
 Specialists' Shopping Centre, 277 Orchard Rd
Marks & Spencer
 Centrepoint, 176 Orchard Rd
Metro
 Far East Plaza, 14 Scotts Rd
 Marina Square, Raffles Blvd
Robinsons
 Centrepoint, 176 Orchard Rd
Seiyu
 Bugis Junction, 230 Victoria St
Yaohan
 80 Marine Parade Rd

WHAT TO BUY

From CDs to luggage and from oriental rugs to model aeroplanes, Singapore's shops have whatever you want. The following information, though only a sample of Singapore's shopping possibilities, suggests places to start looking.

Arts, Crafts & Antiques

Singapore has no shortage of arts and antiques, mostly Chinese but also from all over Asia. When buying antiques, ask for a certificate of antiquity, which is required in many countries to avoid paying customs duty. A good guide is *Antiques, Arts & Crafts in Singapore* by Ann Jones.

Tanglin Shopping Centre (Map 4) on Tanglin Rd is one of the easiest places to find arts and antiques. Check out Antiques of the Orient which has a fascinating collection of antiquarian books, maps and prints. Marina Square (Map 6) in the colonial district also has some shops specialising in expensive oriental arts.

In the Holland Road Shopping Centre in Holland Village (Map 7), dozens of shops sell everything from cloisonné ware to Korean chests.

Upper Paya Lebar Rd, well to the northeast of the city centre, has a number of antique shops, including Mansion Antique House at No 107 and Just Anthony at No 379.

The Singapore Handicraft Centre, which is in Chinatown Point (Map 6) in Chinatown, has dozens of shops selling Chinese lacquerware, pottery and jewellery, as well as some Indonesian and other Asian crafts. Riverwalk Galleria (Map 6), also in Chinatown, has a number of art galleries and shops selling Chinese pottery and antiques on the 4th floor, while on the 1st floor are jewellery and jade shops.

Arab St (Map 5) is a good place for South-East Asian crafts, such as caneware, batik and leather goods. In Chinatown around Smith St, shops sell goods ranging from trinkets and souvenirs, basketware, fans and silk dressing gowns to more expensive curios and antique pottery.

Books

Singapore's main bookshop chains are MPH and Times, with a huge range of books in English. MPH's main shop (Map 6) at 71-7 Stamford Rd, in the colonial district, has been extensively renovated and is probably the best general bookshop in the region. It is also the most salubrious and has a coffee shop and a record shop. MPH has other shops on the 4th floor of Centrepoint on Orchard Rd, on Robinson Rd and at Changi airport.

Times also has a large bookshop on the 4th level of Centrepoint on Orchard Rd, and others at Lucky Plaza, Holland Village, Changi airport, Marina Square and Raffles City.

The Bras Basah Complex (Map 5) on North Bridge Rd specialises in textbooks and stationery but has a few good general bookshops, including Popular Book, which occupies four floors and has a good collection of computer books and books about the region.

Select Books on the 3rd floor of the Tanglin Shopping Centre (Map 4) at 19 Tanglin Rd, north of the Orchard Rd area, specialises in general and academic books on Asia and is the best in Singapore for books on South-East Asia.

Borders is a newer bookshop at 501 Orchard Rd in the Liat Towers complex (Map 4). It boasts a very extensive collection of books, newspapers and magazines and provides comfy chairs for browsers to relax in.

Kinokuniya, the Japanese chain, has some interesting collections and good books on the region. Its main shop is in the Shaw Centre (Map 4) on the corner of Scotts and Orchard Rds and features a large collection of books in Japanese. There are also book and magazine stalls in many of the larger hotels.

Cameras & Film

Cameras are available throughout the city, though camera equipment is not such a bargain these days as camera prices are often as heavily discounted in the west as in Singapore or Hong Kong.

When buying film, bargain for lower prices if you're buying in bulk – 10 films should cost less than 10 times one film.

For information on the costs of developing films in Singapore see the Photography & Video section in the Facts for the Visitor chapter.

Clothes & Shoes

Clothes and shoes – imported, locally made and made to measure – are widely available, but Singapore is not as cheap as some other Asian countries. Singapore is good, however, for top brands and designer labels, and you can be sure of the authenticity and quality. Shoes and brand-name sneakers (Reebok, Nike, Adidas) are a good buy.

Many of the department stores have reasonably priced clothes: Nison in the People's Park Complex (Map 6) in Chinatown has cheap clothes. Lucky Plaza (Map 4) on Orchard Rd is also a good centre for cheap clothes and shoes, but bargain hard for everything. The Peninsula Shopping Centre in the Peninsula Hotel (Map 6) is good for men's shoes.

Wisma Atria, Orchard C&E and OG department store are good places on Orchard Rd for clothes. There are plenty of boutiques selling expensive designer labels: try The Promenade and The Paragon shopping centres and Ngee Ann City, all in the Orchard Rd area.

Computers

Computer systems and laptops are a good buy, though for US-made or Japanese-made name-brand hardware, the prices are good but not necessarily as low as in the countries of origin. Be wary of the cheap, no-name brands, mostly from Taiwan, that you won't be able to get support for back home. Computer components and accessories that are made in Singapore, such as hard disks, are very competitively priced, as are blank diskettes and accessories.

Singapore is enforcing international copyright laws, so cheap software and software manuals are not openly on display as in other Asian countries. The Funan Centre (Map 6) on North Bridge Rd is the main computer centre, with dozens of computer shops on the top floors as well as a large Challenger Superstore. The top floors of Sim Lim Square (Map 5), on the corner of Bencoolen St and Rochor Canal Rd, are good for cheap computers and peripherals.

Electronic Goods

TVs, CDs, VCRs, VCDs, DVDs – you name it, all the latest high-tech audiovisual equipment is available all over Singapore, much of it at very competitive prices. With such a range to choose from, it's difficult to know what to buy; it pays to do a little research into makes and models before you arrive. Make sure your guarantees are worldwide, your receipts are properly dated and stamped, and your goods are compatible with electricity supplies and systems in your country of origin. (See the Buyer Beware section earlier in this chapter for more information.)

There are two main types of TV system used: PAL in Australia and much of Europe and NTSC in the USA and Japan – video recorders must be compatible with the system you use.

Sim Lim Square (Map 5), on the corner of Bencoolen St and Rochor Canal Rd, has a concentrated range of electronics shops, and Sim Lim Tower, nearby on Jalan Besar, has everything from cassette players to capacitors, but be wary and be prepared to bargain hard. Serangoon Plaza (Map 5) at the top end of Serangoon Rd in Little India has a good range of electrical goods at no-nonsense prices, as does the Mustafa Centre, just round the corner on Syed Alwi Rd.

Jewellery

Gold jewellery is sold according to weight and quite often the design and work is thrown in for next to nothing. The gold used is often 22 to 24 carat and you should always retain a receipt showing weight and carat. Gold shops are all over town, but you'll find a concentration in Little India (Map 5) and the People's Park Complex in Chinatown (Map 6).

Singapore is a good place to buy pearls and gemstones but you really need to know the market.

Jade is a Chinese favourite and is expensive. In general, the lighter the colour the more expensive it is. Beware of imitation jade and don't pay too much for cheap jade, such as the dark Indian variety. Examine solid jade pieces for flaws, as these may be potential crack lines.

Music
Guitars, keyboards, flutes, drums, electronic instruments and recording equipment are all good buys, though not necessarily as cheap as the country of origin. A good shop to try is City Music, No 02-12 Peace Centre (Map 4), on the corner of Selegie Rd. Yamaha has a number of showrooms, including one in the Suntec City complex.

Cheap pirated tapes are things of the past but legitimate tapes and CDs are reasonably priced. CDs cost around S$16 to S$20 in department stores and discount bins, and around S$20 to S$25 for more obscure imports. Tower Records, on the 4th floor of the Pacific Plaza (Map 4), 9 Scotts Rd, near the corner of Orchard Rd, has a large selection at higher prices, but Borders in the Liat Towers complex (Map 4) and HMV at 260 Orchard Rd would be hard to beat for its very impressive selection of often obscure and hard-to-find CDS.

Sporting Goods
Almost every shopping centre in Singapore has a sports shop offering brand-name equipment and sportswear at good prices. Most of the department stores also have well-stocked sports sections. For general sports shops, try the Far East Shopping Centre on Orchard Rd. Lucky Plaza on Orchard Rd also has sports shops, including diving shops.

For brand-name bicycles and components, try Soon Watt & Co, 482 Changi Rd, one block south of Kembangan MRT station. For equestrian gear go to Connoisseurs, 613 Bukit Timah Rd (it's about 1km west of the Botanic Gardens).

Excursions

Singapore is only a stone's throw from its two larger neighbours, Malaysia and Indonesia. On weekends and holidays large numbers flee the Lion City in search of fun and sun. The beach resorts and towns of southern Malaysia are just across the Causeway, while Indonesia's Riau Archipelago includes Batam and Bintan islands, which have well developed tourist facilities.

Travel agents in Singapore offer a host of package tours, and the fierce competition results in some good deals. These offer an easy way to explore attractions in Malaysia or Indonesia if your time is limited. Look in the *Straits Times* for advertised tours.

Some examples of cheap tours from Singapore, including transport and accommodation, are:

Bali
  four days for S$400
Batam Island
  one day for S$45, two days for S$80
Desaru
  two days for S$125
Melaka
  one day for S$40, two days for S$70
Danua Toba (Lake Toba)
  five days for S$400
Penang
  three days, including air-fare for S$320, or S$160 by bus
Tioman Island
  three days, including air-fare for S$320

Travel in Malaysia is covered in detail in Lonely Planet's *Malaysia, Singapore & Brunei*, while our *Indonesia*, *Java* and *Bali & Lombok* guides cover the world's largest archipelago. Lonely Planet's *Indonesian phrasebook* and *Malay phrasebook* may also come in useful.

NATURAL SINGAPORE

Singapore is not all shopping and entertainment – as the Singaporeans are belatedly discovering. Day excursions can be made to a few locations scattered across the island that allow visitors to get a feel for what Singapore was like before modernisation and progress took hold.

About the furthest you get away from the high-rises is Pulau Ubin, a small island off the north-east coast of Singapore. It is a good place for people who enjoy walking or cycling. The beaches and camp site are a little tatty however, which is a pity because there is no real other overnight option except camping.

The authorities that look after Pulau Ubin are keen to see the island develop as some kind of eco-Sentosa. It's an idea that has some promise, but the result could just as easily be a spoiling of what 'natural' features remain.

The Bukit Timah Nature Reserve and the Sungei Buloh Nature Park are for visitors serious about flora, birds and other fauna. These are essentially day trips since there

PAUL HELLANDER

Drive up Rifle Range Rd and you will usually see troupes of long-tailed macaques sitting along the roadside. They are also often found in the Bukit Timah Nature Reserve and near the car parks at the Upper Seletar and Lower Pierce reservations.

are no accommodation possibilities at either site. Both locations could be covered in a fairly hectic one day excursion.

See the Things to See & Do chapter for more details on all these places.

Malaysia

Just across the Causeway, Malaysia has a host of attractions, many of which can be visited on day trips from Singapore. Johor Bahru is almost a suburb of Singapore, and the seaside village of Kukup, the waterfalls at Kota Tinggi and the beach resort of Desaru are also within easy reach.

If you have a couple of days or more to spare, further afield is the historic town of Melaka and the beautiful islands off the east coast of Malaysia, of which Tioman is the largest and most popular.

Heading further inland and to the north are the hill resorts of Fraser's Hill and Cameron Highlands, which can be reached via Malaysia's thriving capital, Kuala Lumpur. Further to the north, on the west coast of Peninsular Malaysia, are the popular islands of Penang and Langkawi. The east coast has a string of good beaches, and Kota Bharu in the very north is a centre for Malay culture. Over on Borneo, Sabah and Sarawak are adventure destinations where you can explore the mountains and jungle, and see some unique wildlife.

For more details and other destinations, contact the Malaysia Tourism Promotion Board (☎ 532 6351; fax 535 6650) on the ground floor of the Ocean building (Map 6), 10 Collyer Quay in Singapore. It's open from 9 am to 4.45 pm weekdays and until 12.30 pm Saturday.

Most visitors to Malaysia do not require a visa; you will usually be given a one or two month entry permit on arrival. Crossing the Causeway is straightforward and clearing immigration and customs normally only takes a few minutes; the exception is at weekends, especially long weekends, and on public

holidays – see the Crossing the Causeway section in the Getting There & Away chapter.

The Malaysian dollar (or ringgit) is a stable currency and exchange rates are:

| Singapore | S$1 | = | RM2.39 |
| USA | US$1 | = | RM3.96 |

JOHOR BAHRU

Capital of the Malaysian state of Johor, which comprises the entire southern tip of the peninsula, Johor Bahru is the southern gateway to Peninsular Malaysia. Connected to Singapore by the 1038m-long Causeway, Johor Bahru (or JB as it's usually known) inevitably suffers as a poor relation to its more glamorous neighbour, yet its lively chaos is an interesting contrast to Singapore's squeaky-clean sterility. It is both a breath of fresh air and a bad aroma.

On weekends and public holidays, Singaporeans flock across the Causeway for vice, shopping and excitement, and at these times Johor Bahru puts on a show. Exotic street entertainment is provided by medicinal vendors dangling snakes and promising penis enlargement with their elixirs, or by turbaned *bomohs* (spiritual healers) selling magical 'love oil'. The *kedai gunting rambut* (barber shops) do a great trade too, but in girls not haircuts.

Aside from the seedy exotica, Johor Bahru has the finest museum in Malaysia and a thriving night market. In the business centre of town are plenty of pavement hawkers and other colourful stalls which are so much a part of Asia but lacking in Singapore.

Be alert, however; Johor Bahru has had some bad press recently, particularly with regard to the personal security of visitors. Keep your wits about you and your belongings close by and you should be OK.

Things to See
The **Royal Abu Bakar Museum**, overlooking the Straits of Johor and Singapore, is the former main palace (Istana Besar) of the Johor royal family. It was built in Victorian style by the Anglophile sultan Abu Bakar in 1866. The palace is now a museum

EXCURSIONS

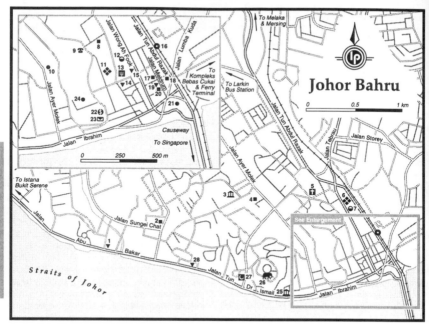

EXCURSIONS

PLACES TO STAY
2 Hyatt Regency
4 Footloose Homestay
8 Puteri Pan Pacific
   Hotel
17 Hawaii Hotel
18 Causeway Inn
20 Top Hotel

PLACES TO EAT
1 Selera Sungei Chat
   Seafood Centre
14 Restoran Nilla
15 Pasar Malam

19 Restoran Medina
28 Tepian Tebrau Food
   Centre

OTHER
3 Johor Art Gallery
5 Church of the Immacu-
   late Conception
6 Komtar Centre
7 Singapore Taxi Station
9 Telekom
10 Immigration Office
11 Plaza Kota Raya
12 Taxi Station

13 Sri Mariamman
   Hindu Temple
16 Railway Station
21 Immigration Check
   Point
22 Hongkong Bank
23 Post Office
24 Bangunan Sultan
   Ibrahim
25 Royal Abu
   Bakar Museum
26 Zoo
27 Sultan Abu
   Bakar Mosque

full of the sultan's possessions, furniture and hunting trophies. There are some superb pieces. The palace is open daily except Friday from 9 am to 6 pm (no entry after 5 pm). Entrance for foreigners is a hefty US$7 per person, payable in ringgit. Despite the price it's well worth a visit.

Not far west of the museum is the magnificent **Sultan Abu Bakar Mosque**. It was built from 1892 to 1900, and executed in a mixture of architectural styles, but with the main influence being, again, Victorian.

Between the museum and mosque and approached through the former palace gardens is a small **zoo**, once the private property of the sultan. It's open from 8 am to 6 pm daily and admission is RM2 for adults, RM1 for children.

The other two city landmarks are the **Istana Bukit Serene**, the actual residence of the Sultan of Johor – highly visible because of its 32m-high tower but closed to the public – and the imposing **Bangunan Sultan Ibrahim** (State Secretariat building) on Bukit Timbalan, overlooking the city centre. The latter has a 64m-high square tower and looks like a medieval fortress transported from Turkey or Mughul India, but it was, in fact, built in the 1940s.

Places to Stay

The only real budget accommodation in Johor Bahru is the *Footloose Homestay* (☎ (07) 224 2881) in a quiet suburban neighbourhood at 4H Jalan Ismail, just off Jalan Yahya Awal. There's one double room for RM28 or six dorm beds for RM14 per person. Be warned though, conditions are basic, especially in the dorm.

The other cheaper hotels are mostly clustered in the Jalan Meldrum neighbourhood, just east of the railway station. Probably the best bet in terms of price and comfort is the *Hawaii Hotel* (☎ (07) 224 0633), 21 Jalan Meldrum, which has carpeted singles/doubles with fan and bath for RM40; rooms with air-con start at RM50. Also good value is the *Top Hotel* (☎ (07) 244 4755), 12 Jalan Meldrum, where rooms with air-con and bath cost RM66.

For anyone willing to spend a little more, the *Causeway Inn* (☎ (07) 224 8811), 6A Jalan Meldrum, is one of the best mid-range hotels, and some rooms have good views across the straits. Clean singles/doubles with air-con and bath cost RM82/92.

Top-end hotels are springing up everywhere in Johor Bahru, mainly to cater for business travellers. The 500 room *Puteri Pan Pacific Hotel* (☎ (07) 223 6622), right in the centre of town, has an impressive range of features, including swimming pool, fitness centre, business centre and four restaurants. Rooms start at RM320/350.

Competing with the Pan Pacific to be the city's top joint is the *Hyatt Regency* (☎ (07) 222 1234) on Jalan Sungei Chat, 2.5km west of the city centre past the Sultan Abu Bakar Mosque. Rooms cost from RM360.

Places to Eat

Johor Bahru can be a good place for dining, especially for seafood, but you have to know where to look. The city also has good hawker venues, the best being the very active *pasar malam* (night market) outside the Hindu temple on Jalan Wong Ah Fook. Divided into three sections – Chinese, Malay and Indian – it has a great selection of dishes. Local specialities to look out for include laksa Johor, relying heavily on coconut, and mee rebus, noodles in a thick sauce, showing a Javanese influence.

The *Plaza Kota Raya* centre near the night market has a selection of western fast-food joints and a supermarket, as well as a good food court on the top floor.

Johor Bahru has some good Indian restaurants, including the ever-busy *Restoran Medina* on the corner of Jalans Meldrum Siew Niam. It serves excellent murtabak, biryani and curries. Right opposite the Sri Mariamman Temple, *Restoran Nilla* specialises in south Indian banana leaf set meals. Most meals are vegetarian but fish-head curry is also on the menu.

The main seafood venues are along the waterfront to the west of the centre but they are not really reachable on foot. The food is great but the sea aspect is spoiled by the very busy road. The *Tepian Tebrau* food centre on Jalan Abu Bakar is famous for its excellent seafood. One kilometre further west is the *Selera Sungei Chat*, another well-patronised seafood centre specialising in ikan bakar (grilled fish).

Although lots of Singaporeans do come across the Causeway to eat seafood in Johor Bahru, given the hassles of crossing the border, changing money and then getting back again, to our minds it just doesn't really seem worth it. The variety and choice of Singapore's culinary offerings takes some beating.

EXCURSIONS

Shopping

Johor Bahru promotes itself as a major shopping destination and new shopping centres are being built at a frantic pace. While Singaporeans still do come across the Causeway to do some of their shopping – notably to buy petrol and groceries – for most goods Singapore has better prices and a far better range.

Major shopping centres in central Johor Bahru are the Kompleks Tun Abdul Razal beneath the Komtar Centre and the much flasher Plaza Kota Raya. Just next to the Church of the Immaculate Conception another giant shopping centre, the Wisma Landmark, is under construction; it most likely will be completed by the time this book is published.

Another shopping complex, designed specifically to cater to the Singaporean market, is the newly completed Kompleks Bebas Cukai (more commonly called the Free Zone Complex), about 2km east of the Causeway. This complex also houses a ferry terminal which handles a lot of the Singapore traffic and a few destinations in Indonesia.

Getting There & Away

See the Getting There & Away chapter for information on getting *to* Johor Bahru from Singapore.

Singapore From Johor Bahru to Singapore there are air-con buses every 15 minutes from 6.30 am to midnight for RM2.10. The bus station is at Larkin, 5km north-west of the Causeway, but buses stop at Malaysian immigration, only a two minute walk from the city centre. You must have a ticket before you can board the bus – they can be bought from the bus station or from the southernmost travel agent in the building across the street from the railway station.

Alternatively, regular bus No 170 also runs to Singapore and you can buy tickets (RM1.20) on board.

Avoid Sunday evening if you can, because things get very busy at both border posts.

Registered taxis to Singapore only leave from the terminal on the 1st level of the car park next to the Komtar Centre on Jalan Wong Ah Fook. The other taxi terminal on Jalan Wong Ah Fook has taxis to the rest of Malaysia. A taxi across the Causeway to the Queen St terminal in Singapore should cost RM28. Other taxis and private cars around town will also offer their services, but bargaining is required. You can negotiate to get dropped off at a hotel in Singapore but expect to pay RM40 to RM60 depending on where you want to go.

Malaysia There are buses from Johor Bahru to Kota Tinggi (RM2.60), Kuala Lumpur (RM16.60 regular or RM22.10 'business class'), Melaka (RM10) and Mersing (RM7).

Regular shared taxis go to Kota Tinggi (RM4.50), Kuala Lumpur (RM40), Melaka (RM30) and Mersing (RM20). All prices are per person.

Getting Around

Taxis around town are metered, but drivers are not always willing to use them. If you have to bargain, you can go almost anywhere in Johor Bahru for RM5, or taxis can be hired at around RM25 per hour for sightseeing.

KUKUP

About 40km south-west of Johor Bahru on the Straits of Melaka, across from Sumatra, this fishing village is famous for its seafood restaurants, most of which are built on stilts over the water. Singaporeans, who are obsessed with the loss of their own kampong life, flock to this village on weekends.

While there is no denying the quality of the seafood, the availability of similar fare in Johor Bahru, and the tattiness of the village make this a low-priority destination.

Next to Kukup is Kampung Air Masin (Salt Water Village), renowned for its top quality *belacan* (shrimp paste). Both villages are largely inhabited by Hokkien Chinese.

Getting There & Away

A chartered taxi all the way from Johor Bahru costs RM60, but if you take a shared taxi to Pontian Kechil and then another to Kukup you'll pay only RM10.

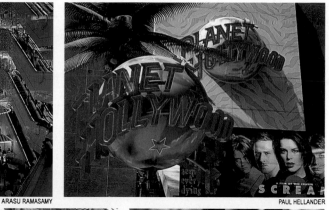

ARASU RAMASAMY

PAUL HELLANDER

PAUL HELLANDER

RICHARD I'ANSON

ARASU RAMASAMY

Shopping in Singapore encompasses the glitter and glamour of Orchard Road's multitude of modern shopping centres (top left, top right and bottom) and the down-to-earth traditional, grab and barter of some fine street markets such as those on Bugis St (middle left) and in Little India (middle right).

VICKI BEALE

RICHARD I'ANSON

CHRIS ROWTHORN

PAUL HELLANDER

Easy excursions from Singapore include the Indonesian islands of the Riau Archipelago (top), the Malay island of Tioman (middle), historical Malay cities like Melaka (bottom right) and the tea plantations of Peninsular Malaysia's Cameron Highlands (left).

Weekend ferries used to leave for Kukup from Singapore's World Trade Centre but at the time of research they seemed to have been suspended.

Day tours from Singapore cost around S$70.

JOHOR BAHRU TO MELAKA

Ayer Hitam is a popular rest stop for buses, taxis and motorists, so the place has lots of small restaurants.

West of Ayer Hitam, Batu Pahat is a riverine town famed for its Chinese cuisine, although it also has a minor reputation as a 'sin city' for jaded Singaporeans. Accommodation can be hard to find here on weekends.

Muar, north-west of Batu Pahat, is a centre of traditional Malay culture, including *ghazal* (female singers) and the *kuda kepang* (prancing horse) dances. This pleasant, lazy city was once home to the Johor sultanate and it still retains a graceful colonial district.

MELAKA

Melaka (Malacca) is Malaysia's most historically interesting city. In the 15th century it rose to become the greatest trading port in South-East Asia before experiencing the complete series of European incursions in Malaysia – Portuguese, Dutch and English.

Under the Melaka sultanates, the city's strategic position on the Straits made it a wealthy centre of spice trade with China, India, Siam and Indonesia. This wealth attracted the attention of the Portuguese who in 1511, led by Alfonso d'Albuquerque, launched an assault on the port. The sultan fled to Johor where he re-established his kingdom.

While Portuguese canons could conquer, they couldn't force merchants to trade in Melaka. Other ports in the area began to challenge for regional supremacy, particularly the Dutch Batavia (modern-day Jakarta). In 1641 the Dutch attacked Melaka and it passed into their hands after a siege lasting eight months.

The Dutch ruled for only about 150 years before, in 1824, they permanently ceded Melaka to the British in exchange for the Sumatran port of Bencoolen.

Under the British, Melaka once more flourished as a trading centre, although it was soon superseded by the growing commercial importance of Singapore.

For long a sleepy backwater town living on memories of past glories, Melaka is starting to catch the economic boom sweeping the rest of the country. Massive land reclamation has seen the historic waterfront retreat inland, and a huge shopping mall and new apartment blocks now enjoy Melaka's sea views.

Despite the modernisation, Melaka is still a place of intriguing Chinese streets filled with antiques shops, old Chinese temples, and nostalgic reminders of the now-departed European colonial powers.

Orientation & Information

Melaka is a small town, easy to find your way around and compact enough to explore on foot. The interesting, older parts are mainly near the river and around the Stadthuys, which is also where you'll find the tourist office (☎ (06) 283 6538); it's open daily from 8.45 am to 5 pm, but closed from 12.15 to 2.45 pm on Friday.

Stadthuys & St Paul's Hill

The **Stadthuys** (town hall), built between 1641 and 1660, is the most imposing relic of the Dutch period and the oldest Dutch building in the east. Close by the Stadthuys is the bright-red **Christ Church** (1753) built with pink bricks brought out from Zeeland, and with old Dutch tombstones laid in the floor.

St Paul's Hill (Bukit St Paul) rises up above the Stadthuys, and on top of it stand the ruins of **St Paul's Church**. Built by the Portuguese in 1571, it was regularly visited by Francis Xavier; the saint's body was buried here before being transferred to Goa in India. The church fell into disuse after the Dutch takeover and was later used as a store for gunpowder. It has been in ruins for 150 years.

The **Porta de Santiago** is all that's left of the old Portuguese fortress, A'Famosa.

EXCURSIONS

EXCURSIONS

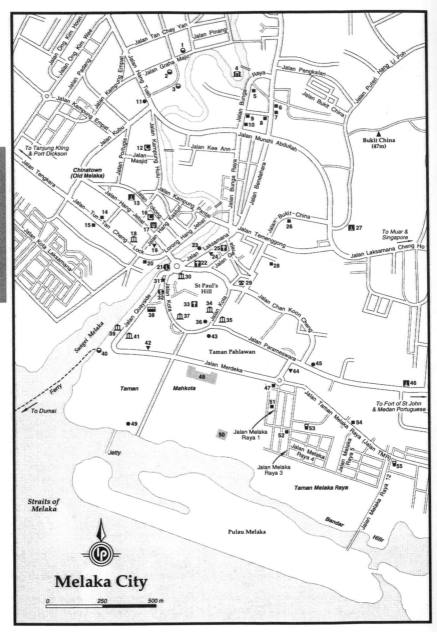

Melaka City

0   250   500 m

PLACES TO STAY
- 5 Majestic Hotel
- 6 City Bayview Hotel
- 7 Orkid Hotel
- 8 Renaissance Hotel
- 9 Ng Fook
- 10 Hong Kong Hotel
- 14 Hotel Puri
- 15 The Baba House
- 20 Heeren House
- 26 Eastern Heritage
  Guest House
- 28 Apple Guest House
- 47 Robin's Nest
- 51 Travellers' Lodge
- 52 Melaka Youth
  Hostel
- 54 Malacca Town
  Holiday Lodge 1

PLACES TO EAT
- 19 Jonkers Melaka
  Restoran
- 24 Restaurant Kim
  Swee Huat

- 42 Glutton's Corner
- 44 Malay Food Stalls

OTHER
- 1 Local Bus Station
- 2 Taxi Station
- 3 Express Bus Station
- 4 Villa Sentosa
- 11 Immigration
- 12 Kampung Hulu Mosque
- 13 Cheng Hoon Teng
  Temple
- 16 Kampung Kling Mosque
- 17 Sri Pogyatha Vinoyagar
  Moorthi Temple
- 18 Baba-Nonya Heritage
  Museum
- 21 Tourist Office
- 22 Christ Church
- 23 Karyaneka Handicrafts
  Emporium
- 25 Church of St Francis
- 27 Sam Po Kong Temple
  & Hang Li Poh Well
- 29 Telekom

- 30 Stadthuys
- 31 Tourist Police
- 32 Hongkong Bank
- 33 St Paul's Church
- 34 Cultural Museum
- 35 Proclamation of
  Independence Hall
- 36 Porta de Santiago
- 37 People's Museum
- 38 Swimming Pool
- 39 Maritime Museum
- 40 Ferries to Dumai·
- 41 Royal Malaysian
  Navy Museum
- 43 Sound & Light Show
- 45 Jin Trading (Bicycle
  Hire)
- 46 Buddhist Temple
- 48 Mahkota Parade
  Shopping Complex
- 49 Mahkota Seaworld
  (under construction)
- 50 Mahkota Medical Centre
- 53 Jam Pub
- 55 Jim's Cottage Pub

EXCURSIONS

Sound and light shows are held here each evening at 8 pm (in Malay) and at 9.30 pm (in English). Entry to the Porta de Santiago is free, but the sound and light show costs RM5.

The **Proclamation of Independence Hall**, in a typical Dutch house dating from 1660, is a small museum displaying events leading up to independence in 1957.

Other museums in the St Paul's Hill area include the **Cultural Museum** (or Muzium Budaya), which is a wooden replica of a Melaka sultan's palace (admission RM1.50) and, south-west of the hill on the quayside, the **Maritime Museum**, housed in a re-creation of a Portuguese ship. The latter has ship models, dioramas and an interesting map room. It's open from 9 am to 9 pm daily (closed Friday from 12.15 to 2.45 pm); entry is RM2.

Chinatown (Old Melaka)
The **Baba-Nonya Heritage Museum**, at 48-50 Jalan Tun Tan Cheng Lock, is a traditional 19th century Peranakan townhouse,

filled with typical Peranakan furniture and artefacts. It is owned by a Baba family who conduct tours of the house. It's open from 10 am to 12.30 pm and from 2 to 4.30 pm daily; admission is RM7.

Old Melaka is a fascinating area around which to wander. Although the city has long lost its importance as a port, ancient-looking junks still sail up the river and moor at the banks.

Jalan Hang Jebat is an intriguing old street full of interesting shops and the odd mosque and Chinese or Hindu temple – the **Sri Pogyatha Vinoyagar Moorthi Temple** (1781) and the Sumatran-style **Kampung Kling Mosque** are both in this area.

Also worth a look is the fascinating **Cheng Hoon Teng Temple** (1646), the oldest Chinese temple in Malaysia. It's on Jalan Tokong, one block north of Jalan Hang Jebat.

Bukit China
In the mid-1400s, the Sultan of Melaka wed the Ming emperor's daughter to seal relations

between the two countries. Their residence was on Bukit China (China Hill). It has been a Chinese area ever since and, together with two adjoining hills, forms a huge Chinese graveyard. At the foot of Bukit China is the **Sam Po Kong Temple** (1795) and nearby is the **Hang Li Poh Well**.

Other Things to See & Do

Roughly 3km east of the city centre is **Medan Portuguese**, or Portuguese Square, an area where many people of Portuguese and Malay descent live. It's a good dining centre.

The **Fort of St John** was originally a Portuguese chapel until it was rebuilt by the Dutch in the 18th century. Today it's just a few walls and cannon emplacements on top of a hill but the views are good. It's east of town, just before the turn-off to Medan Portuguese.

Daily **riverboat tours** of Melaka leave from the quay behind the tourist office. The trip takes 45 minutes and costs RM7 per person (minimum six people); departures are at 11 am, noon and 1 pm, depending on demand.

Places to Stay

Most guesthouses are in the area known as Taman Melaka Raya, which is the reclaimed land south-east of St Paul's Hill. Dorms start at RM8 and singles/doubles cost from RM12/15.

Robin's Nest (☎ (06) 282 9142), at 205B Jalan Melaka Raya 1 (the street running south off the roundabout), and the *Travellers' Lodge* (☎ (06) 281 4793), at 214B of the same street, are two of the most popular places.

The *Melaka Youth Hostel* (Asrama Belia) (☎ (06) 282 7915), just east on Jalan Melaka Raya 3, is spotless and well run with beds in fan-cooled dorms for RM10, or RM14 in the air-con dorm.

The *Malacca Town Holiday Lodge 1* (☎ (06) 284 8830), 148B Jalan Taman Melaka Raya (the main thoroughfare in this area), has no dorms but decent singles/doubles for RM15/20.

Away from Taman Melaka Raya there are a number of other guesthouses dotted around. The pick of them is the *Eastern Heritage Guest House* (☎ (06) 283 3026), 8 Jalan

TONY WHEELER

The Melaka River (Sungei Melaka), once a main artery of the spice trade but these days a sleepy backwater.

Bukit China, in a superb old building from 1918. Rooms cost from RM15/18 to RM30. One street away, the *Apple Guest House* (☎ (010) 667 8744), 24-1 Lorong Banda Kaba, is very good value with rooms at RM12.50/18.

Of the many cheap hotels *Ng Fook* (☎ (06) 282 8055), 154 Jalan Bunga Raya, is basic but OK with rooms from RM23 up to RM41 for air-con and bath. The *Hong Kong Hotel* (☎ (06) 282 3392) a few doors away is slightly cheaper.

For a few ringgits more, the rambling old *Majestic Hotel* (☎ (06) 282 2455), 188 Jalan Bunga Raya, is a classic old place with swishing fans and a cool, lazy atmosphere. Rooms range from RM27 for a small room with fan up to RM63 for a large room with air-con and bathroom.

Melaka's crumbling Chinatown has three new hotels in restored buildings. The newest and undoubtedly the best of the bunch is the *Hotel Puri* (☎ (06) 282 5588; fax 281 5588) at 118 Jalan Tun Tan Cheng Lock – a bright-yellow building which is hard to miss. There's a quiet garden for drinks and the foyer is cool and welcoming. A very comfortable standard room costs RM100. *The Baba House* (☎ (06) 281 1216), 125 Jalan Tun Tan Cheng Lock, has loads of style but some rooms don't have windows. Comfortable rooms with bath cost RM99. For position and style it's hard to beat the six rooms of *Heeren House* (☎ (06) 281 4241), 1 Jalan Tun Tan Cheng Lock, right in the heart of town. Immaculate rooms in this refurbished godown cost RM99, or RM119 on weekends.

At the upper end of the scale, the *Orkid Hotel* (☎ (06) 282 5555; fax 282 7777) at 138 Jalan Bendahara, not far from the bus stations, is a new, private business hotel finished in smart black and green marble. Fairly swish rooms start at RM250.

The *City Bayview Hotel* (☎ (06) 283 9888; fax 283 6699), also on Jalan Bendahara, has rooms from RM275, while across the road the *Renaissance Melaka Hotel* (☎ (06) 284 8888; fax 284 9269) is the best hotel in town and charges from RM350 per night.

Places to Eat

Melaka has no shortage of places to eat. On Jalan Merdeka, previously the waterfront, the *Glutton's Corner* food stalls serve all the usual food centre specialities. Try the *Bunga Raya Restaurant* at No 40 which has excellent steamed crabs, though they are not that cheap at RM35 a serve.

The *Mahkota Parade* shopping complex nearby is mostly a centre for western fast food, though the food court on the 1st floor serves the usual hawker favourites.

On Jalan Laksamana, right in the centre of town, the *Restaurant Kim Swee Huat* at No 38 is a cheap restaurant that does good Chinese food and western breakfasts.

Good, if slightly expensive, daytime cafes for Nonya dishes can be found in restored Peranakan houses in Chinatown. The *Heeren House* guesthouse has a cafe with a delightful atmosphere and is good for cakes and Peranakan and Portuguese food. It also serves western breakfasts. *Jonkers Melaka Restoran*, 17 Jalan Hang Jebat, is a craft shop with a courtyard restaurant. It's a good place for a snack and serves Nonya dishes, including a Nonya set lunch.

At *Medan Portugese* (Portuguese Square) you can sample Malay-Portuguese cuisine at tables facing the sea. Excellent seafood is served, and for around RM25 per person you can eat very well. Just outside the square is a Malay-Portuguese restaurant, the *San Pedro*. The food is similar to that on offer in the square but the atmosphere is more intimate – and the prices higher.

Getting There & Away

Melaka is 216km north-west of Johor Bahru. It can be visited as a day trip from Singapore if you have your own car; it's about 3½ to four hours away on the expressway. By bus, it takes 4½ hours, so a visit really requires two days. Tour companies from Singapore offer 12 to 14 hour day tours for around S$75.

Buses from Singapore can be booked at the Lavender St Malaysia bus station (Map 5) or from an agent operating out of Lavender MRT station. From Melaka express

EXCURSIONS

buses to Singapore leave hourly from 8 am to 6 pm from the express bus stand and the fare is RM11.50.

You can also take the train to Melaka via Tampin, where you have to disembark and continue the journey by taxi for around RM30. From Singapore to Tampin by train costs S$22. In order to get back to Singapore by train you must call the Tampin railway station (☎ (06) 441 1034) to make your reservation and get to Tampin by 9 am if you want to catch the early train. From Tampin to Singapore costs RM25.

Getting Around
A bicycle rickshaw is the ideal way of getting around compact and slow-moving Melaka. To hire by the hour a rickshaw should cost about RM20, or RM6 for any one-way trip within the town, but you'll have to bargain. Taxis are unmetered, and similarly charge RM6 for a trip anywhere around town.

KOTA TINGGI
The small town of Kota Tinggi is 64km north-east of Singapore on the road to Mersing. Waterfalls, 15km north-west of the town, cascade through a series of pools which are ideal for a cooling dip. Entry to the falls is RM1.

At the falls, *Kota Tinggi Waterfall Resort* (☎ (07) 833 1146) has air-con chalets from RM150 on weekends and RM110 on weekdays. Weekend bookings are heavy.

Getting There & Away
From Singapore, it is a 1½ hour drive to Kota Tinggi. From Johor Bahru regular buses (No 41, RM2) and taxis (RM4) go to Kota Tinggi. Take bus No 43 from Kota Tinggi to the waterfalls.

DESARU
On a 20km stretch of beach at Tanjung Penawar, 88km east of Johor Bahru – and also reached via Kota Tinggi – this resort area is a popular weekend escape for Singaporeans. The beach is quite good, but it's not particularly interesting for other international visitors to Malaysia.

Places to Stay & Eat
Accommodation at Desaru is provided by expensive resorts. The *Desaru Garden Beach Resort* (☎ (07) 822 1101) does, however, have a camping ground with sites at RM7 per head, and dorm beds at RM15 per head. The beach resort, like its companion, the *Desaru View* (☎ (07) 822 1221), also has top-end accommodation with a full range of amenities from S$180. Prices rise significantly on weekends.

At Batu Layar, 16km south of Desaru, the *Batu Layar Beach Resort* (☎ (07) 822 1835) is a newish place with garishly painted A-frame chalets from RM75 (the rates go up at weekends).

Getting There & Away
Buses (RM5) and taxis operate from Kota Tinggi. A popular way for Singaporeans to reach Desaru is to take the ferry to Tanjung Belungkor from the Changi ferry terminal, and from there a taxi to Desaru for RM30.

MERSING
Mersing is a small, picturesque fishing village about 150km north of Singapore on the east coast of Peninsular Malaysia. It's the departure point for the beautiful South China Sea islands, including Tioman. If you need to overnight here it has plenty of cheap hotels.

The Mersing jetty is a five minute walk from the town centre and you'll find the offices for boats to all the islands in this area.

Getting There & Away
From Singapore it takes 2½ hours to reach Mersing by car. Alternatively, you can catch direct buses from Singapore or from Johor Bahru.

For information on ferry services to/from Tioman call BCIC Tioman Ferry Services (☎/fax (09) 799 5063). Ferry schedules depend to a large degree on the tides, so all departure and arrival times vary.

TIOMAN ISLAND (PULAU TIOMAN)
The largest and most spectacular of the east coast islands, Tioman has beautiful beaches, clear water and coral for snorkelling or

diving enthusiasts. Its major attraction, however, has to be the diversity it offers – high mountains and dense jungle are only a short walk away from the coast.

Tioman is the most popular destination on the east coast and it can get quite crowded at peak times, particularly in July and August. The island has a host of cheap accommodation at the popular backpackers' beaches of Air Batang, Salang, Juara and Tekek. Accommodation is mostly in very simple huts, longhouse rooms or more comfortable chalets. Expect to pay at least RM20 for a small hut, and up to RM60 for an air-con chalet for two persons.

Of the accommodation options, Salang is probably the best choice if you want a modicum of comfort, a selection of restaurants and bars and money-changing facilities. The only way in and out is by water taxi and they don't come too cheap: count on RM20 from Tekek Village (Kampung Tekek) to Salang, or RM25 from the Berjaya Imperial Island Resort. The beaches and accommodation choices just north of Tekek Village are average to not-so-hot.

Midway in the accommodation options is the *Persona Island Resort* (☎/fax (09) 414 6213) just five minutes walk south of the jetty at Tekek Village. It's a small, low-key resort with comfortable rooms starting at RM80 for a standard room with a fan. It's right on a pretty decent beach and sports a small restaurant and bar.

The *Berjaya Imperial Island Resort* (☎ (09) 419 1000; fax 419 1718; tod@hr. berjaya.com.my) is the only international-class hotel on the island. Rooms cost from RM245 and there is a very impressive range of facilities: a beautiful golf course, tennis, horse riding, jet skis, scuba diving etc.

A number of smaller islands near Tioman also have superb beaches and accommodation, including Rawa, Sibu, Babi Besar and Tengah.

Getting There & Away
Air Silk Air and Pelangi Air have daily flights to/from Singapore's Seletar airport for RM197 (S$115). Pelangi also flies four

times daily to Kuala Lumpur (RM181), and daily to Kuantan (RM119). Berjaya is another small feeder airline with daily flights to Kuala Lumpur for the same price. All prices include the RM40 departure tax.

The booking office for Berjaya tickets is in the Berjaya Imperial Island Resort while for Pelangi it's on the 2nd level of a small building just outside the airport entrance gate.

Boat There's a daily high-speed catamaran service between Singapore's Tanah Merah ferry terminal and Tioman. See the Getting

EXCURSIONS

There & Away chapter for details. On Tioman, bookings can be made at the desk in the lobby of the Berjaya Imperial Island Resort.

Other boats go from Mersing, and a few go from Tanjong Gemok on the border of Pahang and Johor states, 38km north of Mersing.

From Mersing there are a variety of services to Tioman, though sailing times vary according to the tide. Most boats are express services, taking around 1½ hours and costing RM25 or RM30. They normally stop at Genting, Paya, the resort, Tekek, Air Batang (ABC Chalets) and Salang. Buying a return ticket saves you about RM5.

From Tanjong Gemok, boats leave twice daily to Tekek during the peak season at 9 am and 2 pm. The cost is RM25.

Indonesia

Indonesia is a fascinating collection of islands and cultures. If you have a few days to spare and the money for airfares, you can make a number of short tours from Singapore. You can arrange a trip independently or there are dozens of packages available from travel agents.

Some easily reached Indonesian highlights are: Danau (Lake) Toba and Bukittinggi in Sumatra; Jakarta, Yogyakarta and Borobudur in Java; and, of course, Bali. For day or overnight trips, there are the islands of the Riau Archipelago, which cover an area of over 170,000 sq km, curving south-east from Sumatra to Kalimantan and north to Malaysia.

RIAU ARCHIPELAGO

Tanjung Pinang on Bintan is the main town in the archipelago, though Batam is now the centre of all activity. Singaporean investors are pouring millions of dollars into the islands, and the Indonesian and Singaporean governments are developing the area as a special economic zone that will support a variety of industries. Batam gets most of the investment and is now the centre for transport in and out of the archipelago.

Both islands can be visited as day trips from Singapore, although if you wish to stay there is a wide variety of accommodation available.

Batam is a duty-free port which used to attract hoards of Singaporean day trippers stocking up on duty-free goods – then the government woke up and decreed that anyone re-entering Singapore within 48 hours of leaving forfeited the right to any duty-free allowance. As a result, Batam attracts mainly Indonesian tourists.

Bintan is the more interesting island, though there are far less ferries and you may have no choice but to spend the night there.

Both islands provide a taste of Indonesia, though not a particularly memorable one. To see the best of the country you really have to travel further afield.

Most nationalities – including citizens of the USA, the UK, Australia, Canada, New Zealand, Ireland, the Netherlands and most other European countries – do not require a visa to Indonesia for a visit of up to 60 days. The proviso is that entry must be at specified ports – Batam and Bintan are visa-free entry ports – otherwise a visa must be obtained.

The Indonesian monetary unit is the rupiah (rp). Exchange rates at the time of research were S$1 = 8865 rp, US$1 = 14,725 rp but this may change dramatically given Indonesia's ongoing woes.

For further information, contact the Indonesia Tourist Promotion Office (☎ 534 2837; fax 533 4287), 15-07 Ocean building (Map 6), 10 Collyer Quay, Singapore. It is open from 9 am to 5 pm (closed for lunch from 1 to 2 pm) weekdays and from 10 am to 1 pm on Saturday.

Batam Island (Pulau Batam)

There are potentially two reasons why you would want to go to Bintam: to catch an onward ferry to other parts of Indonesia, or to cruise the Riau islands on an organised tour. Shopping for cheap, good quality clothing is also another, though perhaps less-compelling, reason to visit.

EXCURSIONS

While Batam has been heavily developed to become virtually an industrial suburb of Singapore, there's still a distinct frontier town atmosphere to this place, with higher prices than elsewhere in Indonesia. Nonetheless, there's a decent array of quality accommodation and restaurants, a vibrant expat community and it's a convenient spot to get a first taste of Indonesia.

From Singapore, most travellers arrive by boat at the port of **Sekupang**. After you clear immigration, there are counters for money exchange, taxis and hotels. It's a five minute walk to the domestic ferry terminal, from where there are speedboats to numerous other Sumatran destinations. Car and passenger ferries to Bintan leave from **Telaga Punggur** in the south-east of the island (bumboats leave from Kabil).

The main town of **Nagoya** is a brash bustling boom town, complete with bars, massage parlours and flash duty-free cars. The old shanties can still be seen between the new hotels, offices and shopping centres. Nagoya's port area of Batu Ampar is just north of town. Unless you are planning to head straight on out of Batam, you are advised to take the ferry to Batu Ampar where you are closer to hotels and other traveller facilities. However, these services are less frequent.

Batam Centre is a new administrative centre that is being built from the stumps up in the north between Nagoya and Hang Nadim airport. The **Nongsa** peninsula in the north-east is ringed by polished golf resorts built with Singapore visitors in mind, who will never get homesick with a view of the Singapore skyline on the horizon. Direct ferry services link Singapore's Tanah Merah ferry terminal with Nongsa.

There's a money-exchange counter at the Sekupang ferry building, but the rates are better in Nagoya where all the major banks are based. You are advised in any case to bring some rupiah with you as the exchange counter may not be open. Singapore dollars are as acceptable as Indonesian rupiah, though if you plan to do any bargaining stick to rupiah. You can buy rupiah at the money-exchange counter at the World Trade Centre in Singapore.

Organised Tours There is really only one enterprise in the Riau islands that operates to show tourists and travellers the hidden beauties of the archipelago; this is Riau Island Adventures (☎ (0778) 45 434; fax 45 639; iabookings@mailhost.net) run by irrepressible expat Australian Evan Jones. Evan organises very popular one to three day cruise and activity breaks for S$100 to S$320. The mini-cruises on a wooden-hulled schooner typically include sailing, trekking, canoeing, cycling, swimming and eating and take in the clear waters of the straits between Batam and Bintan.

Places to Stay Budget accommodation is limited to rooming houses known as *KOST*, and *wismas* which are small, unofficial guesthouses. These are both geared primarily to the Indonesian visitor and so while they do offer good value with room prices ranging from 25,000 to 50,000 rupiah, few of them will have anyone who speaks English and the quality does vary enormously.

There is a wide scattering of wisma and rooming houses around the centre of Nagoya all within shouting distance of the main drags, Jalan Teuku Umar and Jalan Imam Bonjoi; look for the signs. Always ask to inspect a room before agreeing to stay.

Batam now has a good range of middle to top-end hotels with rates that are considerably below what you would pay in Singapore for an equivalent standard. Prices are usually quoted in Singapore dollars, and singles/doubles start at around S$40 and peak at around S$80.

The *Horisona* (☎ (0778) 457 111) has singles/doubles for S$45/60 and a good central location on Jalan S Rahman. The welcoming *Puri Garden Hotel* (☎ (0778) 458 888; fax 456 333) on Jalan Teuku Umar, run by affable expat Kenneth Dowd, is a pleasant oasis amid the rough and tumble of Nagoya. Comfortable singles/doubles go for S$59/90.

EXCURSIONS

The *Novotel Batam* (☎ (0778) 425 555), on Jalan Durung, Sei Johoh, is a newie with singles/doubles for around S$60.

The best hotel in Nagoya is the *Melia Panorama* (☎ (0778) 452 888; fax 452 555; meliapan@indosat.net.id), a swish hotel (part of the Komplek Tanjung Pantun) in a slightly seedy neighbourhood. Listed room rates kick in at S$198 but discounted rates are often far below that figure.

The beach resorts around Nongsa are mainly for package visitors from Singapore. Some of the places are of a good standard and the beaches are passable, but there is nothing to see or do outside of the resorts.

Places to Eat The best budget eating in Nagoya is at the night food stalls (*pujasera*) which are to be found all over town. The *Pujasera Matahari* is about the most central and easiest to find.

About a block east of the Melia Panorama hotel are a couple of places worth checking; the *Kedai Kopi Indah* is a popular Chinese coffee shop with a good range of eats, while nearby is *Lucy's Oar House Tavern* which offers tasty western food.

There is a posh Japanese restaurant called *Tan Kyu* (pun intended) on the 17th floor of the Melia Panorama and the restaurant of the *Puri Garden Hotel* has a good range of European and Asian dishes. The beer is cheap too.

There are a number of waterfront seafood places dotted around the coast of the island, particularly around the resorts at Nongsa. Prices tend to be on a par with Singapore so don't come expecting bargain dining.

Entertainment Entertainment is confined to any number of bars – with or without karaoke – that have sprouted in pretty well every corner of town. The *Sugar Pub* behind the Mandarin Regency is a favourite watering hole for expats and the *Skylight Disco* at the Bumi Nusantara Hotel on the south side of town is the weekend haunt of hundreds of lonely, single Indonesian female factory workers seeking the company of similarly lonely and preferably unattached males.

Getting There & Away No international services land at Hang Nadim airport but it is a major hub for domestic flights.

See the Getting There & Away chapter for details of the ferries from Singapore. The most frequent and convenient services are those in and out of the international ferry terminal at Sekupang (to Singapore ferries leave constantly from 7.40 am to 7 pm).

A less frequent but cheaper service (S$10 one way) also links Singapore's WTC with Teluk Senimba south of Sekupang.

The main reason most travellers come to Batam is to catch a boat to Pekanbaru on Sumatra. Boats leave from Sekupang's domestic wharf, just 100m south of the international terminal. The trip to Pekanbaru involves a four hour boat trip to Tanjung Buton on the Sumatran mainland, via Selat Panjang (on Pulau Tebingtinggi), followed by a three hour bus ride. The combined ticket costs about 35,000 rp. There are no services to Pekanbaru after 10 am, so you'll need to make an early start if you're coming from Singapore.

Other destinations from Sekupang include: Pulau Karimun (16,500 rp); Pulau Kundur (17,000 rp); Dumai (35,000 rp); and Kuala Tungkal, on the Jambi coast (60,000 rp).

Speedboats to Tanjung Pinang on neighbouring Bintan leave from Telaga Punggur, 30km south-east of Nagoya. There's a steady flow of departures from 8 am to 5.15 pm. The trip takes 45 minutes and costs 10,000 rp one way, plus 1000 rp port tax.

Getting Around There is an island-wide bus service linking Nagoya with Tanjung Uncang, Nongsa, Telaga Punggur and Sekupang for around 600 rp, but most people use the share taxis that cruise the island – just stand by the roadside and call out your destination to passing cabs. Sample fares from Sekupang include 3000 rp to Nagoya and 10,000 rp to Telaga Punggur. You will need to make it clear that you are paying for a seat, not the whole taxi. Avoid the potentially lethal *ojak* motorcycle 'taxis' and their reckless drivers; accidents are frequent and often fatal.

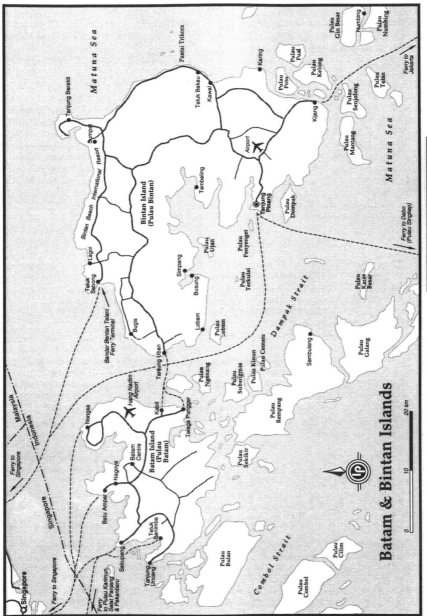

Batam & Bintan Islands

EXCURSIONS

Bintan Island (Pulau Bintan)

Bintan is considerably larger than Batam and much more interesting. Singaporean development is, at present, on a much lower key on Bintan, with the exception of a cluster of golf resorts on the north coast around Lagoi.

The main attractions are the old town of Tanjung Pinang (a visa-free entry/exit point), Penyenget Island (Pulau Penyenget), the beaches of the east coast, and the resort strip in the north of the island.

Tanjung Pinang can be visited as a day trip from Singapore, but ferry connections don't leave much time for exploring the city and you really need to stay overnight. A couple of tour operators in Singapore have two day/one night tours to Bintan for around S$130, and plenty of packages to the beach resorts are also available.

Tanjung Pinang After development-mad Batam, Tanjung Pinang comes as a very pleasant surprise. It may be the largest town in the Riau Archipelago but it retains much of its old-time charm, particularly the picturesque, stilted section of the town that juts over the sea around Jalan Plantar II. The harbour sees a constant stream of shipping of every shape and size, varying from tiny sampans to large freighters.

Senggarang is a fascinating village across the harbour from Tanjung Pinang. Its star attraction is an old **Chinese temple** held together by the roots of a huge banyan tree that has grown up through it.

The temple is to the left at the end of the pier, coming by boat from Tanjung Pinang. Half a kilometre along the waterfront is a big square with three **Chinese temples** side by side. Boats to Senggarang leave from the end of Jalan Plantar II.

You can charter a sampan along the **Snake River** (Sungei Ular) through the mangroves to the **Chinese temple**, with its gory murals of the trials and tortures of hell.

Tiny **Penyenget Island** is in the harbour across from Tanjung Pinang. It was once capital of the kingdom and the whole place is steeped in history. The **ruins** of the old palace of Raja Ali and the **tombs** and **graveyards** of Raja Jaafar and Raja Ali are clearly signposted inland. The most impressive site is the sulphur-coloured **mosque** with its many domes and minarets. Frequent boats go to the island from Bintan's main pier for 1000 rp per person.

Beaches Most of Bintan's beaches are relatively untouched, apart from the inevitable 'drift plastic'. The best beaches are along the eastern coast, where there is also good snorkelling outside the November to March monsoon period. Getting there can be a battle, but there is a choice of accommodation at the main beach, Pantai Trikora (see the following Places to Stay section). There are buses to Trikora for 2500 rp from the bus station in Tanjung Pinang, otherwise a taxi costs around 30,000 rp.

All the main activity is in the north. The huge International Beach Resort development takes up the entire north coast of the island. It comprises a number of hotels, chalets, golf courses and property developments all financed by, and directed toward, Singaporean interests. Much of it is still under construction and, though the beaches are quite good and the resorts sophisticated, over-development threatens to destroy the natural attractions. Ferries run directly to Singapore's Tanah Merah ferry terminal.

Places to Stay – Tanjung Pinang You'll find some good but still pretty spartan budget accommodation in Tanjung Pinang. Lorong Bintan II, a small alley between Jalan Bintan and Jalan Yusuf Khahar in the centre of town, is the place to look. The popular *Bong's Homestay* at No 20 has dorm beds for 10,000 rp and doubles for 15,000 rp, including breakfast. *Johnny's Homestay*, next door at No 22, acts as an overflow.

The *Hotel Surya* (☎ (0771) 21 811) on Jalan Bintan has clean, simple singles/doubles with fan for 21,000/25,000 rp. The *Wisma Riau* (☎ (0771) 21 023) and the *Sampurna Inn* (☎ (0771) 21 555), side by side on Jalan Yusuf Khahar, have air-con rooms with TV for 40,000 rp.

The best hotel in town is the *Asean Hotel* (☎ (0771) 22 161, Singapore ☎ 271 6643) on Jalan Gudang Minyek.

Places to Stay – Pantai Trikora *Yasin's Guesthouse* (☎ (0771) 26 770) at the 36km marker near the village of Teluk Bakau, is a laid-back place with half a dozen simple palm huts right on the beach. It charges 25,000 rp per person per day, including three meals. *Bukit Berbunga Cottages*, right next door, has very similar accommodation. It charges 25,000/30,000 rp for singles/doubles, including breakfast. At the 38km marker, the flashier *Trikora Beach Resort* has singles from S$85 to S$105.

Most of the resorts in the north are Singaporean owned, and packages are offered by the hotels and travel agents in Singapore. Their Singapore telephone numbers are listed below. In the pipeline are marinas, water theme parks, a Club Med and a Shangri-La hotel. Already opened are the *Hotel Sedona Bintan Lagoon* (☎ (0771) 337 3577), a 416 room deluxe hotel with a golf course, and the much smaller *Mayang Sari Beach Resort* (☎ (0771) 732 8515), which has cheaper air-con chalets. The *Banyan Tree Bintan* (☎ (0771) 325 4193) is very popular with Singaporeans. It's a number of luxury villas that rent for S$240 to S$390 during the week, S$340 to S$520 on weekends.

Places to Eat Tanjung Pinang used to have a superb *night market* in the bus station on Jalan Teuku Umar, however, it wasn't there on our last visit and may have gone for good.

During the day, there are several pleasant cafes with outdoor eating areas in front of the basketball stadium on Jalan Teuku Umar; try *Flipper* or *Sunkist*. There are some pretty basic Padang food places along Jalan Plantar II where you can get a tasty fish curry for 1500 rp, or jackfruit curry (kare nangka) for 800 rp.

For a bit of extra comfort the *Indra Jaya* opposite the stadium is a decent place and there is a restaurant in the *Sampurna Inn* that manages to put a reasonable meal together.

Getting There & Away Bintan's airport at Kijang has taken something of a back seat following the upgrading of Batam. Sempati has daily direct flights to Jakarta (290,500 rp) and Pekanbaru (150,800 rp). Air-ticket prices overall may have increased dramatically by the time you read this or Sempati may even be out of business, such is the current economic uncertainty.

Ferries run from Singapore's WTC to Tanjung Pinang. Other ferries run from Singapore's Tanah Merah ferry terminal to the Bandar Bentan Telani ferry terminal at the Bintan Beach Resort in the north of the island. See the Getting There & Away chapter for information on getting to Bintan from Singapore.

There are also a few international ferries running between Tanjung Pinang and Johor Bahru in Malaysia.

Tanjung Pinang retains its traditional role as the hub of Riau's inter-island shipping, with boats to Tanjung Balai on Pulau Karimun (22,000 rp, 2½ hours) and Dabo on Pulau Singkep (25,000 rp, three hours). There are regular speedboats to Telaga Panggur on Batam (11,000 rp, 45 minutes), as well as three boats a day direct to Sekupang (13,000 rp, 1½ hours). Most services leave from the main pier at the southern end of Jalan Merdeka, but check when you buy your ticket. New Oriental Tours & Travel, Jalan Merdeka 61, is a reliable ticket agent.

To Jakarta, Pelni's KM *Bukit Siguntang* and KM *Umsini* sail from the port of Kijang, in the south-eastern corner of the island, every Monday. The journey takes 28 hours. The alternative is the MV *Samudera Jaya*, which leaves Tanjung Pinang every Thursday and does the trip in 18 hours for 95,000 rp. The Pelni office (☎ (0771) 21 513) in Tanjung Pinang is 5km east of the town centre.

Getting Around Taxis charge a standard 15,000 rp for the 17km run from the airport to Tanjung Pinang. Buses and share taxis to other parts of Bintan leave from the bus and taxi station on Jalan Teuku Umar.

EXCURSIONS

Glossary

For a glossary of Singaporean food types and words connected with food, see the Places to Eat chapter.

adat – Malay customary law
adat temenggong – Malay law with Indian modifications. Adat temenggong is the law governing the customs and ceremonies of the sultans.
ang pow – red packets of money used as offerings, payment or gifts
arak – the local (aniseed-based) alcohol spirit drink
ASEAN – Association of South-East Asia Nations
atap – roof thatching

Baba – male *Peranakan*
bandar – port
batang – stem, tree trunk, the main branch of a river
batik – technique for imprinting cloth with dye to produce multicoloured patterns
batu – stone, rock, milepost
bukit – hill
bumiputra – indigenous Malaysians (literally 'sons of the soil')

CBD – Central Business District
chettiar – Indian moneylender
Chingay – annual festival celebrated by a multicoloured parade down Orchard Rd by Chinese and other cultural groups

Deepavali – Hindu festival celebrating the victory of Rama over Ravana, the demon king
dharma – Hindu notion of natural law
dusun – small town

EDB – Economic Development Board
entrepôt – French word for commercial centre

feng shui – literally 'wind-water'; Chinese system of geomancy used in designing living space

five-foot-ways – raised porch area fronting traditional buildings

godown – river warehouse
gopuram – colourful, ornate tower over the entrance gate to Hindu temples

haji – man who has made the pilgrimage to Mecca; feminine version is *hajjah*
hajj – Muslim pilgrimage to Mecca
Hari Raya Haji – Muslim festival in honour of those who have made the pilgrimage to Mecca
Hari Raya Puasa – Malay celebration marking the end of *Ramadan*
HDB – Housing Development Board; state body responsible for the provision of public housing

imam – Islamic leader
istana – palace

jalan – road
jinricksha – rickshaw

kallang – shipyard
kampong – traditional Malay village
kavadi – heavy, spiked metal frames decorated with peacock feathers, fruit and flowers used in the *Thaipusam* parade and carried by Hindu devotees
kelong – fish trap on stilts
keramat – Malay shrine associated with animism
kongsi – Chinese clan organisations for mutual assistance, known variously as ritual brotherhoods, heaven-man-earth societies, triads and secret societies; see also *Triad*
kopi tiam – traditional coffee shop
kota – fort, city
KTM – Keretapi Tanah Malayu (Malaysian Railways System)
kuala – river mouth, place where a tributary joins a larger river
Kuomintang Party – Chinese political party formed in 1911 with strong Communist leanings

lawa – fishing stake that forms part of a *kelong*

lorong – narrow street, alley

LRT – Light Rapid Transport railway system

MAS – Monetary Authority of Singapore

masjid – mosque

Merlion – half-lion, half-fish animal and symbol of Singapore

moksha – the Hindu notion of spiritual salvation

MRT – Mass Rapid Transport railway system

muezzin – the official of a mosque, who calls the faithful to prayer

Navarathri – Hindu festival of the 'Nine Nights'

Nonya – female *Peranakan*

padang – open grassy area; usually the city square

pantai – beach

PAP – People's Action Party; main political party of Singapore

pasar – market

pasar malam – night market

Peranakan – literally 'half-caste', the term refers to the Straits Chinese, the original Chinese settlers in Singapore, who intermarried with Malays and adopted many Malay customs

PIE – Pan-Island Expressway, one of Singapore's main road arteries

pintu pagar – swing doors common in Chinese shop houses

pulau – island

Punggal – Indian harvest festival

Qing Ming – Chinese festival celebrating 'All Soul's Day'

raja – prince, ruler

Ramadan – Islamic month of fasting

rotan – cane made of rattan used to punish criminals

sampan – bumboat

Singlish – variation of English spoken in Singapore

STB – Singapore Tourism Board

STDB – Singapore Trade Development Board

sungei – river

tanjung – headland

temenggong – Malay administrator

Thaipusam – Hindu festival in which devotees honour Lord Subraniam with acts of amazing masochism

Thimithi – Hindu fire-walking ceremony

thola – Indian unit of weight

towkang – Chinese junk

Triad – Chinese secret organised crime society; see also *kongsi*

Vedas – the four Hindu books of divine knowledge

Vesak day – festival celebrating Buddha's birth

wayang – Chinese street opera

wayang kulit – shadow puppet play

wet market – produce market

WTC – World Trade Centre

Index

Maps

Arab St Walking Tour 92
Around Singapore **Map 1**
Batam & Bintan Islands 187
Central Singapore **Map 3**
Chinatown Walking Tour 95
City Centre **Map 6**

Geylang & East Coast **Map 8**
Johor Bahru 174
Jurong **Map 7**
Little India & Arab St **Map 5**
Little India Walking Tour 89
Melaka City 178

Orchard Rd **Map 4**
Sentosa Island **Map 9**
Singapore **Map 2**
Singapore MRT **Map 10**
Tioman Island (Pulau Tioman) 183

Boxed Text

Automated City, The 25
Caning in Singapore 28
Controlling the Internet 54
Cost of a Car, The 65
Costs 49
Drinks 154
Ferry Schedule to Kusu & St
  John's Islands 109
Fines 62
Free Internet Faxing to
  Singapore 53

Hawker Centres on the Web 136
HDBs 111
Hotels Online 125
Kampong Life 104
Kelongs 110
Kiasu or What? 26
More Recommended Eating 150
Old Trades of Chinatown, The 97
Recommended Eating 138
Rogue Trader – Nick Leeson
  160

Singapore-Malaysia Relations
  13
Singapore on a Shoestring? 60
Singapore Sling, The 83
Singlish 42
Speak Mandarin, Please! 41
Sugarcane Deliverance 63
Train Fares From Singapore to
  Malaysia 70

Text

Map references are in **bold** type.
Illustration references are in
  bold italic type.

Abdul Gaffoor Mosque 33, 91
accommodation 118-29
  camping 121
  renting 128-9
activities, *see* individual entries
air travel 66-9
  airline offices 66
  airport departure tax 66
  Australia 67-8
  Changi airport 74-5
  Europe 67
  Indonesia 68-9
  Malaysia 68
  New Zealand 68
  Seletar airport 75
  travel agents 66
  USA & Canada 67
Al-Abrar Mosque 94
Anderson Bridge 81
ang pow 27
antiques 169
Arab St 98, **Map 5**

Sultan Mosque 32-3, 91-2, 98,
  32, *91*
  walking tour 91-3, **92**
archery 115
Armenian church, *see* Church of
  St Gregory the Illuminator
Art Museum 85
arts 23-4
  Chinese opera 23, 163
  film 24
  lion dance 23-4
  literature 24
  Singapore Dance Theatre 85
Asian Civilisations Museum 85-6
Association of South-East Asian
  Nations 163
ATMs 48
Aw Boon Haw 11, 56

Baba-Nonya Heritage Museum
  (Melaka) 179, *21*
Babas, *see* Peranakans
badminton 115
bangsawan, see Malay opera
bargaining 49, *see also* shopping
Barings Bank, *see* Leeson, Nick

bars 157-62
Batam Island 184-6, **187**
Battle Box 85
beaches 105, 108, 182-3, 188
bicycle, *see* cycling
Big Splash 105
Bintan Island 188-9, **187**
birds 15, 57
  Jurong Bird Park 101
  Sunday Morning Bird
    Singing 112
Boat Quay 81, 159, *159*, **Map 6**
boat travel 79
books 55-7, *see also* literature
  bookshops 169
  fiction 56-7
  general 57
  guidebooks 55
  history 55-6
  Lonely Planet 55
  people & society 56
  politics 56
Botanic Gardens 111-12
bowling 115
Buddhism 29-30
Bukit Batok 114

Bukit Timah Nature Reserve
    113-14, 172
Bukit Turf Club 163
bus travel
    Farecards 76
    Malaysia 69
    Singapore 76-7
    Thailand 71
    tourist buses 77
business hours 61-2
business services 51
Bussorah St 92
Butterfly Park, *see* Sentosa
    Island

camping 121
caning 28
Cantonese food 137-9
car travel 77-8
    car parking 78
    car rental 77
    cost 65
    driving licence 46
cathedrals, *see* churches &
    cathedrals
Cathedral of the Good Shepherd
    84
Causeway, the 71
Cavenagh Bridge 81
cemeteries
    Kampong Glam cemetery
        93
    old Christian cemetery 85
censorship 54, 56, 57
central business district (CBD)
    86, **Map 6**
Changi **Map 2**
    airport 74-5
    prison 11, 28, 105
    Village 105
Chettiar Hindu Temple 99
children, travel with 60-1
Chinaman Scholars Gallery 96
Chinatown 97-8, **Map 6**
    Sri Mariamman Temple 36,
        97, *36*
    Thian Hock Keng Temple 34,
        97, *34*
    walking tour 93-6, **95**
Chinese
    clans 22
    customs 26-7
    food 137-42
    funerals 26
    gardens 101
    language 41
    lion dance 23-4
    opera 23, 163

people 22
religion 29-30
temples 34-5
weddings 26
Church of St Gregory the
    Illuminator 85
churches & cathedrals
    Cathedral of the Good
        Shepherd 84
    Church of St Gregory the
        Illuminator 85
    St Andrew's Cathedral 84
cinema 162
City Hall 82
clans 22
Clarke Quay 81, 159-61, **Map 6**
Clifford Pier 86
climate 14, 44
Colonial Singapore 81-6, **Maps
    5&6**
computers 25, 170
Confucianism 29-30
costs 48-9
    Singapore on a shoestring? 60
credit cards 48
cricket 116
Crocodilarium 105
cuisine, *see* food
cultural centres 61
cultural considerations 24-9, 62
    caning 28
    dress 29
    fines 62
    spitting 29
Cuppage, William 99
currency 47
currency crisis 17
customs 47
cybercafes, *see* email & Internet
    services
cycling 79, 108, 116

department stores 168-9
Desaru 182
Dick Lee 157
dining, *see* food
disabled travellers 59
discos 157-62
Discovery Centre 102
drinks 134, 154
    high tea 155
drugs 47, 61
durians 141, 155
duty free, *see* customs

East Coast 102-5, **Map 8**
    East Coast Park 104-5
    Geylang 103

Katong 103-4
East Coast Lagoon 105
East Coast Park 104-5, **Map 8**
    Big Splash 105
    East Coast Lagoon 105
    East Coast Recreation Centre
        105
    Singapore Crocodilarium 105
East India Company 9, 10, 98
ecology, *see* environmental issues
Economic Development Board
    (EDB) 50
economy 16-17
electricity 59, 166
electronic goods 170
Elgin Bridge 81
email & Internet services 53-5
    free Internet faxing 53
    hawker centres on the Web 136
    hotels online 125
embassies 46-7
Empress Place building 81
environmental issues 14-15
exchanging money 47-8

Fantasy Island, *see* Sentosa
    Island
Farecards 76
Farquhar, William 9
fauna 15-16, *see also* birds
    Butterfly Park 107
    Crocodilarium 105
    Insect Kingdom Museum 107
    Jurong Reptile Park 101
    long-tailed macaques 15, 172,
        172
    zoo (Johor Bahru) 175
    Zoological Gardens 112-13
fax services 53
    free Internet faxing 53
Fay, Michael 28
feng shui 30
film 24
fines 62
five-foot-ways 11
flora 15-16, *see also* gardens
food 130-57
    breakfast, snacks, delis 153-5
    Burmese 149
    Chinese 137-42
    fast food 152
    food festival 64
    French 152
    fruit 155-6
    hawker food 131-7
    Indian 142-3
    Indonesian 148
    Italian 152

194 Index

food continued
  Japanese 149-50
  Korean 150-1
  Malay 148
  Nonya 148-9
  recommendations 130, 138, 150
  seafood 141
  Singaporean 149
  supermarkets 156
  Taiwanese 151
  Thai 151
  vegetarian 140-1
  Vietnamese 151
Forbidden Hill 9, 85
Fort Canning 85
Fort Siloso, *see* Sentosa Island
fruit, *see* food

gardens
  Botanic Gardens 111-12
  Chinese gardens 101
  Japanese gardens 101
  Mandai Orchid Gardens 113
  National Orchid Garden 111-12
  Sentosa Orchid Gardens 107
  Zoological Gardens 112-13
gay travellers 59
  bars & clubs 161, 162
geography 14
Geylang 103, **Map 8**
  Geylang Serai Market 103
  Malay Cultural Village 103
Goh Chok Tong 13
golf 116
government & politics 16
  books 56
  People's Action Party (PAP) 12
  Singapore Democratic Party 16
Government House, *see* Istana
Grand Hotel de L'Europe 83
Great Singapore Sale 64, 166-7
Gurdwara Sahib Yishun Sikh Temple 38, *38*

Hainanese food 139
Hajjah Fatimah Mosque 92
harbour 86
Harry's bar 159, 160, *160*
Haw Par Villa 100-1, *100*
hawker food 131-7
HDB housing 111
health 59
Hinduism 40-3
  Hindu temples 36-7
history 8-13
  books 55-6

colonial-era 8
early empires 8
Emergency, the 12
Japanese occupation 11
Lee Kuan Yew's Singapore 12-13
life after Lee 13
postwar alienation 11-12
Raffles' city emerges 8-10
Veranda Riots 11
Hokkien food 139
Holland Village 115
horse racing 163-4
hotels, *see* accommodation
House of Tan Yeok Nee 99

Images of Singapore, *see* Sentosa Island
Indian
  customs 28-9
  food 142-3
  people 23
  religion 40-3
  weddings 28
Indonesia 184-90
  air travel 68-9
  Batam Island 184-6, **187**
  Bintan Island 188-9, **187**
  food 148
  Riau Archipelago 184-90
  sea travel 72-3
Insect Kingdom Museum, *see* Sentosa Island
insurance 45-6
International Convention & Exhibition Centre 51
Internet cafes, *see* email & Internet services
Internet resources, *see* email & internet services
Islam 30, 40
  hajj 40
  mosques 32-3
  Ramadan 40
islands, *see* individual entries
Istana 99
Istana Kampong Glam 92

Japanese
  food 149-50
  gardens 101
  supermarkets 156
Jinriksha station 95
Johor Bahru 173-6, **174**
  getting around 176
  getting there & away 176
  places to eat 175
  places to stay 175

shopping 176
  things to see 173-5
Jurong 99-102, **Map 7**
  Bird Park 101
  Chinese & Japanese gardens 101
  Haw Par Villa 100-1
  New Ming Village & Pewter Museum 102
  Reptile Park 101
  Singapore Discovery Centre 102
  Singapore Mint Coin Gallery 102
  Singapore Science Centre 101-2
  Tang Dynasty City 102

Kampung Days Museum, *see* Malay Cultural Village
Kampung Kling Mosque 179
Katong 103-4, **Map 8**
  Katong Antique House 104
  Peranakan terrace houses 103
kelongs 110
kiasu 26
Kipling, Rudyard 84
Kong Meng San Phor Kark See Temple 115
kongsi, *see* Chinese clans
Kopi Kat Klan 157
kopi tiam 130
Kota Tinggi 182
Kranji War Memorial 115
Kuan Yin Temple 35, 86, **31**
Kuomintang Party 11
Kusu Island 108-9

language 41-3
  Mandarin 41
  Peranakan 19
  Singlish 42, 43
laundry 59
Lee Kuan Yew 12, 13
Leeson, Nick 56, 160
Leong San See Temple 91
lesbian travellers 59
  bars & clubs 161, 162
libraries 61
lion dance 23-4
Little India 88-91, 98, **Map 5**
  Temple of 1000 Lights 98
  walking tour 88-91, **89**
Lower Seletar Reservoir 114

MacRitchie Reservoir 114
Malabar Muslim Jama-Ath Mosque 33, 93, *87*, *93*

Malay
  Cultural Village 103
  customs 27-8
  food 148
  opera 24
  people 22
  weddings 27-8
Malayan Communist Party 11
Malayan Democratic Union 12
Malayan Union 11
Malaysia 173-84
  air travel 68
  bus travel 69-70
  Desaru 182
  Johor Bahru 173-6, **174**
  Kota Tinggi 182
  Kukup 176
  Melaka 177-82, **178**
  Mersing 182
  sea travel 72
  Singapore relations 13
  taxi travel 70-1
  Tioman Island 182-4, **183**
  train travel 72
Mandai Orchid Gardens 113
maps 44
Marco Polo 8
Maritime Museum 107
Maritime Museum (Melaka) 179
markets
  flea market 91
  Geylang Serai Market 103
  New Bugis St 86
  Telok Ayer Centre 86
  thieves' market 94
  Zhujiao Centre 88
Mass Rapid Transit (MRT)
  system 13, 75-6
  fare guides 74
Maugham, Somerset 56-7, 84,
  84
medical treatment, *see* health
Melaka 8, 177-82, **178**
  Bukit China 179-80
  Chinatown (Old Melaka) 179
  getting around 182
  getting there & away 181-2
  orientation & information 177
  places to eat 181
  places to stay 180-1
  Stadthuys & St Paul's Hill
    177-9
  sultanate of 8
Merlion 81, 107, **107**
Mersing 182
Mint Coin Gallery 102
Monetary Authority of
  Singapore (MAS) 17

money 47-50
  ATMs 48
  bargaining 49
  costs 48-9
  credit cards 48
  exchange rates 47
  exchanging money 47
  taxes 49-51, 130, 166
  tipping 49
  travellers cheques 48
mosques 32-3
  Abdul Gaffoor Mosque 33, 91
  Al-Abrar Mosque 94
  Hajjah Fatimah Mosque 92
  Kampung Kling Mosque 179
  Malabar Muslim Jama-Ath
    Mosque 33, 93, **87**, **93**
  Nagore Durgha Shrine 94, **94**
  Sultan Abu Bakar Mosque
    (Johor Bahru) 174
  Sultan Mosque 32-3, 91-2, 98,
    32, **91**
Mt Faber Park 114
museums
  Art Museum 85
  Asian Civilisations Museum
    85-6
  Baba-Nonya Heritage
    Museum (Melaka) 179, **21**
  Battle Box 85
  Changi Prison Museum 105
  Chinaman Scholars Gallery
    96
  Cultural Museum (Melaka)
    179
  Images of Singapore 106
  Insect Kingdom Museum 107
  Kampung Days Museum 103
  Maritime Museum 107
  Maritime Museum (Melaka)
    179
  National Museum 85
  Peranakan Showhouse
    Museum 99
  Pewter Museum 102
  Philatelic Museum 86
  Proclamation of
    Independence Hall
    (Melaka) 179
  Raffles Hotel Museum 84
  Royal Abu Bakar Museum
    (Johor Bahru) 173
  Sun Yatsen Villa 115
  Tong Chai Medical Institute 96
music
  classical 163
  music shops 171
  rock, jazz & blues 157-62

Nagore Durgha Shrine 94, **94**
National Library 61
National Museum 85
National Orchid Garden 111-112
nature reserves 15, 172-3
  Bukit Timah Nature Reserve
    113-14, 172
  Pasir Ris Park 114
  Sungei Buloh Nature Park
    114, 172
New Bugis St 86
New Ming Village & Pewter
  Museum 102
newspapers 57
nightclubs 157-62
Night Safari, *see* Zoological
  Gardens

Omni Theatre, *see* Singapore
  Science Centre
opera, Chinese 23, 163
opium 10
Orchard Rd 99, **Map 4**
  Chettiar Hindu Temple 99
  House of Tan Yeok Nee 99
  Istana 99
  Peranakan Place 99

Padang, the 82-3
Palembang 8
Parliament House 82
Pasir Ris Park 114
People Like Us 59
People's Action Party (PAP) 12
Peranakan Place 99, **18**
Peranakans 11, 18-21, 56, 85
  architecture 103, **18**
  Baba-Nonya Heritage
    Museum (Melaka) 179, **21**
  culture 19
  dress 18
  food 20-1, 148-9
  houses 19-20
  Katong Antique House 104
  language 19
Peranakan Showhouse Museum 99
Pewter Museum 102
Philatelic Museum 86
photography 58
  cameras & film 169-70
politics, *see* government
population 17
postal services 51-2
Proclamation of Independence
  Hall (Melaka) 179
public holidays 62-5
Pulau Tioman, *see* Tioman Island
Pulau Ubin 110, 172

radio 57-8
Raffles Hotel 10, 83, 127-8, 161
Raffles Place 86
Raffles, Stamford 8-10, 85, **9**
   statue 81
Ramadan, *see* Islam
religion 29-30, 40-1, 62
   Buddhism 29-30
   Confucianism 29-30
   festivals 62-5
   Hinduism 40-1
   Islam 30, 40
   keramat worship 109
   places of worship 31-9
   Taoism 29-30
rental, *see* car travel
Riau Archipelago 184-90
rickshaws, *see* trishaws
rotan 28
Royal Abu Bakar Museum
   (Johor Bahru) 173

safety 61
Sakaya Muni Buddha Gaya
   Temple, *see* Temple of 1000
   Lights
Science Centre 101-2
sea travel 71-3
   cruises 73
   Indonesia 72-3
   Malaysia 72
   World Trade Centre 71
Seletar airport 75
senior travellers 59
Sentosa Island 105-8, **Map 9**
   Asian Village 107
   beaches 108
   Butterfly Park & Insect
      Kingdom Museum 107
   Fantasy Island 106
   Fort Siloso 106
   getting there & away 108
   Images of Singapore 106
   Maritime Museum 107
   Merlion Tower 108
   Sentosa Orchid Gardens 107
   Underwater World 106
Shanghainese food 139
shopping, *see also* individual
   entries 165-71
   bargaining 165
   department stores 168-9
   Great Singapore Sale 64, 166-7
   guarantees 165-6
   service 166
   taxes 166
   what to buy 169-71
   where to shop 167-8

Singapore Democratic Party 16
Singapore International
   Chamber of Commerce 50
Singapore river 81-2
Singapore Sling 83
Singapore Tourism Board, *see*
   tourist offices
Singapore Trade Development
   Board (STDB) 50
Singlish 42
Siong Lim Temple 35, 115
sports, *see* individual entries
   sports shops 171
squash 116
Sri Guru Singh Sabha Sikh
   Temple 39
Sri Krishnan Temple 86
Sri Mariamman Temple 36, 97, **36**
Sri Srinivasa Perumal Temple
   90
Sri Veeramakaliamman Temple
   88, 90, **88**
Sriwijaya 8
Stadthuys (Melaka) 177-9
St Andrew's Cathedral 84
St John's Island 108-9
St Paul's Hill (Melaka) 177-9
Straits Settlements 9
Straits Times, *see* newspapers
student cards 46
Sultan Abu Bakar Mosque
   (Johor Bahru) 174
Sultan Hussein 9
Sultan Mosque 32-3, 91-2, 98,
   32, **91**
Sun Yatsen Villa 115
Sunday Morning Bird Singing
   112
Sungei Buloh Nature Park 114,
   172
supermarkets 156
Supreme Court 82, **82**
swimming 116
   Big Splash 105
Syonan 11
Szechuan food 139-40

Tang Dynasty City 102
Tanjong Pagar Heritage
   Exhibition 95
Taoism 29-30
taxes 49-51, 130, 166
taxi travel 70-1, 77
   Malaysia 70-1
telephone services 52
Telok Ayer Centre 86
Temasek 8
Temple of 1000 Lights 91, 98

temples 34-42
   Chettiar Hindu Temple 99
   Chinese temples 34-5
   Gurdwara Sahib Yishun Sikh
      temple 38, **38**
   Hindu temples 36-7
   Kong Meng San Phor Kark
      See Temple 115
   Kuan Yin Temple 35, 86, **31**
   Leong San See Temple 91
   Sikh temples 38-9
   Siong Lim Temple 35, 115
   Sri Guru Nanak Sat Sangh
      Sabha Sikh Temple 104
   Sri Guru Singh Sabha Sikh
      Temple 39
   Sri Krishnan Temple 86
   Sri Mariamman Temple 36,
      97, **36**
   Sri Senpaga Vinayagar
      Temple 104
   Sri Srinivasa Perumal Temple
      90
   Sri Veeramakaliamman
      Temple 88, 90, **88**
   Temple of 1000 Lights 91, 98
   Thai Buddhist Temple 110
   Thian Hock Keng Temple 34,
      97, **34**
   Tua Pek Kong Temple 109
   Wak Hai Cheng Bio Temple
      93
tennis 117
Teochew food 140
Thailand 71
   bus travel 71
   train travel 71
theatre 85, 162-3
   Singapore Dance Theatre 85
Thian Hock Keng Temple 34,
   97, **34**
Tiger Balm King, *see* Aw Boon
   Haw
tigers 10
time 58
Tioman Island 182-4, **183**
tipping 49
Tong Chai Medical Institute
   96
tourist offices 45
tours
   cruises 73
   harbour cruises 80
   organised tours 79
   river cruises 80
   riverboat tours 82
   walking tours of Singapore
      87-96

train travel
    Malaysia 70
    Thailand 71
transvestites 86, 163
travel agents 66
travel insurance, *see* insurance
travellers cheques 48
trishaws 78, 97, **78**
TV 57-8

Ubin, *see* Pulau Ubin
Under One Roof 58
Underwater World, *see* Sentosa
    Island
United Malays National
    Organisation 12

universities 61
Upper Seletar Reservoir 114

vegetarian food 140-1
Veranda Riots 11
Victoria Theatre & Concert Hall
    82
video, *see* photography
visas 45
Volcano Land, *see* Sentosa Island

Wak Hai Cheng Bio Temple 93
walking 79
    Arab St walking tour 91-3, **92**
    Chinatown walking tour
        93-6, **95**

Little India walking tour
    88-91, **89**
    nature walk 107
water sports 117
wayang, *see* Chinese
    opera
weights & measures 59
women travellers 59
work 65
World Trade Centre 71

Yunnanese food 140

zoo (Johor Bahru) 175
Zoological Gardens
    112-13

LONELY PLANET PHRASEBOOKS

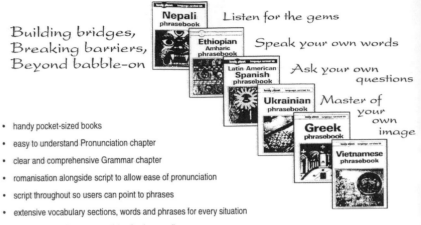

Building bridges,
Breaking barriers,
Beyond babble-on

Listen for the gems

Speak your own words

Ask your own questions

Master of your own image

- handy pocket-sized books
- easy to understand Pronunciation chapter
- clear and comprehensive Grammar chapter
- romanisation alongside script to allow ease of pronunciation
- script throughout so users can point to phrases
- extensive vocabulary sections, words and phrases for every situation
- full of cultural information and tips for the traveller

'...vital for a real DIY spirit and attitude in language learning' – Backpacker

'the phrasebooks have good cultural backgrounders and offer solid advice for challenging situations in remote locations' – San Francisco Examiner

'...they are unbeatable for their coverage of the world's more obscure languages' – The Geographical Magazine

---

Arabic (Egyptian)
Arabic (Moroccan)
Australia
  Australian English, Aboriginal and Torres Strait languages
Baltic States
  Estonian, Latvian, Lithuanian
Bengali
Brazilian
Burmese
Cantonese
Central Asia
Central Europe
  Czech, French, German, Hungarian, Italian and Slovak
Eastern Europe
  Bulgarian, Czech, Hungarian, Polish, Romanian and Slovak
Ethiopian (Amharic)
Fijian
French
German
Greek

Hindi/Urdu
Indonesian
Italian
Japanese
Korean
Lao
Latin American Spanish
Malay
Mandarin
Mediterranean Europe
  Albanian, Croatian, Greek, Italian, Macedonian, Maltese, Serbian and Slovene
Mongolian
Nepali
Papua New Guinea
Pilipino (Tagalog)
Quechua
Russian
Scandinavian Europe
  Danish, Finnish, Icelandic, Norwegian and Swedish

South-East Asia
  Burmese, Indonesian, Khmer, Lao, Malay, Tagalog (Pilipino), Thai and Vietnamese
Spanish (Castilian)
  Basque, Catalan and Galician
Sri Lanka
Swahili
Thai
Thai Hill Tribes
Tibetan
Turkish
Ukrainian
USA
  US English, Vernacular, Native American languages and Hawaiian
Vietnamese
Western Europe
  Basque, Catalan, Dutch, French, German, Irish, Italian, Portuguese, Scottish Gaelic, Spanish (Castilian) and Welsh

---

LONELY PLANET JOURNEYS

JOURNEYS is a unique collection of travel writing – published by the company that understands travel better than anyone else. It is a series for anyone who has ever experienced – or dreamed of – the magical moment when they encountered a strange culture or saw a place for the first time. They are tales to read while you're planning a trip, while you're on the road or while you're in an armchair, in front of a fire.

JOURNEYS books catch the spirit of a place, illuminate a culture, recount a crazy adventure, or introduce a fascinating way of life. They always entertain, and always enrich the experience of travel.

ISLANDS IN THE CLOUDS
Travels in the Highlands of New Guinea
Isabella Tree

Isabella Tree's remarkable journey takes us to the heart of the remote and beautiful Highlands of Papua New Guinea and Irian Jaya – one of the most extraordinary and dangerous regions on earth. Funny and tragic by turns, *Islands in the Clouds* is her moving story of the Highland people and the changes transforming their world.

Isabella Tree, who lives in England, has worked as a freelance journalist on a variety of newspapers and magazines, including a stint as senior travel correspondent for the *Evening Standard*. A fellow of the Royal Geographical Society, she has also written a biography of the Victorian ornithologist John Gould.

'One of the most accomplished travel writers to appear on the horizon for many years . . . the dialogue is brilliant' – Eric Newby

---

SEAN & DAVID'S LONG DRIVE
Sean Condon

Sean Condon is young, urban and a connoisseur of hair wax. He can't drive, and he doesn't really travel well. So when Sean and his friend David set out to explore Australia in a 1966 Ford Falcon, the result is a decidedly offbeat look at life on the road. Over 14,000 death-defying kilometres, our heroes check out the re-runs on tv, get fabulously drunk, listen to Neil Young cassettes and wonder why they ever left home.

Sean Condon lives in Melbourne. He played drums in several mediocre bands until he found his way into advertising and an above-average band called Boilersuit. *Sean & David's Long Drive* is his first book.

'Funny, pithy, kitsch and surreal . . . This book will do for Australia what Chernobyl did for Kiev, but hey you'll laugh as the stereotypes go boom'
– *Time Out*

LONELY PLANET TRAVEL ATLASES

Lonely Planet has long been famous for the number and quality of its guidebook maps. Now we've gone one step further and produced a handy companion series: Lonely Planet travel atlases – maps of a country produced in book form.

Unlike other maps, which look good but lead travellers astray, our travel atlases have been researched on the road by Lonely Planet's experienced team of writers. All details are carefully checked to ensure the atlas corresponds with the equivalent Lonely Planet guidebook.

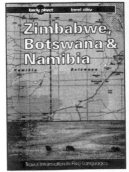

The handy atlas format means no holes, wrinkles, torn sections or constant folding and unfolding. These atlases can survive long periods on the road, unlike cumbersome fold-out maps. The comprehensive index ensures easy reference.

- full-colour throughout
- maps researched and checked by Lonely Planet authors
- place names correspond with Lonely Planet guidebooks
  – no confusing spelling differences
- legend and travelling information in English, French, German, Japanese and Spanish
- size: 230 x 160 mm

Available now:
Chile & Easter Island • Egypt • India & Bangladesh • Israel & the Palestinian Territories •Jordan, Syria & Lebanon • Kenya • Laos • Portugal • South Africa, Lesotho & Swaziland • Thailand • Turkey • Vietnam • Zimbabwe, Botswana & Namibia

---

LONELY PLANET TV SERIES & VIDEOS

Lonely Planet travel guides have been brought to life on television screens around the world. Like our guides, the programmes are based on the joy of independent travel, and look honestly at some of the most exciting, picturesque and frustrating places in the world. Each show is presented by one of three travellers from Australia, England or the USA and combines an innovative mixture of video, Super-8 film, atmospheric soundscapes and original music.

Videos of each episode – containing additional footage not shown on television – are available from good book and video shops, but the availability of individual videos varies with regional screening schedules.

Video destinations include: Alaska • American Rockies • Australia – The South-East • Baja California & the Copper Canyon • Brazil • Central Asia • Chile & Easter Island • Corsica, Sicily & Sardinia – The Mediterranean Islands • East Africa (Tanzania & Zanzibar) • Ecuador & the Galapagos Islands • Greenland & Iceland • Indonesia • Israel & the Sinai Desert • Jamaica • Japan • La Ruta Maya • Morocco • New York • North India • Pacific Islands (Fiji, Solomon Islands & Vanuatu) • South India • South West China • Turkey • Vietnam • West Africa • Zimbabwe, Botswana & Namibia

The Lonely Planet TV series is produced by:
Pilot Productions
The Old Studio
18 Middle Row
London W10 5AT UK

For video availability and ordering information contact your nearest Lonely Planet office.

Music from the TV series is available on CD & cassette.

PLANET TALK

Lonely Planet's FREE quarterly newsletter

We love hearing from you and think you'd like to hear from us.

When...is the right time to see reindeer in Finland?
Where...can you hear the best palm-wine music in Ghana?
How...do you get from Asunción to Areguá by steam train?
What...is the best way to see India?

For the answer to these and many other questions read PLANET TALK.

Every issue is packed with up-to-date travel news and advice including:

- a letter from Lonely Planet co-founders Tony and Maureen Wheeler
- go behind the scenes on the road with a Lonely Planet author
- feature article on an important and topical travel issue
- a selection of recent letters from travellers
- details on forthcoming Lonely Planet promotions
- complete list of Lonely Planet products

To join our mailing list contact any Lonely Planet office.

Also available: Lonely Planet T-shirts. 100% heavyweight cotton.

LONELY PLANET ONLINE

Get the latest travel information before you leave or while you're on the road

Whether you've just begun planning your next trip, or you're chasing down specific info on currency regulations or visa requirements, check out Lonely Planet Online for up-to-the minute travel information.

As well as travel profiles of your favourite destinations (including maps and photos), you'll find current reports from our researchers and other travellers, updates on health and visas, travel advisories, and discussion of the ecological and political issues you need to be aware of as you travel.

There's also an online travellers' forum where you can share your experience of life on the road, meet travel companions and ask other travellers for their recommendations and advice. We also have plenty of links to other online sites useful to independent travellers.

And of course we have a complete and up-to-date list of all Lonely Planet travel products including guides, phrasebooks, atlases, Journeys and videos and a simple online ordering facility if you can't find the book you want elsewhere.

www.lonelyplanet.com
or
AOL keyword: lp

LONELY PLANET PRODUCTS

Lonely Planet is known worldwide for publishing practical, reliable and no-nonsense travel information in our guides and on our web site. The Lonely Planet list covers just about every accessible part of the world. Currently there are nine series: *travel guides, shoestring guides, walking guides, city guides, phrasebooks, audio packs, travel atlases, Journeys – a unique collection of travel writing and Pisces Books - diving and snorkeling guides.*

EUROPE

Amsterdam • Austria • Baltic States phrasebook • Berlin • Britain • Canary Islands• Central Europe on a shoestring • Central Europe phrasebook • Czech & Slovak Republics • Denmark • Dublin • Eastern Europe on a shoestring • Eastern Europe phrasebook • Estonia, Latvia & Lithuania • Finland • France • French phrasebook • Germany • German phrasebook • Greece • Greek phrasebook • Hungary • Iceland, Greenland & the Faroe Islands • Ireland • Italian phrasebook • Italy • Lisbon • London • Mediterranean Europe on a shoestring • Mediterranean Europe phrasebook • Paris • Poland • Portugal • Portugal travel atlas • Prague • Romania & Moldova • Russia, Ukraine & Belarus • Russian phrasebook • Scandinavian & Baltic Europe on a shoestring • Scandinavian Europe phrasebook • Slovenia • Spain • Spanish phrasebook • St Petersburg • Switzerland •Trekking in Spain • Ukrainian phrasebook • Vienna • Walking in Britain • Walking in Italy • Walking in Switzerland • Western Europe on a shoestring • Western Europe phrasebook

Travel Literature: The Olive Grove: Travels in Greece

NORTH AMERICA

Alaska • Backpacking in Alaska • Baja California • California & Nevada • Canada • Chicago • Deep South• Florida • Hawaii • Honolulu • Los Angeles • Mexico • Mexico City • Miami • New England • New Orleans • New York City • New York, New Jersey & Pennsylvania • Pacific Northwest USA • Rocky Mountain States • San Francisco • Seattle • Southwest USA • USA phrasebook • Washington, DC & the Capital Region

Travel Literature: Drive thru America

CENTRAL AMERICA & THE CARIBBEAN

•Bahamas and Turks & Caicos •Bermuda •Central America on a shoestring • Costa Rica • Cuba •Eastern Caribbean •Guatemala, Belize & Yucatán: La Ruta Maya • Jamaica

Travel Literature Green Dreams: Travels in Central America

SOUTH AMERICA

Argentina, Uruguay & Paraguay • Bolivia • Brazil • Brazilian phrasebook • Buenos Aires • Chile & Easter Island • Chile & Easter Island travel atlas • Colombia Ecuador & the Galápagos Islands • Latin American Spanish phrasebook • Peru • Quechua phrasebook • Rio de Janeiro • South America on a shoestring • Trekking in the Patagonian Andes • Venezuela

Travel Literature: Full Circle: A South American Journey

ISLANDS OF THE INDIAN OCEAN

Madagascar & Comoros • Maldives• Mauritius, Réunion & Seychelles

AFRICA

Africa - the South • Africa on a shoestring • Arabic (Moroccan) phrasebook • Cairo • Cape Town • Central Africa • East Africa • Egypt • Egypt travel atlas• Ethiopian (Amharic) phrasebook • Kenya • Kenya travel atlas • Malawi, Mozambique & Zambia • Morocco • North Africa • South Africa, Lesotho & Swaziland • South Africa, Lesotho & Swaziland travel atlas • Swahili phrasebook • Tunisia • Trekking in East Africa • West Africa • Zimbabwe, Botswana & Namibia • Zimbabwe, Botswana & Namibia travel atlas

Travel Literature: The Rainbird: A Central African Journey • Songs to an African Sunset: A Zimbabwean Story

MAIL ORDER

Lonely Planet products are distributed worldwide. They are also available by mail order from Lonely Planet, so if you have difficulty finding a title please write to us. North American and South American residents should write to 150 Linden St, Oakland CA 94607, USA; European and African residents should write to 10a Spring Place, London NW5 3BH; and residents of other countries to PO Box 617, Hawthorn, Victoria 3122, Australia.

NORTH-EAST ASIA

Beijing • Cantonese phrasebook • China • Hong Kong • Hong Kong, Macau & Guangzhou • Japan • Japanese phrasebook • Japanese audio pack • Korea • Korean phrasebook • Mandarin phrasebook • Mongolia • Mongolian phrasebook • North-East Asia on a shoestring • Seoul • Taiwan • Tibet • Tibet phrasebook • Tokyo

Travel Literature: Lost Japan

MIDDLE EAST & CENTRAL ASIA

Arab Gulf States • Arabic (Egyptian) phrasebook • Central Asia • Central Asia phrasebook • Iran • Israel & the Palestinian Territories • Israel & the Palestinian Territories travel atlas • Istanbul • Jerusalem • Jordan & Syria • Jordan, Syria & Lebanon travel atlas • Lebanon • Middle East • Turkey • Turkish phrasebook • Turkey travel atlas • Yemen

Travel Literature: The Gates of Damascus • Kingdom of the Film Stars: Journey into Jordan

ALSO AVAILABLE:

Brief Encounters • Travel with Children • Traveller's Tales

INDIAN SUBCONTINENT

Bangladesh • Bengali phrasebook • Delhi • Goa • Hindi/Urdu phrasebook • India • India & Bangladesh travel atlas • Indian Himalaya • Karakoram Highway • Nepal • Nepali phrasebook • Pakistan • Rajasthan • Sri Lanka • Sri Lanka phrasebook • Trekking in the Indian Himalaya • Trekking in the Karakoram & Hindukush • Trekking in the Nepal Himalaya

Travel Literature: In Rajasthan • Shopping for Buddhas

SOUTH-EAST ASIA

Bali & Lombok • Bangkok • Burmese phrasebook • Cambodia • Ho Chi Minh City • Indonesia • Indonesian phrasebook • Indonesian audio pack • Indonesia's Eastern Islands • Jakarta • Java • Laos • Lao phrasebook • Laos travel atlas • Malay phrasebook • Malaysia, Singapore & Brunei • Myanmar (Burma) • Philippines • Pilipino phrasebook • Singapore • South-East Asia on a shoestring • South-East Asia phrasebook • Thailand • Thailand's Islands & Beaches • Thailand travel atlas • Thai phrasebook • Thai audio pack • Thai Hill Tribes phrasebook • Vietnam • Vietnamese phrasebook • Vietnam travel atlas

AUSTRALIA & THE PACIFIC

Australia • Australian phrasebook • Bushwalking in Australia • Bushwalking in Papua New Guinea • Fiji • Fijian phrasebook • Islands of Australia's Great Barrier Reef • Melbourne • Micronesia • New Caledonia • New South Wales • New Zealand • Northern Territory • Outback Australia • Papua New Guinea • Papua New Guinea phrasebook • Queensland • Rarotonga & the Cook Islands • Samoa • Solomon Islands • South Australia • Sydney • Tahiti & French Polynesia • Tasmania • Tonga • Tramping in New Zealand • Vanuatu • Victoria • Western Australia

Travel Literature: Islands in the Clouds • Sean & David's Long Drive

ANTARCTICA

Antarctica

THE LONELY PLANET STORY

Lonely Planet published its first book in 1973 in response to the numerous 'How did you do it?' questions Maureen and Tony Wheeler were asked after driving, busing, hitching, sailing and railing their way from England to Australia.

Written at a kitchen table and hand collated, trimmed and stapled, *Across Asia on the Cheap* became an instant local bestseller, inspiring thoughts of another book.

Eighteen months in South-East Asia resulted in their second guide, *South-East Asia on a shoestring*, which they put together in a backstreet Chinese hotel in Singapore in 1975. The 'yellow bible', as it quickly became known to backpackers around the world, soon became *the* guide to the region. It has sold well over half a million copies and is now in its 9th edition, still retaining its familiar yellow cover.

Today there are over 350 titles, including travel guides, walking guides, language kits & phrasebooks, travel atlases and travel literature. The company is the largest independent travel publisher in the world. Although Lonely Planet initially specialised in guides to Asia, today there are few corners of the globe that have not been covered.

The emphasis continues to be on travel for independent travellers. Tony and Maureen still travel for several months of each year and play an active part in the writing, updating and quality control of Lonely Planet's guides.

They have been joined by over 80 authors and 200 staff at our offices in Melbourne (Australia), Oakland (USA), London (UK) and Paris (France). Travellers themselves also make a valuable contribution to the guides through the feedback we receive in thousands of letters each year and on our web site.

The people at Lonely Planet strongly believe that travellers can make a positive contribution to the countries they visit, both through their appreciation of the countries' culture, wildlife and natural features, and through the money they spend. In addition, the company makes a direct contribution to the countries and regions it covers. Since 1986 a percentage of the income from each book has been donated to ventures such as famine relief in Africa; aid projects in India; agricultural projects in Central America; Greenpeace's efforts to halt French nuclear testing in the Pacific; and Amnesty International.

'I hope we send people out with the right attitude about travel. You realise when you travel that there are so many different perspectives about the world, so we hope these books will make people more interested in what they see. Guidebooks can't really guide people. All you can do is point them in the right direction.'

– Tony Wheeler

LONELY PLANET PUBLICATIONS

Australia
PO Box 617, Hawthorn 3122, Victoria
tel: (03) 9819 1877 fax: (03) 9819 6459
e-mail: talk2us@lonelyplanet.com.au

USA
150 Linden St
Oakland, CA 94607
tel: (510) 893 8555 TOLL FREE: 800 275-8555
fax: (510) 893 8572
e-mail: info@lonelyplanet.com

UK
10a Spring Place,
London NW5 3BH
tel: (0171) 428 4800 fax: (0171) 428 4828
e-mail: go@lonelyplanet.co.uk

France:
71 bis rue du Cardinal Lemoine, 75005 Paris
tel: 01 44 32 06 20 fax: 01 46 34 72 55
e-mail: bip@lonelyplanet.fr

**World Wide Web: http://www.lonelyplanet.com
or *AOL keyword: lp***

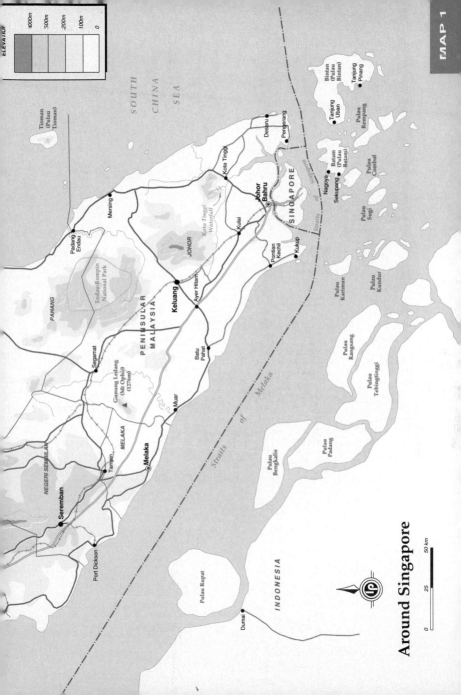

MAP 1

Around Singapore

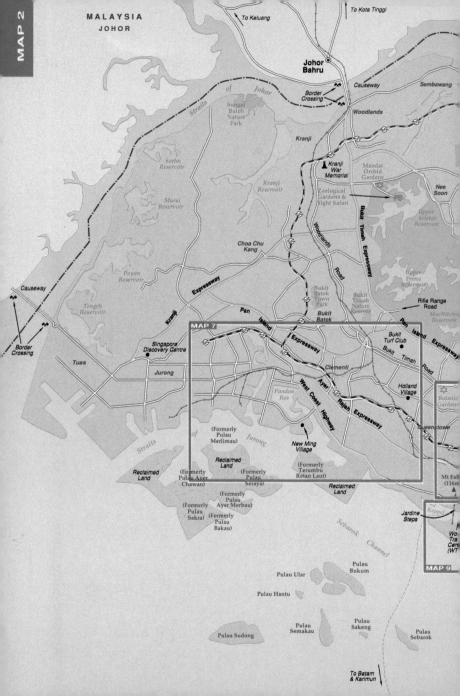

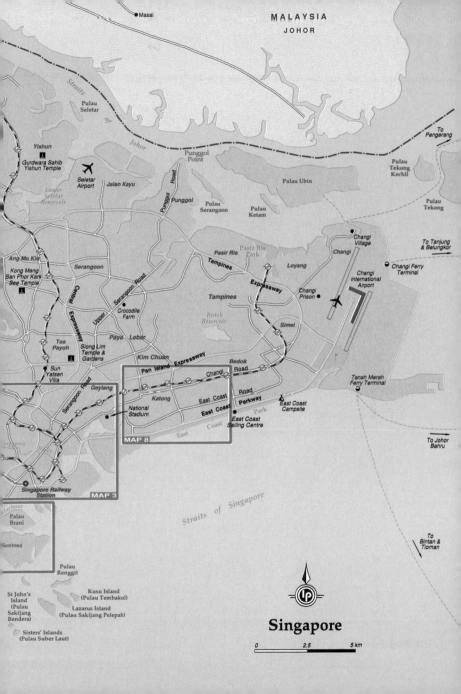

MALAYSIA
JOHOR

• Masai

Straits of Johor

Pulau Seletar

To Pengerang

Punggol Point

Pulau Tekong Kechil

Yishun
Gurdwara Sahib
Yishun Temple

Seletar Airport

Jalan Kayu

Pulau Ubin

Pulau Tekong

Lower Seletar Reservoir

Punggol Road

Punggol

Pulau Serangoon

Pulau Ketam

Changi Village

To Tanjung & Belungkor

Ang Mo Kio

Serangoon

Pasir Ris

Pasir Ris Park

Changi

Changi Ferry Terminal

Kong Meng San Phor Kark See Temple

Tampines

Loyang

Changi International Airport

Serangoon Road

Crocodile Farm

Tampines

Changi Prison

Central Expressway

Upper

Toa Payoh

Siong Lim Temple & Gardens

Paya Lebar

Bedok Reservoir

Simei

Sun Yatsen Villa

Kim Chuan

Pan Island Expressway

Bedok Road

Serangoon Road

Geylang

Changi

Road

Tanah Merah Ferry Terminal

Katong

East Coast Road

Parkway

East Coast Campsite

National Stadium

East Coast

East Coast Sailing Centre

MAP 8

East Coast Park

To Johor Bahru

Singapore River

Singapore Railway Station

MAP 3

Straits of Singapore

To Bintan & Tioman

Harbour
Pulau Brani

Sentosa

Pulau Renggit

St John's Island
(Pulau Sakijang Bendera)

Kusu Island
(Pulau Tembakul)

Lazarus Island
(Pulau Sakijang Pelepah)

Sisters' Islands
(Pulau Suber Laut)

Singapore

0   2.5   5 km

MAP 3

Novotel Orchid Hotel

Singapore
Botanic
Gardens

MAP 4

Dunearn Road

Bukit Timah Road

Farrer Road

Balmoral Road

Stevens Road

Newton

Napier Road

Orange Grove Road

Anderson Road

Scotts Road

Cairnhill Road

Cavanagh Road

Singapore
Botanic
Gardens

Napier Road

Tanglin Road

Orchard Road

Orchard Boulevard

Orchard

Orchard
Road

Cuscaden Road

Central Expressway

Orchard Road

Grange Road

Exeter

Somerset
Road

River Valley Road

Alexandra Canal

Tanglin Road

MAP 6

Zion Road

Jalan Bukit Ho Swee Road

Singapore River

Alexandra Road

Tiong Bahru Road

Redhill

Alexandra Road

Havelock Road

Tiong
Bahru

Tiong Bahru Road

Pearl's
Hill
City
Park

Jalan Bukit Merah

Henderson Road

Outram Road

Outram
Park

Ayer Rajah Expressway

Central Expressway

Nail Road

Cantonment Road

Alkaff Mansion

Lower Delta Road

Jalan Bukit Merah

Singapore
Railway
Station

Central Singapore

Mt Faber
(116m)

Mt Faber
Park

To World Trade
Centre (1km)

Ayer Rajah Expressway

0   0.5   1 km

MAP 5

Novena

Moulmein Road

Expressway

Central

Farrer
Park
Fields

Kampong
Java
Park

Bukit Timah Road
Bukit Timah Road

Little
India

Lavender St
Bus Terminal

Kelink
River

Kallang

Geylang Road

Kallang Road

Mountbatten Road

Syed Alwi Road

Canal

Lavender

Immigration
Department
Head Office

Queen St
Bus Terminal

Bridge Road

Nicoll Highway

National
Stadium

Stadium Boulevard

Kallang
Theatre

Bugis

Golden
Mile
Complex

Singapore
Indoor
Stadium

Dhoby
Ghaut

Penang Road

Colonial
District

Geylang River

East Coast Parkway

East Coast Park

Fort
Canning
Park

River Valley Road

Coleman Street

City
Hall

The
Padang

Raffles

Boulevard

Raffles Avenue

Marina Promenade

Chinatown

Chulia Street

Upper Pickering Street

Cross Street

Raffles
Place

CBD

Clifford
Pier

Marina
Bay

Marina
City
Park

Tanjong
Pagar

Shenton Way

Robinson Road

East Coast Parkway

Marina Bay

Finger Pier

Straits of Singapore

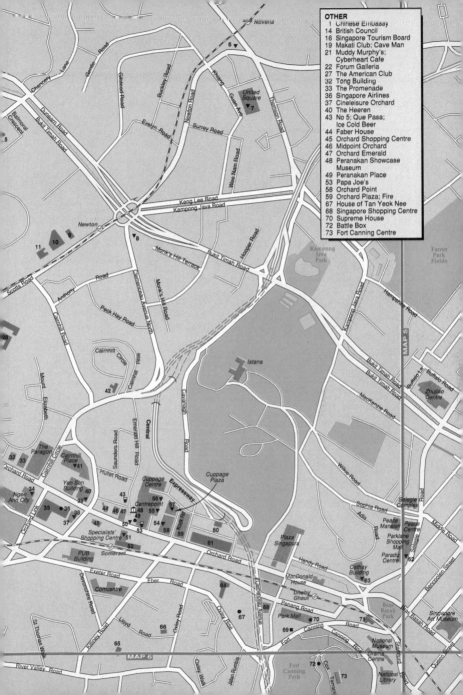

MAP 5

PLACES TO STAY

1 Kam Leng
3 International Hotel
5 Tai Hoe Hotel
6 Mustafa Hotel
7 New Park Hotel
8 Fortuna Hotel
9 Starlet Hotel
10 Penta Hotel
11 Ali's Nest
12 Broadway Hotel
13 Grandmet Hotel
15 Comfort Hotel
16 Little India Guest House
22 Kerbau Hotel
28 Albert Court Hotel; Azizas Restaurant
31 Perak Lodge
32 Dickson Court Hotel
33 Boon Wah Hotel
37 Mayo Inn
46 Golden Landmark Hotel
51 Goh's Homestay; Hawaii Hostel
52 Sun Sun Hotel
54 Peony Mansion Travellers' Lodge; Green Curtains
55 South-East Asia Hotel
61 Lee Boarding House; Peony Mansions; Latin House
62 San Wah Hotel
63 Bayview Inn
64 Bencoolen House
65 Strand Hotel
68 Waterloo Hostel
71 Allson Hotel
73 Hotel InterContinental
74 Willy's
75 Sunderbone Homestay
76 Waffles Homestay
77 Ah Chew Hotel
78 New 7th Storey Hotel
79 New Backpackers' Lodge
80 Cozy Corner Lodge
81 Beach Hotel
83 Lee Traveller's Club
84 Shang Onn
85 Metropole Hotel
88 Carlton Hotel

PLACES TO EAT

2 Lavender Food Centre
4 Fut Sai Kai
14 Berseh Food Centre
18 Muthu's Curry Restaurant
19 Delhi Restaurant
20 Banana Leaf Apolo Restaurant
21 D' Deli Pubb & Restaurant
23 Andhra Curry
24 Komala Vilas
25 Madras New Woodlands Restaurant
29 Anadda Bhavan
30 Sri Krishnan Vilas
34 Bobby-O Claypot Curry
36 Tenco Food Centre
38 Islamic Restaurant
39 Jubilee Classic Restaurant
40 Victory; Zam Zam Restaurant
42 Rumah Makan Minang
47 Parco Bugis Junction; Loy Kee Chicken Rice; Sumo
48 Xiang Yuan
49 Albert Centre Food Centre
50 Fatty's Eating House
55 OM Moosa Restaurant
59 ABC Eating House; Yi Song; Eastern Vegetarian Food; Golden Dragon Inn
66 Regency Palace
69 Koh Fong Restaurant; Yuan Xiang Vegetarian Food
70 Victoria St Food Court
72 Xiang Man Lou Food Court; Esquire Kitchen
85 Tropical Makan Palace; Good Family
86 Yet Con

OTHER

17 Sri Veeramakaliamman Temple
26 Jewelry Shops
27 Little India Arcade
35 Abdul Gaffoor Mosque
41 Sultan Mosque
43 Istana Kampong Glam
44 Airpower Travel
45 Kazura
53 Airpower Travel
57 Kuan Yin Temple
58 Sri Krishnan Temple
60 Bencoolen Mosque
82 Maghain Aboth Synagogue
82 Central Police Station
89 Cathedral of the Good Shepherd

Little India & Arab Street

0   200   400 m

RICHARD I'ANSON

RICHARD I'ANSON

RICHARD I'ANSON

Top: Clarke Quay (Map 6), along with nearby Boat Quay, is Singapore's busiest nightlife area with plenty of good riverside dining options too.
Bottom: Arab St (Map 5) is the place to look for leather bags, basketware and other traditional craftsmarkets.

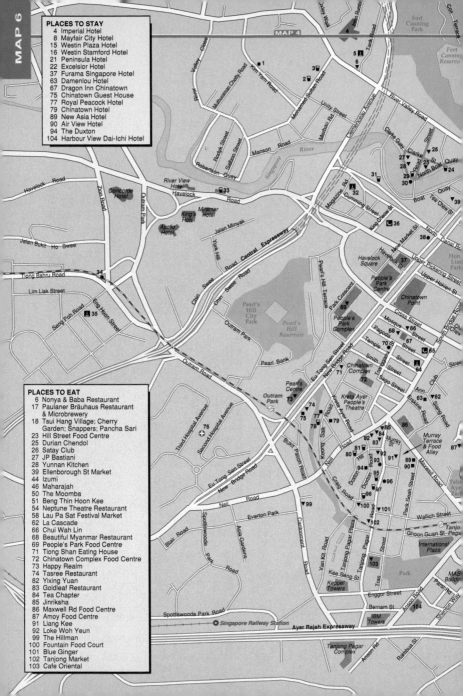

MAP 6

MAP 4

PLACES TO STAY
- 4 Imperial Hotel
- 8 Mayfair City Hotel
- 15 Westin Plaza Hotel
- 16 Westin Stamford Hotel
- 21 Peninsula Hotel
- 22 Excelsior Hotel
- 37 Furama Singapore Hotel
- 63 Damenlou Hotel
- 67 Dragon Inn Chinatown
- 75 Chinatown Guest House
- 77 Royal Peacock Hotel
- 79 Chinatown Hotel
- 89 New Asia Hotel
- 90 Air View Hotel
- 94 The Duxton
- 104 Harbour View Dai-Ichi Hotel

PLACES TO EAT
- 6 Nonya & Baba Restaurant
- 17 Paulaner Bräuhaus Restaurant & Microbrewery
- 18 Tsui Hang Village; Cherry Garden; Snappers; Pancha Sari
- 23 Hill Street Food Centre
- 25 Durian Chendol
- 26 Satay Club
- 27 JP Bastiani
- 28 Yunnan Kitchen
- 39 Ellenborough St Market
- 44 Izumi
- 46 Maharajah
- 50 The Moomba
- 51 Beng Thin Hoon Kee
- 58 Neptune Theatre Restaurant
- 58 Lau Pa Sat Festival Market
- 62 La Cascade
- 66 Chui Wah Lin
- 68 Beautiful Myanmar Restaurant
- 69 People's Park Food Centre
- 71 Tiong Shan Eating House
- 72 Chinatown Complex Food Centre
- 73 Happy Realm
- 74 Tasree Restaurant
- 82 Yixing Yuan
- 83 Goldleaf Restaurant
- 84 Tea Chapter
- 85 Jinriksha
- 86 Maxwell Rd Food Centre
- 87 Amoy Food Centre
- 91 Liang Kee
- 92 Loke Woh Yeun
- 99 The Hillman
- 100 Fountain Food Court
- 101 Blue Ginger
- 102 Tanjong Market
- 103 Cafe Oriental

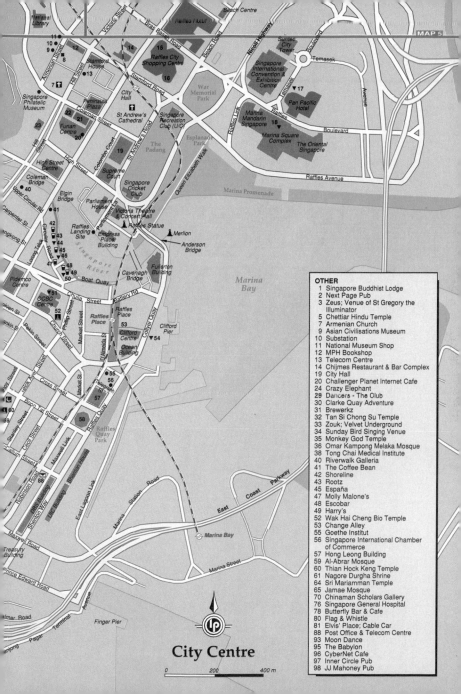

MAP 5

National Library
Beach Centre
Raffles Hotel
Bras Basah Road
Victoria Street
Suntec City Tower
Singapore International Convention & Exhibition Centre
Temasek
Nicoll Highway
11
10
9
8
12
15
14
Stamford House
Raffles City Shopping Centre
16
13
Stamford Road
City Hall
War Memorial Park
17
Pan Pacific Hotel
Lemsek
Marina Mandarin Singapore
18
Singapore Philatelic Museum
Peninsula Plaza
St Andrew's Cathedral
Singapore Recreation Club (U/C)
Marina Square Complex
The Oriental Singapore
7
22
21
Coleman Street
Funan Centre
20
23
St Andrew's Road
Esplanade Park
Raffles Avenue
High Street Centre
Coleman Bridge
40
19
Supreme Court
The Padang
Marina Promenade
Elgin Bridge
Parliament House
Singapore Cricket Club
Queen Elizabeth Walk
Marina Bay
Upper Circular Rd
41
Victoria Theatre & Concert Hall
Raffles Statue
42
Raffles Landing Site
Empress Place Building
Merlion
Anderson Bridge
43
44
45
46
47
48
49
50
Cavenagh Bridge
Fullerton Building
Boat Quay
Singapore River
Pidemco Centre
51
OCBC Centre
52
Chulia Street
Battery Rd
53
Raffles Place
Clifford Centre
Clifford Pier
Ocean Building
54
Market Street
Collyer Quay
55
56
Telok Ayer Street
57
58
Raffles Quay
Raffles Quay Park
88
Shenton Way
East Coast Parkway
Marina Bay
Station Road
Marina Street
Treasury Building
Prince Edward Road
Finger Pier

City Centre

0   200   400 m

OTHER

1 Singapore Buddhist Lodge
2 Next Page Pub
3 Zeus; Venue of St Gregory the Illuminator
5 Chettiar Hindu Temple
7 Armenian Church
9 Asian Civilisations Museum
10 Substation
11 National Museum Shop
12 MPH Bookshop
13 Telecom Centre
14 Chijmes Restaurant & Bar Complex
19 City Hall
20 Challenger Planet Internet Cafe
24 Crazy Elephant
29 Dancers - The Club
30 Clarke Quay Adventure
31 Brewerkz
32 Tan Si Chong Su Temple
33 Zouk; Velvet Underground
34 Sunday Bird Singing Venue
35 Monkey God Temple
36 Omar Kampong Melaka Mosque
37 Tong Chai Medical Institute
40 Riverwalk Galleria
41 The Coffee Bean
42 Shoreline
43 Rootz
45 España
47 Molly Malone's
48 Escobar
49 Harry's
52 Wak Hai Cheng Bio Temple
53 Change Alley
55 Goethe Institut
56 Singapore International Chamber of Commerce
57 Hong Leong Building
59 Al-Abrar Mosque
60 Thian Hock Keng Temple
61 Nagore Durgha Shrine
64 Sri Mariamman Temple
65 Jamae Mosque
70 Chinaman Scholars Gallery
76 Singapore General Hospital
78 Butterfly Bar & Cafe
80 Flag & Whistle
81 Elvis' Place; Cable Car
82 Post Office & Telecom Centre
93 Moon Dance
95 The Babylon
96 CyberNet Cafe
97 Inner Circle Pub
98 JJ Mahoney Pub

MAP 7

Jurong

0   0.5   1 km

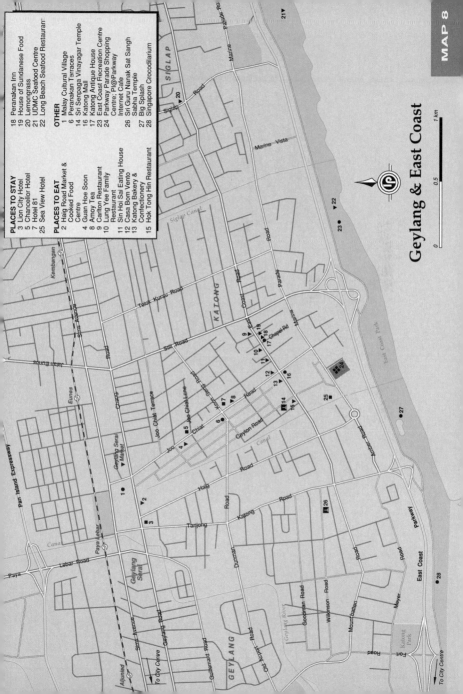

MAP 8

PLACES TO STAY
3 Lion City Hotel
5 Chancellor Hotel
7 Hotel 81
25 Sea View Hotel

PLACES TO EAT
2 Haig Road Market &
   Cooked Food
   Centre
4 Guan Hoe Soon
8 Amoy Tea
9 Carlton Restaurant
10 Lung Yee Family
   Restaurant
11 Sin Hoi Sai Eating House
12 Casa Bom Vento
13 Katong Bakery &
   Confectionery
15 Hok Tong Hin Restaurant

18 Peranakan Inn
19 House of Sundanese Food
20 Lemongrass
21 UDMC Seafood Centre
22 Long Beach Seafood Restaurant

OTHER
1 Malay Cultural Village
6 Peranakan Terraces
14 Sri Senpaga Vinayagar Temple
16 Katong Mall
17 Katong Antique House
23 East Coast Recreation Centre
24 Parkway Parade Shopping
   Centre; Pit@Parkway
   Internet Cafe
26 Sri Guru Nanak Sat Sangh
   Sabha Temple
27 Big Splash
28 Singapore Crocodilarium

Geylang & East Coast

0   0.5   1 km

MAP 9

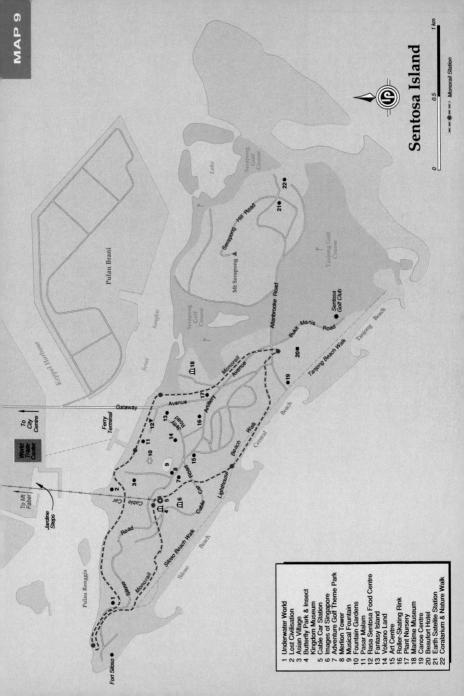

Sentosa Island

1 Underwater World
2 Lost Civilisation
3 Asian Village
4 Butterfly Park & Insect
  Kingdom Museum
5 Cable Car Station
6 Images of Singapore
7 Adventure Golf Theme Park
8 Merlion Tower
9 Musical Fountain
10 Fountain Gardens
11 Pasar Malam
12 Rasa Sentosa Food Centre
13 Fantasy Island
14 Volcano Land
15 Art Centre
16 Roller-Skating Rink
17 Plant Nursery
18 Maritime Museum
19 Canoe Centre
20 Beaufort Hotel
21 Earth Satellite Station
22 Coralarium & Nature Walk

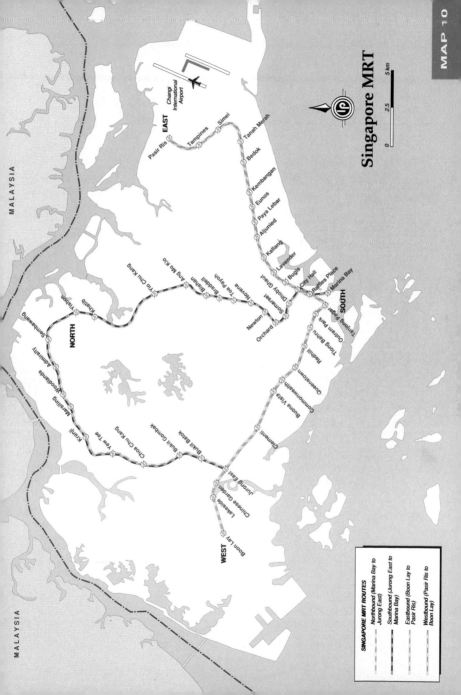

MAP 10

Singapore MRT

Map Legend

BOUNDARIES

.... International Boundary

.... Provincial Boundary

ROUTES

....Freeway, with Route Number `25`

.... Major Road

.... Minor Road

.... Minor Road - Unsealed

.... City Road

.... City Street

.... City Lane

.... Train Route, with Station

.... Metro Route, with Station

.... Cable Car or Chairlift

.... Ferry Route

.... Walking Track

AREA FEATURES

.... Building

.... Cemetery

...............................Hotel

.... Market

.... Park, Gardens

.... Pedestrian Mall

.... Urban Area

HYDROGRAPHIC FEATURES

...........................Canal

.... Coastline

.... Creek, River

.... Lake, Intermittent Lake

.... Rapids, Waterfalls

.... Salt Lake

.... Swamp

SYMBOLS

✪ **CAPITAL** ...... National Capital		✈ .... Airport		🏛 .... Museum		
◉ **CAPITAL** ..... Provincial Capital		Ancient or City Wall		← ...... One Way Street		
● **CITY** .... City		∴ ...Archaeological Site		🄿 .... Parking		
● **Town** .... Town		⊖ .... Bank		★ ....Police Station		
● Village .... Village		✦✦ ...... Border Crossing		✉ .... Post Office		
■ .... Place to Stay		🜨 .... Castle or Fort		❖ ..... Shopping Centre		
		Church		🄰 .... Shrine/Temple		
		Cliff or Escarpment		🏛 .... Stately Home		
▼ .... Place to Eat		♀ .... Embassy		⌷ ....Swimming Pool		
🍺 ....Pub or Bar		W .... Hindu Temple		◌ .... Synagogue		
		✛ ....Hospital		☎ .... Telephone		
		☀ ....Lookout		❶ ... Tourist Information		
		⚊ .... Monument		◓ .... Transport		
		◖ .... Mosque		🐘 .... Zoo		

Note: not all symbols displayed above appear in this book